AFTER THE COUP

MYANMAR'S POLITICAL AND HUMANITARIAN CRISES

AFTER THE COUP

MYANMAR'S POLITICAL AND HUMANITARIAN CRISES

EDITED BY ANTHONY WARE
AND MONIQUE SKIDMORE

Australian
National
University

ANU PRESS

Australian
National
University

ANU PRESS

Published by ANU Press
The Australian National University
Canberra ACT 2600, Australia
Email: anupress@anu.edu.au

Available to download for free at press.anu.edu.au

ISBN (print): 9781760466138
ISBN (online): 9781760466145

WorldCat (print): 1403852647
WorldCat (online): 1403846591

DOI: 10.22459/AC.2023

Cover design and layout by ANU Press

Cover photograph: The scene on a bridge after protesters clash with security forces in
Yangon, Myanmar, on March 16, 2021. Photograph by *The New York Times*. Used with
permission.

This book is published under the aegis of the Social Sciences editorial committee
of ANU Press.

Contents

Acronyms

AA	Arakan Army
AAPP	Assistance Association for Political Prisoners
ANU	The Australian National University
APA	Arakan People's Authority
ARI	Asia Research Institute
ARSA	Arakan Rohingya Salvation Army
ASEAN	Association of Southeast Asian Nations
ASEANSAI	ASEAN Supreme Audit Institutions
BRI	Belt and Road Initiative
CBO	community-based organisations
CCP	Chinese Communist Party
CDM	Civil Disobedience Movement
CRPH	Committee Representing Pyidaungsu Hluttaw
CSO	civil society organisation
DDoS	distributed denial-of-service
EAO	ethnic armed organisations
EC	European Commission
FDC	Federal Democracy Charter
FFM	Fact-Finding Mission on Myanmar
GAD	General Administration Department
GNLM	*Global New Light of Myanmar*
HE	higher education
HEI	higher education institutions
IASC	Inter-Agency Standing Committee

ICC	International Criminal Court
ICJ	International Court of Justice
IDP	internally displaced persons
IFRC	International Federation of the Red Cross
IIE	Institute of International Education
IIMM	Independent Investigative Mechanism for Myanmar
INGO	international NGO
ISEAS	Institute of Southeast Asian Studies
ISP	Institute for Strategy and Policy – Myanmar
MCRB	Myanmar Centre for Responsible Business
MEC	Myanmar Economic Corporation
MEHL	Myanma Economic Holdings Limited
MLHN	Myanmar Local Humanitarian Network
MoE	Ministry of Education
MOGE	Myanmar Oil and Gas Enterprise
MoU	memorandum of understanding
NGO	non-government organisations
NLD	National League for Democracy
NUCC	National Unity Consultative Council
NUG	National Unity Government
OECD	Organisation for Economic Co-Operation and Development
PDF	People's Defence Force
SAC	State Administration Council
SEZ	Special Economic Zone
SUM	Spring University Myanmar
TCG	Tripartite Core Group
UEC	Union Election Commission
ULA	United League of Arakan
UN	United Nations
UNESCO	United Nations Educational, Scientific and Cultural Organization

UNHCR	United Nations High Commission for Refugees
UNHRC	United Nations Human Rights Council
UNTFHS	United Nations Trust Fund for Human Security
USAID	US Aid
USDP	Union Solidarity and Development Party
VFU	Virtual Federal University
VPN	virtual private network

Contributors

Dr Adam Simpson is a senior lecturer in international studies within Justice & Society, University of South Australia. He has held a six-month visiting research fellowship at the Centre for Southeast Asian Studies, Kyoto University, and visiting scholar positions at School of Oriental and African Studies, University of London, Queen Mary, University of London and Keele University. His articles have appeared in journals such as *Environmental Politics, Third World Quarterly, Society & Natural Resources* and *Pacific Review*. He is the author of *Energy, Governance and Security in Thailand and Myanmar (Burma): A Critical Approach to Environmental Politics in the South* (Routledge, 2014; NIAS Press, 2017) and is lead editor of the *Routledge Handbook of Contemporary Myanmar* (2018) and *Myanmar: Politics, Economy and Society* (Routledge, 2021).

Dr Anne Décobert is a development studies scholar, anthropologist of development and development practitioner who has worked since 2009 on questions related to conflict and peace-building, humanitarianism, development and the struggles for rights and justice of minority groups in Myanmar. Strongly committed to ethically engaged research, she is particularly interested in approaches to addressing inequities and injustices faced by marginalised communities whose lives are shaped by structural violence and conflict. Her work to date has notably explored how those who are often wrongly labelled as passive 'victims' of violence and injustices themselves challenge, and potentially redefine, humanitarian and development systems and approaches as part of wider attempts to achieve recognition and social justice. Anne is the author of *The Politics of Aid to Burma: A Humanitarian Struggle on the Thai-Burmese Border* (Routledge, 2016), as well as academic articles, reports and media pieces focusing on humanitarianism, development and peace-building in conflict situations. In addition to her academic work, Anne also continues to act as a consultant with aid agencies in Myanmar.

Associate Professor Anthony Ware is an associate professor of International & Community Development at Deakin University, and convenor of the Development-Humanitarian Research Group. He was director of the Australia Myanmar Institute (2013–17), secretary of the Development Studies Association of Australia (2019–22) and is a thematic editor of *Development in Practice*. He has published over 50 academic papers/chapters and four books (two monographs, two edited collections), including, as lead author, the highly regarded *Myanmar's 'Rohingya' Conflict* (Hurst/Oxford University Press, 2018, with Costas Laoutides). His research focuses on humanitarian/international development approaches in conflict-affected situations, with a particular interest in conflict sensitivity, do no harm, everyday peace, peace-building and countering violent/hateful extremism via community-led programming. His major field of research has been Myanmar.

Dr Aung Naing (pseudonym) is an independent researcher who has spent much of the past two decades studying social protection, poverty reduction and inequalities in Myanmar, as well as training successive generations of new scholars in social research.

Dr Cecile Medail holds a PhD in international political studies from the University of New South Wales. Her main research interests include democratisation, state-building and ethnic identity in Myanmar. Prior to her doctoral studies, she worked with Burmese grassroots organisations in Thailand and in Myanmar for eight years. She provided capacity building support to young community activists from various ethnic backgrounds, advocating for genuine democracy in Myanmar and campaigning for an economic development respectful of the rights of local indigenous communities. She is now a visiting fellow at the Department of Political and Social Change, Coral Bell School of Asia Pacific Affairs, The Australian National University (ANU).

Dr Charlotte Galloway has been researching in Myanmar for over 20 years. An art historian, Charlotte has been actively involved with capacity building in the museum and heritage sector. She has participated in collaborative projects within the Ministry of Religious Affairs and Culture, and was a United Nations Educational, Scientific and Cultural Organization (UNESCO) expert for the preparation of Bagan's world heritage nomination dossier. An experienced educator, she has been visiting faculty at the University of Yangon and has extensive involvement in capacity building and research activities for Myanmar's higher education sector, including working with international donors. Immediately prior to the coup, Charlotte was involved in drafting the higher education components for the National Education Strategic Plan 2 (NESP2) (2021–30) for the Myanmar Ministry of Education. She is currently engaged in a project to investigate and develop alternative modes of education delivery for students in conflict areas.

Associate Professor Costas Laoutides is an associate professor of international relations at Deakin University, Australia. His area of expertise is ethno-political and separatist conflict, and its resolution. He is the co-author of *Myanmar's 'Rohingya' Conflict* (Hurst/Oxford University Press, 2018, with Anthony Ware) and the sole author of *Self-Determination and Collective Responsibility in Secessionist Struggle* (Routledge).

Diya Jiang is a researcher specialising in the fields of international relations and political economy. Her research interests include non-state actors in international relations, foreign influence and democratisation. Following her experience conducting quantitative research for the Center for Policing Equity (policingequity.org/) in New York, she further developed expertise in comparative democratisation and international soft power dynamics during her postgraduate degree in international political economy at the London School of Economics and Political Science. She now pursues her research endeavours at the Central European Institute of Asian Studies (www.ceias. eu), where she has assisted on multiple projects including the Myanmar Coup Tracker (myanmarcouptracker.eu). She is an incoming PhD student in political science at McGill University.

Dr Gerard McCarthy is a research fellow at National University of Singapore's Asia Research Institute (ARI) where he works on the politics of welfare and development in Southeast Asia, especially Myanmar. He also co-leads ARI's archival project 'Living with COVID-19 in Southeast Asia: Personal and visual experiences of crisis, control & Community'. His writing and commentary on welfare politics, non-state social actors, military capitalism and conflict has been published in outlets including *Conflict, Security & Development* and *Journal of Contemporary Asia* along with *The New York Times,* the *Economist* and the *Washington Post.* His book *Outsourcing the Polity: Non-State Welfare, Inequality and Resistance in Myanmar* will be published in 2023 by Cornell University Press. He earned his DPhil from the Department of Political and Social Change at ANU where he was associate director of the ANU Myanmar Research Centre from 2017 to 2019.

Jadyn (pseudonym) is a former computer engineer with diverse experiences including political analysis and monitoring, political campaigning, civic education and media. As a computer engineer during the 2007 Saffron Revolution, he witnessed how the power of the internet carried voices from within Myanmar throughout the entire world. When the country was still closed, Jadyn researched and presented internationally about the internet and the political situation in Myanmar. When the country opened up, he researched and presented locally on civic engagement with the media, politics in cyberspace and political trends in Myanmar.

Juliette McIntyre is a lecturer in law at the University of South Australia, and a PhD candidate at the University of Melbourne. Her PhD thesis examines the rules of procedure of the International Court of Justice. She holds a first-class LLM in international law from the University of Cambridge and is a recipient of the Law Foundation of South Australia Fellowship. She also has significant litigation experience, including before the International Court of Justice. She has published in several leading international journals such as the *Michigan Journal of International Law*, the *Leiden Journal of International Law* and *AJIL Unbound*.

Dr Kristina Kironska is a socially engaged interdisciplinary academic with experience in Myanmar affairs, Taiwan affairs, Central and Eastern Europe – China relations, campaigns and activism. In 2015–16, she lived in Myanmar, where she worked for a local non-governmental organisation (NGO) and conducted research on the 2015 elections, the political transition of the country and the issue of the Rohingya. In 2017–18, she worked for Amnesty International as a campaigner. In 2019–20, she lived in Taipei where she conducted research under the Taiwan Fellowship program, lectured at the University of Taipei and organised monthly human rights talks. Currently, she is the advocacy director at the Central European Institute of Asian Studies (www.ceias.eu) and a senior researcher at the Palacky University in Olomouc, Czech Republic.

Moe Thuzar is senior fellow at the Institute of Southeast Asian Studies (ISEAS)-Yusof Ishak Institute, Singapore, and coordinator of the Myanmar studies program. Moe joined ISEAS in 2008, serving as a lead researcher in the ASEAN Studies Centre up to August 2019. Prior to joining ISEAS, Moe spent 10 years at the Association of Southeast Asian Nations (ASEAN) Secretariat, where she headed the Human Development Unit from 2004 to 2007. A former diplomat, she is researching Burma's foreign policy implementation from 1948 to 1988 for her PhD studies at the National

University of Singapore. Moe has contributed to several compendia on ASEAN and on Myanmar, including *Myanmar: Life After Nargis* (ISEAS, 2009), a co-authored report with Pavin Chachavalpongpun on ASEAN's response to the 2008 Cyclone Nargis in Myanmar, and a coedited volume with Yap Kioe Sheng on *Urbanisation in Southeast Asia: Issues and Implications* (ISEAS, 2012).

Professor Monique Skidmore is an honorary professor with Deakin University's Alfred Deakin Institute. She is an award- and grant-winning Burmese political and medical anthropologist, and international expert media commentator. She has published seven books on Myanmar, including the very highly regarded *Karaoke Fascism: Burma and the Politics of Fear* (University of Pennsylvania Press, 2004). She convened the Burma Studies Update at ANU for eight years, and has held senior positions at the University of Tasmania, University of Queensland and ANU, among other institutions. She is the current director of the Australia Myanmar Institute.

Associate Professor Nicholas Coppel is an adjunct associate professor (practice) at Monash University and a former career diplomat and ambassador. He was Australia's ambassador to Myanmar for four years from 2015 to 2018. Previous postings were as special coordinator of the Regional Assistance Mission to Solomon Islands, deputy high commissioner to Papua New Guinea, deputy ambassador to the Philippines and first secretary in the Australian Embassy, Washington DC. The Solomon Islands government awarded him with the Cross of Solomon Islands for his work towards restoring peace and governance. Among various roles in Canberra, he headed the Economic Analytical Unit in the Department of Foreign Affairs and Trade where he oversaw and contributed to the research, writing and publication of 10 reports covering major trade and economic issues. He holds a Bachelor of Economics degree from ANU and a Master of Business Administration degree from London Business School. From 2004 to 2010 he was on the Editorial Advisory Board of *Asia-Pacific Economic Literature*.

Professor Nicholas Farrelly studied at ANU and the University of Oxford. Over the past 20 years he has researched political conflict and social change across the borderlands where Myanmar meets Thailand, India, Bangladesh and China. In 2006, he founded *New Mandala*, a website that has become a prominent public forum in Southeast Asian studies. He then held a range of academic positions in the College of Asia and the Pacific at ANU, including as deputy director of the Coral Bell School of Asia Pacific Affairs and as director of the Myanmar Research Centre. From 2017 to 2019, Nicholas was an associate dean in the College of Asia and the Pacific, ANU. In 2020, he was appointed to the Board of the Australia-ASEAN Council. As head of the School of Social Sciences at the University of Tasmania, Nicholas leads a vibrant multidisciplinary academic team.

Saw Moo (pseudonym) is a social researcher and project manager currently working with an international organisation in Myanmar. He holds a master's degree in development studies from the University of Melbourne.

Dr Tamas Wells is an academic at the University of Melbourne where he is also coordinator of the university's Myanmar Research Network. His research focuses on contested meanings of democracy, human rights and accountability in Southeast Asia, and the impact of these on development policy. His book *Narrating Democracy in Myanmar* (Cambridge University Press, 2021) examines the Burmese opposition movement in the lead up to the historic 2015 elections in Myanmar and diverging narratives of democracy within the movement and among its international supporters. Before entering academia, he worked as an aid and development adviser and consultant with various NGOs including Save the Children, with seven years living and working in Myanmar. He has been active in developing stronger connections between academics and practitioners in the field of aid and development and is the editor of the *PK Forum*, an online discussion forum on aid and development in Myanmar.

Tay Zar Myo Win is a lecturer at the Faculty of Political Science, Ubon Ratchathani University. His main research interests include analysing electoral systems, decentralisation, democratisation, federalism, social conflict and human rights, both in Myanmar and in the wider Southeast Asian context. His current research projects are the communal conflict in Rakhine State, Myanmar, and the rights of the Rohingya people and the Civil Disobedience Movement in Myanmar's democratisation process. Apart from his research work, Tay Zar has longstanding experience working in development practice, focusing on civic education, democracy and electoral support. Collaborating with civil society organisations and international NGOs in Myanmar, he was involved in developing a series of civic education curricula for young students and adult learners and managed training and workshops. He also closely worked with the Union Election Commission in Myanmar as a member of a technical support team to assist national and local elections in Myanmar.

Dr Ye Min Zaw is an independent researcher and writer in contemporary politics and conflict in Myanmar. His research is focused on sub-national conflict, peace-building and social cohesion in Myanmar, and humanitarian assistance in protracted and fragile conflicts. He has been working in the humanitarian and development sectors for 10 years, with a wide range of international non-profit organisations and the United Nations.

1

Post-Coup Myanmar's Political and Humanitarian Crises

Anthony Ware

Associate Professor, School of Humanities and Social Sciences,
Deakin University, Australia

Monique Skidmore

Professor, Alfred Deakin Institute, Deakin University, Australia

Abstract

Myanmar's coup on 1 February 2021 abruptly ended a decade of (limited) economic and political liberalisations and plunged the country into civil war and a deep humanitarian crisis. This introductory chapter to the volume tracks the key events of the coup, and subsequently, to lay a foundation of facts and details for the analysis offered in the following chapters. It highlights the brutality of the military as they have tried to consolidate power, as well as documenting the emergence of the Committee Representing Pyidaungsu Hluttaw, National Unity Government, Civil Disobedience Movement and People's Defence Force. It documents the current situation regarding numbers of civilian deaths, arbitrary arrests, death sentences, houses destroyed, and people displaced internally and across borders. The chapter concludes that the strength and organisation of resistance clearly took the military leadership by surprise, but this has only increased their brutality. The military face a high rate of defections and are increasingly spread very thinly, but the resistance does not look like it can take control of the country either, leading us to conclude that the conflict is almost certainly destined for a prolonged, bloody stalemate. The chapter then provides a summary of the key contributions of each of the other chapters in the volume, as an outline of the book.

***

The Myanmar military[1] executed a coup d'état in the early hours of Monday morning, 1 February 2021, abruptly ending a decade-long flirtation with (limited) economic and political liberalisation. In a series of pre-dawn raids, the military arrested State Counsellor Aung San Suu Kyi, President Win Myint and other senior members of the elected National League for Democracy (NLD) government (Pietromarchi & Gadzo 2021), and declared a one-year state of emergency, later extended to 18 months, then two years, with further extensions likely. They imposed a national curfew and moved to take control of the key institutions of state. Phone and internet connections were disrupted in Naypyidaw and Yangon (expanding to other centres as resistance spread), state television was taken off air, and financial and banking services were interrupted. In Naypyidaw, military trucks blockaded the parliamentary residential quarter, effectively quarantining hundreds of other elected members of parliament from communications, the media and their constituents. The moves on that first day were swift, decisive, well planned and tightly executed. They were effective in cutting elected representatives and the NLD off from control over any part of the state apparatus.

The coup came just hours before the new parliament had been due to sit for the first time after the 8 November 2020 election. The NLD had won that election with a landslide. It had been widely viewed as a referendum on Aung San Suu Kyi's first five years in office, and the voice of the people was decisive. The NLD won 396 elected seats (83 per cent) in the Union Parliament, an increase from the 370 seats they won in the 2015 election, and well over the 67 per cent super-majority needed to outvote the combined pro-military bloc (once the military-appointed 25 per cent of seats [160 seats] is factored in). The military-backed Union Solidarity and

---

1 The Myanmar military calls itself the 'Tatmadaw', a name that was long adopted by the academic community. However, many in the resistance to the coup refuse to use the name, which literally translates as 'royal armed forces'. As Myanmar is no longer a kingdom, the contemporary use of the name implies 'glorious' more than 'belonging to the king'. In solidarity with the Myanmar people, this chapter, indeed this whole volume, refuses to use the name and usually simply uses the term 'Myanmar military', to avoid implying it is in any way a glorious or meritorious institution. Desmond (2022) makes this case, arguing for use of the term *sit-tat* instead, although Aung Kaung Myat (2022) critiques this as problematic.

Development Party (USDP) won just 33 out of the possible 476 seats in the election, down from 42 seats in 2015, a serious snub by voters that served to further reduce the military's influence in the national parliament to under 200 seats across the two houses. Addressing that, together with NLD campaigning for changes to the 2008 Constitution of the Republic of the Union of Myanmar, were critical motivations behind the coup, because the military would have definitely seen a challenge to its military bloc voting rights in the constitution occur during the next parliamentary term. (That said, it is worth noting that, even then, constitutional change would have required a super-majority of over 75 per cent of parliament voting in favour, and with the military appointing 25 per cent of seats under their 2008 Constitution, so long as the military appointees voted as a bloc, they already had effective power of veto).

The military justified the coup by alleging widespread election fraud, and immediately pledged to clean up politics and run free and fair elections one year after their intervention. These elections have now been deferred until August 2023, and, if they proceed at all, it is clear they will do so without Aung San Suu Kyi or the NLD, in defiance of the will of the people. At best, if they do occur, it seems clear they will be stage-managed and engineered to elect only military-backed parties and candidates to a puppet government. Regardless, to consolidate control, the day after the coup the generals set up the junta-controlled State Administration Council (SAC) to replace the elected government. Chaired by Commander-in-Chief Senior General Min Aung Hlaing and comprising, initially, 11 loyal military personnel, it was expanded to include military-aligned civilian party leaders. In August 2021, it was named as the provisional government, with Senior General Min Aung Hlaing serving as both head of the armed forces and prime minister.

Meanwhile, President Win Myint and Aung San Suu Kyi were permanently sidelined by being charged with a series of trumped-up offences. Win Myint was charged with breaching campaign guidelines and COVID-19 pandemic restrictions, while Aung San Suu Kyi was charged with importing walkie-talkies for her security team (which are restricted in Myanmar and need clearance from military) as well as breaching emergency COVID-19 laws (Myat Thura & Min Wathan 2021). Further charges have been added, with Aung San Suu Kyi facing at least 18 charges including corruption, violating the Official Secrets Act and intent to incite public unrest (*Frontier Myanmar* 2021a). Combined, these charges carry a maximum jail terms of nearly 190 years! By mid-October 2022, the 77-year-old Suu Kyi has already been sentenced to 26 years in jail, some sentences including hard labour, with most charges still to come to court (Mogul & Kwon 2022). The arrogant display of raw power, in the marginalisation of the people's clearly expressed will, is obscene.

While most commentators did not believe the military would institute a coup after the 2020 election, there were many warnings from the military and indications they were considering doing so. On 14 August 2020, three months before the election, 34 pro-military parties including the USDP met with Min Aung Hlaing, seeking to have the military intervene in the event of 'electoral integrity issues' (San Yasmin Aung 2021). Critics were alarmed that the commander-in-chief came out of that meeting bragging, 'I am brave enough to do anything' (San Yasmin Aung 2021), fearing it was a clear threat to institute a coup if they did not win at the ballot box. Then, six days prior to the election, the military issued a statement asserting that the Union Election Commission (UEC) was mishandling preparations for the election (*Irrawaddy* 2021a). Clearly, they were setting up a narrative to support a potential coup. Nonetheless, on election day, 8 November 2020, Min Aung Hlaing did make the comment that, 'I'll have to accept the people's wish and the results that come with it' (Sithu Aung Myint 2021). Observers relaxed, hoping he was committed to respecting the electoral outcome. Immediately after the election, however, he announced the military would review the electoral process—a power it does not constitutionally have— then went on a campaign to discredit the election results, repeatedly alleging irregularities throughout December 2020 and January 2021 (San Yasmin Aung 2021). The coup was thus a surprise, yet not really a surprise.

A week after the coup, 70 UEC officials were taken into custody (ANFREL 2021), replaced by junta appointees who quickly called for the NLD to be disbanded and party leaders to be prosecuted as 'traitors', echoing the senior general's pretext for the coup. That has not (yet) formally occurred, but de facto, through military power and arrests, the NLD has been sidelined from power. If the junta does eventually run new elections, it seems clear that the NLD and other democratic parties will be prevented from contesting. In July 2022, three of the senior UEC officials who administrated the 2020 election were sentenced to prison terms, including the UEC chair Hla Thein (Ko Cho 2022).

Coercive force and civilian resistance

Opposition to the coup was rapidly mobilised. The NLD published a statement on the party's official Facebook account shortly after the coup began unfolding on 1 February, purportedly written by Aung San Suu Kyi before she was detained, urging people to resist the coup (*BBC News* 2021). Whether this came from her, or the NLD media team, elected politicians countered quickly and strategically. Four days after the coup, on 5 February, elected representatives who were not in detention held an emergency parliamentary session, releasing a public claim to be the only legitimate government of Myanmar and appointing a Cabinet. They formed the Committee Representing Pyidaungsu Hluttaw (CRPH) to serve as the legitimate parliament, a body that quickly included over 300 elected representatives from a spectrum of political parties spanning the two houses of parliament (Pyidaungsu Hluttaw 2021; CRPH 2021; *Irrawaddy* 2021b). On 31 March, the CRPH declared the country's 2008 Constitution void and put forward an interim replacement, the Federal Democracy Charter, hoping to woo an alliance with the armed organisations[2] of the country's many borderland minority groups (AP News 2021). On 16 April, the CRPH appointed a National Unity Government (NUG), with representatives from parties beyond the NLD, to form government under the CRPH. The NUG appointed a full Cabinet with ministers and departments (see www.nugmyanmar.org/en/), as well as representatives in several countries including the United States, United Kingdom, France, Czech Republic, Australia and South Korea as they quickly sought international recognition.

The broader public initially resisted the coup by banging pots and pans at 8pm, as the curfew came into effect, which has been a traditional way to ward off evil spirits for centuries (Vossion 1891, 109; Lovett 2021). While minimal, it did signal to the military on the streets how little popular support they had. Two days after the coup, healthcare workers went on strike, quickly followed by civil servants in other sectors across Myanmar (ANFREL 2021). This was the beginning of the Civil Disobedience Movement (CDM), in which civil servants, workers in government health and education sectors, and others connected to government (and beyond),

---

2   These armies, from the country's many minority groups in the borderlands, are often referred to as ethnic armed organisations. Given the damage the ethnicisation of identities has done in Myanmar, particularly the hegemonic adoption of 'ethnicity' in political identities, we prefer avoiding the term completely. 'Ethnicity' is an intellectually lazy conception of minority groups, to be avoided wherever possible.

simply refused to work for the regime, striking until the junta reversed the coup and freed their elected leaders. At its peak, the CDM boasted more than 360,000 members, most of whom chose to walk away from state jobs, and was nominated for the 2022 Nobel Peace Prize (Lipes 2022a). The CDM also became a force online, widely sharing creative forms of resistance and photos of groups supporting the CDM to promote solidarity. By the end of the first week after the coup, tens of thousands of civilians were flooding the streets daily in peaceful protests (Al Jazeera 2021a), with up to 90 per cent of the staff in some government ministries on strike (*Frontier Myanmar* 2021b). Initially, the security forces showed some restraint, for example by sending the police rather than the military to control protests. As the police stood in formation, not advancing, protesters attempted to use moral shame to win them over; however, this only resulted in the military being deployed in many locations. Within weeks, demonstrators were widely beaten, arrested and fired upon. Police and soldiers responded in Mandalay, Bago and Naypyidaw with water cannons, tear gas and both live and rubber bullets (ANFREL 2021). Fortify Rights and Yale Law School's Schell Center claim the junta created a special command a day after the coup, responsible for the operation of troops in urban areas, and authorised lethal attacks on unarmed civilians (Fortify Rights 2022). They claim the junta primarily deployed snipers to kill protesters to instil fear, while soldiers were instructed to arbitrarily arrest protesters and activists.

For weeks, the military crackdown only spurred on the peaceful protest movement. Demonstrations grew to hundreds of thousands of people on the streets across the country (Al Jazeera 2021b; *Guardian* 2021)—this despite expanded curfews, internet cuts, Facebook/WhatsApp/Twitter being completely blocked for days, the deployment of armoured vehicles in city streets (Safi 2021) and security forces firing on protesters (Hallam 2021; Paddock 2021). However, the mass demonstrations finally dissipated as the weeks of mass arrests and the overwhelming use of military force against the civilians took its toll. Eventually, soldiers took to mowing down demonstrators with machine guns and destroying barricades with rocket propelled grenades—for example, in Bago on 9 April 2021 where at least 82 were killed and corpses piled high in the grounds of a local Buddhist temple (Gerin 2021; Strangio 2021).

As this coercive force against the civilians mounted, and numbers protesting peacefully on the streets dwindled, the resistance movement split into those that continued to pursue non-violent civil disobedience and those who wished to use violent means to resist the coup (Lovett & Safi 2021).

Armed resistance groups self-organised, attempting to ambush junta forces and fight back with homemade weapons (Strangio 2021). By early April, for example, activists in Sagaing Region, in northern Myanmar, had armed themselves with rudimentary rifles and adopted the name 'Kalay Civil Army'. With the multiplication of such militias increasing, the NUG announced the formation of a nationwide 'People's Defence Force' (PDF) on 5 May 2021, declaring it a forerunner of a truly federal armed forces institution that would include soldiers from all anti-regime armed groups (*Irrawaddy* 2021c). Their aim was to militarily depose those who took power by force, in cooperation with minority group armies who would work with them. The NUG suggested that 'preparations for this army were made a long time ago' and announced both military training for new recruits and a weapons acquisition department under the NUG's Ministry of Defence (Whong 2021). Unsurprisingly, the military immediately labelled the PDFs as 'terrorist' organisations. But they grew. By 7 September 2021, the NUG's Ministry of Defence announced the launch of a 'defensive war' and called for a 'nationwide revolution' against the military. By October 2021, it had formed a central military command to coordinate resistance operations across the country (Al Jazeera 2021c; Reuters 2021).

Fast forward to the situation as this book is being compiled in late 2022, a year and three-quarters after the coup, and the situation remains highly contested. What started as civil disobedience has now turned into a civil war, taking a horrific toll on the people as the junta rolls out a military campaign across the country to eliminate all opposition to its rule. The financial and human toll, on both sides, means both sides now appear to be losing steam, and the situation risks becoming a grinding stalemate in which neither side can be completely victorious.

The PDF, for their part, claim to be stronger than ever (Lipes 2022b), with new recruits drawn from all walks of life: deposed members of parliament, artists, celebrities, students, farmers and defected soldiers. In May 2022, the NUG Ministry of Defence claimed the PDF had 257 units based in 250 townships across Myanmar, with strong links with more than 400 other local resistance militias. By November 2022, the *Irrawaddy* (Banyar Aung 2022) assessed their operational capacity at over 300 PDF battalions of 200–500 members each, right across the country, 221 of them under the direct command of the NUG, with a further 63 battalions waiting for recognition by the NUG. Combined PDF membership, according to this report, is now over 65,000, excluding the 400 or more Local Defence Force militias not formally affiliated with either the NUG or the established armies of minority groups. Certainly, reports suggest the regime now controls barely half of the country (Min Min 2022a). Over 12,900 soldiers and police have defected to the PDF (MPM 2022; Min Min 2022a). The NUG has raised and spent over USD55 million on military equipment, arms and training for the PDF, and commenced payments to PDF soldiers (Banyar Aung 2022)—in part through innovative fundraising for a government-in-exile, such as selling shares in coup leader Min Aung Hlaing's mansion in Yangon (*Irrawaddy* 2022c) and selling NUG 'treasury bonds'—that latter of which had raised USD38 million by June 2022 (PTV 2022). They also claim to have set up production of single-shot firearms, automatic submachine guns, land mines and bombs to be dropped by drones, outside of factory settings across Myanmar (Lipes 2022c).

However, the NUG/PDF are struggling. Another USD100 million would be required to properly arm the PDF (*Irrawaddy* 2022d), with only 25 per cent of PDF forces fully armed, and another 40 per cent carrying homemade weapons (Banyar Aung 2022). This prompts the uncomfortable question of whether external powers should be more active in arming and training the opposition movement. At present, PDF forces can only employ guerrilla tactics and are unable to face the military head-on (Lipes 2022b). In addition, the CDM is losing steam amid junta crackdowns that have made peaceful opposition too dangerous. The NUG President's Office has conceded that more than a third of people who walked away from state jobs to take part in peaceful anti-junta CDM action have since returned to those jobs, buckling under personal and financial insecurity (Lipes 2022a).

At the same time, though, the Myanmar military are also struggling. In March 2022, Min Aung Hlaing said the military would 'annihilate [its opponents] until the end' (Al Jazeera 2022). They have made extensive new weapons purchases, including jet fighters, armoured vehicles, surface-to-air missiles and mobile defence systems from Russia (Ohmar 2022), as well as other weapons from China (Lipes 2022c). However, weapons alone cannot win against the people, and morale is low and defections high. Prior to the coup, the military was estimated to have around 400,000 troops; it is likely now that they are down to only half that (Min Min 2022a). One contributing factor is the failure of the military company Myanma Economic Holdings Limited (MEHL) to distribute dividends. MEHL is a massive conglomerate, with 56 subsidiary companies operating across 14 industries. Its revenue is a primary means by which the military has self-financed and remained in power for decades. It has been mandatory for more than 20 years for all ranks to buy MEHL shares, and the share dividends are effectively seen as a salary component, becoming a pension after retirement. However, while MEHL's financial losses are not public, as recently as mid-2022 it was clear that the dividend payment due in September 2021 remained unpaid (Min Min 2022b; Zaw Ye Thwe 2022), meaning the regime had not been able to pay current and former soldiers their full salary since the coup. It is not clear in late 2022 whether they have yet been paid, but while MEHL and other military companies are struggling financially, the military will continue to be cash-starved and morale is likely to decline.

The outcome is a terrible, ongoing conflict that has devastated the country and, in our estimation, seems destined for stalemate. The NUG and military would disagree, but we do not see the tide turning any time soon. The result is an acute political and humanitarian crisis affecting the entire population, destroying lives and livelihoods. As of 23 November 2022, according to data from the Assistance Association for Political Prisoners (AAPP 2022a), 2,533 civilians have been verified as killed by the junta, including well over 400 children, with 16,403 arrests for participating in anti-coup activities including the CDM. At that time, some 12,976 remained detained by the military, despite just 1,608 having been charged and sentenced. This figure *may* be less now, after the junta released 5,774 prisoners in an amnesty on 17 November 2022 for National Day, but the AAPP had only been able to verify that 402 of the political prisoners on their list had been released by 23 November (AAPP 2022b, 2022c). Meanwhile, a total of 128 civilians have now been sentenced to death, the first four of whom were executed on 25 July amid global outcry.

The Institute for Strategy and Policy – Myanmar record at least 2,299 civilians shot by the military while protesting and another 701 who died in the process of being arrested by the SAC (ISP 2022a). They confirm that at least 36,000 houses and buildings were destroyed in military raids since the coup (ISP 2022b), resulting in more than 1.6 million people now internally displaced (ISP 2022c)—taking the combined total of internally displaced people plus refugees from Myanmar to almost 3 million people (ISP 2022d; Al Jazeera 2022). The NUG allege around 2,800 separate war crimes have been committed by the military, including arbitrary killings, extrajudicial executions, rape, the use of torture, using civilians as human shields, air and artillery strikes on civilian targets, and the looting and burning of houses (*Irrawaddy* 2022e). On the other side, however, the SAC allege over 3,542 civilians have been killed by resistance forces in targeted assassinations as alleged military informants (ISP 2022a). This has not been independently verified, but, if true, it would take the total civilians killed in violence since the coup to over 7,000 people. Evidence of atrocities on both sides is mounting (Pedroletti 2022).

What is clear is that the strength and organisation of resistance clearly took the military leadership by surprise, and its effectiveness and longevity has surprised most international commentators. The CDM, NUG and PDF have prevented the military from consolidating control. By any analysis, the coup has been only partially successful, at best, in delivering control of the country to the generals, who still have only limited control over the bureaucracy, health and education systems, international relations and, indeed, territory across Myanmar. Their ongoing campaign has not only highlighted their brutality and bloody-mindedness, but also the incompetence of the military. Its need to resort to brutal tactics and overwhelming force, and still be unable to succeed, underscores its total ineptitude. The high rate of defections of soldiers and police to the PDFs have become an increasing concern for the military and have helped to sustain and grow the PDF resistance (Esther J & Min Min 2022). The military are increasingly spread very thin, fighting insurgents on a multitude of fronts, to the point that they have needed to draft police to serve on the frontlines against PDF forces (*Irrawaddy* 2022b) and form armed pro-military civilian militias (*Irrawaddy* 2022a). Reports suggest they have had to resort to airstrikes because ground troops are reluctant to fight (BNI 2022).

There are a range of deeply concerning factors in the events since the coup. These include the military's use of battlefield tactics against civilians in urban areas, particularly the coercive violent repression of unarmed, peaceful civilians in the first months after the coup; renewed warfare between the military and several of the minority group armies, including the use of aerial bombardment for the first time in two decades; increasing strategic engagement of Russia and China; decline, outlawing or suborning of the institutions that previously supported civil society and democratisation, specifically the Buddhist monkhood (Sangha), the NLD and the media; and the rapid breakdown of institutional capacity and increase in state fragility, with a decimation of the economy and rapid impoverishment of the country. The interlinked political, economic and humanitarian crises are severe and deeply intertwined.

Origins and outline of the book

This brief overview of events since the coup sets the stage for the chapters that follow. The contributions in the volume further analyse key aspects of the political and humanitarian crises precipitated by the coup. They explore the implications of various aspects of the coup and its potential responses.

This volume emerged from a two-day research roundtable symposium hosted online and in person by Deakin University on 1–2 February 2022, to mark the one-year anniversary of the coup. A call for chapters was circulated internationally in August 2021, but, with closed borders for COVID-19, most interest came from within Australia and similar time zones. The chapter submissions were selected for relevance and coherence. From there, contributors were required to submit a first draft of their paper prior to the roundtable, and to attend the full two days. Papers were then presented and discussed in-depth by participants on 1–2 February 2022 at the roundtable symposium, which was also open to other selected academics, policymakers and aid sector representatives. Based on the discussions during the roundtable about each paper and the debates about some of the key challenges and issues, authors revised their contributions through several rounds of editorial review—and then the manuscript underwent double peer review by the publisher. All papers are up to date with events as of November 2022, but their focus is not so much on current events as much as on the implications of key aspects of the coup, and the sorts of policy and practical responses international actors have, could and perhaps should make. This analysis is likely to be relevant for years to come.

The remainder of the volume consists of 13 chapter contributions from various scholars, experts and practitioners on topics ranging from the role of social media and disruptive technologies, multinational enterprise behaviour, justice and accountability mechanisms being pursued in international courts, relations with China and ASEAN, whether the Federal Democracy Charter offers a potential path to peace in a post-coup Myanmar, the changing situation in Rakhine State, weaponisation of the pandemic response, appropriate aid approaches and the political resistance dimensions being embraced by local actors, and Myanmar's higher education sector. There are, of course, many more aspects of the political and humanitarian crises precipitated by the coup that need analysis. It is clear that the bloody reintroduction of absolute military rule means that all previous policy settings towards Myanmar are no longer valid—whether in retrospect they ever really were. There is now an urgent need for new policy settings, and for practical engagement based on revised understandings, new goals, new modes and different sorts of partnerships with local actors and/or recipient groups. This volume has a very practical policy focus, exploring the issues presented here in detail, to arrive at policy implications and responses. These are presented by each contributor, within their chapters, but are also then summarised in our final chapter, 'The Aftermath: Policy Responses to Myanmar's Political and Humanitarian Crises'.

There is, of course, a deep tension between our conclusion that the most likely scenario is a drawn-out stalemate in the civil war, most likely until something changes within military itself, and the very idea of policy recommendations premised on the notion that outsiders can have some influence. Nonetheless, we do believe there are ways international actors can show solidarity with and aid the Myanmar people, even if the extent of impact is limited. Perhaps, even, this support may even contribute, in some tiny way, to precipitating internal changes and ending this horrendous predicament.

Looking at the contributions of each of the chapters in turn, Chapter 2, by Professor Nicholas Farrelly, lays out four possible future scenarios for post-coup Myanmar, and thus various potential political and humanitarian conditions in the country over the years ahead. Each of Farrelly's four possible scenarios—coup success, coup failure, centrifugal unravelling and implosion—has long-term implications about the sorts of crises, plausible humanitarian conditions and, thus, international policy and aid responses that may be necessary to support the Myanmar people. The analysis draws on the erratic imbalance of forces, ideas, politics and strategies that have energised Myanmar's turbulence since the recent coup and that, in many respects, influence the range of potential responses. The scenarios are examined separately, and yet, in practice, aspects of each of the potential futures are part of a complex set of trajectories. The analysis highlights the intense challenges any future Myanmar government will face, and those faced by international partners seeking to influence developments in a more positive direction in the meantime. The advantage of looking at the scenarios as distinct future possibilities is that they imply medium-term outcomes that have significant, perhaps permanent, implications for Myanmar, for its immediate neighbours and indeed for the wider Asian region. These scenarios should be kept in mind as each of the subsequent chapters are read.

Chapter 3, by Jadyn (pseudonym), Professor Monique Skidmore and Dr Cecile Medail, explores the role of social media and disruptive technologies in the post-coup conflict. Since the coup, the junta has attempted to expand its authoritarian control over cyberspace, deploying the latest encryption and cybersecurity surveillance technologies to extend its existing physical and psychological warfare battlefields online. In response, anti-coup forces have adapted and innovatively used digital technologies to support the revolution, making the digital space a new, key frontline in the battle between the military and the people of Myanmar. In this chapter, Jayden, Skidmore and Medail analyse the deployment and implications of these new technologies by a military state with techno-totalitarian ambitions, and the ways the resistance movement, civil and armed, has countered with the adoption of disruptive technologies to organise, share real-time information, finance revolution and counter the regime's fearmongering through propaganda.

Multinational enterprises have come under sustained pressure since the coup to review their operations in Myanmar and exit any relationships they have with military-controlled entities. In Chapter 4, former Australian ambassador to Myanmar Associate Professor Nicholas Coppel examines this pressure, the extent and significance of corporate relationships with the military, their responses to the coup and the impact this has had on the junta. Coppel finds that very few foreign firms were in joint venture or had other commercial relations with military-owned or controlled entities, and that companies that left Myanmar mostly did so for security, commercial or reputational reasons. Moreover, leaving was not always easy or helpful to Myanmar's citizens and, in some instances, even benefited the military. Overestimation of the extent and significance of such relationships has distracted policymakers and activists from considering policies focused on the role the business community could play to strengthen human rights in Myanmar. Taken together, targeted sanctions and activist pressure run the risk of stigmatising all business with Myanmar, including legitimate, non-sanctioned activity.

Three separate international justice processes commenced prior to the 2020 coup to hold the Myanmar military accountable for the atrocities committed against the Rohingya. Chapter 5, by Dr Adam Simpson and Juliette McIntyre, considers the implications of Myanmar's 2021 coup for these mechanisms of international justice, and whether the military (or any other groups in Myanmar) could be prosecuted for crimes committed during and since the February 2021 coup using any of these mechanisms. Simpson and

McIntyre find that while the influence and authority of international courts are important, their ability to respond to Myanmar's many crises is limited. At best, the chapter argues, one can anticipate that the joint pressures of the ICC investigation, the ICJ proceedings and work of fact-finding missions and other human rights agencies will lead to an international consensus to refuse the junta recognition.

Chapters 6 and 7 explore China–Myanmar relations and ASEAN's response to the coup. Chapter 6, by Dr Kristina Kironska and Diya Jiang, examines China's shifting response to the coup. China has significant interests in Myanmar and is perhaps the most powerful external actor in relationship with Myanmar; it is thus interesting that Beijing has remained more cautious than other countries in its response to the coup. Kironska and Jiang examine the detailed exchanges between China and Myanmar since the coup, and analyse the two countries' strategic interaction, offering an explanation for why China has gradually changed from a (seemingly) neutral stance immediately after the coup to one more in favour of the military regime. The chapter argues that, initially, ambiguity was logical and beneficial, but, as time went by, appearing neutral became costly to China's strategic interests. China's initial hesitation stemmed largely from the perceived risk of a negative impact on its global economic and political interests, and the risk of security issues surrounding its interests within Myanmar. However, as international attention on Myanmar has lessened, China has once again been motivated primarily by its geostrategic interests in Myanmar, and priority to advance its Belt and Road Initiative projects and further its long-term, two-ocean strategy.

Moe Thuzar, a former head of the Human Development Unit at the ASEAN Secretariat, examines ASEAN's response to the coup in Chapter 7. Myanmar has posed a dilemma for ASEAN ever since its admission into the grouping in 1997, even during its decade of democratisation (2011–21). The February 2021 coup presents the most serious crisis for ASEAN since Myanmar joined the association. Thuzar reviews two historical crises to illustrate ASEAN's Myanmar dilemma: the response to Cyclone Nargis in 2007 dealing with an earlier military regime, and the Rohingya refugee crisis in 2017, which erupted during the democratically elected NLD government's tenure. Using these to frame analysis of ASEAN's responses to date towards the 2021 Myanmar coup, Thuzar argues that new precedents may be emerging that offer some insights into the opportunities and limitations of ASEAN's engagement with recalcitrant members. Myanmar's value to and in ASEAN, and Myanmar's capacity to meet its commitments/obligations as an ASEAN member, present a dilemma for the regional bloc. The chapter concludes with a number of clear policy recommendations for ASEAN based on this analysis.

As noted in the summary of events above, less than two months after the coup, the CRPH (i.e. the representatives elected in the November 2020 election but denied power by the coup) declared the country's 2008 Constitution void and put forward an interim replacement, the Federal Democracy Charter. A key aim of the charter was to woo an alliance with the armed organisations of the country's many borderland minority groups. Chapter 8, by Associate Professor Costas Laoutides, explores this charter, and, in particular, whether it holds the potential to end decades of intergroup conflict and unify the minorities in a common effort to oust the brutal military regime. Laoutides examines the charter in light of international experiences in power sharing agreements designed to mediate the potential harm of majoritarian democracy, and finds that its continued framing around ethnicity as the basis for political identity problematic. In particular, issues emerge around the right to self-determination granted to federal states, and collective rights granted to ethnic groups who may be more geographically dispersed. Laoutides concludes that the charter has not offered a compelling vision to unite minorities, and, despite appearing progressive, its semi-consociational approach around ideas of ethnic identity remains locked in the problematic past rather than paving the way for a future that unites the people.

In Chapter 9, Associate Professor Anthony Ware and Associate Professor Costas Laoutides explore the surprisingly rapid expansion of control over large parts of Rakhine State by the Arakan Army as they take advantage of an informal ceasefire. Ware and Laoutides document the expansion of de facto state institutional functionings by the Arakan Army since the coup, having implemented new judicial, taxation, conflict resolution and security functions, taken a leading role in the COVID-19 response and overturned major aspects of Rohingya policy at the local level. The chapter argues that this is a significant power shift, likely to reshape Rakhine State and (perhaps) politics for decades to come. This chapter explore the likely trajectory of these changes, and the implications for both domestic politics and international aid/peace-building. These developments will have significant implications for the Rohingya, but the nature of these implications is not yet clear or resolved, given that the underlying issues for the Rohingya remain unaltered.

Chapters 9 and 10 consider the impact of the coup on Rakhine State; on intercommunal relations with the Rohingya; and on the emergence of parallel, de facto, state-like institutions under the Arakan Army. Chapter 10, by Ye Min Zaw and Tay Zar Myo Win, examines how the national crisis impacted communal tensions between Arakanese and Rohingya communities in Rakhine State, and the changes in social tension given both the expansion of territorial control by the Arakan Army and the resurgence of Rohingya identity. It explores how the political crisis has impacted communal tensions in Rakhine State and how the communities have responded. Noting significantly improved intercommunal relations, Ye Min Zaw and Tay Zar Myo Win argue that, under the surface of the seemingly stable situation, an atmosphere of fear remains—principally, the fear that violence may resume at any time, as the underlying issues remain unresolved.

Chapter 11 considers the COVID-19 pandemic response and non-state welfare before and after the coup, and how this has impacted Myanmar's vibrant non-state charitable sector. Dr Gerard McCarthy and Saw Moo (pseudonym) draw on a national survey conducted in January 2021, with follow-up work since the coup, to trace the ways in which both the elected government of Aung San Suu Kyi and then then military regime since February 2021 have exploited the COVID-19 response to benefit their political allies and entrench their social dominance. They find that despite issues with the NLD government response, they did encourage and support non-state social responses during 2020. However, after seizing power in February 2021, the SAC weaponised the COVID-19 response to brutally suppress political opposition in ways that have disrupted the non-state pandemic response: suppressing perceived dissenters, empowering loyalists and disciplining charitable actors. As a result, the nascent state–societal cooperation of the NLD-era came to a dramatic end in the wake of the coup, deepening the reliance of ordinary people on private and non-state providers who receive no government or official support. In this sense, the weaponisation of COVID-19 by the junta has compounded the process of social outsourcing that has been ongoing for decades, entrenching societal reliance on non-state social actors both to survive and resist dictatorship. McCarthy and Saw Moo thus urge greater international support to non-state welfare provision in the short term.

Chapters 12 and 13 explore humanitarian aid and responses to the crises in Myanmar: what is possible, what it would look like and how it would be delivered. Chapter 12, by Dr Anne Décobert, reassesses ongoing debates about international humanitarian engagement in Myanmar in light of the coup, arguing that responses to the humanitarian crises precipitated by the coup demonstrate the effectiveness of localised aid. Arguing that neutrality of aid is not possible or desirable in such a context, she focuses attention on humanitarian autonomy, rights and justice. Décobert sees not just ongoing resistance against the military regime in the response by local aid agencies, but also growing resistance towards unequal and unjust international aid systems. In this, Décobert calls for significantly more localisation of aid to Myanmar, supporting local organisations in planning and response, noting that the activist agenda of most localised humanitarian response demands a solidarity-based approach rather than insistence on aid neutrality. While recognising that there are no simple answers to difficult issues, Décobert argues that, in a context where normative neutrality can do harm, reframing 'good humanitarianism' as promoting local agency and autonomy provides a moral compass for international actors to navigate complex political and ethical dilemmas.

Dr Aung Naing (pseudonym) and Dr Tamas Wells follow this up in Chapter 13, examining the impacts of the February 2021 coup on local organisations delivering humanitarian aid in Myanmar. Exploring findings from a recent survey of civil society organisations (CSOs) in Myanmar, they explore ways in which CSOs use local relief to resist military rule—not through overt opposition, but, instead, through localised fulfilment of what should be state functions by non-state CSOs. In this sense, Aung Naing and Wells argue that, through welfare, CSOs demonstrate a particular form of resistance, embodying a viable, legitimate and internally sustainable alternative to the current military government's claims and approach. This chapter urges a reorientation of humanitarian policy towards Myanmar that embraces the complexity, ambiguity and latent potential of emergent, volunteer welfare groups as not only a means of delivering aid in ways that avoid entanglement and dependency on coup-controlled processes, but also enable and promote active citizenship in local communities, which is itself a critical step towards re-establishing community life and institutional integrity in Myanmar.

The final contribution to the volume, Chapter 14 by Professor Charlotte Galloway, examines the impact of the coup on Myanmar's higher education system and the likely implications for future foreign engagement. Galloway identifies how the coup has completely disrupted the progress made within the sector over the last decade, and this almost certainly applies to all levels of the education sector in Myanmar. But, unique to the tertiary sector, the military leaders' lack of trust in engagement with foreign researchers and entities, and their inability to accept even the mildest criticism of their own policy positions, is crippling the higher education sector. The consequences of another lost generation on Myanmar's future prosperity are dire. Without homegrown expertise there will, by necessity, be reliance on external actors to achieve any economic and social development, as the military brutality deters even international students from returning to Myanmar, further eroding Myanmar's knowledge-based capacities. It is difficult to see how the higher education system can recover, and there is no expectation that higher education reform will be a military regime priority.

Thus, on most fronts, the situation in Myanmar is dire. The local response and resistance to the regime is impressive and has defied most predictions. There is an enormous amount for the international community to learn from the local civil disobedience, organising, active citizenship and humanitarian response. However, it is hard to move away from the conclusion that a grinding stalemate is becoming entrenched that only further impoverishes the country and destroys its people and institutions. Chapter 15 returns to the question of future trajectory and international policy and aid responses to the political and humanitarian crises in Myanmar. This final chapter summarises the major findings and implications from the previous chapters. There are no good options. There is no easy solution, no way to force the military to retreat from this brutal and destructive path. Nor is there any good way to change the circumstances of tens of millions of ordinary people who are suffering. Resolution of the complex crises in Myanmar can only come from within the country, and, most likely, from within the Myanmar military hierarchy. However unlikely, we implore them to change, to step back and hand over power to the people. Meanwhile, the research and solid analysis in this volume points to some of the possibilities that exist to improve our response, in coordination with and support of the locals at the frontlines of resistance, to perhaps make a small difference. That is our hope, as we complete this volume.

One final note: conducting any research in Myanmar at this time is very challenging. It is almost impossible, and probably very unwise, for Westerners (at least) to travel to the country for research. And the environment is not a lot easier for local researchers. Travel can be dangerous, asking questions can be potentially problematic, and carrying research data and notes is potentially risky. All contributors to this volume have worked closely with local informants and researchers, whether explicitly recognised in the authorship or subsumed to protect anonymity, and their analysis is based on years of collaboration and engagement. We truly thank these mostly unnamed colleagues for their partnership and seek to amplify their voices through this volume, even if we cannot name most of them at this time. For their sake, we hope this analysis resonates, and impacts policy and practice in ways that lead to change, to the extent any foreign engagement may be able to influence the dire situation in Myanmar.

References

AAPP (Assistance Association for Political Prisoners). 2022a. 'Daily Briefing in Relation to the Military Coup'. 23 November. aappb.org/?p=23521

AAPP (Assistance Association for Political Prisoners). 2022b. 'Press Statement: Burma's 2022 National Day Prison Releases'. 23 November. aappb.org/?p=23470

AAPP (Assistance Association for Political Prisoners). 2022c. 'Statement Update on November 17 Political Prisoner Releases'. 23 November. aappb.org/?p=23503

Al Jazeera. 2021a. 'Thousands of Myanmar Protesters in Standoff with Police in Yangon'. 6 February. www.aljazeera.com/news/2021/2/6/thousands-of-myanmar-protesters-face-off-with-police-in-yangon

Al Jazeera. 2021b. 'Hundreds of Thousands Swell Myanmar Protests against Coup'. 11 February. www.aljazeera.com/news/2021/2/11/us-treasury-sanctions-10-burmese-military-leaders-for-coup-role

Al Jazeera. 2021c. 'Myanmar Shadow Government Calls for Uprising against Military'. 7 September. www.aljazeera.com/news/2021/9/7/myanmar-shadow-government-launches-peoples-defensive-war

Al Jazeera. 2022. 'More Than 1 Million People Displaced in Myanmar: UN'. 1 June. www.aljazeera.com/news/2022/6/1/more-than-1-million-people-displaced-in-myanmar-un

ANFREL (Asian Network for Free Elections). 2021. 'Myanmar Situation Update (1 to 14 February 2021)'. 15 February. anfrel.org/wp-content/uploads/2021/03/Myanmar-Situation-Update-1-to-14-February-2021.pdf

AP News. 2021. 'Junta's Foes Woo Ethnic Allies with New Myanmar Constitution'. 1 April. apnews.com/article/thailand-yangon-myanmar-587c55a3227917ccf3 4ea9052bea41ee

Aung Kaung Myat. 2022. 'Sit-Tat or Tatmadaw? Debates on What to Call the Most Powerful Institution in Burma'. *Tea Circle*, 3 October. teacircleoxford. com/politics/sit-tat-or-tatmadaw-debates-on-what-to-call-the-most-powerful-institution-in-burma/

Banyar Aung. 2022. 'An Assessment of Myanmar's Parallel Civilian Govt after Almost 2 Years of Revolution'. *Irrawaddy*, 24 November. www.irrawaddy.com/opinion/ analysis/an-assessment-of-myanmars-parallel-civilian-govt-after-almost-2-years-of-revolution.html

BBC News. 2021. 'Myanmar Coup: Aung San Suu Kyi Detained as Military Seizes Control'. 1 February. www.bbc.com/news/world-asia-55882489

BNI (Burma News International). 2022. 'Karen State: 2,190 Burma Army Soldiers Killed—KNU Claims Junta Now Resorting to Airstrikes as Its Ground Troops Reluctant to Fight'. 17 January. www.bnionline.net/en/news/karen-state-2190-burma-army-soldiers-killed-knu-claims-junta-now-resorting-airstrikes-its

CRPH (Committee Representing Pyidaungsu Hluttaw). 2021. *Announcement No (1/2021)*. 8 February. crphmyanmar.org/declarationeng-1-2021-8-feb-2021/ (page discontinued).

Desmond. 2022. 'Please Don't Call Myanmar Military Tatmadaw'. *Irrawaddy*, 25 May. www.irrawaddy.com/opinion/guest-column/please-dont-call-myanmar-military-tatmadaw.html

Esther J and Min Min. 2022. 'Head of Myanmar's Junta Urges Unity as Military Defections Continue'. *Myanmar Now*, 29 March. myanmar-now.org/en/news/ head-of-myanmars-junta-urges-unity-as-military-defections-continue

Fortify Rights. 2022. *'Nowhere Is Safe': The Myanmar Junta's Crimes against Humanity Following the* Coup D'état. Fortify Rights & Yale Law School's Schell Center, 27 March. www.fortifyrights.org/downloads/Nowhere%20is%20Safe%20-%20 Fortify%20Rights%20Report.pdf

Frontier Myanmar. 2021a. 'Aung San Suu Kyi Hit with Two New Criminal Charges'. 1 March. www.frontiermyanmar.net/en/aung-san-suu-kyi-hit-with-two-new-criminal-charges/

Frontier Myanmar. 2021b. 'Striking Government Workers Say They Are "Ready to Face the Worst"'. 8 March. www.frontiermyanmar.net/en/striking-government-workers-say-they-are-ready-to-face-the-worst/

Gerin, Roseanne. 2021. 'Myanmar Junta Kills Scores of Protesters in Bago, Decrees Death Penalty for 19 in Yangon'. *Radio Free Asia*, 9 April. www.rfa.org/english/ news/myanmar/bago-protesters-04092021192417.html

Guardian. 2021. 'Myanmar: More Than 100,000 Protest in Streets against Coup'. 18 February. www.theguardian.com/world/2021/feb/17/suu-kyi-myanmar-trial-protests-military

Hallam, Jonny. 2021. 'Myanmar Police Open Fire on Protesters in Mandalay Leaving at Least Two Dead, Say Reports'. *CNN*, 20 February. edition.cnn.com/2021/02/20/asia/myanmar-police-protestors-reports-shooting-intl/index.html

Irrawaddy. 2021a. 'NLD Govt Slams Myanmar's Military for Attacking Election Body'. 4 February. www.irrawaddy.com/news/burma/nld-govt-slams-myanmars-military-attacking-election-body.html

Irrawaddy. 2021b. 'Amid Coup, Myanmar's NLD Lawmakers Form Committee to Serve as Legitimate Parliament'. 8 February. www.irrawaddy.com/news/burma/amid-coup-myanmars-nld-lawmakers-form-committee-serve-legitimate-parliament.html

Irrawaddy. 2021c. 'Myanmar's Shadow Government Forms People's Defense Force'. 5 May. www.irrawaddy.com/news/burma/myanmars-shadow-government-forms-peoples-defense-force.html

Irrawaddy. 2022a. 'Myanmar Junta Arming, Training Civilians as Losses, Defections Mount'. 18 January. www.irrawaddy.com/news/burma/myanmar-junta-arming-training-civilians-as-losses-defections-mount.html

Irrawaddy. 2022b. 'Myanmar Junta Enacts Law Allowing It to Deploy Police to Front Lines'. 29 March. www.irrawaddy.com/news/burma/myanmar-junta-enacts-law-allowing-it-to-deploy-police-to-front-lines.html

Irrawaddy. 2022c. 'Sale of Myanmar Coup Leader's Mansion Raises US$2 Million in Three Days'. 9 May. www.irrawaddy.com/news/burma/sale-of-myanmar-coup-leaders-mansion-raises-us2-million-in-three-days.html

Irrawaddy. 2022d. 'NUG Plans More Weapons and Funds for Revolution Against Myanmar Junta'. 26 May. www.irrawaddy.com/news/burma/nug-plans-more-weapons-and-funds-for-revolution-against-myanmar-junta.html

Irrawaddy. 2022e. 'Myanmar Regime Committed Almost 2,800 War Crimes in Last Six Months: NUG'. 13 June. www.irrawaddy.com/news/burma/myanmar-regime-committed-almost-2800-war-crimes-in-last-six-months-nug.html

ISP (Institute for Strategy and Policy – Myanmar). 2022a. 'Over 7,000 Civilian Deaths since the Military Coup'. *Data Matters*, no. 32, 18 October. www.ispmyanmar.com/over-7000-civilian-deaths-since-the-military-coup/

ISP (Institute for Strategy and Policy – Myanmar). 2022b. 'Over 36,000 Houses And Buildings Burned and Destroyed since the Coup'. *Data Matters* 30: www.isp myanmar.com/more-than-36000-homes-and-buildings-torched-after-the-coup

ISP (Institute for Strategy and Policy – Myanmar). 2022c. 'IDPs Spread Across 96 Townships'. *Data Matters*, no. 34, 2 November. www.ispmyanmar.com/idps-spread-across-in-96-townships/

ISP (Institute for Strategy and Policy – Myanmar). 2022d. 'Almost 3 Million Internally Displaced and Exiled Refugees in Myanmar'. *Data Matters*, no. 28, 2 September. www.ispmyanmar.com/almost-3-million-internally-displaced-and-exiled-refugees-in-myanmar-2/

Ko Cho. 2022. 'Myanmar Junta Sentences Three UEC Heads to Prison'. *Myanmar Now*, 11 July. myanmar-now.org/en/news/myanmar-junta-sentences-three-uec-heads-to-prison/

Lipes, Joshua. 2022a. 'Myanmar Civil Disobedience Movement "Losing Steam" amid Junta Crackdowns'. *Radio Free Asia*, 26 April. www.rfa.org/english/news/myanmar/cdm-04262022211343.html

Lipes, Joshua. 2022b. 'Conflict Seen Escalating in Myanmar on Anniversary of PDF'. *Radio Free Asia*, 11 May. www.rfa.org/english/news/myanmar/anniversary-05112022202816.html

Lipes, Joshua. 2022c. 'Defector Group Says 4 Combat Weapons in Production for Fight against Myanmar Junta'. *Radio Free Asia*, 6 June. www.rfa.org/english/news/myanmar/weapons-06102022164120.html

Lovett, Lorcan. 2021. 'The Nights of Pots and Pans are Back, on Myanmar's Fearful Streets'. *Guardian*, 2 February. www.theguardian.com/global-development/2021/feb/02/the-nights-of-pots-and-pans-are-back-on-myanmar-fearful-streets

Lovett, Lorcan and Michael Safi. 2021. 'Myanmar's Besieged Resistance Dreams of "People's Army" to Counter Junta'. *Guardian*, 21 March. www.theguardian.com/world/2021/mar/20/myanmars-besieged-resistance-dreams-of-peoples-army-to-counter-junta

Min Min. 2022a. 'Is Myanmar's Military Becoming a Spent Force?' *Myanmar Now*, 8 May. myanmar-now.org/en/news/is-myanmars-military-becoming-a-spent-force

Min Min. 2022b. 'It's Certain That the Military Is Losing Ground'. *Myanmar Now*, 6 May. myanmar-now.org/en/news/its-certain-that-the-military-is-losing-ground

Mogul, Rhea and Jake Kwon. 2022. 'Myanmar Court Extends Aung San Suu Kyi's Prison Sentence to 26 Years'. *CNN*, 12 October. edition.cnn.com/2022/10/12/asia/aung-san-suu-kyi-myanmar-court-corruption-intl-hnk/index.html

MPM (Myanmar Peace Monitor). 2022. 'Coup Dashboard: October 2022'. 6 November. www.mmpeacemonitor.org/314605/coup-dashboard-october-2022/

Myat Thura and Min Wathan. 2021. 'Myanmar State Counsellor and President Charged, Detained for 2 More Weeks'. *Myanmar Times*, 4 February. www.mmtimes.com/news/myanmar-state-counsellor-and-president-charged-detained-2-more-weeks.html (page discontinued).

Ohmar, Khin. 2022. 'To Stop Russian Aggression, US Must Act on Myanmar'. *Myanmar Now*, 13 May. myanmar-now.org/en/news/to-stop-russian-aggression-us-must-act-on-myanmar

Paddock, Richard C. 2021. 'Myanmar Security Forces Open Fire on Protesters, Killing 2'. *The New York Times*, 20 February. www.nytimes.com/2021/02/20/world/asia/myanmar-protesters-killed.html

Pedroletti, Brice. 2022. 'Myanmar: Army Atrocities Are on the Rise in the Central Plains'. *Le Monde*, 27 June. www.lemonde.fr/en/international/article/2022/06/27/myanmar-army-atrocities-are-on-the-rise-in-the-central-plains_5988064_4.html

Pietromarchi, Virginia and Mersiha Gadzo. 2021. 'Myanmar's Military Stages Coup D'etat'. *Aljazera Live News*, 1 February. www.aljazeera.com/news/2021/2/1/myanmar-military-stages-coup-against-aung-san-suu-kyi-live

PTV (Public Voice Television). 2022. 'Public Voice Television'. Facebook, 22 June. www.facebook.com/pvtvmyanmar/photos/a.107260768162692/368852755336824

Pyidaungsu Hluttaw. 2021. 'Statement by the Representatives of the Pyidaungsu Hluttaw (National League For Democracy) (2/2021)'. Pyidaungsu Hluttaw, 5 February. www.burmalibrary.org/sites/burmalibrary.org/files/obl/2021-02-05-Statement-by-the-Representatives-of_the-Pyidaungsu-Hluttaw_NLD_2-2012-en-tu-red.pdf

Reuters. 2021. 'Myanmar Shadow Government Calls for Revolt against Military Rule'. 7 September. www.reuters.com/world/asia-pacific/myanmar-shadow-government-unveils-new-strategy-oppose-military-rule-2021-09-07/

Safi, Michael. 2021. 'Myanmar: Armoured Vehicles Roll into Cities as Internet Shut Down'. *Guardian*, 15 February. www.theguardian.com/world/2021/feb/14/tanks-on-streets-of-myanmar-city-prompt-us-embassy-warning

San Yasmin Aung. 2021. 'Updated Timeline: Tracing Military's Interference in Myanmar Election'. *Irrawaddy*, 20 January. www.irrawaddy.com/specials/timeline-tracing-militarys-interference-in-myanmar-ele.html

Sithu Aung Myint. 2021. 'Min Aung Hlaing's Constitutional Crisis'. *Frontier Myanmar*, 12 February. www.frontiermyanmar.net/en/min-aung-hlaings-constitutional-crisis/

Strangio, Sebastian. 2021. 'Myanmar Sees Another Day of Bloodshed, as Armed Resistance Rises'. *Diplomat*, 12 April. thediplomat.com/2021/04/myanmar-sees-another-day-of-bloodshed-as-armed-resistance-rises/

Vossion, Louis. 1891. 'Nat-Worship among the Burmese', *Journal of American Folklore* 4, no. 13: 107–14.

Whong, Eugene. 2021. 'Myanmar Shadow Government Forms Militia to Oppose Military Junta'. *Radio Free Asia*, 4 May. www.rfa.org/english/news/myanmar/pdf-05052021221913.html

Zaw Ye Thwe. 2022. 'Why Thousands Have Left Myanmar's Military—and Why Most Stay'. *Myanmar Now*, 5 June. myanmar-now.org/en/news/why-thousands-have-left-myanmars-military-and-why-most-stay/

2

Scenarios for Understanding Myanmar's Political and Humanitarian Crises

Nicholas Farrelly

Head of School, School of Social Sciences,
University of Tasmania

Abstract

This chapter explores four interlinked scenarios about Myanmar's trajectory since the February 2021 military coup, with specific attention to plausible humanitarian conditions in the years ahead. The analysis draws on the erratic imbalance of forces, ideas, politics and strategies that have energised Myanmar's turbulence since the most recent coup and that, in many respects, influence the range of potential responses to the multiple, ongoing humanitarian crises. The examination of hypotheticals, such as these scenarios, requires attention to history, to current conditions and to foreseeable future outcomes. The scenarios are explored in the hope that, by better understanding recent events, we may be able to better appreciate future trajectories. The analysis highlights the intense challenges for any future Myanmar government and for international partners seeking to influence developments in a more positive direction.

Thinking about the future of Myanmar's coup

Part of the dark calculation in Naypyidaw for Myanmar's 2021 coup was that powerful international players, divided by intense geostrategic rivalries and diminished by the response to the first year of the COVID-19 pandemic, would struggle to mount any substantial response. Exhausted by almost two decades of active military and humanitarian intervention across the Middle East and Central Asia, the United States and key allies have signalled, for years, increasing reluctance to directly support teetering, or toppled, democratic regimes. Enthusiasm for the process of contested institution-building, especially in places where there are only modest strategic interests at stake, has waned dramatically.

In the Myanmar situation, the generals and their enablers in the civilian bureaucracy have many years of direct experience manipulating Association of Southeast Asian Nations (ASEAN) diplomacy towards outcomes favourable to the entrenchment of military power. Under these circumstances, the generals would have judged, with some confidence, that the room for external powers to make dramatic pronouncements and then actively build momentum against the re-entrenchment of military power was very limited. Yet, well after the coup, the new military regime has struggled to consolidate its control of territory and remains deeply unpopular across the breadth of Myanmar society. Brazen anti-coup tactics, like silent strikes, reinforce the overwhelming perception that the 2021 coup could still fail, although the trigger for a calamitous breakdown in the military regime has proved elusive. In the past, Myanmar's military decision-makers have also usually succeeded in avoiding real scrutiny or consequences when called to account for human rights abuses (Shukri 2021, 258). Since the coup, there have been admirably thorough efforts to document the range of distressing allegations that have emerged (A. A. & Gaborit 2021, 56).

In this strategic and historical context, this analysis draws on the erratic imbalance of forces, ideas, politics and strategies that have energised Myanmar's turbulence since the most recent coup and that, in many respects, influence the range of potential responses to the multiple, ongoing humanitarian crises. With the Myanmar military now fighting a much wider range of opponents, including the People's Defence Force militias that formed in 2021, the entire Myanmar state system is being tested by those prepared to mount 'revolutionary responses' (Prasse-Freeman & Ko

Kabya 2021). Where the previous compact for power sharing in Myanmar, which grew from 2011 onwards, between democratic, militarist, ethnic and chauvinist groups was always uneasy (Renshaw & Lidauer 2021), most parts of the country avoided large-scale humanitarian issues. The key exception—the Rakhine State—saw almost a million people flee across the border to Bangladesh in 2017, generating a substantial international and Bangladeshi humanitarian response (Halim et al. 2021, 199; also Ahmed & Das 2022). That crisis led to the Myanmar government facing accusations of genocide in the International Court of Justice in The Hague. Aung San Suu Kyi led the government's defence of its actions in what was, at the time, a striking signal of the popularity of anti-Rohingya violence and the uneasy working coalition between the military and elected officials from the National League for Democracy (NLD).[1] Aung San Suu Kyi is now, again, detained by the military and faces years of imprisonment on charges laid after the coup.

There remains deep concern internationally about the direction of events in Myanmar and the humanitarian crises that have evolved since the 2021 coup have not been completely ignored. Obviously, any major breakdown of state institutions will further galvanise local, national and regional responses, including more robust attention to the structure of Myanmar's future political system (for an early contribution, see Kipgen 2021), but it would be bold to predict that Myanmar is ever more than a peripheral concern among great powers, except, of course, for China's regional ambitions. What is also apparent is that the carefully curated and heavily controlled institutions that allowed for increased popular participation in politics from 2011 to 2021 are gone, with no clear indications of how alternative models of governance will be created (Thant Myint-U 2020). After the coup, the State Administration Council apparently expected that its repudiation of the NLD's 2020 electoral triumph would only lead to modest and short-lived opposition. That judgement was plainly wrong and, once again, brings into question the strategic acumen of Naypyidaw's powerbrokers (for helpful and wideranging analysis, see Selth 2020).

---

1   In the wake of the coup there has been some commentary on these issues. For example:

The case of Myanmar unfolding before our eyes shows us that calling for accountability is something that the private sector operating and investing in Myanmar should do: in this case, they should insist that a reinstalled democratic leadership embrace the jurisdiction of the International Criminal Court. To finally and firmly entrench democracy in Myanmar, there will be a need for accountability for both the military and the political actors involved in perpetrating the genocide. (Triponel & Williams 2021)

With this history and the challenging contexts in mind, this chapter explores how the Myanmar people confront four volatile and heavily contested scenarios. Each scenario has long-term implications for the resolution of the country's multiple crises across the full spectrum of humanitarian domains. The discussion is, by its nature, somewhat speculative, but I have also sought, where possible, to draw on a wide reading of the strategic, political, cultural and historical conditions that led to the 2021 coup, and that will shape Myanmar's further development over the next five to 10 years.

State institutions and state fragility

This chapter explores these four interlinked scenarios pertaining to Myanmar's post-coup trajectory, with specific attention to plausible humanitarian conditions in the years ahead. The examination of hypotheticals, such as these scenarios, requires attention to history, current conditions and foreseeable future outcomes. The scenarios are presented here in the hope that, by better understanding recent events, we may be able to better appreciate future trajectories. The analysis highlights the intense challenges for any future Myanmar government and for international partners seeking to influence developments in a more positive direction.

Coup is consolidated

First, there is a scenario in which the post-coup military regime consolidates its power. This is the baseline scenario, partly due to the country's history of coup consolidation. Myanmar's previous military coups, in 1962 and in 1988, both faced resistance, which, in both cases, was only ever partly eliminated. Nonetheless, the most serious opposition, at least in terms of armed response, was eventually pushed to the margins, usually to the mountains along Myanmar's borders. After 1962, it was the Communist Party of Burma, and various Shan, Karen, Mon and Kachin armed groups, that fought, often over decades, against central government control. From 1988, Myanmar's battlegrounds were even more fractious, with ceasefires, stalemates and open warfare all coexisting. The conflict situation since February 2021 has challenged the new junta in different ways. The military government has fought hard to maintain its control of state institutions, a posture that has generated sustained opposition both in the Bamar-majority regions and across the ethnic minority–dominated peripheries.

In a consolidation scenario, there will still be resistance to the army, other security agencies and the wide range of other representatives of government authority, with continued armed opposition.

In this scenario, the blurred threats of ongoing violence, continued displacement, appalling human rights abuses and economic paralysis would likely create increased pressure on all of Myanmar's neighbours, with acute outcomes for Thailand, and potentially for Bangladesh and India. Many Myanmar people do not want to live under military rule ever again. Since the coup, over 440,000 people have been displaced by fighting, and some have left the country, most heading to Thailand and Malaysia, with smaller numbers offered rare pandemic-era permission to travel to countries across the democratic West. In this scenario, with the new junta able to consolidate its rule, the Rohingya and other marginalised groups would continue to suffer greatly while the Myanmar Army limits their access to meaningful civil and economic rights.

Where the NLD and Union Solidarity and Development Party (USDP) governments may have been receptive to some types of advocacy around human rights issues, the coup also gives senior decision-makers the chance to reverse even some of the modest improvements that had occurred. For instance, the National Human Rights Commission, established in 2011, cannot continue with its work, and there is no prospect of its modest functions and influence being transferred to any other body. In late 2021, Senior General Min Aung Hlaing announced that an election would be held in mid-2023, extending an earlier schedule that had implied an election in 2022. The military will seek to manipulate this timetable to its own advantage and, obviously, has much experience using the rules and procedures available through formal mechanisms to develop 'compromises' that further its institutional agenda. The USDP, which won an undemocratic election in 2010, and then ruled from 2011 to 2016, is now a greatly diminished vehicle for the presentation of a civilianised group of post-coup military leaders.

There will never again be any confidence that the USDP, or a similar political configuration, could surrender power to genuinely elected representatives, as they did after the 2015 general election victory by the NLD. As such, a scenario in which the coup is consolidated likely draws on many of the organisational, cultural and personal resources built up during the last period of sustained military dominance, which only ended in 2011. Obviously many aspects of military rule were used to define political, economic and strategic direction after the USDP took power. Almost all its senior figures were previously key players in the State Peace and Development Council military regime and those who helped to make up the legislative numbers, at the local and national levels, also tended to have enjoyed long careers within, or adjacent to, the military regime's bureaucracy. Their subsequent failure in open electoral competition—at the 2012 by-election, the 2015 general election and then again at the 2020 general election—ultimately created the conditions for the coup. For the USDP, and for its sponsors still in army uniforms, the dominance of the NLD as an electoral force undermined their ability to secure the outcomes, in terms of political balance, on which they always insisted.

For this scenario, the ASEAN region offers a number of models, historically and today, for guided, managed and, indeed, authoritarian electoral systems. Some analysts have speculated that the Myanmar generals take inspiration from General Prayuth Chano-ocha in Thailand, whose 2014 coup finally ended the electoral dominance of the Shinawatra family, under prime ministers Thaksin and Yingluck Shinawatra. While Thailand held an election in 2019, its outcome was predetermined by the limits on competition set by the military-drafted constitution. The result kept General Prayuth in charge, his situation improved by the extra legitimacy even a flawed electoral process often eventually delivers. Long-serving regimes in Singapore and Cambodia have similarly utilised multifaceted restrictions on political opponents, alongside regular elections, to ensure the continuity in power of dominant individuals and political parties. In each case, they benefit from a nexus of bureaucratic, cultural and military power, in which, over decades, the national elite has regenerated its capacity to exert control to the exclusion of alternative forces. The problem, in the final judgement, is that Myanmar's generals will struggle to ever regain the type of support and interest that was generated after the USDP government took power in 2011.

With the consolidated coup scenario, the role of the NLD and other electorally successful forces would be managed closely by military leaders who would remain wary, perhaps on a permanent basis, of those who so strongly and effectively opposed the coup. The prospect of Aung San Suu Kyi's ongoing incarceration would obviously weigh heavily on any chance of the NLD re-emerging as a political force; she may face decades in gaol. The NLD has been obliterated and would struggle for space for even a compromised role in any new political structure. Indeed, in the consolidation scenario, many anti-coup activists are likely to remain imprisoned, or in exile, or struggling to survive under constant surveillance, marginalised by the military's ongoing entrenchment of its power. Restrictions on the free flow of information would be a key part of the military regime's ongoing strategy. We understand Chinese technicians have worked with their Myanmar counterparts since the coup to better monitor, and perhaps in the future fully control, the digital realm (see Lintner 2021).

Such issues obviously highlight some of the differences between circumstances this decade and those during previous periods of military rule. The fact is, after 2011, Myanmar society changed rapidly, with information, education, technology, international travel and exchange, political experimentation and open electoral competition all working to further expand the horizons and possibilities for millions of Myanmar people. The backlash against the coup, which apparently surprised key leaders in Naypyidaw, is a consequence, partly, of the enormous shifts experienced by the Myanmar people. They have enjoyed the benefits of a more liberal, transparent, lively and unpredictable political and economic environment. The nationwide and almost universal opposition to the coup is a strong signal of just how highly the average Myanmar person has valued the changes that occurred from 2011 to 2021. It is on the basis of these changes that the resistance to the coup has organised itself to battle against the dominance of military figures in the country's political future.

Coup fails

Second, it is important to fully consider the implications of a scenario in which the Myanmar military is forced to surrender its claimed status ruling from Naypyidaw. Since the coup, ASEAN foreign ministers have raised concerns about the legitimacy of the post-coup regime, indicating that, even within orthodox foreign policy circles, there are grave misgivings about the legitimacy of the military's authoritarian rule. The State Peace and Development Council government that ruled from 1996 to 2011 became skilled, after its inclusion in ASEAN from 1997, at using regional forums, and the legitimacy it could draw from its welcome to the ASEAN family, to manage its engagement with the global system.

In this coup failure scenario, Myanmar's pre-coup political arrangements may provide some inspiration for the management of the country's diverse geographies and cultures, and yet there would be a strong incentive for a revolutionary government to dispense with the foundational expectations of previous regimes. In such a scenario there would still be increased state fragility, with the prospect that some conflicts would continue between a new central government and other armed forces. Even in a best case scenario, it is unlikely there would be a sustained consensus about Myanmar's future political direction (for context, see Sadan 2016). Would the NLD, for instance, remain the key player in a future revolutionary system?

The answer likely depends on the ability of senior NLD figures to position themselves as the legitimate guardians of the revolutionary spirit. During 2021 it became apparent that the elected democratic forces, both Bamar and from ethnic minorities, were only part of the story of resistance to the coup. Some groups and individuals have sought to redefine their struggles beyond the scope of earlier democratic movements. Part of this shift is generational, with young activists often still only in their teens and twenties taking enormous risks. They may be reluctant to empower senior figures who they may judge made the wrong concessions to the military or, perhaps most tellingly, compromised Myanmar's democratic values on policies of exclusion—even genocide. Working through these types of foundational and existential questions would be a major test for any new, revolutionary regime.

As such, a revolutionary regime would also need to determine, quickly, what it stood for, balancing the interests of the National Unity Government (NUG), NLD and other stakeholders. Even within the NLD, which has over 30 years of political experience and maturity, the space for alternative perspectives has often been limited greatly by the policy authority of a small number of senior decision-makers, led by Aung San Suu Kyi (Farrelly 2016). For instance, members of the 88-Generation, which has a similarly long history of democratic activism and opposition to military rule, found themselves excluded from the NLD's political vehicle after 2011. Other major political groups, such as the Kachin Independence Organisation, the Arakan National Party, the New Mon State Party and the Kachin State Democracy Party, are wholly defined by the interests of small elites, many of whom have worked together closely for decades. Bringing in new voices, embracing youth-inspired debate and finding mechanisms to generate genuine popular engagement have proved difficult.

Looking closely at a scenario in which the coup fails, it is important to consider, as Su Mon Thant (2021, 10–12) has done, the variety of anti-coup forces that exist. She calls them 'democrats', 'federalists' and 'intersectionalists'. From her perspective:

The causes of the democrats are direct and narrow, focusing on the immediate actions they see as needed to put the nation back on track. This group has the advantage of wide public participation, but its limited goals do not satisfy the other two groups, who are actively engaging and leading the resistance movement. While the aim of federalists is to best guarantee a federal state for ethnic minorities, agreeing on federal terms in parallel to the anti-coup movement costs time. While intersectionalists have strong and equitable ideals for a post-revolution society, this requires long-term commitment and devotion. (Su Mon Thant 2021, 11–12)

Her useful summary of the situation is a strong reminder of the significant challenges ahead for this new generation of political actors in a scenario in which they are, for the first time, given the opportunity to more directly influence political outcomes. Their ideals will be tested both by the realities of entrenched conflict and disadvantage, and also by the ongoing battles for influence among senior figures unwilling to surrender their status to more youthful voices.

For the coup to fail, in a comprehensive sense, requires some other type of significant change likely at both the local and global levels. For now, the Myanmar military regime draws on support from Russia and China, which dramatically improves its battlefield options. The fuller mobilisation of external military support, including the proliferation of heavier weaponry among different anti-regime forces, would likely be part of any such coup failure scenario. Where foreign support for Myanmar's resistance forces exists, it would be fair to assume it is kept as quiet (and deniable) as possible. The style of foreign support made available to Ukraine as it resisted Russian invasion in 2022 is not possible due to the double bind of ASEAN hesitation and Chinese opposition to any hint of military escalation near its border. The stalemate that may appear to exist between the Myanmar Army and its many opponents is, however, made less stable by the prospect of fresh injections of trained and well-equipped fighters on either side, and by the unpredictable use of both new and old technology, both military and civilian, in shaping the rapidly changing battlefield. In this context, openly arming anti-regime forces would introduce other unpredictable dynamics, especially in terms of the response from both China and Russia.

Centrifugal unravelling

Then there is the third scenario, in which Myanmar unravels. Indeed, the further diminution of state control, in either of the first two scenarios, could add weight to the centrifugal forces that pull, on an almost permanent basis, at the unifying agenda emphasised by leaders in Naypyidaw over the past 15 years (Farrelly 2018). Avoiding the fragmentation of Myanmar has been a stated objective of all its post-independence governments, but the current crisis is a new test for the decades-long project of Myanmar nation-building (Walton 2015; also Meehan 2015). The Myanmar Army's capacity to coopt powerful ethnic minority groups, especially those with their own large fighting forces and economic engines, will remain in question (Brenner 2015; McCarthy & Farrelly 2020).

While any hypothetical declarations of independence from a 'Kachinland' or a 'Kawthoolei' or, perhaps, a 'Wa Union' would need to draw on foreign powers for credibility, in this scenario there could simply be alternative quasi-state institutions that, over time and perhaps incrementally, create alternative identities at the margins of a crumbling Myanmar state. Some are already reasonably well placed to make the transition into more formally constituted state-like entities. In parts of Shan State, for instance, the United Wa State Army controls significant territory, and has, for the past three decades, maintained its strength through a narcotics and weapons-based economy. It is active along both the Chinese and Thai borders, and has been able, through the large army that it fields, to carve out an independent sphere of influence. Analysts speculate that much of its capability is the outcome of support received from Chinese actors. They would be essential, it seems, to any further development of Wa political institutions.

The political economy of these 'illiberal' sub-national governance arrangements have been explored in detail elsewhere (including McCarthy & Farrelly 2020). What is still unclear is how any future micro-states would sustain themselves economically. There would be only limited international interest in providing subsidies to the weakest of these new statelets, meaning, in practice, that illicit economies would continue to offer alternative streams of personal and institutional revenue. Some parts of Myanmar, perhaps most notably the Kachin State, are rich in resource wealth, and they could, in theory, build reasonably strong economies on local jade, gold, tin, timber and energy industries. Yet almost all of these resources would still be exported in a relatively unprocessed form. Industrialisation of Kachin

State seems implausible. And it would be many years before tourism or other service industries could offer much to the people of even Myanmar's richest area.

In the unravelling scenario, the poor corners of the country, such as the Chin and Rakhine states, would be in a very difficult position if Myanmar's central government was to collapse. Local conflicts, such as those along the Muslim–Buddhist faultline, or between different Chin language groups, could quickly overwhelm the modest capabilities of any fragile new micro-state. In a scenario in which centrifugal unravelling occurs, there would be uneven outcomes and different responses from neighbouring governments. In the Rakhine and Chin examples, both Bangladesh and India have sufficient concerns about instability spilling over their borders that there would be the possibility, at least, for some level of foreign military intervention.

Implosion, war, chaos

Fourth, it is possible that the Myanmar system implodes more dramatically, with no clear mandate for a post-coup government, and with sparring between the other significant military factions and other political players in the cities and elsewhere. For this scenario, what could lead to such a dramatic deterioration? There are many possibilities, all of which imply the comprehensive breakdown of faith in the emergence of a stable political situation. Open conflict between military regime forces is the likeliest trigger for such a breakdown, with violent military factionalisation encouraging new coalitions, including the opportunistically multi-ethnic, to strike hard against their opponents. Such an implosion, followed by vendettas, war and chaos, would also be the culmination of other things going wrong. If we seek historical examples for potential triggers, then it is killing of specific types, especially assassinations or mass atrocities, that can lead to such a tragic unravelling. Whatever the trigger, such breakdowns can also often draw their strength from deeper structural and historical conditions.

Such a scenario would likely be predicated on, and then would further encourage, the involvement of neighbouring powers particularly Thailand, China and India, and potentially even Bangladesh. In terms of the hypotheticals considered in this analysis, this is the scenario that would, in the medium term, likely cause the greatest damage to Myanmar's people, to the economies on which they rely and to the future sovereignty of the political system(s) they have sought to build. The scenario, which is still low likelihood, could have significant and permanent consequences for the entire Asian region. It would imply that other efforts to avoid calamity have failed, and that the cultural, political and strategic restraints on expected action have completely fallen away. The prospect of remnant forces—drawing their fighting strength from the former Myanmar Army, from the People's Defence Forces and from various ethnic armies—that could reconvene and then regroup in different formations, would make it very difficult to understand the ideological or other basis on which groups were working.

The outcomes would be unpredictable; however, if core strategic interests were believed to be at stake, including the security of China's pipelines across central Myanmar, then the scenario would be primed for regional armed forces to (perhaps very reluctantly) become more involved (Ahamed, Rahman & Hossain 2020). A push by the People's Liberation Army into Myanmar territory would make the country, perhaps only temporarily, a global flashpoint, requiring attention at the United Nations and elsewhere. How other countries would respond to a Chinese expeditionary force deep in Myanmar territory is difficult to judge. The United States and its allies like Japan and Australia would also probably have some level of active involvement. Thailand would be the obvious launch-pad for their support, but the Thai government, under former coup commander General Prayuth Chano-ocha would be reluctant to become too heavily involved in a conflict that, ordinarily, it would judge is the responsibility of Myanmar authorities to resolve. But what if Myanmar's authorities have dissolved?

Factors to consider in all scenarios

Compared to any of Myanmar's previous crises there are some new factors that make the conditions in 2023 and beyond different. These factors require serious attention because we are all inclined to dwell on historical examples, analogies and interpretative speculation, as it allows us to seek to find a good fit for any judgements about Myanmar's current and future trajectory. One of the most important issues that differentiates Myanmar's political situation since the 2021 coup is the proliferation of the internet and internet-enabled devices in Myanmar. Technology for taking photos, video-recording, editing, broadcasting and then engaging is almost universal. The early protests against the coup were remarkable for the speed and clarity with which information about events could circulate within the country and, to a lesser extent, the outside world. On Facebook, Twitter and elsewhere, the implication of current footage and information was significant, drawing many people to the Myanmar situation during the early, somewhat upbeat, coverage of popular defiance. The deterioration of conditions since the coup has put extra pressure on internet access, with the military government keen to ensure it can monitor subversive materials and crackdown on resistance activities. Like in so many other parts of life, the effort to put the genie back in the bottle struggles against years of rapid rollout of high-quality and cost-effective technologies supporting economic, cultural and political activity across Myanmar.

The related change is to the expectations of the Myanmar people at large, many of whom have enjoyed greater opportunities for education, enrichment, travel and interaction than ever before. While many parts of the country remain poor, the country's economic growth has been significant over the past decade. In 2012, gross domestic product per capita, a reasonable proxy in this context for economic activity and also for key aspects of social wellbeing, was USD936—the lowest in Southeast Asia, and one of the world's lowest outside sub-Saharan Africa. By 2015, this had grown to USD1,144. By 2019, Myanmar had risen even further, to USD1,362. Yet, since the coup, the economy has contracted dramatically, with the World Bank estimating that it is almost 20 per cent smaller than at the start of 2021, after already suffering through the initial pandemic upheavals of 2020 (Robinson 2022). Such a calamitous decline in domestic product is accompanied by deep pockets of poverty and disadvantage. Some parts of the country have seen waves of displacement and depopulation since the coup, with estimates that very large numbers of people, in, for instance, the Kayah State capital, Loikaw, have now left for what they hope is relative safety in the mountains or near the Thai border. Relentless attacks by the military regime make it impossible for ordinary life to continue, and even basic necessities are now hard to come by in many parts of Myanmar.

Further, it now seems very unlikely that Myanmar's democrats will ever again tolerate the types of concessions that were accepted, and indeed were acceptable, during the decade from 2011 to 2021. Many now look at this period as a strategic blunder, one in which the NLD and other anti-military forces gave up too much of their credibility to legitimise the military's continued role in politics. While it campaigned hard on the need to change the constitutional arrangements that kept Aung San Suu Kyi out of the presidential palace, and the military's constitutionally mandated 25 per cent of allocated seats as a handbrake on further changes, the NLD never managed to make the strategic or tactical changes that it sought. And yet, even the small chance that a new NLD government would push harder for the military to surrender its residual vetoes and dominance was enough for the coup to be launched, and for so much further suffering and violence to occur. It is for this reason that the calls for change are nowadays much more forceful: there is a mood for revolution, for the destruction of the Myanmar Army as a political force and, perhaps, even for its final disbanding.

For these reasons, planning around political and humanitarian scenarios requires attention to Myanmar's specifics, and also a broader imagining of what might be possible under these conditions. What are the meaningful comparisons? The Balkanisation that followed the end of unified Yugoslavia? The end of the Khmer Rouge regime in Cambodia and the civil war that followed? The Rwandan genocide? The toppling of the Suharto regime in Indonesia? While there may be some common elements and analytically useful threads, the situation in Myanmar is not so readily comparable in ways that make for the creation of easy models or straightforward comparisons.

How to avoid disaster?

Considering these four scenarios as interlinked versions of Myanmar's future development after the coup is designed to encourage reflection on the humanitarian, economic and political consequences of the forces unleashed over the past year. Opportunities to build effective political institutions will require careful attention to the range of calculations being made by the Myanmar military itself, within well-established ethnic armed organisations, and across the spectrum of new militia and political organisations. Policymaking and advocacy interests, within ASEAN and beyond, will need to confront the possibility that further deterioration will lead to hard decisions about the resources required to avoid an even more complex humanitarian catastrophe (with examples from recent experience of peace-building still relevant to the discussion, see Roy, Ware & Laoutides 2021; Mathieson 2021).

In any of these scenarios, Myanmar will lag far behind its neighbours for years to come due to the upheavals generated by the coup, and through the parallel health and economic degradation that has occurred (Myo Nyein Aung, Shiu & Chen 2021; also Wunna Tun 2021, 50). With a shrinking economy, even more widespread poverty, the persistent threat of violence, stark limitations on foreign involvement and new political disagreements adding fuel to old enmities, the overall outcome is likely to be bleak for tens of millions of people (for recent analysis of livelihood issues across Myanmar, see Thawnghmung 2019; also Moos, Roberts & Mo Aye 2021). Avoiding the worst hardships and the most damaging violence would mean Myanmar needs to receive much more attention from regional and global players than was available in the first two years after the coup.

In Naypyidaw the expectation remains that exhaustion with Myanmar's tragic situation, and the related inability of ASEAN governments to build a more proactive policy position, will give the post-coup government sufficient time to eventually consolidate its rule. Yet this perspective is based on a general assessment, with judgements predicated on patterns that existed before the coup, about the effectiveness of resistance forces. Those forces look very different in 2022, and have improved their fighting capabilities in every domain. For instance, urban guerrillas prepared to target junta forces in their moments of vulnerability make the job of securing Myanmar's vast cities and sprawling hinterlands an almost impossible one. With the economy in such a parlous condition, it is difficult to see how Senior General Min Aung Hlaing and his key strategists can firm up their positions without further alienating the vast majority of Myanmar people, already dissatisfied with the coup and the violence of 2021.

Where Myanmar goes next is, as ever, a question for the Myanmar people, the NUG, the People's Defence Forces, and the strongest of the ethnic armed groups who are working towards toppling the powers in Naypyidaw once and for all. It is worth reflecting, finally, on what such an outcome might mean in both political and humanitarian terms. To leave behind the rule of the Myanmar Army and its top generals would not imply a future without conflicts or, indeed, violence. Of course, one of the key ideas justifying military rule in Myanmar is that the country would spiral into the abyss without firm management from a central, Bamar-dominated political institution. There is no escaping the same difficulties faced by Aung San Suu Kyi and the NLD as they sought to broker the nationwide ceasefire through the Union Peace Conference under the auspices of the 21st Century Panglong framework. Any future government, elected through a free vote after the collapse of the post-coup regime, would need to navigate perilous political terrain, with no guarantee that the country's many large armed groups would be prepared to accept the range of concessions and compromises required for a genuinely united front.

Final thoughts on the future of the four scenarios

The four scenarios examined in this chapter have been explored side-by-side, and yet, in practice, there are likely to be times when aspects of each of the potential futures are part of a complex set of trajectories. The advantage of looking at the scenarios as distinct future possibilities is that they imply medium-term outcomes that could have significant, perhaps permanent, implications for Myanmar, for its immediate neighbours and, indeed, for the wider Asian region.

In the first scenario—with the coup consolidated, and with a new military regime able to impose its will on Myanmar society and continue to largely define the scope of political action—the country's democratic activists are likely to face years, even decades, of dismay and punishment. Foreign investors and institutions from the Western democracies, such as the universities that committed resources to Myanmar's earlier liberalisation, will be unlikely to ever return with substantial investments. The country's international links will, once again, be defined by ties with ASEAN, and also with countries that pay little or no heed to human rights expectations. Countries with their own antagonistic relations with the West—such as China, Russia and North Korea—have historically proved the most consistent supporters of Myanmar's military. Yet it is doubtful there will ever be much, if any, enthusiasm for their active involvement in society among the vast mass of Myanmar people. China, as the largest, most powerful and most proximate of these countries, is also the international player that faces the greatest risk of pushback from the Myanmar people. Russia is also preoccupied with other conflicts, most acutely in Ukraine.

In the second scenario, in which the coup fails and a democratic revolution prevails, the efforts to unravel generations of military dominance and to create a viable institutional basis for alternative political cultures would require substantial external support. In this scenario, a wide range of countries, such as the United States, the United Kingdom, Thailand, Japan, Germany, Singapore and Australia, are likely to commit significant resources across humanitarian, commercial, educational and political domains. Efforts to influence the next generation of decision-makers, and to help shape the model of national governance, would need to be carefully managed, especially as the debates between Myanmar stakeholders would, like before the coup, rarely lead to consensus. A peace process, truth and justice mechanisms, and the ultimate path towards some type of national reckoning, or hypothetical reconciliation, would take time and test the patience of those seeking immediate and decisive change. Any new government, even one that can draw on all of the country's policy and political talent, would still need to manage Myanmar's long history of trauma, poverty, exclusion and distrust. One core requirement would be the creation, training and resourcing of military forces that could help to unite the entire country.

Yet the risks for those who might encourage the coup to fail outright should be contemplated too. There appears to be a sense, among policymakers around the world, that effectively managing the failure of the coup would require an enormous investment of resources and ideas, perhaps well beyond apparent appetites. Recognising the political and military forces opposed to the coup will always need both symbolic and practical components, and the practicalties are expensive, fraught with danger and, perhaps, only justified where other strategic interests are at stake. These assessments point back towards the initial calculations in Naypyidaw about the willingness of democratic powers to actively oppose the coup. The implication is that the United States and its key allies now lack the will, and perhaps the imagination, for the vast nation-building projects that accompanied the early twenty-first-century interventions in the Middle East and Central Asia. Myanmar, treated the wrong way, is a strategic nightmare from which there would be no meaningful retreat.

There is no avoiding the problem. The political conundrum in both the first and second scenarios is the need to find a sustainable set of understandings between Myanmar's largest ethnic group, the Bamar, and the country's many ethnic minorities. In the scenarios in which the coup is consolidated or fails, the longer-term prospects of any future government would be determined, to a large extent, by the ability of key decision-makers to effectively manage the political grievances they would face, almost inevitably, along ethnic lines. It is in scenario three that those grievances could prove most destabilising, with centrifugal forces ultimately unravelling Myanmar claims to a single union. A process of unravelling would be uneven, in the sense that some areas and leaders would be better prepared to take advantage of the failure of central authorities to maintain the unified order.

What would happen to the Bamar-majority areas of central Myanmar in such a scenario would be a further test. The possibility of ongoing discontent and conflict would be real, especially given the very mixed population patterns across most areas of Myanmar. There are almost no parts of the country where the Bamar do not currently live, and many other ethnic groups, perhaps most notably the Karen, Mon, Kachin and Shan, all have large populations outside their ethnic states. Any process of partition on ethnic lines would create messy and probably violent upheavals. A process of new nation-state-building would probably create a number of failures along the way.

The fourth scenario implies a much wider failure of Myanmar governance, and one that would, therefore, almost certainly motivate foreign diplomatic, and then military, intervention. Avoiding this scenario, should, on humanitarian grounds alone, be a high priority for national, regional and global leaders. Does that imply accepting the restoration of some political and economic stability under the new military dictatorship if it means avoiding greater calamity and, if only marginally, improving the lives of millions of destitute Myanmar people at the same time? This question matters regionally too, because Myanmar's implosion would be especially difficult for the near neighbours with the most to lose: Thailand and China. For them, a failed state, whatever form that took, would be a problem with deep strategic and economic implications, especially if millions of Myanmar people sought refuge in their borderlands. Deploying military forces into Myanmar would also not be a smooth process, and would almost inevitably draw in all of the world's most militarily significant players, especially in the context of the hypothetical leadership of the United Nations. China's role would obviously be crucial and it would be a profound test of the Communist Party's willingness to use Chinese power beyond their own borders to secure economic and strategic linkages, and also to avoid further deterioration in the regional security landscape.

References

A. A. (Myanmar researcher) and Liv S. Gaborit. 2021. 'Dancing with the Junta Again: Mistreatment of Women Activists by the Tatmadaw Following the Military Coup in Myanmar. *Anthropology in Action*, 28 (2): 51–6. doi.org/10.3167/aia.2021.280207

Ahamed, Akkas, Md Sayedur Rahman and Nur Hossain. 2020. 'China–Myanmar Bilateral Relations: An Analytical Study of Some Geostrategic and Economic Issues'. *Journal of Public Administration and Governance*, 10 (3): 321343. doi.org/10.5296/jpag.v10i3.17704

Ahmed, Meherun and Suparna Das. 2022. 'A Deplorable Future for the Stateless Rohingya Ethnic Minority? NGO Intervention in Refugee Camps in Bangladesh'. In *Forced Displacement and NGOs in Asia and the Pacific*, edited by Gül İnanç and Themba Lewis, 48–70. London: Routledge. doi.org/10.4324/9781003145233-4

Brenner, David. 2015. 'Ashes of Co-Optation: From Armed Group Fragmentation to the Rebuilding of Popular Insurgency in Myanmar'. *Conflict, Security & Development*, 15 (4): 337–58. doi.org/10.1080/14678802.2015.1071974

Farrelly, Nicholas. 2016. 'The NLD's Iron-Fisted Gerontocracy'. *Myanmar Times*, 1 February. www.mmtimes.com/opinion/18759-the-nld-s-iron-fisted-gerontocracy.html (page discontinued).

Farrelly, Nicholas. 2018. 'The Capital'. In *Routledge Handbook of Contemporary Myanmar*, edited by Adam Simpson and Nicholas Farrelly, 55–63. Oxford: Routledge. doi.org/10.4324/9781315743677-6

Halim, Md. Abdul, Sumiya Majumder Rinta, Md. Al Amin, Azmira Khatun and Adnan Habib Robin. 2021. 'The Environmental Implications of the Rohingya Refugee Crisis in Bangladesh'. *Asian Journal of Environment & Ecology*, 16 (4): 189–203. doi.org/10.9734/ajee/2021/v16i430269

Kipgen, Nehginpao. 2021. 'The 2020 Myanmar Election and the 2021 Coup: Deepening Democracy or Widening Division?' *Asian Affairs*, 52 (1): 1–17. doi.org/10.1080/03068374.2021.1886429

Lintner, Bertil. 2021. 'China Showing Myanmar Junta How to Firewall the Internet'. *Asia Times*, 24 December. asiatimes.com/2021/12/china-showing-myanmar-how-to-firewall-the-internet/

Mathieson, David. 2021. 'Myanmar's Nationwide Ceasefire Agreement Is Dead'. *Irrawaddy*, 15 October. www.irrawaddy.com/opinion/guest-column/myanmars-nationwide-ceasefire-agreement-is-dead.html

McCarthy, Gerard and Nicholas Farrelly. 2020. 'Peri-Conflict Peace: Brokerage, Development and Illiberal Ceasefires in Myanmar's Borderlands'. *Conflict, Security & Development*, 20 (1): 141–63. doi.org/10.1080/14678802.2019.1705072

Meehan, Patrick. 2015. 'Fortifying or Fragmenting the State? The Political Economy of the Opium/Heroin Trade in Shan State, Myanmar, 1988–2013'. *Critical Asian Studies*, 47 (2): 253–82. doi.org/10.1080/14672715.2015.1041280

Moos, Bethany, Russell Roberts and Mo Aye. 2021. 'The Myanmar Military Coup: Propelling the 2030 Milestones for Neglected Tropical Diseases Further Out of Reach'. *PLoS Neglected Tropical Diseases*, 15 (7). doi.org/10.1371/journal.pntd. 0009532

Myo Nyein Aung, Chengshi Shiu and Wei-Ti Chen. 2021. 'Amid Political and Civil Unrest in Myanmar, Health Services Are Inaccessible'. *The Lancet*, 397 (10283): 1446. doi.org/10.1016/S0140-6736(21)00780-7

Prasse-Freeman, Elliott and Ko Kabya. 2021. 'Revolutionary Responses to the Myanmar Coup'. *Anthropology Today*, 37 (3): 1–2. doi.org/10.1111/1467-8322. 12649

Renshaw, Catherine and Michael Lidauer. 2021. 'The Union Election Commission of Myanmar 2010–2020'. *Asian Journal of Comparative Law*, 16 (S1): 1–20. doi.org/10.1017/asjcl.2021.33

Robinson, Gwen. 2022. 'Myanmar's "Critically Weak Economy" to Grow 1% in 2022: World Bank'. *Nikkei Asia*, 26 January. asia.nikkei.com/Spotlight/Myanmar-Crisis/Myanmar-s-critically-weak-economy-to-grow-1-in-2022-World-Bank

Roy, Chiraag, Anthony Ware and Costas Laoutides. 2021. 'The Political Economy of Norwegian Peacemaking in Myanmar's Peace Process'. *Third World Quarterly*, 42 (9): 2172–88. doi.org/10.1080/01436597.2021.1909467

Sadan, Mandy. 2016. 'Can Democracy Cure Myanmar's Ethnic Conflicts?' *Current History*, 115 (782): 214–19. doi.org/10.1525/curh.2016.115.782.214

Saito, Eisuke. 2021. 'Ethical Challenges for Teacher Educators in Myanmar Due to the February 2021 Coup'. *Power and Education*, 13 (3): 205–12. doi.org/10.1177/ 17577438211037202

Selth, Andrew. 2020. *Interpreting Myanmar: A Decade of Analysis*. Canberra: ANU Press. doi.org/10.22459/IM.2020

Shukri, Shazwanis. 2021. 'The Rohingya Refugee Crisis in Southeast Asia: ASEAN's Role and Way Forward'. *Journal of International Studies*, 17: 239–63. doi.org/ 10.32890/jis2021.17.10

Su Mon Thant. 2021. *In the Wake of the Coup: How Myanmar Youth Arose to Fight for the Nation*. Brussels: Heinrich-Böll-Stiftung. eu.boell.org/sites/default/files/ 2021-12/Myanmar%20youth_FINAL.pdf

Thant Myint-U. 2020. *The Hidden History of Burma: A Crisis of Race and Capitalism*. London: Atlantic Books.

Thawnghmung, Ardeth Maung. 2019. *Everyday Economic Survival in Myanmar*. Madison: University of Wisconsin Press. doi.org/10.2307/j.ctvfjczf5

Triponel, Anna and Paul R Williams. 2021. 'Responding to the Military Coup in Myanmar: What Business Can and Should Do'. *LSE Business Review*, 9 February. blogs.lse.ac.uk/businessreview/2021/02/09/responding-to-the-military-coup-in-myanmar-what-business-can-and-should-do/

Walton, Matthew J. 2015. 'The Disciplining Discourse of Unity in Burmese Politics'. *Journal of Burma Studies*, 19 (1): 1–26. doi.org/10.1353/jbs.2015.0003

Wunna Tun. 2021. 'How Myanmar Doctors Taking Care of Patients under Heavy Fire in the Time of COVID-19 and Military Coup'. *World Medical Journal*, 67 (3): 48.

3

The Role of Social Media and Disruptive Technologies in Post-Coup Democracy Activism

Jaydn (pseudonym)

Consulting firm director, conducting political and business analysis for international companies in Myanmar

Monique Skidmore

Professor, Alfred Deakin Institute, Deakin University, Australia

Cecile Medail

Visiting Fellow, Department of Social and Political Change, The Australian National University

Abstract

This chapter reflects upon the effectiveness of censorship and surveillance technologies in asserting totalitarian control versus the power of disruptive cyber technologies to overthrow dictatorships. From hacktivism, to doxing, to cryptocurrency donations, to financial bond sales and 'click-to-donate' websites, a new generation of IT-savvy democracy activists in Myanmar are fighting for their right to live in a democratic state by harnessing their skills to disrupt authoritarian control. In a context in which the country's economy has become dependent upon the internet, app-based payment and communication technologies, we argue that the junta is struggling to maintain and extend its control of this new sphere of conflict. By contrast, a creative and diverse use of digital technologies enables the anti-coup movement to disrupt the military's repressive attempts to conquer the virtual battlefield.

Fighting in cyberspace

The nature of civil war is fundamentally changing due to repressed populations having widespread access to cyberspace and state deployment of online encryption and surveillance technologies (e.g. Ethiopia; ICG 2021). Myanmar is the first East Asian conflict zone in which social media and encryption technologies may be deciding factors. This chapter analyses the deployment and implications of new technologies by a military state with techno-totalitarian ambitions, and the resistance movement's adoption of disruptive technologies.

The 1 February 2021 military coup in Myanmar has been fiercely resisted in urban and village battlefields across the country. Meanwhile, a third territory has opened up in this fight for democracy: cyberspace. The Myanmar military has demonstrated totalitarian ambition for decades, waging physical and psychological warfare to establish authoritarian structures of control over its people. Totalitarianism is at the heart of the Myanmar military mindset (Selth 2021; Skidmore 2003). The logic of totalitarianism is one of fighting a continual war of attrition of the spirit—of placing physical and psychological boundaries around a population so that, over time, resistance is reduced to easily extinguished spot fires by an ever more experienced apparatus of repression (Skidmore 2004, 2007).

After the reprise of liberalisations in the Burman heartlands (but not borderlands) over the past decade, the military have sought to rapidly extend their control over cyberspace. They have doubled down on these efforts since the coup and the unexpected resistance they have received from their captive population. The coup marks a shift in the military's online strategy. No longer able to use social media to promote its authoritarian agenda, Myanmar's military, led by the State Administration Council (SAC), is now rapidly deploying the internet as an extension of the existing battlefields in which physical and psychological warfare are waged. Since the coup, a contest between the latest encryption and cybersecurity surveillance technologies has become one of several new frontiers.

The widespread availability and use of the internet and social media apps constitutes a main difference between the post-coup mass resistance and the 2007 Saffron Revolution, which was the last time the population sought to overthrow the military junta (Skidmore & Wilson 2008). The internet has played an increasingly crucial role in facilitating Burmese pro-democracy diaspora activism since the 1990s (Danitz & Strobel 1999), and in disseminating vital information securely via nascent online platforms during the Saffron Revolution (Chowdhury 2008; Brough & Li 2013).

The phenomenon of democracy communication and mobilisation against authoritarian rulers has been documented in Africa and the Middle East, and it is not surprising that a new generation of Burmese have turned to apps and the internet to organise resistance. Since the coup, cyberspace has become a critical workplace for many of the key actors at the forefront of the current resistance, notably the National Unity Government (NUG), the People's Defence Forces (PDFs) and the Civil Disobedience Movement (CDM). This chapter examines the use of new technologies employed by civil and armed resistance groups against the junta for their utility in allowing more effective organisation and communication. We see the strategic use of disruptive technologies to finance revolution and to counter the regime's fearmongering through propaganda as being both novel and potentially the most effective form of resistance to date.

The use of Facebook as a new terrain of authoritarian control

Facebook provides a good illustration of the junta's use of cyberspace to expand its authoritarian control. Its role has changed from an unregulated channel for military propaganda to a temporary platform of resistance against the coup. Facebook's efforts to stop hate speech and deplatform the military after the coup eventually blunted the junta's online strategy, which rapidly shifted to restriction and repression.

Myanmar is the East Asian nation that was most quickly dominated by Facebook. The rapid uptake occurred in a similar fashion to the extraordinarily fast adoption of mobile phone telephony from 2013. Akin only to North Korea, until 2011, mobile phone subscriptions in Myanmar were between one and two per 100 persons (ITU 2013) with a cost of over USD3,000 for a single subscription (Petulla 2013). When Ooredoo then Telenor were given network licences in 2013, subscriptions fell to USD1.50—and Ooredoo sold 1 million subscriptions in three weeks, while Telenor sold 500,000 (*Economist* 2015; Ling et al. 2015).

Similarly, the Facebook platform rapidly became very powerful in Myanmar: by 2021, Facebook users represented 51.5 per cent of the population with 28.7 million users, 12.4 million being between 25 and 34 years of age (NapoleonCat 2021). Considering the levels of poverty, internet connectivity and remoteness of parts of the country, this is an extraordinary statistic. Accounting for over 93 per cent of all internet traffic in April 2022, Facebook enjoys a unique level of popularity and a quasi-monopoly on social media use and information sharing (Statcounter 2022). In 2016, the global body representing mobile operators found that in Myanmar many people considered Facebook as their entry point for online information and perceived postings as news (Hogan & Safi 2018). For the average Myanmar phone user, Facebook is synonymous with the internet and most people do not use internet browsers to search for information. Such success is largely due to Facebook's quick development of a Burmese language version and the fact that Facebook was typically pre-installed on phones, and that some phone plans did not charge for time spent on Facebook.

The changing role of the platform during Myanmar's quasi-democratic period has been discussed elsewhere (Tønnesson, Min Zaw Oo & Ne Lynn Aung 2022). In this section, we look at Facebook as a case study of the military's expansion of its authoritarian control over cyberspace. Facebook is now at the centre of the junta's repression, censorship and surveillance efforts deployed to impose its authoritarian control over cyberspace and attempts to defeat the resistance movement's free access to information and its potential for digital disruption.

The centrality of Facebook throughout Myanmar society

During Myanmar's quasi-democratic period, widespread access to smartphones and the rapid growth of internet use enabled a broad range of actors to use Facebook as their primary channel of communication. Media outlets, the general public, Buddhist figures, and military and government officials, as well as minority ethnic armed organisations, all began posting on Facebook. As a central forum of discussion that has also become a main outlet for traditional media, Facebook has allowed a broad spectrum of people to engage with social and political issues, offering them a new way to access information, express their opinions and connect with others.

However, the platform has also contributed to the polarisation and reinforcement of pre-existing opinions among communities sharing the same interests (McCarthy 2018). Facebook facilitated the spread of ultra-nationalist sentiment reflected in leading monk U Wirathu's sermons, supported the propagation of negative prejudice towards Muslim men (McCarthy & Menager 2017) and enabled the production of narratives of fear and Buddhist–Muslim antagonisms (Schissler 2015). The platform eventually played a major role in the spread of hate speech, enabling users to participate in the co-production of nationalism and the construction of a potential Muslim threat (Prasse-Freeman 2021).

The pace of social media's spread in the 2010s is also reflected in the way government authorities communicated with the public. The use of official social media channels by high-level military and civilian government offices to promote their narratives became the norm. Facebook, in particular, became the main platform for partisan political communication used by the government and its supporters (Aung Khant 2017; Dowling 2019; Nyi Nyi Kyaw 2019). Finally, ethnic armed groups also use Facebook as a tool of communication with their constituents to mobilise support and legitimise their role. For some armed groups, such as the Arakan Army, their intelligence gathering and successful military operations against Myanmar's armed forces relied heavily on social media until the army pushed the civilian government to impose the world's longest internet shutdown between June 2019 and February 2021, in Rakhine and Chin states (Tønnesson, Min Zaw Oo & Ne Lynn Aung 2022; Kyaw Hsan Hlaing & Fishbein 2021).

Military Facebook: Promoting the authoritarian agenda

The army's psychological warfare department is believed to have trained hundreds of officers to run multiple Facebook accounts, attracting followers and spreading fake news to foment religious and racial crises. Officials of the Thein Sein government used posts from the minister of information—known as 'the Minister of Facebook'—refuting allegations of human rights abuses in order to spread hate speech (*Irrawaddy* 2018). In 2014, U Wirathu, the notoriously anti-Muslim monk leader of the Mabatha movement, shared a Facebook post with fabricated accusations of rape that went viral, resulting in another incident of intercommunal violence.

The fact that the NLD government relied on Facebook for their own partisan political communication represented a great challenge to the regulation and sanction of fake news in Myanmar (Nyi Nyi Kyaw 2019). Senior officials, including the military leadership and civilian wing of the government, did not persuasively condemn the Buddhist-nationalist narrative in their official media outlets or on their Facebook accounts; neither did they use the 2013 Telecommunication Law to charge individuals involved in promoting religious hate speech, such as the extremist monk U Wirathu (Fink 2018). By contrast, authorities used this law just before the 2020 election to prosecute hundreds of Facebook users for mocking Senior General Min Aung Hlaing (Yan Naung Oak & Brooten 2019).

During the peak of military and civilian violence against Muslims in 2016 and 2017, hate speech on Facebook multiplied and socially licensed the brutal military operations that led to the displacement of 700,000 Rohingya to Bangladesh. The crackdown on the Rohingya was supported by top Myanmar officials, including the leader of the military, Senior General Min Aung Hlaing, and the leader of the National League for Democracy, Aung San Suu Kyi, who asserted that testimonies from refugee camps and the international depiction of the crisis were biased. This claim was reinforced by viral posts on social media (Kinseth 2019). Since state media and Buddhist-nationalist Facebook pages only relayed the displacement of Buddhists and Hindus, many citizens expressed support on Facebook for the counterinsurgency operations against Rohingya militants (Fink 2018).

The end of impunity and the blunting of the junta's online strategy

In early 2018, Facebook was in the spotlight for spreading hate speech against the Rohingya minority, as investigators from the UN Human Rights Council's Fact-Finding Mission on Myanmar indicated that social media, which in Myanmar is Facebook, played a 'determining role' in the level of conflict within the public (Miles 2018). The Fact-Finding Mission report, released later in the year, described Facebook as 'slow and ineffective' at stopping hate speech (HRC 2018).

Soon after Facebook's role was first officially criticised, and as a result of pressure from digital rights activists, the platform took some steps to actively remove hate speech and ban military officials.[1] By August 2018, 18 Facebook accounts, and 52 Facebook pages representing almost 12 million followers, were removed. This ban included the account of Min Aung Hlaing, the leader of the coup, and the armed forces' Myawaddy television channel. By the end of the year, another 438 pages, 145 accounts and 17 groups were removed for being linked to the military (Meta 2018).[2] According to *Frontier Myanmar* (2018), taking the unprecedentedly popular Facebook platform away from top army officials and outlets represented the strongest punishment the international community could hope to inflict.

However, such measures had a limited impact, as the armed forces remained in control of other pages, such as the Ministry of Defence page, and could possibly use other pages managed by the civilian government to spread its propaganda (*Frontier Myanmar* 2018).

In the weeks following the coup, Facebook banned the remaining military state and media pages, groups and accounts, including the Ministry of Defence page, as well as ads from commercial entities linked to the armed forces, which were eventually removed at the end of 2021. The banning of these military-linked businesses from the platform occurred just after a group of Rohingya refugees filed a lawsuit against Facebook for allowing the spread of hate speech, which led to large-scale violence against the ethnic minority group (Milmo 2021). Despite these moves, a report released in March 2022 revealed that Facebook was still approving ads with hate speech content inciting violence against the Rohingya (*GW* 2022).

---

1   Facebook has certainly restricted its Myanmar users for not following its 'community standards' before its role in the propagation of hate speech was officially exposed. However, restrictions had been applied unevenly (Fink 2018). While Rohingya users have complained that Facebook was silencing them by quickly suspending or closing their accounts for documenting human rights abuses committed by the military (Osborne 2017), U Wirathu's account was only permanently shut down in January 2018, after being able to propagate hate speech for years, despite reports that his page was spreading inflammatory content. Even after his account was shut down, his videos remained in circulation (Barron 2018). In addition, despite the hiring of dozens of Burmese speakers to review hate speech content, announced in April 2018, a Reuters report exposed in August 2018 that more than a thousand posts, images or comments attacking Rohingya had been up for up to five years (Reuters 2018).
2   Additionally, in February 2019, Facebook deplatformed four armed groups who were members of the Northern Alliance, which the National League for Democracy government had previously characterised as terrorist organisations. Although this label is no longer held by the NUG, Facebook's censorship of these armed groups remains, which the anti-coup movement perceives as very detrimental because it restricts the flow of information and, hence, their ability to organise (Kyaw Hsan Hlaing 2021).

Nevertheless, ending years of military use of the platform with impunity, Facebook's deplatforming of Myanmar's armed forces blunted the junta's online strategy by limiting its outreach capacity while bolstering the anti-coup movement. As the chapter will develop further, activists have used Facebook extensively to mobilise people, organise protests, urge civil servants to join the CDM, fundraise, document military abuses, share information and encouragements or give advice on protest tactics and safety. Countless users have changed their profile pictures to express their support for the NUG. The coup thus marked a huge change in the military's online strategy: instead of using Facebook to spread its propaganda, the junta started restricting and punishing its use.

Post-coup military crackdown on social media and internet access

The junta's subsequent attempts to control the virtual battlefield through internet shutdowns, the establishment of its own intranet with limited services, and its increased surveillance and repression of groups and individuals significantly impacted social media use and Facebook use in particular.

After seizing power, the SAC enacted amendments to the Electronic Transactions Law to allow them to access user data and then sue prominent opponents (HRW 2021). It also sought to win the communications battle by temporarily shutting down access to the internet. During the first few hours of the coup, the SAC completely shut down the internet in Myanmar. This effectively cut the flow of information via social media to prevent the organisation of a resistance. However, this quickly resulted in chaos as the banking system shut down, halting the functioning of sectors of the economy. The junta then instituted a nightly ban on internet services and shut down mobile internet services, which is the main source of web access.

These measures lasted only three months. The internet is a major development factor of Myanmar's economy (OBG 2019). In a context in which pandemic restrictions have increased the dependency of Myanmar's economy on internet banking and ecommerce, many businesses require reliable internet access for their transactions. In 2020 alone, 38 per cent of Myanmar firms moved to online platforms, resulting in a 73 per cent increase in e-transactions (Chen 2021). The SAC also remains dependent on the internet for its surveillance efforts, which rely on platforms like

Facebook. The *dalan* (pro-military civilian informants) have been deployed across the platform to monitor posts and activity, including in private groups (Duncan & Mendelson 2021).

Employing a strategy used by the government in 2020 to silence critical voices (Nyan Hlaing Lin 2020), the junta pressured mobile operators and internet service providers to restrict access to certain websites and also virtual private networks (VPNs) that can bypass internet filtering. In an attempt to develop a national intranet, the junta whitelisted more than 1,200 web services used for business purposes, such as internet banking and some social media apps like WhatsApp, Zoom and Instagram (Strangio 2021). In some conflict areas, the SAC ordered a total internet shutdown and sporadic mobile communications cuts.

The fact that the SAC has been applying the same measures previously used against the Arakan Army suggests it has yet to develop alternative strategies to limit digital disruption without incurring a socioeconomic toll (ICG 2021). The SAC also attempted to restrict internet access by raising the price of sim cards from USD1.50 to USD11 and internet services by 50 per cent. It also drafted a Cybersecurity Law to punish the use of VPNs, which has already been enforced, although it has yet to be passed as a law (*Irrawaddy* 2022a; Haffner 2022; Dobberstein 2022).

Since Facebook is banned and the use of VPNs is risky and does not get around *dalan* surveillance, the number of Facebook users has decreased as people move to safer encrypted apps. In early 2022, the number of active social media users dropped to about 38 per cent of the Myanmar population, against 53 per cent the previous year (Statistica 2022). Similarly, the number of Facebook users decreased to 21 million people one year after the coup as opposed to almost 28 million people—more than half of Myanmar's 54 million population—just before the coup (NapoleonCat 2021, 2022). As of June 2022, the predominance of Facebook in social media traffic has dropped from 93 per cent to 77 per cent (Statcounter 2022). While direct comparison with figures from previous years should be made with caution, this general trend seems to reflect the realities of internet shutdowns, restrictions on certain social media platforms such as Facebook and the increased prices of mobile data connection. Some people fear being arrested with their smartphones and charged under the Cybersecurity Bill, so they delete Facebook and their VPN when taking their phone outside their home. The junta's use of the Counter-Terrorism Law to seize the property of democracy supporters has led to the confiscation of more than

547 properties since the NUG's declaration of war in September 2021 (*Irrawaddy* 2022b). As a result, fewer people express support for the NUG on Facebook. In addition, the junta continues to expand its control over cyberspace with the development of a national identity database and the adoption of a new sim card regulation, which requires users to register their sim cards with their national ID card number. This, combined with the fact that telecom providers are either controlled by the junta or believed to be controlled by military-aligned entities, enables the junta to control users' personal data and arrest people more easily (RFA 2022).

As an illustration of military rule in cyberspace, the case of Facebook's rise and decline in Myanmar shows how the junta has used a central part of cyberspace as a new terrain of authoritarian control, and how it has changed its tactics since the coup. After initially simply moving their crude propaganda and psychological warfare strategies into cyberspace and throttling internet connectivity to disrupt opposition communications, the junta have now imported new cyber-surveillance technologies from China, Russia, the United States, Israel and Sweden (Beech 2021). Nonetheless, the use of Facebook and social media and the internet in general has not been uncontested. The civil resistance and armed movements in Myanmar have adopted new technologies to push back military control of the Myanmar cyber-sphere.

The resistance fights back: Disruptive technologies v. authoritarian control

Despite the SAC's fierce attempts to control cyberspace, democracy activists have so far been one step ahead in their use of new technologies. According to Ryan and Tran (2022), this has been possible because pro-democracy activists were able to sharpen their 'digitalized capacity' prior to the coup, through the development of training programs and advocacy campaigns directed towards social media platforms, government authorities and internet users. Building on these skills, the anti-coup movements harnessed the cyber-sphere for disruptive purposes: they have been successful in digitally organising protests, fundraising and sharing information about events inside the country, with each other and the world. While Facebook continues to be instrumental to the anti-coup movement, Myanmar's digital activism has predominantly relied on other tools that require little knowledge or skill, such as free VPNs and encrypted messaging services.

In a review of the literature on digital activism, George and Leidner (2019) divide digital activism into three broad categories: digital spectatorship, digital transition activities and digital gladiatorial activities. They describe digital spectator activities as clicktivism, mentioning and assertion; digital transitional activities as e-funding, political consumerism, digital petitions and botivism; and digital gladiatorial activities as data activism, exposure and hacktivism. Hacktivism has been taken up by Myanmar democracy activists. Jordan (2002) has described hacktivism as the attempt to achieve social and political objectives through hacking. George and Leidner (2019) further differentiate hacktivists into cyberterrorists, civic hackers and patriotic hackers. Myanmar's nascent hacktivist political activism is a little of each of these subcategories, with the aim being to disable the regime's ability to govern and to spread propaganda. This section discusses, in particular, the use of social media for counterpropaganda and real-time communication, and the effectiveness of digital gladiatorial activities such as hacktivism and doxing, and digital transitional methods of e-financing, in preventing the SAC from consolidating its control on the ground.

Counterpropaganda and real-time communication

The use of social media makes the regime's censorship of media outlets and restrictions of social media platforms less effective by publishing evidence that is contrary to the regime's statements and accounts. For example, images of deserted cities posted on Facebook counter the regime's illustrations in media outlets showing congested streets during the nationwide 'silent strikes'. Armed resistance groups routinely use Facebook pages to report battles and attacks in real time through photo and video uploads of fighting and human rights abuses. One group may have several pages. One of the reasons for the SAC's attempted shutdown of the internet has been to try and stop information reaching rank and file soldiers so as to preserve morale and limit further defections (ICG 2021).

Social media apps have allowed widespread publishing of real-time military movements, numbers and weaponry. Different tools have been used in Yangon and Mandalay, mainly during the peak of the attacks. Some websites such as Myanmarmap.live[3] have provided real-time map information. Facebook messenger groups have been used to get security information in

---

3   Site no longer accessible.

various neighbourhoods and townships and to relay it to people directly in the line of advancing SAC columns.[4] After the banning of Facebook, resistance groups have massively moved to encrypted apps such as Telegram and Signal to share sensitive information. The Fifth Column Telegram channel gathers and shares military intelligence information with resistance groups. The walkie talkie app Zello has also been used as a channel to communicate between trusted parties (as joining a Zello channel requires a recommendation from a group member). These tools provided grassroots-level information for resistance groups to organise protests, avoid arrests and attack military supporters—for example, when five police officers were killed on a train in Yangon (*Myanmar Now* 2021). In addition, people have been using them in their daily lives to plan safe travel routes.

Hacktivism and doxing

Hacktivism in Myanmar is used to block military propaganda by preventing public access to government websites and, in some cases, display a protest message. For instance, the government-owned news websites *Global New Light of Myanmar* and *Myanmar Digital News* have been targeted, with messages such as 'Stop arresting people illegally at midnight; Save Myanmar'. Although hacktivism is a 'gladiatorial' activity with the ability to have the most significant effects upon the regime's ability to govern and propagandise, as yet the Myanmar resistance forces lack the capacity to create mass DDoS (distributed denial-of-service) attacks and so hacktivism has been largely symbolic.

Doxing has proven a more successful, albeit small-scale, resistance tactic. Doxing is a social punishment strategy used in cyberspace, which consists of naming and shaming individuals affiliated with the junta or related to military officers. This social punishment campaign, which started soon after the coup, works as a kind of retribution for the junta's past social exclusion of democracy activists that goes far beyond cyberbullying.

Anonymous activists have set up a database listing targets in the armed forces, their locations, photographs and the type of offence they have committed. Individuals have also created Facebook groups and viral posts that publish the personal details of family members of military officers and pro-regime celebrities. In addition to the widespread incitement to bully senior officers'

---

4   See, for example, the closed South Okkalapa township Facebook group, www.facebook.com/grou ps/419886232433483/?ref=share

children,[5] the tactic allowed the boycott of military-linked businesses and had the effect of decreasing the legitimacy of the junta by shrinking the number of influential and well-known Burmese (such as entertainers or social media influencers) willing to be associated with them (Sithu Aung Myint 2021). The deportation and freezing of assets of military family members and associates living abroad has been a key motivation for the diaspora movement engaging in doxing (McMichael 2021). For instance, the Australian Government launched an investigation into junta relatives living in Australia following calls from human rights advocates and Burmese Australians who prepared a list naming 15 relatives of senior junta members (Galloway & McKenzie 2021).

Doxing has also had concrete effects on the ground, including the murder of at least four military supporters and informants as the direct result of revealing their identity and personal details on Facebook. In November 2021, local armed groups killed two military informants and a ward administrator as well as a teacher who did not join the CDM (*Irrawaddy* 2021a; Maung Maung Thein 2021). In addition to exposing the teacher's identity, resistance supporters specifically asked her to stop collaborating with the military (Maung Maung Thein 2021).

Reliable sources indicate that, in some cases, people have been wrongly identified as pro-military, with real-life consequences. For instance, the supposed addresses of Myanmar Air Force Officers were published in a public Facebook group. This wrongly led to the bombing of a residence that was later identified as that of a local singer (Ko Korozan 2022). In addition, this climate of social punishment has trickled down to civilians, with increased tensions and polarisation, which the youth feel strongly (Chiu 2022). The fear of being publicly shamed and labelled as pro-military causes social anxiety and results in self-censorship: people can be ostracised simply for using Facebook to share their intention to study abroad or go back to university (Chiu 2022).

Doxing has been a small-scale but effective strategy deployed by activists inside and outside the country, and has also been a deadly tactic used by the SAC's intelligence apparatus to hunt pro-democracy supporters.

---

5   For example, in March 2021, the personal information of the son of a general was published on Facebook. The post incited people to use it for cyberbullying, phone bullying and even offline bullying. Later, the post was removed from Facebook.

The identity and details of active resistance supporters have been exposed on social media, leading to their arrests, and there are credible reports of extrajudicial killings.[6]

One of the biggest recent changes is the use of Telegram channels by both pro-democracy and pro-military groups. A Telegram channel allows its owner to broadcast messages to an unlimited number of subscribers who cannot send their own messages—unless the channel owner links it to a discussion group and enables comments. While the pro-resistance channel 'Digging SAC' is mainly used to share information, the pro-military channels 'Han Nyein Oo' and 'Ko Lu Ngwe' are used to crowdsource information about pro-democracy activists through their subscribers, the online *dalans*, who can safely denounce members of the resistance through a private account created for this purpose. Members of the resistance have been arrested or killed through these channels. For instance, two National League for Democracy supporters were killed in Mandalay in response to a pro-military militia's launch of a counterinsurgency operation circulated on the Han Nyein Oo channel (*Irrawaddy* 2022d).

While doxing has had a concrete impact and sometimes led to deaths, its effectiveness in undermining the junta's consolidation is limited because of its infrequent and small-scale uses and also because this tactic is used against the resistance itself. Digital financing represents the real game changer in the short term as it offers a new frontier.

Digital financing

Digital financing is used to fund the resistance against the coup, both non-violent and violent, through three main avenues: the parallel government, grassroots actors and, more recently, through click-to-donate websites and apps.

The NUG is able to finance the resistance movement through its innovative use of crowdfunding. In late 2021, the NUG announced a target budget of about USD800 million (MMK1.4 trillion) to cover social and humanitarian support, including health care, education, welfare and funding for striking civil servants as well as defecting military personnel and police officers (Nachemson 2021; *Irrawaddy* 2021b). This budget did not officially

---

6   See, for instance, the arrest of a bank employee, www.facebook.com/ngerdopnaingmarpar/posts/191226889878748

include defence spending, but, in June 2022, the NUG declared that it had already spent over 45 million—about 95 per cent of its available funds—on arming PDFs. More money is desperately needed, however, as funding the armed resistance would require at least USD10 million monthly (*Irrawaddy* 2022f).

The alternative government was able to raise this money through innovative initiatives, such as the purchase of lottery ticket sales, bonds, participating in a 'voluntary tax' regime, and through sales of military property shares and cryptocurrency. The online lottery sale pilot scheme launched in August 2021 raised USD8 million. The bond sale began in November 2021, with USD2 million worth of bonds sold within the first two hours (Nachemson 2021). The voluntary tax, which can be paid online through a voluntary self-assessment process, raised about USD150,000 in a month (*Mizzima* 2021; Nyan Hlaing Lin 2021). The Ministry of Finance also launched an unexpected scheme at the end of April 2022 whereby properties owned by military leaders would be reclaimed and sold in shares to support the revolution. In the first three days that Min Aung Hlaing's residence was put on sale for USD10 million (a third of its value), USD2 million was raised in the sale of shares (*Irrawaddy* 2022e). Such a fundraising move is revolutionary in that it is simultaneously delegitimising the junta, bestowing legitimacy on the NUG and potentially supporting violent action. Finally, the NUG encourages the use of cryptocurrency, which is hard to trace. The Ministry of Finance announced in December 2021 the use of the stable coin Tether as its official currency, to ensure the safety of donations made to the NUG (Al Jazeera 2021). Then, in June 2022, the NUG launched NUG Pay, a digital platform using a new blockchain digital currency, the Digital Myanmar Kyat. With this technology, the NUG is able to circumvent the formal banking sector without SAC interference (Abuza 2022).

In addition to NUG funding, the resistance movement is widely using grassroots fundraising techniques to support striking civil servants as well as local PDFs. Such grassroots fundraising is organised by individuals, celebrities and armed groups and includes platforms such as We Pledge CDM Myanmar, which receives donations supporting CDM participants and humanitarian aid. Digital wallet platforms, such as KBZ Pay, are widely used to support armed resistance. Any group can post its digital wallet ID or QR code on Facebook for donors to transfer money. It is not easy for the junta to trace such fund movements. However, in some cases, the use of transfer names like 'Revolution' or 'PDF' enabled the junta to identify several accounts and freeze them. To further crack down on people funding the anti-junta movement, the Central Bank announced a new restrictive regulation in September 2022 whereby mobile payments would be cancelled unless transfers were registered with the user's correct identification details (*GNLM* 2022).

Donating money via digital wallet platforms has thus become increasingly risky. The junta has been charging NUG or PDF supporters with funding terrorism under the 2014 Counter-Terrorism Law. Almost 200 people have been prosecuted since the coup, and face up to 10 years imprisonment, no matter how small the donation (*Irrawaddy* 2022c). In one instance, two university students received a seven-year sentence for donating MMK5,000 or USD3 (*Irrawaddy* 2022c). Where funding for pro-democracy and armed resistance groups has been stopped by the SAC, some have turned to cryptocurrency. When Myanmar celebrity Htar Htet Htet's digital wallet code was revealed by regime supporters in August 2021, she encouraged her followers to make donations to the NUG through different countries and platforms, which include Binance, Bitcoin and PayPal. While the use of NUG Pay is increasing among NUG supporters, KBZ Pay remains the main payment method. Responding to increasing challenges in accessing, transferring and raising funds in Myanmar, the PDFs have instituted other innovative fundraising systems that rely on internet advertising revenue rather than on individual donations. Revenue is generated through the YouTube channels views and likes as well as through click-to-donate websites. Users typically generate a donation to the website owner by clicking on ads without spending their own money. While each donation only generates a few cents, the objective is to accrue enough clicks to produce significant amounts. Donations are encouraged on Facebook's Click2donate page, which also shares daily reports of funds raised by a total of 10 sites. Facebook is still used for the promotion of this innovative crowdfunding system, which offers a much safer way to donate to the resistance and generates a significant amount daily. For example, on 5 May 2022 alone, almost USD10,000 was generated. Tech savvy resistance youth have also developed several click-to-donate apps—for instance, the news app 'Tha Din' and the gaming app 'The PDF Game'—whereby the user generates a donation each time an ad shows up as the app is loading. These new fundraising strategies represent a much safer option than posting a QR code on a Facebook account, which could easily be traced if the post became viral. It is also a simple act, which does not cost anything to the user but can make a significant difference when used collectively. Tapping into the global advertising networks moves resistance funding into the mainstream and provides an ongoing and passive source of income.

Despite continuous attempts to repress the use of cyberspace, the junta has not been able to stop digital financing because they do not have the capacity to shut down the internet, which continues to be used by a highly creative pro-democracy resistance. Yet, the impact of digital financing is beyond cyberspace as it provides the resistance with more capacity to buy weapons and, therefore, has the potential to directly influence the result of the war on the ground.

Conclusion

Counterinsurgency strategies have proved too costly for the junta to implement digitally as for the moment, it inhibits their economy and banking system. By employing innovative digital techniques that go beyond Facebook's quasi-monopoly to maintain its access to information and sustain the resistance movement, pro-democracy groups have been able to blunt the pro-totalitarianism military's fear-making apparatus that includes its own propaganda, surveillance and censorship methods. At this early stage of disruptive technology use in the developing cyber-world of Myanmar, connectivity to the internet is critical for the resistance movement to access funds through digital financing and to communicate through social media. In the short and medium term, digital financing of the resistance has the potential to affect the outcome on the physical battleground: the PDFs are better armed this year and the junta is unable to consolidate its coup.

But all authoritarian regimes have been confronted with these new opportunities for democracy activism. The 2011 Arab Spring movement is considered the first social media–enabled resistance movement, but theorists have written on the formation of such virtual communities in terms of 'Slacktivism', an ultimately ineffective form of protest or adjunct to physical resistance. We only need to look to Myanmar's northern border to see how authoritarian governments over time are mastering these tools to building their own cyberworlds. In the Chinese Splinternet, for example, an authoritarian metaverse is being created that is as tightly bound and defended as their physical territories (Griffiths 2019).

The junta has studied longstanding autocracies such as China and Russia to understand how they have been able to neutralise the power of the internet and social media to resist their rule and to turn it into an extension of their social control. As a result, the regime is working hard on making the everyday use of the internet and social media too expensive and risky. The junta can buy spyware and other tools and start creating its own internet. The purchase of new cyber-surveillance technologies is ongoing, as illustrated by the visit in early April of a private open-source intelligence expert from Russia selling a public opinion monitoring system on social media, Telegram channels and the darknet (IO 2022). This might explain the internet shutdown that affected the whole country mid-March. We should expect more measures designed to deny Burmese citizens access to the cyber-world as the junta learns to navigate and create their own cyber-sphere. Techno-totalitarianism may eventually win in Myanmar, as it is winning in its more cyber-developed neighbour China. But, until a time comes when the junta is able to control access to cyberspace, Myanmar activists will continue to use social media and the internet not just to organise and publicise alternate politics and visions of the future, but also to dull the resonance of the regime's propaganda. Last but not least, with the ability to digitally fund armed resistance in the physical battlefield, cyberspace offers ways, if only in the short term, to even up the stakes on the ground.

References

Abuza, Zachary. 2022. 'The NUG's Economic War on Myanmar's Military'. *Stimson*, 27 September. www.stimson.org/2022/the-nugs-economic-war-on-myanmars-military/

Al Jazeera. 2021. 'Myanmar Shadow Government Approves Crypto as Official Currency'. 14 December. www.aljazeera.com/economy/2021/12/14/myanmar-shadow-government-approves-crypto-as-official-currency

Aung Khant, Alex. 2017. 'Who to Believe in a Time of Crisis?' *Tea Circle*, 29 September. teacircleoxford.com/opinion/who-to-believe-in-a-time-of-crisis/

Barron, Laignee. 2018. 'Nationalist Monk Known as the "Burmese Bin Laden" Has Been Stopped from Spreading Hate on Facebook', *Time*, 28 February. time.com/5178790/facebook-removes-wirathu/

Beech, Hannah. 2021. 'Myanmar's Military Deploys Digital Arsenal of Repression in Crackdown'. *The New York Times*, 1 March. www.nytimes.com/2021/03/01/world/asia/myanmar-coup-military-surveillance.html

Brough, M. and Z. Li. 2013. 'Media Systems Dependency, Symbolic Power, and Human Rights Online Video: Learning from Burma's "Saffron Revolution" and WITNESS's Hub'. *International Journal of Communication*, 7 (1): 281–304.

Chen, Estey. 2021. 'Months after Coup, Myanmar Accelerates toward Surveillance State'. *Diplomat*, 2 September. thediplomat.com/2021/09/months-after-coup-myanmar-accelerates-toward-surveillance-state/

Chiu, Francesca. 2022. 'Personal Struggles, Political Lens: How the Coup Unites and Divides Myanmar's Youth'. *Tea Circle*, 17 January. teacircleoxford.com/essay/personal-struggles-political-lens-how-the-coup-unites-and-divides-myanmars-youth/

Chowdhury, Mridul. 2008. 'The Role of the Internet in Burma's Saffron Revolution'. *Berkman Center Research Publication*, no. 2008-8. doi.org/10.2139/ssrn.1537703

Danitz, Tiffany and Warren P. Strobel. 1999. 'The Internet's Impact on Activism: The Case of Burma'. *Studies in Conflict & Terrorism*, 22 (3): 257–69. doi.org/10.1080/105761099265766

Dobberstein, Laura. 2022. 'Myanmar's Military Junta Seeks Ban on VPNs and Digital Currency'. *Register*, 24 January. www.theregister.com/2022/01/24/myanmar_military_junta_bans_vpns_crypto/

Dowling, Thomas. 2019. 'Shooting the (Facebook) Messenger (Part I)'. *Tea Circle*, 21 January. teacircleoxford.com/essay/shooting-the-facebook-messenger-part-i/

Duncan, Kiana and Allegra Mendelson. 2021. 'The Tatmadaw Has Mass Surveillance Technology, but How Well Is It Used?' *Globe*, 7 June. southeastasiaglobe.com/myanmar-military-surveillance/

Economist. 2015. 'Land of Temples and Tech'. 25 March. www.economist.com/business/2015/03/26/land-of-temples-and-tech

Fink, Christina. 2018. 'Dangerous Speech, Anti-Muslim Violence, and Facebook in Myanmar'. *The Journal of International Affairs*, 71 (1.5): 43–52.

Frontier Myanmar. 2018. 'A Clear Message'. 28 August. www.frontiermyanmar.net/en/a-clear-message/ (page discontinued).

Galloway, Anthony and Nick McKenzie. 2021. 'Home Affairs Investigating Relatives of Myanmar Military in Australia'. *Sydney Herald Tribune*, 5 May. www.smh.com.au/politics/federal/home-affairs-investigating-relatives-of-myanmar-military-in-australia-20210504-p57ood.html

George, J. J. and D. E. Leidner. 2019. 'From Clicktivism to Hacktivism: Understanding Digital Activism'. *Information and Organization* 29 (3): 100249. doi.org/10.1016/j.infoandorg.2019.04.001

GNLM (*Global New Light of Myanmar*). 2022. 'Mobile Money Transfer Accounts Will be Cancelled Unless They Are Level 2: CBM'. 18 September. www.gnlm.com.mm/mobile-money-transfer-accounts-will-be-cancelled-unless-they-are-level-2-cbm/

Griffiths, James. 2019. *The Great Firewall of China: How to Build and Control an Alternative Version of the Internet*. London: Zed Books. doi.org/10.5040/9781350225497

GW (*Global Witness*). 2022. 'Facebook Approves Adverts Containing Hate Speech Inciting Violence and Genocide against the Rohingya'. 20 March. www.globalwitness.org/en/campaigns/digital-threats/rohingya-facebook-hate-speech/

Haffner, Andrew. 2022. 'Myanmar's Internet Gets Pricier for Dissenters, Apolitical Alike'. Al Jazeera, 11 February. www.aljazeera.com/economy/2022/2/11/myanmars-internet-gets-pricier-for-dissenters-apolitical-alike

Hogan, Libby and Michael Safi. 2018. 'Revealed: Facebook Hate Speech Exploded in Myanmar during Rohingya Crisis'. *Guardian*, 3 April. www.theguardian.com/world/2018/apr/03/revealed-facebook-hate-speech-exploded-in-myanmar-during-rohingya-crisis

HRC (Human Rights Council). 2018. 'Report of the Independent International Fact-Finding Mission on Myanmar'. 10–28 September. www.ohchr.org/sites/default/files/Documents/HRBodies/HRCouncil/FFM-Myanmar/A_HRC_39_64.pdf

HRW (Human Rights Watch). 2021. 'Myanmar: Post-Coup Legal Changes Erode Human Rights'. 2 March. www.hrw.org/news/2021/03/02/myanmar-post-coup-legal-changes-erode-human-rights

ICG (International Crisis Group). 2021. *Myanmar's Military Struggles to Control the Virtual Battlefield*. Report No. 314. www.crisisgroup.org/asia/south-east-asia/myanmar/314-myanmars-military-struggles-control-virtual-battlefield

IO (Intelligence Online). 2022. 'Kremlin's Favourite OSINT Expert Helps Russian Plans in Myanmar'. 13 April. www.intelligenceonline.com/surveillance--interception/2022/04/13/kremlin-s-favourite-osint-expert-helps-russian-plans-in-myanmar,109767698-gra

Irrawaddy. 2018. 'Facebook Slow to React to Violence, Hate Speech in Myanmar'. 20 April. www.irrawaddy.com/opinion/editorial/facebook-slow-react-violence-hate-speech-myanmar.html

Irrawaddy. 2021a. 'Myanmar Junta Informants and Officials Killed in Yangon Attacks'. 6 August. www.irrawaddy.com/news/burma/myanmar-junta-informants-and-officials-killed-in-yangon-attacks.html

Irrawaddy. 2021b. 'Myanmar's Civilian Government to Start Selling Bonds to Fund Revolution'. 5 November. www.irrawaddy.com/news/burma/myanmars-civilian-government-to-start-selling-bonds-to-fund-revolution.html

Irrawaddy. 2022a. 'Myanmar Junta Raises SIM and Internet Taxes to Silence Opposition'. 12 January. www.irrawaddy.com/news/burma/myanmar-junta-raises-sim-and-internet-taxes-to-silence-opposition.html

Irrawaddy. 2022b. 'Myanmar's Junta Seizes More Than 547 Properties of Anti-Regime Activists'. 5 April. www.irrawaddy.com/news/burma/myanmars-junta-seizes-more-than-547-properties-of-anti-regime-activists.html

Irrawaddy. 2022c. 'Myanmar Regime Jails Women over Alleged Donations'. 7 April. www.irrawaddy.com/news/burma/myanmar-regime-jails-women-over-alleged-donations.html

Irrawaddy. 2022d. 'Pro-Junta Militia Kills NLD Supporters in Myanmar'. 25 April. www.irrawaddy.com/news/burma/pro-junta-militia-kills-nld-supporters-in-myanmar.html

Irrawaddy. 2022e. 'Sale of Myanmar Coup Leader's Mansion Raises US$2 Million in Three Days'. 9 May. www.irrawaddy.com/news/burma/sale-of-myanmar-coup-leaders-mansion-raises-us2-million-in-three-days.html

Irrawaddy. 2022f. 'Myanmar's Armed Resistance Groups Ready to Go on Offensive: NUG'. 22 June. www.irrawaddy.com/news/burma/myanmars-armed-resistance-groups-ready-to-go-on-offensive-nug.html

Jordan, T. 2002. *Activism! Direct Action, Hacktivism and the Future of Society*. Reaktion Books.

Kinseth, Ashley S. 2018. 'Genocide in the Modern Era: Social Media and the Proliferation of Hate Speech in Myanmar', *Tea Circle*, 10 May. teacircleoxford.com/2018-year-in-review/genocide-in-the-modern-era-social-media-and-the-proliferation-of-hate-speech-in-myanmar/

Ko Korozan. 2022. 'My U Khin Maung Win (Rozan)'s House'. Facebook post, 1 February. www.facebook.com/100000642633928/posts/5079630962068275/?d=n (page discontinued).

Kyaw Hsan Hlaing. 2021. 'Facebook Is Still Censoring Groups Fighting the Military Coup in Myanmar'. *Rest of World*, 14 May. restofworld.org/2021/facebook-is-still-censoring-groups-fighting-the-military-coup-in-myanmar/

Kyaw Hsan Hlaing and Emily Fishbein. 2021. 'In Myanmar, One Blackout Ends, Another Begins'. *Rest of World*, 10 February. restofworld.org/2021/myanmar-one-blackout-ends-another-begins/

Ling, Rich, Elisa Oreglia, May Lwin, Chitra Panchpakesan and Rajiv Aricat, eds. 2015. 'Mobile Phones among Trishaw Operators'. *International Journal of Communication*, 9 (1): 3583–600.

Maung Maung Thein. 2021. 'North Okkalapa #PDF Fire with Gun to High School Teacher Daw Hla Hla Than'. Tweet, 5 November. twitter.com/MgMg Thein1973/status/14571540368141271111

McCarthy, Gerard. 2018. 'Cyber-Spaces'. In *The Routledge Handbook of Contemporary Myanmar*, edited by Ian Holliday, Nicholas Farrelly and Adam Simpson, 92–105. Milton Park: Routledge. doi.org/10.4324/9781315743677-10

McCarthy, Gerard and Jacqueline Menager. 2017. 'Gendered Rumours and the Muslim Scapegoat in Myanmar's Transition'. *Journal of Contemporary Asia*, 47 (3): 396–412. doi.org/10.1080/00472336.2017.1304563

McMichael, Clara. 2021. 'Myanmar's Social Punishment'. *Future Tense*, 23 April. slate.com/technology/2021/04/myanmar-coup-social-punishment.html

Meta. 2018. 'Removing Myanmar Military Officials from Facebook'. 28 August. about.fb.com/news/2018/08/removing-myanmar-officials/

Miles, Tom. 2018. 'UN Investigators Cite Facebook Role in Myanmar Crisis'. Reuters, 13 March. www.reuters.com/article/us-myanmar-rohingya-facebook/u-n-investigators-cite-facebook-role-in-myanmar-crisis-idUSKCN1GO2PN

Milmo, Dan. 2021. 'Rohingya Sue Facebook for £150bn over Myanmar Genocide'. *Guardian*, 7 December. www.theguardian.com/technology/2021/dec/06/rohingya-sue-facebook-myanmar-genocide-us-uk-legal-action-social-media-violence

Mizzima. 2021. 'People Can Now Pay Their Taxes to NUG Online'. 5 October. mizzima.com/article/people-can-now-pay-their-taxes-nug-online

Myanmar Now. 2021. 'Five Police Officers Shot Dead in Attack on Yangon Train'. 15 August. www.myanmar-now.org/en/news/five-police-officers-shot-dead-in-attack-on-yangon-train (page discontinued).

Nachemson, Andrew. 2021. 'Cost of War: Myanmar Rebels Crowdfund Resistance to Military Coup'. Al Jazeera, 13 December. www.aljazeera.com/economy/2021/12/13/cost-of-war-myanmar-rebels-crowdfund-armed-resistance-to-junta

NapoleonCat. 2021. 'Facebook Users in Myanmar'. napoleoncat.com/stats/facebook-users-in-myanmar/2021/01/

NapoleonCat. 2022. 'Facebook Users in Myanmar'. napoleoncat.com/stats/facebook-users-in-myanmar/2022/02/

Nyan Hlaing Lin. 2020. 'Government Blocks More Websites It Claims Have "Terrorist" Links'. *Myanmar Now*, 14 May. myanmar-now.org/en/news/government-blocks-more-websites-it-claims-have-terrorist-links?page=19

Nyan Hlaing Lin. 2021. 'Myanmar's Shadow Government Launches Plan to Tax Business Owners'. *Myanmar Now*, 6 November. www.myanmar-now.org/en/news/myanmars-shadow-government-launches-plan-to-tax-business-owners

Nyi Nyi Kyaw. 2019. 'Facebooking in Myanmar: From Hate Speech to Fake News to Partisan Political Communication'. *ISEAS Perspective No. 36*. Singapore: ISEAS-Yusof Ishak Institute.

OBG (Oxford Business Group). 2019. 'Growth of Mobile and Internet Usage Make Myanmar ICT More Competitive'. In *The Report: Myanmar 2019*. oxfordbusinessgroup.com/overview/tech-transformation-mobile-and-internet-usage-rise-sector-set-expand-and-become-more-competitive

Osborne, Samuel. 2017. 'Facebook Is "Silencing" Rohingya Muslim Reports of "Ethnic Cleansing"'. *Independent*, 19 September. www.independent.co.uk/tech/facebook-rohingya-muslim-women-ethnic-cleansing-burma-myanmar-socila-network-rakhine-state-a7954791.html

Petulla, S. 2013. 'This SIM Card Used to Cost $3,000. Democracy May Bring It Down to Zero'. *Quartz*, 15 March. qz.com/62523/this-sim-card-used-to-cost-3000-democracy-may-bring-it-down-tozero/

Prasse-Freeman, Elliott. 2021. 'Hate Bait, Micro-Publics, and National(ist) Conversations on Burmese Facebook'. In 'Politics of Exclusion and Inclusion in Myanmar', special issue, *Independent Journal of Burmese Scholarship*, 1 (December): 144–204.

RFA (*Radio Free Asia*). 2022. 'Myanmar Activists Say Junta Will Use SIM Card Registration to Target Opposition'. 3 October. www.rfa.org/english/news/myanmar/simcards-10032022211504.html

Ryan, Megan and Mai Van Tran. 2022. 'Democratic Backsliding Disrupted: The Role of Digitalized Resistance in Myanmar'. *Asian Journal of Contemporary Politics*. doi.org/10.1177/20578911221125511

Schissler, Matt. 2015. 'New Technologies, Established Practices: Developing Narratives of Muslim Threat in Myanmar'. In *Islam and the State in Myanmar: Muslim–Buddhist Relations and the Politics of Belonging*, edited by Melissa Crouch, 211–33. Oxford: Oxford University Press. doi.org/10.1093/acprof:oso/9780199461202.003.0009

Selth, Andrew. 2021. *Myanmar Military's Mindset: An Exploratory Study*. Gold Coast: Griffith University.

Sithu Aung Myint. 2021. '"Social Punishment" Campaign Turns the Tables on Military Elite'. *Frontier Myanmar*, 18 March. www.frontiermyanmar.net/en/social-punishment-campaign-turns-the-tables-on-military-elite/

Skidmore, Monique. 2003. 'Darker Than Midnight: Fear, Vulnerability, and Terror Making in Urban Burma (Myanmar)'. *American Ethnologist*, 30 (1): 5–21. doi.org/10.1525/ae.2003.30.1.5

Skidmore, Monique. 2004. *Karaoke Fascism: Burma and the Politics of Fear.* Philadelphia: University of Pennsylvania Press. doi.org/10.9783/9780812204766

Skidmore, Monique. 2007. 'Buddha's Mother and the Billboard Queens: Contesting Moral Power in Burma'. In *Women and the Contested State: Religion, Violence, and Agency in South and Southeast Asia*, edited by Monique Skidmore and Patricia Lawrence, 171–87. Indiana: University of Notre Dame Press.

Skidmore, Monique and Trevor Wilson, eds. 2008. *Dictatorship, Disorder, and Decline in Myanmar*. Canberra: ANU EPress. doi.org/10.22459/DDDM.12.2008

StatCounter. 2022. 'Social Media Stats Myanmar'. gs.statcounter.com/social-media-stats/all/myanmar

Statistica. 2022. 'Active Social Media Users as a Share of the Total Population in Myanmar from 2016 to 2022'. www.statista.com/statistics/883751/myanmar-social-media-penetration/

Strangio, Sebastian. 2021. 'Internet "Whitelist" Highlights Myanmar Military's Wishful Economic Thinking'. *Diplomat*, 26 May. thediplomat.com/2021/05/internet-whitelist-highlights-myanmar-militarys-wishful-economic-thinking/

Tønnesson, Stein, Min Zaw Oo and Ne Lynn Aung. 2022. 'Pretending to be States: The Use of Facebook by Armed Groups in Myanmar'. *Journal of Contemporary Asia*, 52 (2): 200–25. doi.org/10.1080/00472336.2021.1905865

Yan Naung Oak and Lisa Brooten. 2019. 'The Tea Shop Meets the 8 O'clock News: Facebook, Convergence and Online Public Spaces'. In *Myanmar Media in Transition: Legacies, Challenges and Change,* edited by L. Brooten, J.M. McElhone and G. Venkiteswaran, 327–65. Singapore: ISEAS – Yusof Ishak Institute. doi.org/10.1355/9789814843409-020

4

Multinational Enterprise Behaviour in Post-Coup Myanmar

Nicholas Coppel

Adjunct Associate Professor (practice), Monash University,
and former Australian ambassador to Myanmar

Abstract

Since the coup, multinational enterprises have come under pressure to review
their operations in Myanmar and exit any relationship they have with military-
controlled entities. Targeted sanctions imposed by the United States, United
Kingdom, Canada and European countries made it a legal requirement in
their jurisdictions. However, very few foreign firms were in joint venture or
had other commercial relations with military-owned or controlled entities,
and the overestimation of the extent and significance of such relationships
has distracted policymakers and activists from considering policies focused
on the role the business community could play to strengthen human rights
in Myanmar. The companies that left Myanmar mostly did so for security,
commercial or reputational reasons. Leaving was not always easy or helpful to
Myanmar's citizens and, in some instances, even benefited the military. This
chapter explores these pressures and responses and argues that policies need
to recognise that change will only come from within Myanmar; thus, the
focus should be less on external actors and more on what the international
community can do to support responsible business practices in the country
that will strengthen human rights and the wellbeing of the people.

***

Following the 1 February 2021 coup d'état, the United Kingdom, United States, Canada, the European Union and other European countries imposed targeted sanctions on the two military-owned and controlled conglomerates, Myanma Economic Holdings Ltd (MEHL) and Myanmar Economic Corporation (MEC), as well as state-owned enterprises and the business interests of named military personnel and their family members. Most of the rest of the world did not follow with their own sanctions, although a number of countries restricted exports of arms and military equipment. The economy-wide sanctions applied by some countries from the 1990s to the 2010s are regarded as having concentrated wealth and power in the hands of regime-linked forces (Jones 2015) and this time were not applied by any country. Notably, none of the sanctioning countries was a significant trading partner of Myanmar (China, Thailand and Japan account for 58 per cent of Myanmar's exports and 50 per cent of imports; World Bank 2021), and none of Myanmar's bordering countries imposed sanctions. But, more significantly, as discussed below, very few foreign firms were actually in joint venture or in other commercial relationships with the Myanmar military or its entities. In this context, sanctions have not had much bite or functioned well as a coercive lever. Foremost, they have been statements of concern and displeasure at the coup and a signal of solidarity with those opposed to it.

The ways in which multinational enterprises responded to the coup were, thus, influenced not so much by the legal requirements of sanctions as by Organisation for Economic Co-Operation and Development (OECD) and United Nations (UN) guidelines, and principles setting voluntary standards of corporate behaviour. Various non-governmental organisations have developed advice specific to the Myanmar context to help guide businesses. Activist organisations, in particular, have targeted companies that lease land from military entities or pay fees to state-owned enterprises, arguing that these companies are complicit in the atrocities and human rights abuses committed by the military. Taken together, targeted sanctions and activist pressure run the risk of stigmatising all business with Myanmar, including legitimate, non-sanctioned activity. Corporate boards and fund managers concerned about their organisation's reputation can be influenced by perceptions. If this sentiment is pervasive, targeted sanctions combined with activist pressure could become similar in effect to damaging economy-wide sanctions.

This chapter explores the extent and significance of corporate relationships with the military, and their responses to the coup, and concludes that withdrawing from the country is not always helpful, and that policies need to recognise that change will only come from within Myanmar. Thus, the focus should be on supporting responsible business practices in-country that can strengthen human rights and the wellbeing of the people.

Multinational enterprises and human rights

The OECD's *Guidelines for Multinational Enterprises* (2011) set out non-binding principles and standards for responsible business conduct. These voluntary, not legally enforceable, guidelines advise that the first obligation of enterprises is to obey domestic laws, and that where domestic law conflicts with the guidelines, enterprises should seek to honour the guidelines in ways that do not place them in direct violation of domestic law. They also suggest that enterprises abstain from improper involvement in local political activities. Most publicly listed companies subscribe to these principles but, as we shall see, they are not comforting principles when the authority issuing the laws and regulations has come to power through the barrel of a gun.

The UN's *Guiding Principles on Business and Human Rights* (UN 2011) state that in conflict-affected areas, the host state of multinational enterprises has a role to play in assisting corporations to ensure that they are not involved with human rights abuses. Business enterprises should seek to prevent or mitigate adverse human rights impacts directly linked to their operations, products or services, even if they have not contributed to those impacts. Where a business has not directly contributed to an adverse human rights impact, and it does not have the leverage to prevent or mitigate the adverse impact, 'the enterprise should consider ending the relationship, taking into account credible assessments of potential adverse human rights impacts of doing so' (UN 2011). Here there is a recognition that, in some cases, enterprises will need to weigh the impact of leaving against the impact of staying.

In Myanmar, the Myanmar Centre for Responsible Business (MCRB) initially responded to the coup with a cautiously worded statement saying that it was watching the developments with growing and deep concern, but was abstaining from politics (MCRB 2021). Reinforcing this, the statement avoided the word 'coup' or condemnation of what had happened. While noting that everyone benefited from respect for human rights, democracy, fundamental freedoms and the rule of law, it said its primary concern was the safety of employees and the continued provision of essential services. The emphasis was on the contribution multinational enterprises could make to human rights and essential services (MCRB 2021). This focus featured also in a statement by several chambers of commerce, which said their members had provided Myanmar people with access to greater opportunities and prosperity (CCI France 2021).

As military atrocities against civilians increased, more was expected of foreign firms than watching with concern. The UK-based Institute for Human Rights and Business, an international think tank that founded the local MCRB, advised businesses to 'ensure they do everything in their power to abide by international standards and avoid complicity in human rights violations being committed by security forces' (Tripathi & Morrison 2021). In response to claims that payments legitimised the regime, funded the military and could be complicit in acts of atrocity, they cautioned businesses 'to avoid and end commercial relationships—direct or indirect— with the military and its economic interests'. But, on the fraught question of whether to pay taxes, they pointed out that tax revenues contributed to preventing a failed state. They suggested that companies should publish what they paid and advocate for taxes to be spent on welfare not warfare.

In further collective advice to businesses, the Institute for Human Rights and Business suggested that foreign enterprises leave Myanmar if they were 'contributing to, or directly linked to, harm and cannot exercise any leverage—collectively or individually—to prevent or mitigate that harm'. Conversely, there was an argument for some enterprises to stay, especially those that:

> have the leverage to ensure at least their own operations, and usually those of their business partners, respect human rights on issues such as worker safety, fair wages, and respecting the rights to freedom of association and expression, and not to be discriminated against, including as a union member. (Tripathi, Morrison & Bowman 2021)

The argument was that, by staying, they would offer a different, more hopeful, vision of the future and be well placed to contribute to the country's eventual revival. That is, the essential step was for enterprises to review their operations and consider whether they were in any way connected to harm. This approach was contested by activist groups who argued that any payment to the Myanmar military regime would support and legitimise the military and make the payer complicit in atrocity crimes and human rights abuses. The respective merits of these competing approaches are considered later in this chapter in light of the impact of companies that did withdraw from the country.

Calls to end commercial relationships with military-owned or controlled entities

Drawing attention to multinational enterprises with commercial relationships with Myanmar's military predates the coup. For example, following the attacks on Myanmar's Rohingya community in Rakhine State in 2017, an Independent International Fact-Finding Mission was mandated by the UN Human Rights Council to investigate. It reported on the military's economic interests, concluding that:

> Foreign companies with joint ventures and other commercial relationships with the Tatmadaw … are in some cases legally implicated in the conduct of the Tatmadaw, and in all cases complicit through their tacit acceptance and approval of the Tatmadaw's actions. (UNHRC 2019, 62)

The Fact-Finding Mission advocated economic isolation of, and disengagement from, the military conglomerates and associated companies. In view of the scale and diversity of the military's business interests, it is surprising that only 14 foreign company joint ventures with military-owned or controlled businesses were identified, and only 44 foreign companies were identified as having other contractual or other commercial ties, such as leasing land (UNHRC 2019).

Continuing this approach, the self-styled Special Advisory Council for Myanmar, a trio of former UN rapporteurs or advisers on Myanmar, advocated a 'cut the cash' strategy involving ending commercial relationships with not only military-owned companies, but also the six state-owned economic enterprises (SAC-M 2021). This approach was supported by other advocacy groups who argued that Myanmar state-owned enterprises—especially the Myanmar Oil and Gas Enterprise—financially benefited the military. Burma Campaign UK maintained a list of multinational enterprises doing business with the Myanmar military and this so-called Dirty List included 101 companies (Burma Campaign UK 2021).

Returning to the UNHRC Fact-Finding Mission report, the 14 joint ventures identified represent just 11 foreign companies, as three foreign companies each had two joint ventures (see Table 4.1). Nine of the joint ventures have partners domiciled in either Korea or Japan, and all bar one are domiciled in Asia.

Table 4.1: Foreign joint venture partnerships with MEHL and MEC

Myanmar company	MEHL or MEC	Foreign company	Domicile	Sector
Coal Mine and Power Plant	MEC	Saraburi Coal Co. Ltd	Hong Kong	Mining
Gold Cement Co.	MEHL	26.4% GC Holdings	Seychelles	Manufacturing
Hanthawaddy Golf & Country Club	MEHL	37% Inno Co. Ltd	Korea	Recreation
JPMD Ltd	MEC	49% Japan Myanmar Development Institution	Japan	Construction
Mandalay Brewery Ltd	MEHL	51% Kirin Holdings	Japan	Manufacturing
Moe Gyo Sulphuric Acid	MEHL	Unknown % NORINCO	China	Manufacturing
Myanmar Brewery Ltd	MEHL	51% Kirin Holdings	Japan	Manufacturing
Myanmar Inno International Ltd	MEHL	44% Inno Co. Ltd	Korea	Real estate
Myanmar Inno Line Co. Ltd	MEHL	18% Inno Co. Ltd	Korea	Real estate
Myanmar POSCO C&C Co. Ltd	MEHL	70% POSCO Coated & Color Steel Co. Ltd	Korea	Manufacturing
Myanmar POSCO Steel Co. Ltd	MEHL	70% POSCO Steel Co. Ltd	Korea	Manufacturing
Myanmar Wise-Pacific Apparel Yangon Co. Ltd	MEHL	55% Pan-Pacific Co. Ltd	Korea	Manufacturing
Telecom Int'l Myanmar Co. Ltd	MEC	49% Viettel	Viet Nam	Communications
Virginia Tobacco Co. Ltd	MEHL	60% Distinction Investment Holdings Pte	Singapore	Tobacco

Source: UNHRC (2019, 96–7).

Of the 11 foreign joint venture partners two, Kirin Holdings Co. Ltd (a Japanese beverage maker) and POSCO Steel, have announced their intention to end their joint ventures. Kirin and MEHL jointly own Myanmar Brewery and Mandalay Brewery. Kirin had pre-existing concerns about their association with MEHL and, in 2020, decided to suspend dividend payments from the two breweries (Goto 2021). After the coup, Kirin initially wanted to retain their Myanmar investment, but without the stigma attached to being in partnership with MEHL and sought to terminate the joint venture. However, in February 2022, it concluded that this would not be possible and decided to sell its stake in the breweries and withdraw completely from Myanmar. Unable to find an outside buyer, Kirin sold its stake to its military joint venture partner (Taguchi & Henmi 2022). Similarly, immediately after the coup, POSCO Coated & Color Steel Co. Ltd announced in February 2021 that it had suspended all dividend payments to joint venture partner MEHL and, two months later, said it would rearrange the joint venture but continue to make steel roofing to improve the housing market, create employment and industrialise and revitalise the economy (POSCO 2021).

Three years after publication of the Fact-Finding Mission's report and 21 months after the coup, only one foreign joint venture had divested and one other hoped to rearrange its joint venture. The limited impact of the Fact-Finding Mission report stems from the misapprehension that the military's large and diversified business interests were integrated into the global economy. However, decades of isolationism, economic mismanagement and the stigma attached to going into a joint venture with a military conglomerate meant there actually were few linkages created over the preceding decades and, hence, limited leverage. Further, those few companies with linkages were from countries not imposing sanctions. This casts doubt on the utility of a response to the coup that targets foreign firms but has no discernible effect on the military's funding or attitude.

Multinational enterprises in other relationships with military entities

Unlike most other companies in some sort of relationship with the military, Facebook received funds from them—it did not make payments to them. Shortly after the coup, Facebook banned the Myanmar military and military-controlled state and media entities from Facebook and Instagram as well as ads from military-linked entities. In December 2021, Meta Platforms Inc. (formerly known as Facebook) expanded its ban and removed pages, groups and accounts representing military-controlled entities such as Myanmar Beer and telecommunications operator Mytel. Meta used the International Fact-Finding Mission report on the economic interests of the military to identify companies to be removed (Frankel 2021).

All bar three of the 44 foreign companies with contractual or commercial ties to the military-owned business conglomerates were domiciled in Asia and one other was domiciled in both Singapore and Lebanon. That is, the foreign enterprises with a direct association with the sanctioned entities were not domiciled in the jurisdictions imposing sanctions. Consequently, the imposition of sanctions did not have much success.

Nevertheless, one company, Adani, felt the impact of sanctions and sustained advocacy and decided to exit. Adani Ports and Special Economic Zone Ltd, an India-based subsidiary of the Adani Group, was subjected to considerable international attention because it leased land from MEC (a sanctioned entity) to develop a port project in Yangon. It did not matter that in 2019 it was the National League for Democracy government that had granted Adani permission to develop, operate and maintain a port on the land. In an example of shareholder activism, Norwegian pension fund KLP said it would divest from Adani Ports and Special Economic Zone Ltd on the grounds that the company's military link breached the fund's responsible investment policy (Fouche 2021). Initially, Adani denied their linkage was inappropriate, but in October 2021 said it would nevertheless work on a plan to exit the company's investment by June 2022 (Sethuraman N.R. & Sudarshan Varadan 2021). This was cautiously welcomed by activist groups who, in an afterthought about the consequences, said:

> Adani Ports must now find a way to exit responsibly by mitigating the impact on their Myanmar workers and recovering what they can of their $90 million payment to MEC so they do not leave a windfall for the terrorist Myanmar military. (ACIJ 2021)

Campaigns to attract public support need also to have regard to the complexity of situations and the range of implications. Ironically, Adani's heralded departure may further enrich the military, while national income and employment will likely be less than what they would be if they stayed.

Australia's sovereign wealth fund, the Future Fund, was criticised for having equity stakes collectively valued at AUD157.9 million across 14 publicly traded companies that maintain business links to the Myanmar military.

Somewhat tenuously, an activist group argued that the Future Fund was 'profiting from the Myanmar military's brutal oppression and campaign of terror' (Justice for Myanmar 2021b). Even more tenuously, it argued that the Australian Government had not directed the fund to divest and was, therefore, 'directly connected to the Myanmar military's grave violations of human rights' (Justice for Myanmar 2021b). The equity stakes were in companies including Adani Ports, Kirin and POSCO. New Zealand's Super Fund was also criticised for investing in Adani (BHRRC 2021). The goal of these campaigns was to create a perception that all commercial connections with Myanmar carry reputational risk and to get the attention of the Australian and New Zealand governments, which had not joined European and North American governments in imposing sanctions. Selling down their relatively small shareholdings in companies listed on international bourses could not seriously be expected to be of any consequence to the situation in Myanmar.

Multinational enterprises in relationships with state-owned enterprises

Myanmar's six state-owned enterprises play a large role in the economy, and the National Unity Government (NUG) called for sanctions to be imposed on them, especially the Myanmar Oil and Gas Enterprise (MOGE) (NUG 2021). The NUG also called on all offshore gas operators to suspend payments to the government until democracy was restored. The US, UK, Canada and European countries have heeded the call and sanctioned some of the state-owned enterprises, but only the EU has sanctioned MOGE.

Publish What You Pay Australia, a civil society coalition, claimed that:

> any international oil and gas company making or facilitating the payment of funds to MOGE is likely to be assisting the Myanmar military in committing extensive human rights abuses and financing and legitimising its claim to be the government of Myanmar. (Moore 2021b, 7)

They also said that asset managers and pension funds were 'exposed to the risk of funding the military through the military's misappropriation of MOGE's cash, supporting its efforts to crush Myanmar's transition to democracy and its human rights abuses' (Moore 2021b, 7). They did not call for production to be halted (two-fifths of Myanmar's power comes from gas) but called on oil and gas companies to place gas sale proceeds into escrow accounts until there is an elected, civilian government. Withholding taxes, however, would place them in violation of domestic law and would not be consistent with OECD guidelines or the approach favoured by the Institute for Human Rights and Business.

MOGE is in four offshore gas joint ventures with multinational enterprises: the Yadana, Shwe, Zawtika and Yetagun projects. Each joint venture comprises a gas production component and a gas transportation component. The main joint venture companies are the French energy group Total; Korea's POSCO International; PTTEP, a subsidiary of the Thai state-owned oil and gas company PTE; and Petronas, Malaysia's state-owned oil and gas company.

Total is the operator of the Yadana Project, which supplies 50 per cent of total gas supply to Myanmar and 11 per cent of Thailand's natural gas. In May 2021, the joint venture suspended cash distributions to shareholders from the project's gas pipeline joint venture, but continued to pay taxes. However, in January 2022, Total and another joint venture partner, Chevron, decided to exit Myanmar, leaving PTTEP, a subsidiary of the Thai state-owned oil and gas company PTE, as the project's operator. Total and Chevron's withdrawal increased the equity share (and future dividend payments) of the remaining partners including MOGE (PTTEP 2022). Given that their withdrawal has only increased the equity of MOGE, it was incorrect for Justice for Myanmar to herald Total's decision to exit Myanmar as 'a major step in cutting off funds to the illegal military junta' (Justice for Myanmar 2022a). Total's exit was a windfall gain for MOGE and is illustrative of the unintended consequences that can come from pressuring foreign firms to exit.

POSCO, the operator of the Shwe Project supplying gas to China, maintained operations, defending its relationship with MOGE on the basis that it predated the coup and that withdrawal might see it replaced by China or other players, which would only benefit the junta and inflict damage to Korea (*Korea Times* 2021). POSCO International is continuing its exploration activities. In July 2021, it extended its contract with Swiss-based driller Transocean (Energy Voice 2021). The Zawtika Project is operated and mostly owned by PTTEP and most of the project's gas is piped to Thailand. PTT is also in a joint venture with MEC to construct a fuel terminal that has attracted criticism (HRW 2021).

In April 2021, Petronas, operator of the Yetagun Project, declared force majeure due to depletion of gas production and said it would temporarily cease production until remedial measures were undertaken to enable its resumption (Petronas 2021). A year later, Petronas and their foreign joint venture partners all withdrew from the project and the military appointed a Thailand-based private oil and gas company as operator, thereby ensuring the continued flow of funds to the military (Justice for Myanmar 2022c).

Certainly, MOGE's revenue is the greatest of all the state-owned enterprises and, consequently, has been the major target in efforts to cut funding to the military. Several foreign joint venture partners have divested, leaving other foreign partners to assume the role of operator. Their divestments have served only to increase MOGE's share in the joint ventures. Despite the attention on international operators, no gas production has halted (other than from the depleted Yetagun Project), and the military's revenue has only increased.

To stay or to leave?

Many multinational enterprises operating in Myanmar are not in a relationship with the military or their owned or controlled entities. Nevertheless, several have, of their own accord, chosen to divest while others have been pressured to do so.

Shortly after the coup, Woodside, an Australian natural gas producer with large offshore petroleum exploration holdings in Myanmar, reduced its presence in Myanmar and demobilised its offshore exploration drilling team. The company subsequently went one step further and withdrew from Myanmar, relinquishing its exploration permits. The company said its conduct was 'guided by the UN Guiding Principles on Business and Human Rights and other relevant international standards' (Woodside 2022). While the company did not have any producing assets or generate any revenue, it had, as required, a production sharing agreement with MOGE that would have become operational if the gas fields were to be developed. The relinquished exploration permits are now open to being offered by MOGE to less principled gas producers from China and Russia. The future possibility of a gas-for-weapons deal cannot be ruled out.

Claims were made that if Myanmar Metals, an Australian explorer and mine developer, did not divest from its Bawdwin joint venture it 'would essentially be in support of the illegal, unconstitutional seizure of power and legitimize the Myanmar military's authority' (Moore 2021a). The company decided to dispose its entire interest to one of its local joint venture partners, but stated other reasons for doing so:

> the lack of stability, clarity, and confidence in Myanmar at this time makes it impossible for us to bring international finance to bear on the project, impossible for us to gain access to it, and impossible for us to meet our obligations in the meantime. (Myanmar Metals 2021)

Civil society groups remained unhappy and lodged a complaint with the Australian national contact point for the OECD guidelines, arguing that the sale could lead to millions of dollars 'lining the pockets of Myanmar's murderous generals once the mine becomes operational' (Barrett 2021).

Telenor Myanmar, a Norwegian-owned mobile telephony provider, is another example of a company that activists criticised for withdrawing from Myanmar. Telenor was criticised not for paying its licence fees but for divesting its Myanmar operations through a sales agreement with the Lebanon-based M1 Group (Justice for Myanmar 2022b). As a condition precedent for regulatory approval, M1 entered into a local partnership to ensure it had a local majority owner (Telenor 2022b). Telenor's decision to write-off its investment was informed by the deteriorating situation and by security, regulatory and compliance issues. Ensuring continuation of operations that provide affordable mobile services to support Myanmar's development and growth was also a consideration (Rostrup 2021). Activist groups were concerned that the business's new owners might be less vigilant in resisting censorship and protecting customer data and claimed Telenor's sale would further embolden the military, 'putting the lives of activists, journalists and anyone opposed to the military junta at greater risk' (Justice for Myanmar 2021a). Telenor explained the dilemma they faced:

> There are no solutions without negative consequences … a key reason for selling Telenor Myanmar is that we do not want to activate intercept equipment, which all operators are required to do … It is precisely this conflict—between the requirement to comply with local law on the one hand and the concern about human rights and the risk of violations of Norwegian and European sanctions on the other—that leaves Telenor with no choice but to sell … selling the business is the least detrimental solution for customers, employees and the broader society. (Telenor 2022a)

These examples from Total, Woodside, Myanmar Metals and Telenor all highlight the risk of unintended consequences from pressuring companies to leave. The Total and Myanmar Metals exits could lead to more revenue for the military and Telenor's exit is not good news for its 18 million subscribers.

Other companies to exit for operational reasons include:

- The German wholesaler Metro, suppliers of food to restaurants and hotels, ceased operations due to 'the volatile investment and business environment' (Metro 2021).
- In October 2021, British American Tobacco said it would cease all operations after evaluating their long-term operational and commercial viability (Petty 2021).
- EDF, a French power group, suspended development of the Shweli 3 hydropower project citing human rights concerns (Reuters 2021).
- Amata Asia (Myanmar), a Thai industrial estate developer, indefinitely suspended the Yangon Amata Smart & Eco City Project (Chan Mya Htwe & Aung Loon 2021).
- Hongkong and Shanghai Hotels Ltd suspended for one year construction of its planned Peninsula Yangon Hotel 'due to the unfortunate situation in Myanmar' (Kawai 2021).
- Sembcorp Industries, a Singapore-based engineering company operating a gas-fired power plant, is 'actively monitoring the situation' and has not made a decision on whether to proceed with its proposed industrial park development (Sembcorp 2021). Its president said: 'we are invested in this country. We are operating this very important infrastructure asset; our immediate priority is to continue to serve the community' (Connors 2021).
- The Swiss-owned Kempinski Hotel in Nay Pyi Taw ceased operating in October 2021, eight months after the coup, suggesting business conditions including the impact of COVID-19 contributed to the decision (*Myanmar Now* 2021).

This chapter has identified over 30 multinational enterprises (Table 4.2) as having made public statements about their Myanmar operations. Those exiting range from franchise operators selling pretzels (Auntie Anne's) or bubble tea (KOI Bubble Tea Shop) to major multinational corporations developing industrial zones (Amata Corporation) or manufacturing cigarettes (British American Tobacco). While there may be more companies that have ceased or been sold since the coup that have not attracted media attention, many of the 1,914 existing foreign investment projects in Myanmar (DICA 2022) are keeping a low profile and continuing. Examples of such companies include Carlsberg, Sumitomo, Marubeni, Mitsubishi (in the Thilawa Special Economic Zone and the Landmark Project) and Accor. Media reports of an exodus of multinational companies abandoning Myanmar (*Nikkei Asia* 2021; *Economist* 2021) are, thus, clearly exaggerated. However, the more significant story is the almost complete end of new foreign investment. According to the Myanmar Investment Commission, the cumulative value of permitted projects increased by less than USD100 million between May 2021 and April 2022, with most of the new investment coming from China and Hong Kong (DICA 2022).

Table 4.2: Multinational enterprise announcements about Myanmar operations

Company	Domicile	Activity	Decision
Adani Ports & SEZ	India	Container terminal	Divest by June 2022
AEON	Japan	Shopping mall developer	Project shelved
Amata Corporation	Thailand	Industrial zone development	Indefinite suspension
Ant Financial	China	Mobile payment services	Not proceeding with purchase of stake in Wave Money
Auntie Anne's	USA	Pretzel retailer	Exited
Bridgestone	Japan	Tyre manufacture	Operations suspended
British American Tobacco	UK	Cigarette sale and production	Ceased operations and will withdraw
Chevron	US	Yadana gas project	Equity transferred to subsidiary
EDF	France	Hydropower development	Development suspended
ENEOS Holdings	Japan	Yetagun gas project	Divested
Hongkong & Shanghai Hotels	Hong Kong	Peninsula Hotel	Construction suspended for a year
Kempinski Hotel	Switzerland	Kempinski Nay Pyi Taw	Operations ceased
Kirin Holdings	Japan	Beer production and sale	Divested
KOI Bubble Tea Shop	Taiwan	Bubble tea retail	Exited
Meta	US	Social media (Facebook)	Military-linked entities banned from platform

Company	Domicile	Activity	Decision
Metro	Germany	Grocery wholesaler	Operations ceased
MGTC	France, US	Gas pipeline	Cash distributions suspended but taxes paid
Mitsubishi	Japan	Yetagun gas project	Divested
Myanmar Metals	Australia	Mining	Divested
Petronas	Malaysia	Yetagun gas project	Divested
Portia Group	UK	Port management	Contract not extended beyond 2021
Ooredoo	Qatar	Mobile telephony	Divested
POSCO International	Korea	Offshore gas	Continuing
POSCO Coated & Color Steel	Korea	Steel roofing	Continuing but seeking new JV partner
PTTEP	Thailand	Yadana gas project	Assuming project operator status
Puma Energy	Switzerland	Aviation fuel	Divested
RMH Singapore	Singapore	Cigarette sale and manufacture	Withdrew from joint venture
Sembcorp	Singapore	Industrial park development	No decision
Sembcorp	Singapore	Gas-fired powerplant operator	Continuing
Telenor	Norway	Mobile telephony	Divested
Telenor	Norway	Mobile payment services	Sold 51% stake in Wave Money
Tokyo Tatemono Co Ltd	Japan	Commercial complex development	Suspended operations
Total SA	France	Yadana gas project	Divested
Toyota	Japan	Hi-lux assembly	Opening postponed
Woodside	Australia	Offshore gas exploration	Exited

Source: Company websites and media reporting.

Twenty-one months after the coup, the main observation is not an exodus of existing foreign investment, but the drying up of new investment, which is in stark contrast to the previous 10 years, which saw an opening of the economy and an influx of foreign investment. To be sure, some prominent firms have left but many others have remained. And almost all of those that have announced their departure or suspension of operations are not those identified as in joint ventures or other commercial relationships with military conglomerates or state-owned enterprises. They were businesses without any military association.

Conclusions and policy recommendations

Multinational enterprises have responded to the coup in ways that largely reflect their equities in the Myanmar economy. Small investors in franchise operations such as Auntie Anne's pretzels and KOI Bubble Tea Shop had no military association but decided to exit the market for commercial reasons. The investments were relatively small and catered to consumers with disposable income. Some multinational enterprises still in the development phase of their investments, such as industrial zone development and hotel development, have suspended operations. In such decisions we see recognition that it was no longer possible, for a combination of commercial and strategic reasons, to continue; yet, the value of the original investment was significant. Suspension leaves open the possibility of returning to extract value from the sunk cost in the event that the political situation improves. Multinational enterprises with fully operational investments, such as mobile telephony services and beer and gas production, faced difficult decisions. Even when the enterprise wished to divest there was a need to do so responsibly. Human rights considerations included the impact on employees, the potential loss of a service benefiting the community and the possibility that a new owner might be more willing to comply with military edicts and be less sensitive to responsible business practices. Telenor Myanmar, for example, was faced with requirements to shut down the internet, block websites, provide data and switch on intercept equipment, and, consequently, decided to divest. However, it was criticised for leaving the business in the hands of others perceived as unlikely to have qualms about complying with military directives. Total's exit will increase MOGE's share of the revenue from the Yadana offshore gas field and increase the resources available to the military. The unintended consequences of these withdrawals need to be considered by all stakeholders concerned about the coup.

For many multinational enterprises, it will not be feasible to operate without having some relationship with a military-controlled regulatory body, such as payment of rent, lease fees, taxes or licence fees. Some argue that such payments fund the military, but this assumes a linear relationship, whereas, given the fungibility of revenue, there is none. We also know that when revenue is constrained, the military prioritises themselves and their operations, reducing funds for health and education. Nevertheless, corporate boards dislike adverse publicity and when accused of being complicit in atrocity crimes will seriously consider divesting. In this sense, stigmatisation of ongoing operations in Myanmar can have the same effect as economy-wide sanctions. Myanmar's earlier period of sanctions did little to change the will or capacity of the military to maintain their power and repressive policies, while adding to the suffering of the population (ICG 2004, 15–18; Jones 2015). The current stigmatisation of continued business operations in Myanmar risks having the same outcomes.

Policy options are limited. UN-mandated targeted sanctions or an arms embargo, howsoever desired, will not be achieved while China and Russia continue to protect Myanmar from UN Security Council resolutions. Unilateral sanctions are possible but will not harm or sway the generals, as they have little regard for international opinion and their business interests are domestically focused. Nevertheless, sanctions can serve as a signal of displeasure at the coup and of solidarity with those opposed to the coup.

Activist pressure ostensibly focused on businesses with connections to military entities has not achieved much, in large part because the prevalence and significance of such ties have been greatly overestimated. The loudness of the calls to cut military ties, despite their insignificance, raises questions about whether the calls are a Trojan horse for those who would countenance collapsing the economy in an attempt to force change. To date, however, military violence and economic mismanagement have done more to cut funds available to the military than the actions of external players.

Foreign government and multinational enterprise policies need to have regard to their impact on the country, the workforce and the businesses themselves, both now and into the future. The policy objective should not be the economic collapse of Myanmar and immiseration of the people. From a broad and long-term human rights perspective, staying can be a responsible option. An isolated and impoverished Myanmar, when eventually restored to democracy, would face heightened challenges of governing with a debilitated commercial sector, small tax base and low-skilled workforce. The departures of Telenor and producers of gas for electricity generation will make life harder, not better, for the people of Myanmar, without adding to the financial pressure the regime faces.

Policymakers need to think more creatively about how foreign businesses in Myanmar can be leveraged to promote human rights. They may not be able to resolve conflict, but they can model good corporate behaviour by respecting human rights on issues such as worker safety, fair wages and freedom of association, as well as by developing employee and managerial skills. As we saw with mobile telephony, circumstances may deny the possibility of operating responsibly and the decision then becomes whether it is more responsible to stay and uphold other elements of corporate responsibility or to divest and leave the business in the hands of cronies or other less principled players. The arrest and sentencing of MCRB's director, Vicky Bowman, shows that responsible business practices are perceived by the military as being in opposition to their regime, placing them at risk and in need of protection. The focus of policymakers needs to be on encouraging and supporting responsible business practices that can make a difference to the lives of Myanmar's citizens. Foreign activist organisations also need to think beyond the standard action playbook focused on large Western corporations and devise Myanmar-focused strategies—that is, strategies that directly assist agents and conditions for change in Myanmar. It is the businesses, organisations and people who remain, not those that have left, that will ultimately bring about change in Myanmar.

References

ACIJ (Australian Centre for International Justice and Justice for Myanmar). 2021. 'Australian and Myanmar Groups Welcome Adani Ports' Withdrawal from Myanmar and Renew Calls to Shelve Carmichael Coal Project'. 28 October. www.justiceformyanmar.org/press-releases/australian-and-myanmar-groups-welcome-adani-ports-withdrawal-from-myanmar-and-renew-calls-to-shelve-carmichael-coal-project

Barrett, Chris. 2021. 'Junta Links Put Spotlight on Sale of Australian Company's Mine in Myanmar'. *Sydney Morning Herald*, 15 September. www.smh.com.au/world/asia/junta-links-put-spotlight-on-sale-of-australian-company-s-mine-in-myanmar-20210914-p58rms.html

BHRRC (Business & Human Rights Resource Centre). 2021. 'National Wants Answers from NZ Super Fund after Links with Myanmar Military Revealed'. 7 April. www.business-humanrights.org/en/latest-news/national-wants-answers-from-nz-super-fund-after-links-with-myanmar-military-revealed/

Burma Campaign UK. 2021. 'The Dirty List'. Accessed October. burmacampaign.org.uk/take-action/dirty-list/

CCI France. 2021. 'Statement on Myanmar by AustCham Myanmar, British Chamber of Commerce Myanmar, CCI France Myanmar, New Zealand Myanmar Chamber of Commerce'. 30 March. www.ccifrance-myanmar.org/sites/ccifrance-myanmar.org/files/joint_chambers_statement_on_myanmar-30_march_2021.pdf

Chan Mya Htwe and Aung Loon. 2021. 'Foreign Investments in Myanmar under Threat'. *Myanmar Times*, 4 February. www.mmtimes.com/news/foreign-investments-myanmar-under-threat.html (page discontinued).

Connors, Emma. 2021. 'Singapore's Sembcorp Warns on Myanmar's Economic Uncertainty'. *Australian Financial Review*, 23 February. www.afr.com/world/asia/singapore-s-sembcorp-warns-on-myanmar-s-economic-uncertainty-2021 0223-p5753m

DICA (Directorate of Investment and Company Administration). 2022. 'Foreign Investment of Permitted Projects (by Country/Region)'. Ministry of Investment and Foreign Economic Relations, Foreign Investment by Country. www.dica.gov.mm/sites/default/files/document-files/fdicountry_0.pdf

Economist. 2021. 'Asian Investors Have Doubts about Myanmar's Military Regime'. 29 May. www.economist.com/asia/2021/05/29/asian-investors-have-doubts-about-myanmars-military-regime

Energy Voice. 2021. 'Transocean Rig Could Keep Drilling Off Myanmar for POSCO'. 23 July. www.energyvoice.com/oilandgas/asia/338851/transocean-rig-could-keep-drilling-off-myanmar-for-posco/

Fouche, Gwladys. 2021. 'Nordic Fund KLP Divests from Adani Ports over Links to Myanmar Military'. Reuters, 22 June. www.reuters.com/business/nordic-fund-klp-divests-adani-ports-over-links-myanmar-military-2021-06-22/

Frankel, Rafael. 2021. 'An Update on the Situation in Myanmar'. Meta, 7 December. about.fb.com/news/2021/02/an-update-on-myanmar/

Goto, Takeru. 2021. 'Japan's Kirin Seeks End to Myanmar Ventures "Within a Year": CEO'. *Nikkei Asia,* 18 February. asia.nikkei.com/Editor-s-Picks/Interview/Japan-s-Kirin-seeks-end-to-Myanmar-ventures-within-a-year-CEO

HRW (Human Rights Watch). 2021. 'Myanmar: Thai State-Owned Company Funds Junta'. 25 May. www.hrw.org/news/2021/05/25/myanmar-thai-state-owned-company-funds-junta

ICG (International Crisis Group). 2004. *Myanmar: Sanctions, Engagement or Another Way Forward?* 26 April. www.crisisgroup.org/asia/south-east-asia/myanmar/myanmar-sanctions-engagement-or-another-way-forward

Jones, Lee. 2015. *Societies under Siege: Exploring how International Economic Sanctions (Do Not) Work*. Oxford: Oxford University Press. doi.org/10.1093/acprof:oso/9780198749325.001.0001

Justice for Myanmar. 2021a. 'Telenor Myanmar's Buyers Have Financed Atrocities and Cosied up to Dictators'. 9 July. www.justiceformyanmar.org/stories/telenor-myanmars-buyers-have-financed-atrocities-and-cosied-up-to-dictators

Justice for Myanmar. 2021b. 'Abusing Myanmar for Australia's "Future"'. 29 November. www.justiceformyanmar.org/stories/abusing-myanmar-for-australias-future

Justice for Myanmar. 2022a. 'Justice for Myanmar Welcomes TotalEnergies' Withdrawal from Myanmar'. 21 January. www.justiceformyanmar.org/press-releases/justice-for-myanmar-welcomes-totalenergies-withdrawal-from-myanmar

Justice for Myanmar. 2022b. 'Telenor Group Is Aiding and Abetting M1 Group to Violate Myanmar Sanctions'. Media release, 22 March. www.justiceformyanmar.org/press-releases/telenor-group-is-aiding-and-abetting-m1-group-to-violate-myanmar-sanctions

Justice for Myanmar. 2022c. 'Petronas, PTTEP, ENEOS, Mitsubishi Corp & Japan Gov Irresponsibly Exiting Yetagun Gas Project'. Media release, 28 June. www.justiceformyanmar.org/press-releases/petronas-pttep-eneos-mitsubishi-corp-japan-gov-irresponsibly-exiting-yetagun-gas-project

Kawai, Kenji. 2021. 'Peninsula Hotels Suspends $130m Yangon Project for a Year'. *Nikkei Asia*, 21 May. asia.nikkei.com/Spotlight/Myanmar-Crisis/Peninsula-Hotels-suspends-130m-Yangon-project-for-a-year

Korea Times. 2021. 'POSCO Denies Profitable Gas Project's Alleged Ties to Myanmar Junta'. 6 April. www.koreatimes.co.kr/www/common/printpreviews.asp?categoryCode=693&newsIdx=306711

MCRB (Myanmar Centre for Responsible Business). 2021. 'Statement by Concerned Businesses Operating in Myanmar'. 19 February. www.myanmar-responsiblebusiness.org/news/statement-concerned-businesses.html

Metro. 2021. 'METRO Will Cease Operations in Myanmar Due to Volatile Business Conditions'. Press release, 1 September. newsroom.metroag.de/en/news/2021/09/01/metro-will-cease-operations-in-myanmar

Moore, Clancy. 2021a. *Extracting the Truth about the Bawdwin Mine*. www.pwyp.org.au/publications/extracting-the-truth-behind-the-bawdwin-mine

Moore, Clancy. 2021b. *Shwe gas project: companies must stop the flow of wealth to the Myanmar military*. www.pwyp.org.au/publications/1162021shwe-gas-project-companies-must-stop-the-flow-of-wealth-to-the-myanmar-military

Myanmar Metals. 2021. 'Chairman's Address – General Meeting 2021'. Address by Chairman and CEO Mr John Lamb, 24 September. www.listcorp.com/asx/myl/mallee-resources-limited/news/chairmans-address-to-shareholders-2597746.html?ref=more_news

Myanmar Now. 2021. 'Naypyitaw's Kempinski Hotel Becomes Latest Victim of Myanmar's Economic Turmoil'. 18 October. www.myanmar-now.org/en/news/naypyitaws-kempinski-hotel-becomes-latest-victim-of-myanmars-economic-turmoil

Nikkei Asia. 2021. 'Farewell, Myanmar: Corporate Exodus Grows, from Europe to India'. 30 October. asia.nikkei.com/Spotlight/Myanmar-Crisis/Farewell-Myanmar-Corporate-exodus-grows-from-Europe-to-India?utm_campaign=GL_asia_daily&utm_medium=email&utm_source=NA_newsletter&utm_content=article_link&del_type=1&pub_date=20211101123000&seq_num=6&si=041229

NUG (National Unity Government). 2021. 'Sanction Policy'. 9 November. www.burmalibrary.org/sites/burmalibrary.org/files/obl/2021-11-09-NUG-policy-on-sanctions-tu-en.pdf

OECD (Organisation for Economic Co-Operation and Development Publishing). 2011. *OECD Guidelines for Multinational Enterprises*. Paris: OECD. doi.org/10.1787/9789264115415-en

Petronas. 2021. 'PETRONAS's Upstream Operations in Myanmar Declares Force Majeure on Its Yetagun Field'. Press release, 2 April. www.petronas.com/media/press-release/petronas-upstream-operations-myanmar-declares-force-majeure-its-yetagun-field

Petty, Martin. 2021. 'British American Tobacco Pulls Out of Army-Ruled Myanmar'. Reuters, 13 October. www.reuters.com/world/asia-pacific/british-american-tobacco-pulls-out-army-ruled-myanmar-2021-10-12/

POSCO. 2021. 'POSCO C&C, Rearrangement of JV Partnership with Myanmar, MEHL'. 16 April. www.posco.co.kr/homepage/docs/eng6/jsp/irinfo/irdata/s91b6000073l.jsp?schidx=379 (page discontinued).

PTTEP. 2022. 'The Change of the Operator of Yadana Project, Myanmar'. 14 March. www.pttep.com/en/InvestorRelations/RegulatorFilings/SETNotification/Thechangeoftheoperatorofyadanaprojectmyanmar.aspx

Reuters. 2021. 'France's EDF Halts Hydropower Project in Myanmar after Junta Coup'. 20 March. www.reuters.com/article/myanmar-politics-edf-idUSL1N2 LH1T5

Rostrup, Jørgen C. Arentz. 2021. 'Values and Choices in an Extraordinary Situation'. Telenor, 12 August. www.telenor.com/media/newsroom/values-and-choices-in-an-extraordinary-situation/index.page

SAC-M (Special Advisory Council for Myanmar). 2021. 'Cut the Cash'. Accessed 10 February 2023. specialadvisorycouncil.org/cut-the-cash/

Sembcorp. 2021. 'Sembcorp Updates on Its Investments in Myanmar'. Media release, 16 February. www.sembcorp.com/en/media/597873/sembcorp-updates-on-its-investments-in-myanmar.pdf

Sethuraman N.R. and Sudarshan Varadan. 2021. 'India's Adani Ports Scraps Myanmar Container Terminal Plans'. Reuters, 27 October. www.reuters.com/world/india/indias-adani-ports-says-it-will-exit-myanmar-investment-2021-10-27/

Taguchi, Shoichiro and Junya Henmi. 2022. 'Kirin to Sell Entire Stake in Venture with Myanmar Military'. *Nikkei Asia*, 30 June. asia.nikkei.com/Spotlight/Myanmar-Crisis/Kirin-to-sell-entire-stake-in-venture-with-Myanmar-military

Telenor. 2022a. 'We Cannot Make Our Employees in Myanmar Delete Data and Break the Law'. Announcement, 19 February. www.telenor.com/media/newsroom/announcement/we-cannot-make-our-employees-in-myanmar-delete-data-and-break-the-law-update-by-jorgen-c-arentz-rostrup-evp-and-head-of-telenor-asia/

Telenor. 2022b. 'Sale of Telenor Myanmar Approved by Myanmar Authorities'. Press release, 18 March. www.telenor.com/media/newsroom/press-releases/sale-of-telenor-myanmar-approved-by-myanmar-authorities/index.page

Tripathi, Salil and John Morrison. 2021. 'Can Companies Continue to Operate Responsibly in Myanmar?' Institute for Human Rights and Business, 1 June. www.ihrb.org/focus-areas/myanmar/commentary-can-companies-continue-to-operate-responsibly-in-myanmar (page discontinued).

Tripathi, Salil, John Morrison and Vicky Bowman. 2021. 'Staying or Leaving Myanmar? What's Needed Is a Human Rights-Led Approach'. Institute for Human Rights and Business, 14 September. www.ihrb.org/other/businesss-role/staying-or-leaving-myanmar-whats-needed-is-a-human-rights-led-approach (page discontinued).

UN (United Nations). 2011. *Guiding Principles on Business and Human Rights*. New York: UN. www.ohchr.org/Documents/Publications/GuidingPrinciples BusinessHR_EN.pdf

UNHRC (United Nations Human Rights Council). 2019. *The Economic Interests of the Myanmar Military*. 5 August. www.ohchr.org/Documents/HRBodies/ HRCouncil/FFM-Myanmar/EconomicInterestsMyanmarMilitary/A_HRC_ 42_CRP_3.pdf

Woodside. 2022. 'Woodside to Withdraw from Myanmar'. ASX announcement, 27 January. www.woodside.com.au/docs/default-source/asx-announcements/ 2022/woodside-to-withdraw-from-myanmar.pdf

World Bank. 2021. 'Myanmar Trade Balance, Exports and Imports by Country 2019'. World Integrated Trade Solution. Accessed 10 February 2023. wits.world bank.org/CountryProfile/en/Country/MMR/Year/2019/TradeFlow/EXPIMP/ Partner/by-country

5

Politics, Justice and Accountability: Myanmar and International Courts

Adam Simpson

Senior Lecturer in International Studies, Justice & Society,
University of South Australia

Juliette McIntyre

Lecturer in Law, Justice & Society, University of South Australia
and PhD candidate, University of Melbourne

Abstract

The military coup in February 2021 has added yet another brutal chapter
to the multiple crises facing Myanmar. Prior to the coup, Myanmar and its
military already faced various charges, including crimes against humanity and
genocide of the Muslim Rohingya minority, in the International Criminal
Court and the International Court of Justice. There are now questions over
whether there have been crimes committed during and since the February
2021 coup, by the military or any other groups in Myanmar, that could be
prosecuted under international law. While the United Nations Independent
Investigative Mechanism for Myanmar gathers evidence of such crimes, it
cannot prosecute, and it is not a court. This chapter investigates the potential
international justice mechanisms available to hold Myanmar to account,
and the issues with these. It finds that various factors, such as restrictions
on jurisdiction, the need for state consent and the significant burden of

establishing criminal acts reaching the threshold of crimes against humanity or genocide, mean that the influence and authority of international courts, while important, remains limited.

***

The military coup in February 2021 has added yet another brutal chapter to the multiple crises facing Myanmar (Simpson 2021a). It has provided a further case study of the Myanmar military's ruthless modus operandi. Prior to the coup, Myanmar and its military already faced various international court proceedings, notably at the International Criminal Court (ICC) and the International Court of Justice (ICJ). The crimes being investigated included crimes against humanity and genocide of the Muslim Rohingya minority.

In 2017, the Myanmar military conducted clearance operations in Rakhine State that resulted in the exodus of 740,000 mostly Rohingya refugees to Bangladesh (Simpson & Farrelly 2021b). These operations involved the commission of serious human rights violations including mass killings, torture, rape and sexual assault, and the destruction of homes and mosques (UNHRC 2018a, 256–60). Myanmar refused to allow independent investigators into the country and vigorously defended its actions in the proceedings, as seen in Aung San Suu Kyi's vigorous defence of the military at the ICJ in November 2019 (Simpson 2020; Simpson & Farrelly 2020).

Since 2019, three separate international justice processes have commenced with the goal of accountability for the atrocities committed against the Rohingya. First, the Independent Investigative Mechanism for Myanmar (IIMM) was established by the United Nations Human Rights Council (UNHRC 2018b) in September 2018. Its mandate was to collect evidence regarding serious international crimes and violations of international law committed in Myanmar since 2011. Second, on 11 November 2019, The Gambia filed suit in the ICJ against Myanmar alleging that Myanmar was responsible for committing genocide against the Rohingya (The Gambia 2019). The Gambia has emphasised that the prohibition of genocide has the character of a peremptory norm and the obligations under the Genocide Convention are owed *erga omnes* (to all states) and *erga omnes partes* (to all other states party to a treaty) (The Gambia 2019, 14). The UK, the Maldives, Canada, and the Netherlands have stated their intention to act as intervenors in the case (Pillai 2020; Simpson 2022b). Third, on 14 November 2019, a Pre-Trial Chamber of the ICC authorised the opening of a full investigation by the Office of the Prosecutor into crimes against humanity committed against the Rohingya that took place, at least in part, on the territory of Bangladesh, which is a state party to the Rome Statute (ICC 2019). These alleged crimes have only been investigated outside of Myanmar since Myanmar is not a state party to the Rome Statute. The former National League for Democracy government, deposed in the 2021 coup, blocked investigations by the relevant agencies within Myanmar's territory.

Other cases in national courts, such as those of Argentina and Germany, have also sought to address the accountability gaps in Myanmar for atrocities against the Rohingya and the rest of the population. In November 2021, the Federal Criminal Court of Argentina confirmed that it would pursue an action against senior Myanmar military officials under the principle of universal jurisdiction, which allows particularly horrific crimes to be prosecuted anywhere in the world, regardless of where the crimes were committed. This allows the court in Argentina to investigate all crimes committed against the Rohingya in Myanmar, giving it a wider remit than the ICC prosecution (Reed 2021). Similarly, in January 2023, the NGO Fortify Rights announced in Bangkok that it had filed a criminal complaint with the federal public prosecutor general of Germany under the principle of universal jurisdiction against senior Myanmar military generals and others for genocide, war crimes and crimes against humanity covering atrocities related to both the Rohingya pogroms and the military coup (Fortify Rights 2023). In this chapter, however, we focus on the international court proceedings since they reflect most clearly a developing international political and legal consensus.

By November 2022, there were reports that more than 2,400 opponents of the military regime had been killed since the February 2021 coup, including almost 250 children, with over 13,000 political prisoners under arrest (AAPP (Burma) 2022). The military regime also tortured detainees to death (Simpson & Farrelly 2021a). Almost a million people remained displaced (Andrews 2022b). These activities may well result in further charges against the military of crimes against humanity, which could be brought before the ICC or other courts. It may, therefore, one day be significant that the exiled National Unity Government (NUG) has declared that it will accept the ICC's jurisdiction with respect to all international crimes committed in Myanmar since 2002 (Simpson 2021b).

This chapter will consider the implications of Myanmar's 2021 coup for these mechanisms of international justice and consider the avenues for increasing accountability under international law through engagement with the NUG. The first section examines the existing international justice processes, including the IIMM investigation and the proceedings before the ICJ and the ICC. The second section addresses the procedural issue of who represents Myanmar in international legal proceedings, whether it be a representative from the junta, the NUG or a civil servant. The third section investigates the actions of the military—and the opposition—since the coup and considers the substantive issue of whether prosecutions under international law are possible or likely. The fourth section addresses the policy implications of international legal considerations for the international community, including the Association of Southeast Asian Nations (ASEAN) and Australia. The chapter concludes by finding that while the influence and authority of international courts are important, their ability to respond to Myanmar's many crises is limited.

Existing international justice processes

There are three active international justice processes investigating war crimes, crimes against humanity in Myanmar and genocide of the Muslim Rohingya ethnic minority. The scope of each of these processes, which are at times intersecting, is outlined below.

Independent investigative mechanism for Myanmar

In response to reports of human rights abuses, the UNHRC has established various independent fact-finding investigations into the situation in Myanmar. The Independent International Fact-Finding Mission on Myanmar (FFM) (with which Myanmar refused to cooperate) was established in April 2017 (UNHRC 2017). It concluded that the actions of Myanmar's military forces in Kachin, Rakhine and Shan states since 2011 constituted consistent patterns of serious human rights violations, crimes against humanity and war crimes (UNHRC 2018a). The FFM proposed that the United Nations (UN) Security Council should refer the situation to the ICC or create an ad hoc international criminal tribunal (UNHRC 2018, 426), neither of which has occurred due to obstruction by Russia and China.

Following the release of the FFM final report, the IIMM was established (UNHRC 2018b). The FFM transferred almost all the material it gathered to the IIMM, and, as such, the two processes may be seen as connected. The role of the IIMM is to collect and preserve evidence of the most serious international crimes and violations of international law committed in Myanmar since 2011. As explained by the head of the body, the necessity of this work derives from the fact that, over time, 'crime scenes get disturbed, bodies decompose, wounds can heal, people's memories can fade, witnesses with information can pass away' (*UN News* 2021). The IIMM works to ensure that evidence is gathered in a way that meets the required technical and procedural standards to be admissible in criminal proceedings. The IIMM may also prepare case files for use by prosecutors where it considers that the information meets the standard required to hold individuals criminally responsible. However, the body itself cannot prosecute or adjudicate cases; it is not a court.

Unlike the FFM, the IIMM is not limited in geographical scope, nor to any particular group of victims or perpetrators. It may investigate any international crime occurring in the territory of Myanmar. It is also mandated to investigate both past and future situations. As such, it has continued to closely monitor events in Myanmar since the coup (IIMM 2021). Indeed, the IIMM reports that it has experienced an 'exponential increase in communications' (IIMM 2021) since the military seized power on 1 February 2021. By July 2022, its repository consisted of nearly 3 million information items, including 'interview statements, documentation, videos, photographs, geospatial imagery and social media material' (IIMM 2022).

The IIMM prioritised the post-coup events for investigation:

> on the basis of a preliminary assessment of the gravity of the crimes concerned, including their scale, nature, manner of commission and impact on victims; the degree of responsibility of alleged perpetrators; the strength of the available evidence; the importance the Mechanism's thematic priorities concerning sexual and gender-based crimes and crimes against children; and the likelihood of a court or tribunal taking jurisdiction over the crime(s) in question. (IIMM 2022)

Thanks to the work of the IIMM, evidence of the atrocities committed by the junta is being collected and collated. But this record-keeping function is insufficient in and of itself as an instrument of justice. The IIMM cannot directly hold perpetrators to account. Indeed, as observed by Mahnad, the model was 'an innovation borne out of desperation' in a situation in which there was no realistic prospect of domestic prosecutions in the near future, a lack jurisdiction on the part of the ICC and 'no path toward it due to a blocked Security Council' (Mahnad 2018).

The International Court of Justice

However, the importance of the FFM and IIMM's evidence-gathering function is demonstrated by the reliance placed on the reports of the FFM by the ICJ in the proceedings brought by The Gambia. The Gambia alleges that Myanmar is responsible for committing genocide against the Rohingya by undertaking operations that were intended to destroy the Rohingya as a group, in whole or in part (The Gambia 2019, 6).

The jurisdiction of the ICJ requires the consent of both parties to the dispute, which can be manifested by 'matters specially provided for … in treaties and conventions in force' (ICJ Statute 1945, Art. 36(1)). In this case, The Gambia and Myanmar are both parties to the Genocide Convention (adopted by the UN in 1950), Article XIII of which provides that disputes relating to the 'interpretation, application or fulfilment' of the treaty shall be submitted to the ICJ. While The Gambia is not directly implicated or impacted by Myanmar's conduct, the ICJ held in accordance with its previous jurisprudence (Longobardo 2021) that:

> any State party to the Genocide Convention, and not only a specially affected State, may invoke the responsibility of another State party with a view to ascertaining the alleged failure to comply with its obligations *erga omnes partes*, and to bring that failure to an end. (ICJ 2020, 17)

In December 2019, the ICJ heard arguments on whether to grant an interim order for provisional measures pursuant to Article 41 of the court's statute; a hearing notorious for the appearance of Nobel Peace Prize laureate and former state counsellor Aung San Suu Kyi as agent for Myanmar, attempting 'to defend her government against allegations that many considered indefensible' (Becker 2020, 428). The court's unanimous order, issued in January 2021, held that Myanmar was required to 'to take all measures within its power to prevent the commission of all acts' of genocide (as defined in Article 2 of the Genocide Convention) in relation to the members of the Rohingya group in its territory, and to report back to the court 'on all measures taken to give effect' to this order within four months, and thereafter every six months, until a final decision on the case was reached by the court (ICJ 2020, 30). Although the reports are confidential, Myanmar appears to have continued to comply with this order even following the coup (*Myanmar Now* 2021, 2; ICJ 2022a, 15).

Prior to making this order, the ICJ needed to establish that the requisite elements of Article 41 were made out (Miles 2017). The court had to be satisfied that the rights asserted by The Gambia were 'at least plausible' (ICJ 2020, 18). In this case, it was

> the right of the Rohingya group in Myanmar and of its members to be protected from acts of genocide and related prohibited acts … and the right of The Gambia to seek compliance by Myanmar with its obligations not to commit, and to prevent and punish genocide in accordance with the Convention. (ICJ 2020, 23)

This is where we return to the reports of the FFM, because, in finding that these rights were plausibly established, the court relied heavily on the conclusions of the FFM investigation (ICJ 2020, 22) to find that the Rohingya were a protected group under the Genocide Convention and that the Rohingya in Myanmar 'remain extremely vulnerable' (ICJ 2020, 26). Vice-President Xue observed that the evidentiary 'weight' of the FFM reports 'cannot be ignored' (ICJ 2020, 35). While there are questions remaining as to the reliance that the court will place on such third-party fact-finding at the merits stage of the case, where the standard of proof is higher (Becker 2019b; Becker 2019a; Devaney 2016), the IIMM has been requested by both parties to share evidence with the court (*UN News* 2021). As such, while the IIMM cannot itself prosecute international crimes, it has an important role to play in providing evidence to decision-makers.

Oral hearings in relation to Myanmar's objections to the ICJ's jurisdiction to hear the case were held on 21–28 February 2022, a year after the coup. This raised issues relating to the legal and legitimate representation of Myanmar at these proceedings, which are explored in the third section.

The International Criminal Court

Finally, in relation to the conduct of the Myanmar authorities prior to the coup, there is the question of the role to be played by the ICC. There are separate questions to be asked regarding the role of the ICC for conduct occurring as part of, or subsequent to, the coup, which will be addressed in the last section.

In November 2019, an investigation into crimes against humanity committed against the Rohingya was authorised by the ICC (ICC 2019). This followed an earlier ruling that the ICC had jurisdiction 'over the alleged deportation of members of the Rohingya people from Myanmar to Bangladesh, provided that such allegations are established to the required threshold' (ICC 2018, 42). The reason for the geographical limitation is that Myanmar is not a party to the Rome Statute, and, as such, the ICC does not have jurisdiction to investigate crimes occurring within the territory of Myanmar without its consent, unless it has a Security Council mandate.

Bangladesh, however, is a party to the Rome Statute, and the ICC may assert jurisdiction pursuant to Article 12(2)(a) of the statute if at least one element of a crime within the jurisdiction of the court or part of such crime is committed on the territory of a state party to the statute. The prosecutor successfully argued that the crime of deportation (Rome Statute 1998, Art. 7(1)(d)) was completed when the victims fled to Bangladesh as a result of coercive acts and a coercive environment (ICC 2019, 24).

However, deportation that falls within the jurisdiction of the ICC must reach the threshold of a crime against humanity (Rome Statute 1998, Art. 7(1)). This requires that the act takes place in a context of 'a widespread or systematic attack directed against any civilian population'. Article 7(2)(a) of the Rome Statute further defines an 'attack directed against any civilian population' as 'a course of conduct involving the multiple commission of acts … against any civilian population, pursuant to or in furtherance of a State or organizational policy to commit such attack'. The underlying crime of deportation must have been committed as part of the attack.

The Pre-Trial Chamber accepted that 'there exists a reasonable basis to believe' that 'widespread and/or systematic acts of violence may have been committed against the Rohingya civilian population' that could qualify as the crime against humanity of deportation across the Myanmar–Bangladesh border (ICC 2019, 42). The chamber did not assess whether other crimes may have been committed, although this line of inquiry could form part of the prosecutor's ongoing investigation.

The Office of the Prosecutor is now undertaking an investigation in relation to any crime, including any future crime, that meets the criteria set down by the Pre-Trial Chamber. That is, in addition to meeting the temporal limitations demanded by the entry into force of the Rome Statute, the alleged crime must be: 1) within the jurisdiction of the ICC, 2) allegedly committed at least in part on the territory of Bangladesh, or on the territory of another state that accepts ICC jurisdiction (i.e. not Myanmar) and 3) sufficiently linked to the situation of the deportation of the Rohingya minority. Therefore, while the prosecutor's investigation is to be welcomed, it is, in fact, extremely limited in its scope.

Who represents Myanmar?

The procedural issue of who represents Myanmar in international law is one that is heavily dependent on international politics. The main practical contest in the international sphere is whether Myanmar is represented by the junta and its representatives, or the NUG and the opposition. This has played out in a variety of fora but most recently in relation to the ICJ case. For the purposes of the court, it is the state of Myanmar and not the government that has standing to appear (ICJ Statute 1945, Art. 34). This was emphasised by the president of the court at the opening to the oral hearings in February 2022, where she stated that 'the parties to a contentious case before the Court are States, not particular governments' (ICJ 2022a, 11). Ko Ko Hlaing, minister for international cooperation under the junta, appeared as agent for Myanmar at these hearings, along with its attorney-general, Thida Oo. Both are subject to US sanctions due to the coup and the violent suppression of resultant peaceful protests. The hearings proceeded as normal, and the ICJ is, at the time of writing, deliberating on its judgement.

But matters could have proceeded very differently. The NUG on 1 February 2022—the one-year anniversary of the coup—issued a statement that withdrew the preliminary objections and asserted that UN Ambassador Kyaw Moe Tun is 'the only person authorised to engage with the Court on behalf of Myanmar' (NUG 2022, n.p.). Had the ICJ accepted this, it could have proceeded immediately to hearing the merits of the case.

The ICJ's choice to permit the junta to appear on behalf of Myanmar creates political difficulties, as other organs of the UN continue to resist acknowledging the junta. For example, in September 2021, the US and China brokered a deal that prevented Myanmar's military rulers from addressing the General Assembly at its 76th session (Lynch, Gramer & Detsch 2021). And while the military junta stated that it had appointed Aung Thurein, a former military commander, as Myanmar's ambassador to the UN, the incumbent representative Kyaw Moe Tun remained the ambassador, as a decision must be taken by the General Assembly credentialing committee and approved according to General Assembly rules before he can be replaced (Simpson 2021c).

The NUG has endeavoured to be seen, both by Myanmar's population and the international community, as the legitimate government and representative of Myanmar. It announced a 'defensive war' that would work with newly formed volunteer People's Defence Force (PDF) units to attack the junta and its interests (Regan & Olarn 2021). To prosecute the war, it developed a 'chain of command' to assist in coordination between disparate groups (*Myanmar Now* 2021). But the junta's appearance at the ICJ has conferred a perception of legitimacy upon the military government that works against the NUG's claims (Simpson & McIntyre 2022; Weller 2022). This was a valuable diplomatic win for the military junta, one that a more powerful nation, such as Russia, may not have been so desperate to achieve (McIntyre & Simpson 2022a).

Within ASEAN, the response has also been mixed. Traditionally, ASEAN has been far more accommodating to military juntas and human rights abuses, partially because of the limited history and culture of democracy across Southeast Asia (Simpson & Smits 2018). With the organisation's mostly timid and laggardly response in the first few months following the Myanmar coup, history seemed to be repeating itself. That changed at the emergency meeting of ASEAN foreign ministers held on 15 October 2021 (Simpson 2021d). The statement released afterwards began with a discussion of the Five-Point Consensus reached with coup leader Min Aung Hlaing in April and the role of the special envoy, who had just cancelled his visit to Myanmar after being refused access to Aung San Suu Kyi and other junta opponents. It went on to hint at Myanmar's intransigence by 'emphasising the need to exercise flexibility', while noting that the situation in Myanmar was having an impact on regional security and the credibility of ASEAN itself.

The statement noted requests by the NUG to represent Myanmar at the meeting and then employed ASEAN's tradition of consensus decision-making to deny representation to both the NUG and the junta, instead deciding to invite a non-political representative from Myanmar, probably a civil servant. This response, pushed by the more progressive quartet of ASEAN—Indonesia, Malaysia, Singapore and the Philippines—and supported by the then ASEAN chair, Brunei, effectively disinvited Min Aung Hlaing to a series of ASEAN-related summits in October 2021, including one with US President Joe Biden.

In November 2021, ASEAN continued its surprising stance when the virtual ASEAN–China Special Summit, a major event to commemorate 30 years of ASEAN–China relations, began with Myanmar's seat embarrassingly empty, a further major snub to the military (Simpson 2021e). The same five governments of Indonesia, Brunei, Malaysia, the Philippines and Singapore joined Myanmar's Civil Disobedience Movement in successfully opposing the junta's attendance at the summit, despite diplomatic lobbying by China. The following day, the Myanmar representative attending an ASEAN climate and disaster conference was a minister of the NUG not the military junta. While this event was relatively independent of the ASEAN Secretariat and did not have the prominence of the leaders' summits, it was still significant: an NUG minister was invited to an ASEAN conference for the first time. It was a sign of growing frustration with the military's brutality and intransigence. Further snubs soon followed, with the junta's foreign minister barred from attending an ASEAN retreat in February 2022 and Myanmar represented by an empty chair at a special US–ASEAN Summit at the White House in May (AFP 2022).

While it might seem somewhat bizarre to contemplate two rival groups fighting to be prosecuted for genocide at the ICJ, this competition should be seen in the context of the politics of international legitimacy and representation. Both groups want to be seen as the legitimate government of Myanmar, although Suu Kyi's previous robust defence of the military at the ICJ would likely evaporate if the NUG was to take the stand.

The ICC will likely follow the UN in its recognition protocols, which is currently in the NUG's favour due to the incumbency of Kyaw Moe Tun. Due to ongoing support from the US and others in the credentialing committee, Kyaw Moe Tun remained in place for the 77th Session of the UN General Assembly in September 2022 and will likely remain so for the foreseeable future (Simpson 2022b).

International proceedings in the future: Prosecuting the coup?

Clearly, the existing ICC and ICJ proceedings demonstrate that there is a case to be answered in international courts in relation to the Rohingya (Becker 2020). A more substantive issue than who represents Myanmar is whether there have been crimes committed during and since the February 2021 coup, by the military or any other groups in Myanmar, that could be prosecuted under international law.

As noted above, the IIMM is mandated to investigate both past and future situations. As such, it has continued to closely monitor events in Myanmar since the coup to gather evidence of potential crimes. However, despite the reliance placed on similar materials by the ICJ in its provisional measures order, there is no capacity for the ICJ to expand the scope of its judgement beyond the question of genocide of the Rohingya. The ICJ is limited by the jurisdictional mandate granted under the Genocide Convention, and by the *non ultra petita* (not beyond the request) principle, by which it cannot independently investigate issues outside of those raised by the parties to the case.

We are, therefore, left with the possibility of criminal prosecution against individuals at the ICC. The Rome Statute grants the ICC jurisdiction in respect of genocide, war crimes, crimes against humanity and the crime of aggression (Rome Statute 1998, Arts 6–8*bis*). In respect of the situation in Myanmar, only the crime of deportation is presently within the scope of the investigation opened by the Office of the Prosecutor.

Putting to one side the question of jurisdiction, as noted above, to reach the threshold of a crime against humanity, the criminal act—murder, rape, torture or other acts as listed in Article 7(1)—must take place in a context of 'a widespread or systematic attack directed against any civilian population'.

Given that the military is an organ of the state of Myanmar (ICL 2001, Art. 4) or at the least that the junta is exercising elements of governmental authority in Myanmar (ICL 2001, Art. 5), it is likely that its acts would be considered to be in furtherance of state or organisational policy.

Regarding the requirement of multiple attacks against civilian populations, as evidence mounts it is becoming clear that the junta's attacks on the opposition may reach the threshold of crimes against humanity with a range of interrelated actions including:

- shooting or otherwise killing or maiming unarmed protesters in multiple peaceful demonstrations over many months, including:
  - a massacre in Yangon on 14 March 2021 when at least 65 unarmed protesters and bystanders were killed
  - on 5 December 2021, security forces driving purposefully into the rear of a protest, followed up by beating and shooting protesters, leaving five dead and many others injured.

- the killing of unarmed civilians or captured members of the opposition (including the PDF) in a variety of villages across the country, including:
  - an attack in Kayah (Karen) State on 24 December 2021 that left more than 30 people dead and burned, including women, children and two staff members from the international non-governmental organisation Save the Children
  - a series of mass killings in Sagaing in July 2021 that resulted in at least 40 men, beaten or tortured to death
  - the burning of 11 unarmed captives, including teenagers, in Sagaing Region in December 2021
  - taking 40 villagers from Magway Region's Myaing Township hostage in May 2022 and using them as human shields, while killing six of them
  - the torture and killing of at least six civilians in Kani Township, Sagaing, in June 2022.
- systematic torture, with at least 110 prisoners dying in police custody, many from torture in the first 24 hours of detention while others died due to being denied medical care.
- execution of four political prisoners in July 2022 (Simpson 2022a).
- indiscriminate attacks on villages that kill civilians including air strikes, shelling and the burning of buildings and entire villages, including:
  - an attack on Thantlang in Chin State in September 2021, which was analysed by the *Washington Post* through videos, photos, satellite imagery, eyewitness accounts and military planning documents, and demonstrated that it was the result of a premeditated campaign that targeted civilians
  - an air raid by military jets in October 2022 that bombed a music festival in Kachin State celebrating the anniversary of the founding of the Kachin Independence Organisation, killing at least 80 people, including musicians and other civilians, and injuring at least 100 (Al Jazeera 2022).
- blocking the transport of humanitarian aid to civilian communities.
- the displacement, arbitrary detention and torture of children (Andrews 2022a).

The mandate of the IIMM does not extend to the overthrow of the constitutional authority via the coup, but, in November 2021, Nicholas Koumjian, the head of the IIMM, suggested that preliminary evidence collected since the coup demonstrated a widespread and systematic attack on civilians 'amounting to crimes against humanity' (Associated Press 2021).

Another issue to consider is whether ethnic armed groups, the PDF and other oppositional actors have committed crimes that might also be prosecuted under international law. There is little doubt that PDFs have been undertaking targeted assassinations of civilians who have assisted with the junta's administration, and clashes have resulted in the death of thousands of military personnel. Any crimes committed against civilians by the opposition should also be investigated, but the opposition does not presently exercise governmental authority, nor are these entities to be equated with organs of the state of Myanmar. As such, even criminal acts on their part would not reach the threshold of crimes against humanity necessary to implicate prosecution at the ICC.

In this regard, the efforts of the NUG to establish itself as Myanmar's legitimate government, with a clear chain of command between itself and the PDFs, may be a double-edged sword, since, although it may be advantageous politically and diplomatically, it may also open it to prosecution under the ICC. While this is a potential outcome in the future, it is likely that for the moment, for the purposes of international state and individual criminal liability, the main perpetrator of international crimes is the instigator of the crisis itself, the Myanmar military led by Min Aung Hlaing.

However, at present the ICC cannot consider any of these acts, whomever commits them, since Myanmar is not a state party to the Rome Statute. The ICC does not have jurisdiction. It is worth noting that there is one way in which the ICC could widen its mandate, and that is through the operation of Article 13(b) of the Rome Statute, which allows the ICC to receive referrals of situations by the Security Council. This has occurred, for example, in respect of the situation in Darfur, notwithstanding that Sudan is not a state party to the Rome Statute (de Wet 2018). With such a referral, the ICC could assume jurisdiction over all crimes listed in the Rome Statute that may have been committed in the territory of Myanmar. To date, however, the non-cooperation of China and Russia has ensured the Security Council has not taken any steps in this direction.

Policy implications for the international community

The international community has a range of levers at its disposal to influence events in Myanmar, many of which can be considered part of the contentious policy known as Responsibility to Protect (R2P) (Simpson 2021a), where the international community intervenes in a country when its government is unable, or unwilling, to protect communities at risk.

Human Rights Watch and other international non-governmental organisations have called for a comprehensive global arms embargo against Myanmar (HRW 2021). Fortify Rights, an organisation focused on Myanmar and its region, called for UN member states to form an emergency coalition to respond to the coup and Myanmar's devastating COVID-19 outbreaks (Fortify Rights 2021). These organisations have some influence in the Western halls of power, but they are still dependent on action from states. States themselves have a range of competing interests and are constrained by the limits of their authority within the international system. Even a UN Security Council resolution banning arms sales to the junta was a bridge too far for China and Russia.

In terms of the ICJ proceedings, the most effective direct action for the international community would be to formally intervene in the genocide case under Article 63 of the ICJ Statute. Such intervention brings moral and legal reinforcement to one side of the case (Fitzmaurice 1958, 127). While many states, such as the UK, Canada, the Netherlands and the Maldives have made statements that they intend to intervene, by November 2022 none had filed a formal declaration of intervention (ICJ 2022b). This is in stark contrast to the other genocide case underway at the ICJ, in which at least 23 countries have formally intervened to support Ukraine against Russia (ICJ 2022c; McIntyre & Simpson 2022b; Simpson 2022c). However, regardless of who joins the Myanmar genocide case, it is highly unlikely that the ICJ will make any reference to the coup.

The ICC cannot act in relation to activities within Myanmar unless there is a Security Council resolution or Myanmar itself becomes a party to the Rome Statute. Since the NUG has committed to joining the Rome Statute if it takes power, it is in the international community's interest for this to happen. The main avenue for international pressure at present is, therefore, to recognise the NUG as Myanmar's legitimate government and accredit

Myanmar's various rebellious ambassadors, including the current UN representative, Kyaw Moe Tun, who have denounced the military coup and been sacked by the military as a result. This would send a potent message to the junta and allow the NUG to fill Myanmar's currently empty seat on the UN Human Rights Council (Simpson 2022b).

Likewise, ASEAN should continue to isolate the military and recognise the NUG. Unfortunately, the visit to Myanmar in January 2022 of Hun Sen, Cambodia's prime minister and the chair of ASEAN for 2022, undermined ASEAN's fragile position by meeting with Min Aung Hlaing, resulting in criticism from Malaysia's foreign minister. Hun Sen was confident that, as a fellow authoritarian, he could make progress in the peace process. However, he came away from the discussions empty handed and, in February, virtually gave up on making any headway (Nachemson 2022).

Another important strategy for the international community is to provide material support to the NUG and the opposition movement. Many participants in the Civil Disobedience Movement have not received any income since February 2021. Since the coup, the real value of Myanmar's currency has collapsed, losing up to 60 per cent of its value, with rampant inflation only exacerbating Myanmar's humanitarian crisis. The NUG has very limited funding with essentially no-one being paid. A substantial international measure, that would assist both the NUG and the rest of the opposition movement, would be for the US to release the USD1 billion frozen in the Federal Reserve to the NUG. Countries such as Australia should also consider applying sanctions against Myanmar's military officials. Australia has recently enacted Magnitsky-style legislation that could be deployed for this purpose.

A more contentious, although still justifiable, policy would be to support the anti-junta PDFs that have emerged, often in conjunction with existing ethnic minority militias, to militarily challenge the Tatmadaw. While many governments are hesitant to arm or support non-state militias, arguing that non-violent methods should be employed, Myanmar's military has shown throughout history that it has no qualms in ruthlessly and brutally crushing non-violent opposition movements. While the conflicts and crises in Myanmar are only likely to be resolved by groups within the country, aid and diplomatic support may well provide the opposition movement with the resources, resolve and recognition that they need to force a negotiated settlement.

Conclusion

The evolving crises facing the people of Myanmar are not limited to violence and political repression. They include the heavy burdens of poverty, food shortages and unemployment, along with the collapse of the healthcare and education systems and the pressure of COVID-19 (Simpson 2021a; Thant Myint-U 2021). A report by the World Bank estimated that Myanmar's economy contracted by 18 per cent in 2021 because of the joint effects of the pandemic and the coup (World Bank Group 2021). It suggested the share of people living in poverty would more than double by the beginning of 2022 compared to 2019. Another crisis waiting in the wings is climate change, which is already disrupting the monsoon, causing droughts and reducing agricultural returns (Simpson & South 2022; Thant Myint-U 2020).

Applying external pressure to the military junta is unlikely to have any significant impact while China, Russia and some ASEAN countries continue to work with the regime. The international community can provide aid and diplomatic support to the opposition, but the conflicts in Myanmar are only likely to be resolved by the groups within the country.

The power of the international judiciary to respond to these intersecting crises in general, and the violence and repression of the coup in particular, are limited. International courts can only act within the legal mandate granted to them by states. Various factors, such as restrictions on jurisdiction, the need for state consent and the significant burden of establishing criminal acts reaching the threshold of crimes against humanity or genocide, mean that their influence and authority, while important, remains limited.

The acts committed by the military junta are abhorrent and, thanks to the work of the IIMM, have been documented for the eyes of the world to see. It is difficult to be optimistic in the face of the military's brutality and incompetence. However, a bleak outlook is no reason not to act on Myanmar, whether at a diplomatic level or via international courts. There is always the possibility of political change, particularly when the vast majority of a country's population is so implacably opposed to its leaders. While some sections of Myanmar's population reluctantly accepted military rule for the half-century prior to 2011, there can be no doubt this time about the level of visceral domestic fury directed towards the military for having, once again, driven the country into the ground and snuffed out the dreams of its long-suffering people. The joint activities of the ICC investigation, the ICJ proceedings related to the Rohingya genocide, and the work of fact-finding missions and other human rights agencies will continue to document crimes and prosecute the military in courts where possible. The wheels of international justice turn slowly but it is hoped that, one day, justice can be done.

References

AAPP (Burma). 2022. 'Daily Update 16/11/22 Day 654'. Twitter. twitter.com/aapp_burma/status/1592838654573293569?s=20&t=4mDD9mpnawp815Vmgm6e_g

AFP. 2022. 'Myanmar Junta Slams US Summit Snub, Lauds Ties with China'. *Jakarta Post*, 16 May. www.thejakartapost.com/world/2022/05/16/myanmar-junta-slams-us-summit-snub-lauds-ties-with-china-.html

Al Jazeera. 2022. 'Death Toll from Air Raids in Myanmar's Kachin Reported to Hit 80'. 25 October. www.aljazeera.com/news/2022/10/25/horrific-air-raids-in-myanmars-kachin-kills-80-reports

Andrews, Thomas H. 2022a. *Conference Room Paper of the Special Rapporteur: 'Losing a Generation: How the Military Junta Is Attacking Myanmar's Children and Stealing Their Future'*. UN Doc. A/HRC/50/CRP.1, Office of the UN High Commissioner for Human Rights, 13 June 2022. www.ohchr.org/en/documents/thematic-reports/ahrc50crp1-conference-room-paper-special-rapporteur-losing-generation

Andrews, Thomas H. 2022b. *Report of the Special Rapporteur on the Situation of Human Rights in Myanmar*. UN General Assembly, 77th Session, UN Doc. A/77/494, 3 October. www.ohchr.org/en/documents/country-reports/a77494-report-special-rapporteur-situation-human-right-myanmar

Associated Press. 2021. 'Attacks on Civilians in Myanmar "Crimes against Humanity": UN'. Al Jazeera, 6 November. www.aljazeera.com/news/2021/11/6/attacks-on-civilians-in-myanmar-crimes-against-humanity-un

Becker, Michael. 2019a. 'The Situation of the Rohingya: Is There a Role for the International Court of Justice?' *University of Cambridge Legal Studies Research Paper Series*, no. 25/2019. doi.org/10.2139/ssrn.3285738

Becker, Michael. 2019b. 'The Challenges for the ICJ in the Reliance on UN Fact-Finding Reports in the Case against Myanmar'. *Blog of the European Journal of International Law*, 14 December. doi.org/10.2139/ssrn.3505272

Becker, Michael. 2020. 'The Plight of the Rohingya: Genocide Allegations and Provisional Measures in The Gambia v Myanmar at the International Court of Justice'. *Melbourne Journal of International Law* 21 (2): 428–49. doi.org/10.2139/ssrn.3688935

de Wet, Erika. 2018. 'Referrals to the International Criminal Court under Chapter VII of the United Nations Charter and the Immunity of Foreign State Officials'. *American Journal of International Law Unbound*, 112: 33–7. doi.org/10.1017/aju.2018.13

Fitzmaurice, Sir Gerald. 1958. 'The Law and Procedure of the International Court of Justice, 1951–4: Questions of Jurisdiction, Competence and Procedure'. *British Yearbook of International Law* 34 (1): 1–161.

Fortify Rights. 2021. 'UN Member States: Form Emergency Coalition to Respond to COVID Outbreak and Coup D'état in Myanmar'. 21 July. www.fortifyrights.org/mya-inv-2021-07-21/

Fortify Rights. 2023. 'Criminal Complaint Filed in Germany against Myanmar Generals for Atrocity Crimes'. 24 January. www.fortifyrights.org/mya-inv-2023-01-24/

The Gambia. 2019. *Application of the Convention on the Prevention and Punishment of the Crime of Genocide (The Gambia v. Myanmar)*. Application instituting proceedings and request for the indication of provisional measures, 11 November.

HRW (Human Rights Watch). 2021. 'Global Civil Society Statement on Myanmar'. 5 May. www.hrw.org/news/2021/05/05/global-civil-society-statement-myanmar

ICC (International Criminal Court). 2018. *Request under Regulation 46(3) of the Regulations of the Court*. ICC-RoC46(3)-01/18, 6 September.

ICC (International Criminal Court). 2019. *Situation in the People's Republic of Bangladesh/Republic of the Union of Myanmar*. ICC-01/19, 14 November.

ICJ (International Court of Justice). 2020. *Application of the Convention on the Prevention and Punishment of the Crime of Genocide (The Gambia v. Myanmar)*. Provisional Measures, 23 January.

ICJ (International Court of Justice). 2022a. *Verbatim Record of the Public Sitting Held on Monday 21 February 2022, at 1.30 p.m., at the Peace Palace, President Donoghue Presiding, in the Case Concerning Application of the Convention on the Prevention and Punishment of the Crime of Genocide (The Gambia v. Myanmar)*. CR 2022/1.

ICJ (International Court of Justice). 2022b. *Application of the Convention on the Prevention and Punishment of the Crime of Genocide (The Gambia v. Myanmar)*. Case 178, 22 July. www.icj-cij.org/en/case/178

ICJ (International Court of Justice). 2022c. *Allegations of Genocide under the Convention on the Prevention and Punishment of the Crime of Genocide (Ukraine v. Russian Federation) – Intervention*. Case 182, 21 July. www.icj-cij.org/en/case/182/intervention

ICL (International Law Commission). 2001. 'Draft Article on the Responsibility of States for Internationally Wrongful Acts, with Commentaries'. *Yearbook of the International Law Commission*, vol.2, part 1. Documents of the 53rd Session, UN. Doc. A/56/10.

IIMM (Independent Investigative Mechanism for Myanmar). 2021. 'Message from the Head of the Mechanism'. *Bulletin* 5, (October).

IIMM (Independent Investigative Mechanism for Myanmar). 2022. *Report of the Independent Investigative Mechanism for Myanmar*. UN Doc. A/HRC/51/4, 12 July.

Longobardo, Marco. 2021. 'The Standing of Indirectly Injured States in the Litigation of Community Interests before the ICJ: Lessons Learned and Future Implications in Light of The Gambia v. Myanmar and Beyond'. *International Community Law Review*. doi.org/10.1163/18719732-12341480

Lynch, Colum, Robbie Gramer and Jack Detsch. 2021. 'U.S. and China Reach Deal to Block Myanmar's Junta from U.N.'. *Foreign Policy*, 13 September. foreignpolicy.com/2021/09/13/myanmar-united-nations-china-biden-general-assembly/

Mahnad, Polina Levina. 2018. 'An Independent Mechanism for Myanmar: A Turning Point in the Pursuit of Accountability for International Crimes'. *Blog of the European Journal of International Law,* 1 October. www.ejiltalk.org/a-turning-point-in-the-pursuit-of-accountability-for-international-crimes/

McIntyre, Juliette and Adam Simpson. 2022a. 'A Tale of Two Genocide Cases: International Justice in Ukraine and Myanmar'. *East Asia Forum*, 26 May. www.eastasiaforum.org/2022/05/26/a-tale-of-two-genocide-cases-international-justice-in-ukraine-and-myanmar/

McIntyre, Juliette and Adam Simpson. 2022b. 'Myanmar's Genocide Overshadowed by Ukraine'. *East Asia Forum*, 5 October. www.eastasiaforum.org/2022/10/05/myanmars-genocide-overshadowed-by-ukraine/

Miles, Cameron. 2017. *Provisional Measures before International Courts and Tribunals*. Cambridge: Cambridge University Press. doi.org/10.1017/97813164 10813

Myanmar Now. 2021. 'NUG Establishes "Chain of Command" in Fight against Regime'. 28 October. www.myanmar-now.org/en/news/nug-establishes-chain-of-command-in-fight-against-regime

Nachemson, Andrew. 2022. 'Misreading the Room: Why Hun Sen Is Failing on Myanmar'. Al Jazeera, 30 March. www.aljazeera.com/news/2022/3/30/misreading-the-room-why-hun-sen-is-failing-on-myanmar

NUG (National Unity Government). 2022. 'Announcement (2/2022) – Myanmar Withdraws all Preliminary Objections to the International Court of Justice Hearing on the Genocide Case'. 1 February. gov.nugmyanmar.org/2022/02/01/announcement-2-2022-myanmar-withdraws-all-preliminary-objections-to-the-international-court-of-justice-hearing-on-the-genocide-case/ (page discontinued).

Pillai, Priya. 2020. 'Canada and The Netherlands: New Intervention in The Gambia v Myanmar at the International Court of Justice'. *Opinio Juris blog*, 3 September. opiniojuris.org/2020/09/03/canada-and-the-netherlands-new-intervention-in-the-gambia-v-myanmar-at-the-international-court-of-justice/

Reed, John. 2021. 'Argentine Court to Hear Myanmar Rohingya Genocide Case'. *Financial Times*, 28 November. www.ft.com/content/0a2c1a4c-269a-4121-b37f-0da41e53a618

Regan, Helen and Kocha Olarn. 2021. 'Myanmar's Shadow Government Launches "People's Defensive War" against the Military Junta'. *CNN*, 8 September. edition.cnn.com/2021/09/07/asia/myanmar-nug-peoples-war-intl-hnk/index.html

Rome Statute. 1998. *Rome Statute of the International Criminal Court*. 17 July. United Nations Diplomatic Conference of Plenipotentiaries on the Establishment of an International Criminal Court: Rome. Entry into force: 1 July 2002, in accordance with Article 126.

Simpson, Adam. 2020. 'The Folly of Aung San Suu Kyi's "Bad Apple" Defence'. *East Asia Forum*, 26 March. www.eastasiaforum.org/2020/03/26/the-folly-of-aung-san-suu-kyis-bad-apple-defence/

Simpson, Adam. 2021a. 'Coups, Conflicts, and COVID-19 in Myanmar: Humanitarian Intervention and Responsibility to Protect in Intractable Crises'. *Brown Journal of World Affairs* 28 (1): 1–19.

Simpson, Adam. 2021b. 'Myanmar's Exile Government Signs up to ICC Prosecutions'. *East Asia Forum*, 17 September. www.eastasiaforum.org/2021/09/17/myanmars-exile-government-signs-up-to-icc-prosecutions/

Simpson, Adam. 2021c. 'Two Governments Claim to Run Myanmar. So, Who Gets the Country's Seat at the UN?' *Conversation*, 24 September. theconversation.com/two-governments-claim-to-run-myanmar-so-who-gets-the-countrys-seat-at-the-un-167885

Simpson, Adam. 2021d. 'ASEAN Finds its Voice as a Military Offensive Looms in Myanmar'. *Strategist*, 22 October. www.aspistrategist.org.au/asean-finds-its-voice-as-a-military-offensive-looms-in-myanmar/

Simpson, Adam. 2021e. 'ASEAN Rebuffs Myanmar's Military Junta as Aung San Suu Kyi Faces Long Jail Term'. *Conversation*, 1 December. theconversation.com/asean-rebuffs-myanmars-military-junta-as-aung-san-suu-kyi-faces-long-jail-term-172619

Simpson, Adam. 2022a. 'Myanmar's Kangaroo Courts Hand Aung San Suu Kyi Another Six-Year Term While Sean Turnell Pleads Not Guilty'. *Australian Outlook*, 18 August. www.internationalaffairs.org.au/australianoutlook/myanmars-kangaroo-courts-hand-aung-san-suu-kyi-another-six-year-term-while-sean-turnell-pleads-not-guilty/

Simpson, Adam. 2022b. 'Myanmar: A Desperate Junta Trying, and Failing, to Shore up its Legitimacy'. *Interpreter*, 29 September. www.lowyinstitute.org/the-interpreter/myanmar-desperate-junta-trying-failing-shore-its-legitimacy

Simpson, Adam. 2022c. 'Relief as Australian Sean Turnell to be Released from Prison in Myanmar, but More Needs to Be Done'. *Conversation*, 17 November. theconversation.com/relief-as-australian-sean-turnell-to-be-released-from-prison-in-myanmar-but-more-needs-to-be-done-194814

Simpson, Adam and Nicholas Farrelly. 2020. 'The Rohingya Crisis and Questions of Accountability'. *Australian Journal of International Affairs* 74 (5): 486–94. doi.org/10.1080/10357718.2020.1813251

Simpson, Adam and Nicholas Farrelly. 2021a. 'As Killings, Beatings and Disappearances Escalate, What's the End Game in Myanmar?' *Conversation*, 11 March. theconversation.com/as-killings-beatings-and-disappearances-escalate-whats-the-end-game-in-myanmar-156752

Simpson, Adam and Nicholas Farrelly. 2021b. 'The Rohingya Crisis: Nationalism and Its Discontents'. In *Myanmar: Politics, Economy and Society*, edited by Adam Simpson and Nicholas Farrelly, 249–64. London: Routledge. doi.org/10.4324/9780429024443-20

Simpson, Adam and Juliette McIntyre. 2022. 'It's a Mistake to Allow Myanmar's Junta to Appear in Rohingya Case'. *Interpreter*, 23 February. www.lowyinstitute.org/the-interpreter/it-s-mistake-allow-myanmar-s-junta-appear-rohingya-case

Simpson, Adam and Mattijs Smits. 2018. 'Transitions to Energy and Climate Security in Southeast Asia? Civil Society Encounters with Illiberalism in Thailand and Myanmar'. *Society and Natural Resources* 31 (5): 580–98. doi.org/10.1080/08941920.2017.1413720

Simpson, Adam and Ashley South. 2022. 'Evolving Climate Change Governance in Myanmar: Limitations and Opportunities in a Political Crisis'. In *Governing Climate Change in Southeast Asia: Critical Perspectives*, edited by Jens Marquardt, Laurence L. Delina and Mattijs Smits, 112–32. London: Routledge.

Statute of the International Court of Justice. 1945. 33 UNTS 99316.

Thant Myint-U. 2020. *The Hidden History of Burma: Race, Capitalism, and the Crisis of Democracy in the 21st Century*. New York: W. W. Norton & Company.

Thant Myint-U. 2021. 'Myanmar's Coming Revolution: What Will Emerge from Collapse?' *Foreign Affairs*, July/August. www.foreignaffairs.com/articles/burma-myanmar/2021-06-11/myanmars-coming-revolution

UNHRC (United Nations Human Rights Council). 2017. *Resolution 34/22: Situation of Human Rights in Myanmar*. 24 March, UN Doc. A/HRC/RES/34/22. ap.ohchr.org/documents/dpage_e.aspx?si=A/HRC/RES/34/22

UNHRC (United Nations Human Rights Council). 2018a. *Report of the Detailed Findings of the Independent International Fact-Finding Mission on Myanmar*. UN Doc. A/HRC/39/CRP.2. digitallibrary.un.org/record/1643079?ln=en

UNHRC (United Nations Human Rights Council). 2018b. *Resolution 39/2: Situation of Human Rights of Rohingya Muslims and Other Minorities in Myanmar*. 3 October, UN Doc. A/HRC/RES/39/2. ap.ohchr.org/documents/dpage_e.aspx?si=A/HRC/RES/39/2

UN News. 2021. 'Myanmar: In race against time, experts collect evidence of rights violations'. 15 October. news.un.org/en/story/2021/10/1103042

Weller, Marc. 2022. 'Is the ICJ at Risk of Providing Cover for the Alleged Genocide in Myanmar?' *Blog of the European Journal of International Law*, 11 February. www.ejiltalk.org/is-the-icj-at-risk-of-providing-cover-for-the-alleged-genocide-in-myanmar/

World Bank Group. 2021. *Myanmar Economic Monitor – Progress Threatened; Resilience Tested*. pubdocs.worldbank.org/en/525471627057268984/Myanmar-Economic-Monitor-July-2021.pdf

6

China–Myanmar Relations after the 1 February Military Coup

Kristina Kironska

Senior Researcher, Department of Asian Studies,
Palacky University Olomouc, Czech Republic

Diya Jiang

PhD candidate, Department of Political Science,
McGill University, Canada

Abstract

Following Myanmar's 1 February military coup, Beijing remained more cautious than other countries in its response. Protesters accused China of supporting the Myanmar generals and torched Chinese factories and boycotted Chinese products. However, did China actually back the Myanmar military? It would be too simplistic to assume that China favoured a return to military rule in Myanmar. Myanmar, with its many Belt and Road Initiative projects, is important for China to achieve its strategic presence in the Indian Ocean; therefore, choosing the appropriate strategy was crucial for a continued relationship. Beijing's initially ambiguous attitude towards the coup did not favour the military; yet, despite having a reasonable relationship with Aung San Suu Kyi, it did not favour the protest movement either. However, as time has passed, China has edged increasingly closer to recognising the military regime, approving funds for infrastructure projects and donating COVID-19 vaccines. Why has this shift occurred?

This chapter argues that, although initially logical and beneficial, appearing neutral ultimately became costly to China's strategic interests as time passed and that, as a consequence, China began moving to closer cooperation with the military.

***

China's reactions to the coup in Myanmar have been very interesting. While Burma was the first non-Communist country to recognise the People's Republic of China in 1949, the relationship between Burma/Myanmar and China over the following decades remained nervously friendly, at best, and at times even hostile. The relationship warmed in 1988, and China became the junta's closest ally after the coup, supporting it economically and diplomatically. With Myanmar's top-down political transition to quasi-civilian rule from 2010 onwards, relations with China soured due to the cancellation of various Chinese-funded projects and Myanmar's expansion of its diplomatic profile following reforms and the country's so-called opening up. Cooperation with China was subsequently revived under the umbrella of the Belt and Road Initiative (BRI) during the Aung San Suu Kyi administration. Then, when the Rohingya crisis broke out and the West criticised the military's actions, China refused to condemn Myanmar and even supported the Myanmar government. So, given the twists and turns in China's relationship with Myanmar's military and democratic forces, the question of how China would react to the 1 February 2021 coup was far from clear-cut.

Myanmar is geopolitically important for China to achieve its strategic presence in the Indian Ocean, to reduce transport time for some of China's trade and to achieve its long-term two-ocean objective. Choosing the right strategy after the coup was crucial to ensure a continued relationship. Beijing's initially ambiguous attitude towards the coup did not favour the Myanmar military but, despite having a reasonable relationship with Aung San Suu Kyi, neither did it favour the protest movement. Yet, remaining neutral was not an option in the long term due to political and other costs. This chapter examines how the Chinese government has gradually shifted its response towards the military, assuming that it would play some role in Myanmar's future. The authors examine exchanges between China and Myanmar in 2021 and early 2022 through process-tracing, analyse the strategic interactions and offer an explanation as to why China changed from a (seemingly) neutral stance immediately after the coup to gradually leaning towards the military in the later months.

The chapter is organised as follows. After the introduction, China's diplomatic interactions immediately after the coup (including the Chinese media's take on the coup) and in the later months (including the advancement of each BRI project summed up in an easily comprehensible table) are described. This is followed by an analysis of China's shifting attitude. Finally, the conclusion sums up the findings of the research.

China's ambiguous stance towards Myanmar following the coup

The relationship between China and Myanmar was relatively warm during the Aung San Suu Kyi administration, which, among other things, suggests that China had relatively few border security concerns (although the authors acknowledge that many specifics are at play along the Myanmar–China border). The interactions between state officials during this period focused mainly on economics. Just a few weeks before the coup, Chinese Foreign Minister Wang Yi visited Myanmar, discussing cooperation with Aung San Suu Kyi and President Win Myint and promising COVID-19 assistance (CMoFA 2021). Wang was the first foreign minister invited to visit Myanmar after its general elections in November 2020, confirming the importance attached to Myanmar's neighbour on the one hand, and China's support for the National League for Democracy (NLD) government (which won a landslide in the elections) on the other.

Immediately following the coup, Beijing was extremely cautious in its comments as to what had happened in Myanmar. While other countries expressed serious concern and denounced the military's actions, China merely took note of the situation and turned a blind eye to the military coup (Tiezzi 2021a). Indeed, to avoid 'picking a side', China opposed the UN Human Rights Council's calls for the release of Aung San Suu Kyi, insisting that Myanmar's 'internal affair' should not be interfered with (Cook 2021). When thousands of Myanmar people took to the streets to join peaceful protests and were shot at by the military, various countries and groupings, such as the European Union and G7, issued statements demanding that the military refrain from violence against demonstrators. On 11 February, the United States announced sanctions on the junta leaders and several companies and other countries followed suit, such as Britain and Canada on 18 February and the European Union on 22 March (ANFREL 2021; Reuters 2021c). Countries such as Japan, India and Australia called for the return of democracy in Myanmar. China remained silent (Reuters 2021a).

China's initial reservations towards the situation in Myanmar are reflected in Chinese media reports. For example, Xinhua, the official Chinese state-run media, referred to the coup as a 'cabinet reshuffle' (Xinhua 2021a) in the newspaper's English-language version. Similar language was adopted by the *People's Daily*, the largest state-controlled newspaper in China. On 2 February, the day after the military deposed the NLD government, Xinhua released an article entitled 'Major Cabinet Reshuffle Announced in Myanmar' (Xinhua 2021a). The same article was published in Chinese, with a direct translation of 'cabinet reshuffle' (政治改组) (Xinhua 2021b). The official website of the *People's Daily* contained a similar report, also avoiding the word 'coup' (政变). The content and reporting style was consistent in both English and Chinese. As the official state media is directly controlled and monitored by the Central Committee of the Chinese Communist Party (CCP), the tone and reporting directly reflected the government's attitude, signalling its reluctance to condemn the military takeover. However, while official state media reports downplayed any mention of the violence that occurred in the wake of the coup, Chinese local media outlets, targeting Chinese audiences, were less hesitant. Large newspapers not directly owned by the CCP, such as the *Southern Weekly* and *Beijing News*, described the military takeover as a coup. Likewise, a page on Baidu Baike, the Chinese version of Wikipedia, was created under the name '2.1 Myanmar Coup' (Baidu 2021). The difference in tone between the official state media (representing the government's stance and targeting foreign audiences) and those directed at Chinese citizens reflected China's dual agenda. Domestically, the long-term objective was to maintain China's own power; in a sense, reporting on the 'undemocratic' misery of foreign nations could be seen as strengthening the government's legitimacy by increasing the relative satisfaction felt by its citizens towards their own national environment. Internationally, however, the government chose to be more reserved in order to optimise its international leverage.

In Myanmar, the image of China has been severely damaged for a long period of time. During the years of military rule in Burma/Myanmar (1962–2011), China provided economic assistance, cheap loans, trade, investment, and military and diplomatic support in return for access to Myanmar's natural resources. Myanmar people remember this support as having neglected the voice of the people under suppression. Mistrust of China also runs deep among the armed forces, and reducing dependency on China was one of the key motivations for the Myanmar military to initiate political reforms to the quasi-democratic system in 2011 (Kironska 2020). Although Myanmar's civilian NLD government cooperated more broadly with the Chinese than its military had done, Chinese projects were still attacked for not creating enough jobs for locals, not treating Myanmar workers the same as Chinese workers and not adhering to environmental standards.

Given this strong anti-Chinese sentiment in Myanmar and Beijing's lack of a firm stance on the Myanmar coup in the initial weeks, it is not surprising that China was accused of involvement in the coup. Many rumours circulated on the internet—for example, that Chinese airplanes had been seen transporting technical staff to Myanmar to help build a firewall and that Chinese soldiers were present in the streets of Myanmar. Chinese officials denied such rumours, calling them 'complete nonsense and totally ridiculous' (*Chinanews* 2021). The Chinese Ambassador to Myanmar Chen Hai stated that China was 'not informed in advance of the political change in Myanmar' and that the situation was not something China wanted to see (EoPRC 2021a). However, Facebook was flooded with posts blaming the Chinese; people in Myanmar began boycotting Chinese products and posting images of what not to buy—for example, big white onions were deemed to have originated in China, and people were encouraged to buy the smaller (local) ones instead. During a protest against China in April, a Chinese flag was burned in Yangon, and pictures were circulated on the internet.

In March 2021, dozens of Chinese-financed factories in Yangon were attacked and some were destroyed by arson. It was not clear how the attacks began, but the Chinese Embassy released a statement saying they were 'completely nasty' (EoPRC 2021b). Taiwan's de facto embassy in Myanmar advised Taiwanese companies operating in the country to fly the island's flag and hang signs stating they were from Taiwan to avoid being confused with Chinese companies (Reuters 2021d). Chinese officials condemned the perpetrators and urged Myanmar officials to prevent any further violence to ensure the safety of Chinese citizens and Chinese-owned businesses in Myanmar. The coup leader reassured Beijing that his regime would protect foreign-funded enterprises and, a few weeks later, the military tribunal sentenced 28 people to 20 years in prison for the attacks, signalling to China the seriousness of this promise (Reuters 2021b). China's reaction to the arson—blaming the protesters and only mentioning financial damage without considering the people killed by the junta—and, later, its presence at a military parade to celebrate the annual Armed Forces Day in Naypyidaw on 27 March (along with representatives from seven other countries), angered Myanmar's pro-democracy movement.

China's assets in Myanmar were again attacked in the following months. In May 2021, guards at the Mandalay off-take station of the oil and gas pipelines were killed (*Irrawaddy* 2021b). In June, a bomb exploded at a Chinese clothing factory in Ayeyarwady Region (*Irrawaddy* 2021a). In January 2022, electricity pylons supplying a China-backed nickel-processing plant in Sagaing Region were blown up by the local People's Defence Forces, forcing production to halt (*Irrawaddy* 2022a). China was concerned with its projects from the onset of the coup and requested as early as February 2021 that the military regime tighten security measures, to which the coup leader gave his reassurances.

China's shift towards an increasingly positive attitude towards the junta

From its initial ambiguity, China moved to officially supporting the efforts of the Association of Southeast Asian Nations (ASEAN) to assist Myanmar to address the situation, basically using the association as a proxy. China emphasised the principle of noninterference in other countries' internal affairs and promoted restoring stability 'the ASEAN way'. Beijing emphasised the 'three avoidances': prevent violence (on all sides), prevent foreign influence and prevent intervention by the Security Council (*China Daily* 2021). This would lessen pressure on the Myanmar military and prevent it from collapsing, which China did not want to see because it expected the military to continue to play a role in Myanmar's future.

Although it took some time, China also made contact with Myanmar's shadow government. China is known for its multilayered approach, utilising its government-to-government, party-to-party and people-to-people policies to widen contacts (and leverage). In the past, following this approach, it managed to play the ethnic armed groups in the border region against the central government, securing for itself an official role in Myanmar's (failed) peace process (Lintner 2021). After a phone call between the Chinese Embassy and a member of the Committee Representing the Pyidaungsu Hluttaw (legislative body in exile, created after the coup) was made public, the NLD was invited to attend an online meeting (as one of four parties from Myanmar and others from South and Southeast Asia) on 'Political Parties' Cooperation in Joint Pursuit of Economic Development' organised by the CCP, a party-to-party platform, in September 2021. At the same time in the international arena, China helped broker an agreement to block the Myanmar junta from addressing the United Nations General Assembly, thereby delaying efforts by the junta to push the United Nations to recognise it as Myanmar's legitimate representative.

With all this balancing, China still edged increasingly closer to recognising Myanmar's military regime, having previously avoided explicitly picking a side. As time passed and the likelihood of the NLD government returning to power diminished, it became more geopolitically beneficial for China to embrace friendly relations with the newly established military regime. After the junta leader and his foreign minister met the Chinese ambassador, the embassy's Facebook statement identified the senior general as the 'Leader of Myanmar' (CEM 2021). Chinese state-run media followed suit. China's lean towards the military junta was confirmed in June 2021 when the junta was invited to the third BRI meeting (held online), the special ASEAN–China Foreign Ministers meeting in Chongqing (where the junta's foreign minister, Wunna Maung Lwin, had a one-on-one informal session with the Chinese foreign minister) and the Mekong-Lancang Cooperation meeting with other foreign ministers from the Mekong region (Tiezzi 2021b). At the last-mentioned meeting, the bloc approved 22 projects to be implemented in Myanmar, for which more than USD6 million was to be transferred from the Chinese government to the Myanmar military (Strangio 2021). China's special envoy for Asia, Sun Guoxiang, also travelled to Myanmar twice (in August and November 2021) to meet with top military leaders and lobby support for the junta's attendance at the China–ASEAN leaders' summit in November; however, ASEAN decided to exclude the military regime from the leaders' summit (*Frontier Myanmar* 2021). China also assisted the junta with the delivery of COVID-19 vaccines, including donating some of them.

In 2022, this trend in the development of China–Myanmar relations persisted; although Myanmar's military continued facing domestic resistance and struggled to consolidate its power, Beijing grew closer to the military regime. In April, China's ambassador to Myanmar, Chen Hai, held meetings with the Union Election Commission to discuss the planned elections, as did India's ambassador (*Irrawaddy* 2022b). That month, Chinese Foreign Minister Wang Yi met with his junta counterpart, Wunna Maung Lwin, in Anhui province, China, where he promised to continue China's COVID-19 support and encouraged the development of deeper relations by pushing forward the China–Myanmar Economic Corridor and other landmark projects (CMoFA 2022). Wang reiterated China's support of 'the ASEAN way' in resolving the conflict in Myanmar and 'working with Myanmar constructively'.

Myanmar civil society reacted to the strengthening of relations between the two states with an open letter to Xi Jinping warning that Chinese projects in Myanmar could be targeted if China continued to cooperate with the junta. The authors of the letter, written on behalf of 558 Myanmar organisations, claimed that China's engagement with the junta was legitimising the military regime in the country (Progressive Voice 2022).

China's strategy in terms of its engagement with Myanmar is driven by its geopolitical and strategic interests in Myanmar. As Myanmar represents a close neighbour, involving a number of important BRI projects and providing important geopolitical access in the Asia-Pacific, China has a strong interest in remaining relatively friendly with the country. The junta, for its part, is eager to advance the previously agreed and commenced projects in the country, as it is again becoming internationally isolated. The junta ousted all civilian government members of the China–Myanmar Economic Corridor Joint Committee and replaced them with their own appointees as it pushed ahead with plans to implement Chinese projects that were part of the BRI. Table 6.1 presents a comprehensive list of, and updates on, the BRI projects in Myanmar following the coup.

Table 6.1: Projects under the BRI's 1,700-kilometre-long China–Myanmar Economic Corridor

She Gas and Oil Pipelines

The 771-kilometre-long gas and oil pipelines, implemented by the China National Petroleum Corporation and Myanmar Oil and Gas Enterprise, have run from Myanmar's Rakhine State to China's Yunnan Province since 2013 (gas) and 2014 (oil). With an annual transport capacity of 22 million tons of oil and 12 billion cubic metres of gas, the pipelines currently run at a quarter gas capacity and half oil capacity. They constitute less than 10 per cent of all piped gas imports to China and about 2 per cent of all oil imports to China.

Development after the coup

Officials from both countries held an emergency meeting in February 2022, at which Chinese officials urged the military regime to tighten security measures for the pipelines, a request first made in September the previous year. In February 2022, a take-off station of the pipelines was damaged as a result of attacks from a local resistance group.

Shwe Natural Gas

This project consists of several offshore gas fields in the Bay of Bengal (discovered in 2004) and is being developed by a consortium of six companies from Myanmar (Myanmar Oil and Gas Enterprise), China, Korea and India. Production began in 2013 after the completion of the first of three phases.

Development after the coup

POSCO DAEWOO Corporation, the project operator, is currently undertaking the second and third phases of development. The first gas from phase two is expected in the second quarter of 2022.

Kyaukphyu Special Economic Zone (SEZ)

The project gives China direct access to the Indian Ocean. A framework agreement for its development by China's state-run CITIC Group was signed in 2018. During Xi Jinping's official visit to Myanmar in 2020, China and Myanmar agreed to push forward with the project.

Development after the coup

Preparations have been made to seize 250 acres of land in the proposed area, and the SEZ management committee has been reorganised. In August 2021, the military regime invited bids to provide legal services to the SEZ and Deep Sea Port projects. In September 2021, CITIC announced that a consortium had signed with another Chinese company to conduct consultancy services and a preliminary field investigation. In October 2022, a gas-fired power plant was opened by the Chinese ambassador to Myanmar, Chen Hai.

Kyaukphyu Deep Sea Port

This project, approved to continue in 2020, is being built by CITIC Group in Myanmar's Rakhine State. It is part of the Kyaukphyu SEZ, 105 kilometres from the Sittwe Port in Rakhine State, a deepwater port constructed by India in 2016. It provides China with direct access to the Indian Ocean and the Bay of Bengal, where India is developing a new naval base for nuclear submarines and ships (Project Varsha).

Development after the coup

In August 2021, the military regime invited bids to provide legal services to the Deep Sea Port and SEZ projects. In September, an agreement to conduct preliminary field investigation work for the project was signed.

Myitsone Dam

The dam project (a cascade of seven dams) in the state of Kachin was being implemented by the state-owned China Power Investment Corporation and the Myanmar conglomerate Asia World and was allegedly designed to supply 90 per cent of its electricity to China. President Thein Sein suspended the project in September 2011, after widespread opposition.

Development after the coup

In February 2021, the junta announced the resumption of an unnamed hydropower project, but the Myitsone Dam project remains suspended.

Letpadaung Copper Mine

The mine is located in the Sagaing Region and, since 2011, has been operated by Wanbao Mining (a subsidiary of NORINCO, a Chinese state-owned conglomerate with interests in arms manufacturing and mining) in partnership with the Union of Myanmar Economic Holdings. The Myanmar government receives 51 per cent of shares from royalties and income tax. It began shipping copper in 2016. Since 2012, locals have been protesting against the project.

Development after the coup

In February 2021, the mine stopped operations after thousands of employees joined the Civil Disobedience Movement (some operations continued to run staffed by Chinese labourers); however, it has since resumed operation. In April 2022, the military promised to deploy troops to protect the mine after several attacks.

127

Three border economic cooperation zones

The three border economic cooperation zones are located in Muse (Shan State), Chin Shwe Haw (Shan State, part of the Kokang Self-Administered Zone; this gateway provides the shortest route from Kunming to Kyaukphyu) and Kanpiketi (Kachin State).

Development after the coup

The junta reorganised the three working committees of the cross-border economic cooperation zones:

1. *Muse:* No update since the second meeting of the bilateral local working group on the China–Myanmar Ruili-Muse Border Economic Cooperation Zone was held in 2020. The border has also been closed due to COVID-19.
2. *Chin Shwe Haw:* In May 2021, the military regime and officials from the Kokang Administration Department discussed reviving the 125 border zone (destroyed in 2017 during attacks by an ethnic armed group).
3. *Kanpiketi:* In May 2021, the regime-controlled investment commission gave the green light to begin the construction of this project.

Kunming–Muse–Mandalay–Kyaukphyu/Yangon railway and road

The project aims to run from Kunming to Mandalay and from there to Kyaukphyu and Yangon. Construction began in 2011 but has been delayed due to fighting between the Myanmar military and ethnic armed groups. The Kunming–Kyaukpyu railway and pipeline constitute one of the most critical veins of the BRI, as it provides China with access to the Indian Ocean.

Development after the coup

On the Chinese side, a new rail line was opened in August 2021 stretching from Chengdu to Lincang (opposite Chin Shwe Haw). On the Myanmar side, there was no development other than a feasibility study. The first trial of the China–Myanmar corridor took place with a cargo of 60 containers being sent by road from Yangon to Chin Shwe Haw, then by train from Lincang to Chengdu.

New Yangon city

This project, on the west bank of the Yangon River and occupying a proposed 20,000-acre area, is led by the Yangon Region Government and the China Communication Construction Company. In January 2021, Xi Jinping referred to the project as one of the three pillars of the China–Myanmar Economic Corridor. The project is controversial because of its flood-prone location and because of corruption allegations against the China Communication Construction Company.

Development after the coup

In March 2021, the military regime held a meeting with officials playing vital roles in the implementation of the project. Officials have been instructed to finalise the land acquisition process to move construction of the project forward.

Source: Compiled by the authors from various sources.

Explaining China's shifting attitude

To analyse and understand this shifting attitude towards Myanmar's military since the coup, we take the lens of China as a strategic player and examine its economic and political interests both domestically and internationally when engaging with the junta. It is important to note that, as Chinese diplomatic exchanges have traditionally been with those holding power, the coup has placed the Myanmar military in the ruling position and, thus, as the main player. Although China's relations with other actors—the shadow government, the NLD and ethnic armed groups—have also been important in the wake of the coup, analysing Beijing's move towards Myanmar's military may provide some insight into the possible future direction of China–Myanmar relations.

Following its rapid economic expansion at the turn of the century, China now presents itself as an important global player, capable of influencing, and seeking to influence, the global norm (Chhabra et al. 2020). Especially since Xi took power in 2012, economic and political influence has been prominent in the Chinese agenda, with the BRI arguably the first step in China's grand strategy (Clarke 2017, 71–9). The BRI constitutes an important part of China's interests, both economically and politically. The expansion and successful completion of BRI projects will help China to become a global norm shaper, attracting more countries to engage with it. The success of the BRI is likely to have an even more important symbolic meaning, especially in light of rising competition from the West, such as the Partnership for Global Infrastructure and Investment (PGII), a G7 initiative aiming to provide investment to developing countries. China's BRI projects also provide effective economic leverage and can be used as coercive tools in socialising countries to behave in ways that favour Chinese interests.

The BRI projects also provide certain leverages to Myanmar. As shown in the previous section, Myanmar is a host to many infrastructure and energy projects. Due to its geographic proximity to China, Myanmar is home to an important section of the belt and road, connecting directly to inner China. In other words, significant parts of the belt and road could not be completed without Myanmar. In this case, a strategic decision that accelerates ongoing projects or one that leads to additional economic engagements could establish further economic and political ties and build a good reputation for the BRI and further Chinese engagement globally. However, a decision that leads to the cancellation of projects or even more stagnation could incur a reputational cost and could potentially have a spillover effect on other recipients, leading them to reject BRI projects in their countries.

The BRI is certainly not the only factor influencing China. Maintaining a certain international reputation is important for China—although this has been variable in recent years. As a member of numerous international bodies, China needs to consider the reaction of the international community when making decisions. It is in China's interest to maintain a favourable image among countries in which it holds a strategic interest, even though some may not align with it ideologically, especially in the Asia-Pacific region. A good and well-maintained reputation can bring additional economic exchanges and help to avoid economic sanctions or trade wars caused by disagreements or hostile public opinions in democratic countries. In the case of Myanmar, ASEAN's opinion is particularly relevant to China. Given the negative attitude of most ASEAN countries towards the coup, China needed to consider the potential downturn of some established relations should it show support for the coup.

Military interests, or security concerns, are arguably the most important of China's strategic interests, as they directly affect the regime's survival. Military interests include both short-term border security as well as long-term geopolitical risks. The Chinese government has historically used nationalism (often arising from territorial concerns and disputes) to enforce its legitimacy and minimising security risks remains a priority for internal stability (Downs & Saunders 1998). Such concerns are especially salient in interactions with neighbouring states (e.g. Myanmar), as geographical proximity can pose immediate threats to border security, including a possible refugee crisis. China, with its strict refugee policy, is neither well equipped nor particularly willing to handle a large inflow of refugees. Further, it has its own security problems (e.g. separatist movements troubling the CCP), making the additional cost of a neighbouring refugee crisis too high.

Comparing the perceived outcomes of the above interests for each possible position China could take helps to explain its shifting attitude towards the Myanmar military. There are three possible stances or attitudes China could adopt: positive, neutral or negative. In the early period immediately following the coup, the attitude of the military, its willingness to work with Beijing and the likelihood of its survival were relatively unknown. Officially endorsing the Myanmar military could have resulted in BRI projects moving (faster) forward if the military was willing to work with Beijing.

However, the coup attracted considerable international attention, and openly supporting the military could have damaged China's international reputation, thus increasing the risk of its relations with the West, and possibly also ASEAN countries, turning negative. Therefore, in the immediate wake of the coup, China's open support of the military could have brought more cost than benefit.

Public condemnation of the regime would also have yielded a negative result, as it would have alienated the military, causing China to lose one of its important allies in the region. A damaged relationship with the Myanmar military may have resulted in less effort being expended to maintain the China–Myanmar border, leading to possible conflicts and unwanted refugees. Moreover, such action could have resulted in the cancellation of many ongoing BRI projects, incurring both economic and reputational costs to China. Consequently, given the level of uncertainty immediately following the coup, taking a definite position of either support for, or condemnation of, the military posed a high risk of negative effects on Chinese interests. Thus, China chose to appear neutral, as this approach was less likely to induce a negative downturn in its relations with Myanmar. This helps to explain the Chinese government's initially ambiguous attitude towards the Myanmar military, including its reluctance to call what occurred a 'coup' while also avoiding statements that would declare the junta a 'government'.

As the months went by, however, the situation changed. International attention diminished and with it the risk to China's reputation, as well as the risk of international sanctions being imposed on China. In fact, holding a seemingly neutral position posed its own risks, including loss of reputation, as it made China appear indecisive. When it became clear that China's apparent neutrality could not be maintained long term, the government was forced to take a position. By then it had become clear that the junta was willing to cooperate with Beijing. As the Myanmar military gradually took decisive control over economic and infrastructure projects across the country (thus increasing its leverage over China), it became clear that holding a positive attitude towards the military could lead to potential economic gains through moving BRI projects forward and deepening political ties with the military. As the alternative—adopting a negative attitude towards the military and/or continuing to appear neutral—would most likely have had negative effects on Chinese interests and incurred other costs, it made sense for China to adopt a more positive and friendly stance towards the military. This helps to explain China's shifting attitude in the later months of the crisis.

Conclusion

Beijing's initially ambiguous attitude towards the coup neither favoured the Myanmar military nor the protest movement headed by the shadow government. As time passed, China edged increasingly closer towards recognising Myanmar's military regime. This chapter has outlined the major exchanges between China and Myanmar following the February 2021 coup and documented Beijing's shifting attitude, in which it first attempted to appear neutral and gradually became more friendly towards the military. Analysing China's strategic interests in relation to Myanmar, the authors found that China's initial hesitation stemmed largely from the possibility of a decline in economic and political power and security issues. In the beginning, when criticism of the military was widely circulating, open support for the military would have damaged China's reputation, increased the risk of possible international sanctions and prompted a decline in China's global political power. Conversely, China's open condemnation of the regime could also have negatively impacted its balance of power and incurred a security risk. Thus, appearing neutral was the option most likely to best serve China's strategic interests.

In the months following the coup, the situation changed. As international attention on the Myanmar crisis lessened, the risk to China's reputation and threat of possible sanctions decreased. At the risk of being seen as an indecisive international actor, China decided to take a more affirmative and supportive stance. The following statement from the 13th National People's Congress of China illustrates China's position: 'No matter how the situation evolves, China will not waver in its commitment to advancing China–Myanmar relations and will not change the course of promoting friendship and cooperation' (Xinhua 2021c). One should not forget that Myanmar is geopolitically important to China in terms of its commitment to advancing its BRI projects and two-ocean strategy.

Although China has traditionally been cautious and avoided direct conflict when dealing with Western countries, the time of cautious diplomatic exchange seems to be over. China's soft power and reputational power is now limited in the West. Consequently, in the future, China is likely to be more direct—even bold—in its condemnation of other countries. Its recent open alignment with bodies such as the Taliban indicates that Beijing is less and less concerned about its reputation in the West. As a result, when dealing with China, Western countries will need to understand that China is likely to be more assertive and, to a certain extent, more extreme.

When dealing with Myanmar, countries such as Australia need to be aware that, as time goes by, China is likely to be a stronger ally to the Myanmar military. Further, China is unlikely to contribute to, and will probably oppose, any moves by international actors to engage with the Myanmar shadow government.

Funding

This work was supported by the European Regional Development Fund, 'Sinophone Borderlands—Interaction at the Edges', CZ.02.1.01/0.0/0.0/ 16_019/0000791.

References

ANFREL (Asian Network for Free Election). 2021. 'Myanmar Situation Update'. 1–14 February. anfrel.org/wp-content/uploads/2021/03/Myanmar-Situation-Update-1-to-14-February-2021.pdf

Baidu. 2021. 'Myanmar in State of Emergency'. 1 February. baike.baidu.com/item/ 2·1缅甸紧急状态/56029899?fr=aladdin&fromtitle=2·1缅甸政变&fromid= 55964656#reference-%5B20%5D-31482699-wrap

CEM (Chinese Embassy in Myanmar). 2021. 'The Leader of Myanmar Senior General Min Aung Hlaing Met with Chinese Ambassador to Myanmar'. Facebook, 5 June. www.facebook.com/paukphawfriendship/posts/4011208475621842

Chhabra, Tarun, Rush Doshi, Ryan Hass and Emilie Kimball. 2020. *Global China: Global Governance and Norms*. Washington, DC: Brookings Institution. www. brookings.edu/research/global-china-global-governance-and-norms/

China Daily. 2021. 'Wang Yi Talks about the "Three Avoidances" for the Situation in Myanmar'. 3 April. cn.chinadaily.com.cn/a/202104/03/WS6067cadda3101 e7ce97476c9.html

Chinanews. 2021. 'People's Daily: The International Community Should Create a Favourable Environment for Myanmar to Properly Resolve Differences'. 4 February. www.chinanews.com.cn/gj/2021/02-04/9404107.shtml

Clarke, Michael. 2017. 'The Belt and Road Initiative: China's New Grand Strategy?' *National Bureau of Asian Research*, no. 24: 71–9. doi.org/10.1353/asp.2017. 0023

CMoFA (Chinese Ministry of Foreign Affairs). 2021. 'Myanmar's President U Win Myint Meets with Wang Yi'. 11 January. www.mfa.gov.cn/ce/cgla//eng/topnews/t1846055.htm (page discontinued).

CMoFA (Chinese Ministry of Foreign Affairs). 2022. 'Wang Yi Holds Talks with Myanmar's Foreign Minister U Wunna Maung Lwin'. 1 April. www.fmprc.gov.cn/eng/zxxx_662805/202204/t20220402_10663718.html

Cook, Pip. 2021. 'Myanmar Coup: UN Human Rights Council Calls for Release of Aung San Suu Kyi'. Geneva Solutions. genevasolutions.news/peace-humanitarian/myanmar-coup-un-human-rights-council-calls-for-release-of-aung-san-suu-kyi

Downs, Erica Strecker and Philip C. Saunders. 1998. 'Legitimacy and the Limits of Nationalism: China and the Diaoyu Islands'. *International Security* 14 (3): 114–46. doi.org/10.2307/2539340

EoPRC (Embassy of the People's Republic of China). 2021a. 'Chinese Embassy Spokesperson Statement'. 14 February. www.mfa.gov.cn/ce/cemm//chn/sgxw/t1860921.htm (page discontinued).

EoPRC (Embassy of the People's Republic of China). 2021b. 'Wang Yi Presents Three Points on the Situation in Myanmar'. 8 March. www.mfa.gov.cn/ce/cemm/chn/sgxw/t1859274.htm (page discontinued).

Frontier Myanmar. 2021. 'The Top Stories in Myanmar This Week'. 26 November. us11.campaign-archive.com/?u=038fcddd300c51ade6a49aad3&id=c3e7733342

Irrawaddy. 2021a. 'Deadly Attack on Pipeline Station Spotlights China's High Stakes in Myanmar'. 6 May. www.irrawaddy.com/news/burma/attack-oil-and-gas-pipelines-china-off-take-station-spotlight-stakes-junta-regime-protect-protesters-arson-attack-strategic-investment-unsc-support.html

Irrawaddy. 2021b. 'Bomb Explodes at Chinese-Backed Factory in Myanmar'. 11 June. www.irrawaddy.com/news/burma/bomb-explodes-at-chinese-backed-factory-in-myanmar.html

Irrawaddy. 2022a. 'Myanmar Resistance Forces China-Backed Nickel Plant Shut Down'. 18 January. www.irrawaddy.com/news/burma/myanmar-resistance-forces-china-backed-nickel-plant-shut-down.html

Irrawaddy. 2022b. 'Interest in Regime's Planned Election Reveals China and India's Disguised Support for Myanmar Junta'. 27 April. www.irrawaddy.com/news/burma/interest-in-regimes-planned-election-reveals-china-and-indias-disguised-support-for-myanmar-junta.html

Kironska, Kristina. 2020. 'The New Era of Sino-Burmese Relations: Changes in the Bilateral Relationship in View of China's Rise and Myanmar's Reforms'. *Journal of Burma Studies* 24 (2): 197–227. doi.org/10.1353/jbs.2020.0009

Lintner, Bertil. 2021. *The Wa of Myanmar and China's Quest for Global Dominance*. Chiang Mai: Silkworm Books.

Progressive Voice. 2022. 'Open Letter to President of People's Republic of China Xi Jinping'. Facebook, 26 April. www.facebook.com/progressivevoice/photos/pcb.10159677132209890/10159677131934890

Reuters. 2021a. 'Japan, US, India, Australia Call for Return of Democracy in Myanmar'. 18 February. jp.reuters.com/article/usa-blinken-quad-myanmar/japan-u-s-india-australia-call-for-return-of-democracy-in-myanmar-idUSKBN2AI208

Reuters. 2021b. 'UK and Canada Impose Sanctions on Myanmar Generals after Coup'. 18 February. www.reuters.com/article/myanmar-politics-int-idUSKBN2AI043

Reuters. 2021c. 'Taiwan Tells Firms in Myanmar to Fly Flags to Distinguish from China'. 15 March. www.reuters.com/article/myanmar-politics-taiwan-int-idUSKBN2B70CQ

Reuters. 2021d. 'Myanmar Military Tribunal Orders 20-Yr Jail Terms for Torching Chinese-Linked Factories'. 28 May. www.reuters.com/world/asia-pacific/myanmar-military-tribunal-orders-20-yr-jail-terms-torching-chinese-linked-2021-05-28/

Strangio, Sebastian. 2021. 'China Announces Aid Dispersal to Myanmar's Military Junta'. *Diplomat*, 11 August. thediplomat.com/2021/08/china-announces-aid-dispersal-to-myanmars-military-junta/

Tiezzi, Shannon. 2021a. 'What the Myanmar Coup Means for China'. *Diplomat*, 3 February. thediplomat.com/2021/02/what-the-myanmar-coup-means-for-china/

Tiezzi, Shannon. 2021b. 'China Holds Slimmed-Down Belt and Road Conference'. *Diplomat*, 25 June. thediplomat.com/2021/06/china-holds-slimmed-down-belt-and-road-conference/

Xinhua. 2021a. 'Major Cabinet Reshuffle Announced in Myanmar'. *Xinhuanet*, 2 February. www.xinhuanet.com/english/2021-02/02/c_139713877.htm

Xinhua. 2021b. 'Myanmar Army Announces Reorganization'. *Xinhuanet*, 2 February. www.xinhuanet.com/2021-02/02/c_1127051916.htm

Xinhua. 2021c. 'Chinese FM Raises Three-Point Proposal on Myanmar Situation'. *Xinhuanet*, 7 March. www.xinhuanet.com/english/2021-03/07/c_139792049.htm

7

Myanmar in ASEAN: Dilemmas, Determinants and Capacity

Moe Thuzar

Fellow, ISEAS-Yusof Ishak Institute, Singapore

Abstract

Myanmar marked a quarter-century as an ASEAN member in 2022. Accepted into the Association of Southeast Asian Nations (ASEAN) fold under a previous military regime amid international criticism, Myanmar's ASEAN membership since 1997 has presented both ASEAN and successive administrations in Myanmar with more hard experiences than teachable moments. The collaborative response to humanitarian needs after Cyclone Nargis in 2008 and the decade of Myanmar's opening and democratic transition (2011–20) offered some optimism that ASEAN's constructive engagement might prove a workable approach for Myanmar. However, the tendency of Myanmar authorities to manipulate the ASEAN space, including in the aftermath of the 2017 Rohingya exodus following military operations, provides another example of how authorities in Myanmar may resort to precedents in managing regional interventions. ASEAN's role in dealing with crises in Myanmar gained more salience after the 1 February 2021 coup. While past precedent still provides a reference, new precedents may be emerging, offering some insight into the opportunities and limitations of ASEAN's engagement with recalcitrant members, and how authorities in Myanmar view their country's membership in, and interactions with, ASEAN and, by extension, with ASEAN's external interlocutors.

***

The year 2022 marks a quarter-century of Myanmar's membership of the Association of Southeast Asian Nations (ASEAN). Myanmar's bid to join ASEAN was initiated by the State Law and Order Restoration Council military regime, which took power in 1988, quelling a nationwide democracy uprising that saw the crumbling of close to three decades of (military-dominant) socialist authoritarian rule. It has become a truism that developments in Myanmar have posed a dilemma for ASEAN, ever since Myanmar's admission into the grouping in 1997, even during the decade of democratisation from 2011 to 2021.

The military's grip on political power and its reluctance to relinquish control of the state presents the most salient aspect of this dilemma. ASEAN's responses to various crisis situations over the two and half decades also indicate the grouping's perceptions of the determinants of the dilemma and the attendant capacities in Myanmar to respond to ASEAN's interventions. The coup on 1 February 2021 presents the most serious crisis for the country, and for ASEAN's response.

This chapter reviews two past crises to illustrate ASEAN's Myanmar dilemmas, and the grouping's responses to each. The analysis seeks to identify the determinants and capacities for ASEAN's response to the current crisis in Myanmar. Specifically, the chapter examines ASEAN's response to Cyclone Nargis in 2008 and its dealings with an earlier military regime, and its response to the Rohingya refugee crisis in 2017, which erupted during the tenure of the democratically elected National League for Democracy (NLD), using these to frame analysis of ASEAN's responses to date towards the 2021 Myanmar coup. The chapter concludes with a number of policy recommendations, including engagement with Myanmar's National Unity Government (NUG)[1] and ethnic armed organisations (EAOs), not just the Tatmadaw, and strengthening work with ASEAN's dialogue partners.

---

1   The NUG emerged in April 2021 as appointees of the Committee Representing Pyidaungsu Hluttaw (CRPH), which was formed primarily with NLD lawmakers who had been initially detained in their dormitories then released in the early days of the coup. The NUG's claim to legitimacy stems from the CRPH's status as elected members of parliament. However, the SAC annulled the results of the 2020 elections, and the NUG itself is an interim entity in the political roadmap towards an envisioned federal democracy.

ASEAN responses to past crises in Myanmar

ASEAN was founded in 1967, originally with five member states.[2] Although criticised for its slow progress, ASEAN has nevertheless developed a unique geopolitical role. Over the last 20 years, it has mitigated a wide range of underlying tensions in East Asia, largely by dint of its central convening role in bringing contesting parties to the table, and a pragmatic balancing of global power pressures.

Mahbubani's (2017) observation that ASEAN's strategic diplomacy has resulted in peaceful relations in Southeast Asia, despite a high degree of ethnic, religious, political and economic diversity, uses ASEAN's experience with Myanmar as one of several examples. However, there are few precedents for ASEAN's success in overcoming internal conflicts among its members. Most ASEAN members have at least one ethnic or communal conflict within their borders that has resisted resolution for decades. Myanmar stands out as a test case, precedent and example for ASEAN's interventions. Two instances provide a benchmark of sorts for ASEAN's response to the political crisis that erupted in Myanmar after the military seized power on 1 February 2021.

Cyclone Nargis

A precedent to justify ASEAN intervening in Myanmar occurred in the aftermath of Cyclone Nargis in 2008. The cyclone devastated Myanmar's Irrawaddy delta region on 2 May 2008, causing over 130,000 fatalities. International focus on the cyclone's aftermath arose when offers of humanitarian assistance were met with reticence from the military regime then in power in Myanmar. On 19 May 2008, the ASEAN foreign ministers held a special meeting to consider assisting Myanmar with humanitarian relief. This meeting—convened by Singapore, ASEAN chair for that year—overcame the ASEAN principle of noninterference in the domestic affairs of its members, leading directly to an ASEAN-coordinated international emergency relief program. Barely six months earlier, in November 2007, Prime Minister of Myanmar Thein Sein had rejected ASEAN's suggestion to have the special envoy of the secretary-general of the United Nations (UN), Ibrahim Gambari, brief the 13th ASEAN Summit in Singapore on the

---

2   The original five were Indonesia, Malaysia, Philippines, Singapore and Thailand. Brunei joined in 1984. Vietnam was admitted in 1995, followed by Laos and Myanmar in 1997, and Cambodia in 1999.

situation in Myanmar following the September 2007 Saffron Revolution. Singapore, as ASEAN chair in 2007, issued the grouping's strongest-worded statement on Myanmar, expressing 'revulsion' at the crackdown on peaceful protests (Singapore Government 2007).[3]

ASEAN's response in May 2008 evolved in the context of a tense standoff between the international community and Myanmar's military regime, caused by the disconnect between the international community's eagerness to send aid and the military's suspicion of their motives. An ASEAN Secretariat report documenting aspects of ASEAN's response mentioned that Singapore's foreign minister, George Yeo, recalled that 'some countries had dispatched warships carrying supplies to the region and even talked openly about invoking the Responsibility to Protect' principle (Marr 2010). Yeo was referring to US Navy vessels off Myanmar's coast (the US Navy was participating in the annual 'Cobra Gold' US–Thailand joint military exercises at the time). He was also referring to the French foreign minister's proposal to invoke the UN's 'Responsibility to Protect' (R2P) clause and deliver aid directly to the Myanmar people without waiting for approval from the military government. Myanmar's military junta saw the R2P invocation as blatantly disrespectful of the ASEAN principle of noninterference in a member country's domestic affairs. But, in May 2008, ASEAN itself played the R2P card as one of three options open to Myanmar:

1. a UN-led mechanism for managing the post-Nargis relief and reconstruction effort
2. an ASEAN-led mechanism, in which ASEAN would be at the forefront of a coalition of neighbouring countries and other competent organisations; specifically, ASEAN would work together with the Myanmar government to manage access by the coalition partners in implementing relief and reconstruction programs in the affected area
3. the delivery of aid by force, if necessary, on the basis of the R2P principle.

The State Peace and Development Council regime acceded to the second option. Four days after the special ASEAN Foreign Ministers' Meeting, it allowed relief workers into the country irrespective of nationality. Subsequently, the international humanitarian community has had the opportunity to openly maintain a presence in Myanmar.

---

3   The statement was issued by Singapore, in its ASEAN chair capacity, on the sidelines of the United Nations General Assembly in New York. It was done with Myanmar's full knowledge and acquiescence.

At the 19 May 2008 meeting, ASEAN foreign ministers also took the first step towards creating an ASEAN-led tripartite coordination mechanism. They established the ASEAN Humanitarian Task Force to work closely with the UN and the Myanmar Government. ASEAN also led the ASEAN–UN Pledging Conference in Yangon on 25 May 2008. Representatives of countries that had been treating Myanmar as a pariah state for its human rights abuses set aside politics and attended the conference along with representatives from ASEAN member countries and other Asian countries. The Humanitarian Task Force established a formal implementation mechanism involving ASEAN, the UN and Myanmar, called the Tripartite Core Group (TCG), to organise immediate assistance and undertake a post-Nargis joint assessment.

Although not an instrument to bring about political change in Myanmar, the TCG mechanism showed Myanmar government officials over the next two years new ways of working with a wide range of interest groups, both domestic and foreign, without upsetting the established political order. Frank discussions in the TCG led to the streamlining of several rigid and lengthy bureaucratic processes, and also exposed Myanmar's military to humanitarian operations.

ASEAN's initiative to broker and lead the coordination of international humanitarian response to Myanmar, and its calling attention to issues requiring special engagement with Myanmar, set a precedent for future ASEAN responses to crises in Myanmar. Since 2008, ASEAN's cross-border coordination role has evolved and expanded, despite the institutional hurdles of the noninterference and consensus principles.[4]

ASEAN and Rohingya repatriation

Another defining moment occurred at a special ASEAN Foreign Ministers' Meeting in Myanmar on 19 November 2016. It was the first time ASEAN foreign ministers had been invited by a member country to discuss a domestic conflict, namely the escalating pattern of attacks in Rakhine State on the Muslim community self-identified as Rohingya. Myanmar's stance up to that point, under both military (pre-2011) and Union Solidarity and Development Party (USDP) (2011–16) regimes, had been to insist on the domestic nature of the issue and refuse to have the topic

---

4   The 'consensus principle' requires that all formal decisions by ASEAN be adopted with the agreement of all ASEAN members.

tabled for ASEAN's discussion agenda. An important factor enabling this meeting was the recognition of the potential trans-boundary impacts of this internal conflict on other ASEAN members (e.g. human trafficking and migration), necessitating discussion of humanitarian and other responses from a regionally coordinated viewpoint. Another factor was that Aung San Suu Kyi, head of the country's new civilian-led government, showed a willingness to brief ASEAN counterparts. This suggests that ASEAN's quiet diplomacy approach, led by Indonesian Foreign Minister Retno Masurdi in this instance, was still preferred for managing sensitive and difficult topics, regardless of whether the Myanmar leadership was civilian or military.

Nonetheless, the careful language used in the Indonesian Ministry of Foreign Affairs' statement on the matter (CabSecRI 2017), and Minister Retno's factual recounting of ASEAN's role and Indonesia's initiative (Asia Society 2017), indicate that the NLD government's willingness to cooperate with ASEAN was still limited to, or framed within, the humanitarian assistance sphere. This attitude constrained any potentially constructive interventions that ASEAN could have initiated or instituted for an ongoing process for addressing the Rohingya issue, even within the bounds of the recommendations presented by the Advisory Commission on Rakhine led by former UN secretary-general Kofi Annan. The NLD government had just announced its commitment to implementing that commission's 88 recommendations when the military crackdown on Rohingya communities commenced on 25 August 2017 (Callahan 2018).

To address the consequences of the 2017 exodus, ASEAN's proposal to assist Myanmar with the Rohingya repatriation followed the Nargis precedent, although the communities in question and attitudes in Myanmar towards the problem could not have been more different. The NLD government started its Rohingya response by emphasising peace and development in Rakhine State, and prioritising a civilian-led coordination of responses to humanitarian needs in Rakhine. It established the Union Enterprise on Humanitarian Assistance, Resettlement and Development in Rakhine on 17 October 2017, with direct oversight by the State Counsellor's Office. The NLD government's emphasis on this initiative as the vehicle for humanitarian and other assistance in Rakhine, and its preference for bilateral initiatives over a regional response, indicate Myanmar's unease with having the Rohingya issue discussed in a regional or multilateral setting, despite the recognition among policymakers dealing with this issue that a do-nothing approach or insistence that this was a domestic matter was no longer an option. If Myanmar had to accept external intervention on this issue, the ASEAN platform presented a more favourable space for the authorities in Myanmar.

The 2019 State of Southeast Asia survey conducted by the ASEAN Studies Centre at the ISEAS-Yusof Ishak Institute reveals Myanmar's preferences. Close to 60 per cent of respondents in Myanmar preferred that ASEAN mediate between the Myanmar government and other stakeholders. A relatively large minority (41.4 per cent) of respondents viewed the issue as Myanmar's domestic affair, and only a few (7.1 per cent) wanted diplomatic pressure on Myanmar. Regionally, the most preferred option was mediation (66.5 per cent), with humanitarian assistance (50.9 per cent) and diplomatic pressure (38 per cent) as second and third preferences, respectively.

The 2017 Rohingya crisis response revealed Myanmar's ability to manoeuvre within the ASEAN space. The deployment of an ASEAN-coordinated needs assessment team for the repatriation process was delayed as a result of the repatriation process itself being delayed. The ASEAN secretary-general visited Myanmar in December 2018 and May 2019 to discuss ASEAN's role in helping Myanmar address repatriation and other related concerns. A preliminary needs assessment report in 2019 identified three potential areas of cooperation: enhancing capacity of reception and transit centres, strengthening information dissemination and supporting the provision of basic services (AHA Centre 2019).

It should be noted that the Rohingya and other sectors of the international community have subsequently been critical of ASEAN's response to the Rohingya crisis. In particular, concerns have been expressed that Myanmar authorities may have used ASEAN's preliminary needs assessment report to downplay the impact of the 2017 violence against Rohingya communities.

Since 2017, ASEAN's key statements have included a paragraph on the current status of the regional response in Myanmar. Hopes for a safe and voluntary return of the Rohingya have been hampered by the security situation in Rakhine State and, more recently, by the COVID-19 pandemic. However, the underlying and main concern behind the Rohingyas' reluctance to be repatriated on a voluntary basis remains the history of persecution and systematic discrimination they have faced, mainly at the hands of Myanmar's security apparatus. The February 2021 coup has further complicated matters. The State Administration Council (SAC) junta initially indicated some interest in restarting repatriation talks with

Bangladesh, but, in an interview with Chinese-language Phoenix Television in May 2021, Senior General Min Aung Hlaing denied the possibility of accepting a return of Rohingya refugees to Myanmar (Reuters 2022a).[5]

ASEAN and Myanmar after the 1 February 2021 coup

When the military seized power in February 2021, deposing the NLD government, ASEAN initially turned to its past experience with military regimes in Myanmar as a way forward. However, there were some nuances in its approach that signalled a different attitude. For example, although occasional references were made to its (only) successful intervention in Myanmar (i.e. the Nargis response), other developments showed that ASEAN was breaking, somewhat, with its past practices regarding Myanmar. It should be noted, however, that these developments only started in October 2021, eight months after the coup began. Prior to that, ASEAN faced a credibility challenge, both in Myanmar and internationally, due to its response to the coup. Further, despite these nuances, some doubts remain as to whether ASEAN can maintain its credibility and centrality in responding to what may constitute its most serious internal challenge to date.

Although ASEAN issued a statement a day after the coup, it was not until March 2021 that ASEAN foreign ministers convened to prepare for a leaders' meeting on Myanmar, which finally took place on 24 April 2021. At the meeting, ASEAN heads of state and government met with Senior General Min Aung Hlaing and agreed upon a Five-Point Consensus[6] that called for a cessation of violence and a mediated dialogue among key stakeholders to find a peaceful solution. The SAC's subsequent conflation of the Five-Point Consensus with its own political roadmap affected internal perceptions

---

5   The Myanmar military channel, Myawady, has published the full transcript (in English) of Min Aung Hlaing's interview, see www.myawady.net.mm/content/phoenix-tv-people%E2%80%99s-republic-china-interviews-chairman-state-administration-council (page discontinued).

6   Appended to the Chairman's Statement on the ASEAN Leaders Meeting of 24 April 2021, the Five-Point Consensus calls for: 1) immediate cessation of violence in Myanmar, 2) constructive dialogue among all parties concerned towards a peaceful solution, 3) a special envoy of the ASEAN chair to facilitate mediation, assisted by the ASEAN secretary-general, 4) humanitarian assistance through the AHA Centre and 5) the special envoy to visit Myanmar to meet with all parties concerned (ASEAN 2021). The full text of the Chairman's Statement and Five-Point Consensus is available at asean.org/wp-content/uploads/Chairmans-Statement-on-ALM-Five-Point-Consensus-24-April-2021-FINAL-a-1.pdf

of ASEAN's response to Myanmar. Meanwhile, the surge of COVID-19 infections and deaths in mid-2021 compounded the effects of the coup. The inability of regional governments (facing pandemic challenges of their own) to urgently respond to the plight of the Myanmar people caused a shift in how people in Myanmar viewed international interventions. Initial calls for R2P-type interventions gave way to calls for self-determination and a growing climate of cynicism towards regional and international diplomacy.

Nevertheless, ASEAN's decision on 15 October 2021 (BMoFA 2021) that the 38th and 39th ASEAN Summits, and related summit meetings for 2021, would invite a 'non-political representative' (i.e. a senior civil servant) from Myanmar raised some hope, as the decision effectively barred the SAC chief and his ministerial-level nominees. Even though accepting any representative associated with the SAC constituted a pragmatic acceptance of the SAC's presence at the regional table, ASEAN persisted with this approach, holding many of its sectoral meetings with SAC representatives in the Myanmar seat, at ministerial, senior official and working group levels.[7]

Currently, Myanmar is the 2022–23 rotational executive director and secretariat for ASEANAPOL, the regional mechanism for cooperation among police forces in the 10 member states. In November 2021, Myanmar assumed the rotational two-year chairmanship of ASEAN's Supreme Audit Institutions (ASEANSAI 2021). In June 2022, the SAC's defence minister attended the Defence Ministers Meeting chaired by Cambodia (MMoI 2022).

The chairman's statement at the emergency ASEAN Foreign Ministers' Meeting on 15 October 2021 (BMoFA 2021) mentioned the NUG by name. Prior to this, ASEAN had remained largely silent on the NUG, although several ASEAN member states had unilaterally made informal contact with NUG representatives. Malaysia's foreign minister, Saifuddin Abdullah, publicised his informal meeting with his NUG counterpart Zin Mar Aung on the sidelines of the ASEAN–US Summit in Washington DC in May 2022 (Reuters 2022b). Prior to this, Saifuddin had publicly called for ASEAN to collectively meet with the NUG, drawing an angry response from the SAC's foreign ministry (*Irrawaddy* 2022b).

---

7   ASEAN insiders have shared that, in the weeks and months following the February 2021 coup, the SAC insisted (in writing) that ASEAN meetings and activities accept its representatives in the Myanmar seat.

It is worth monitoring whether ASEAN's think tank community will engage more fully with NUG representatives. On 27 January 2022, the Center for Strategic and International Studies in Indonesia convened an online panel discussion on Myanmar, inviting the NUG's ambassador to ASEAN to discuss ASEAN's role in dealing with the Myanmar crisis (CSIS-Indonesia 2022). This, and another panel on 17 November featuring the NUG's deputy foreign minister discussing Indonesia's role as ASEAN chair and the Myanmar crisis, have been the only publicised instances to date.[8]

In response to ASEAN's October 2021 decision, the SAC retaliated by refusing to attend the summits under Brunei's chairmanship, and challenged ASEAN on its charter provisions regarding participation at ASEAN meetings, citing the principle of equality. ASEAN, however, upheld its decision and convened the 2021 summits, with Myanmar's Zoom screen blank.[9] ASEAN held to this default position for the ASEAN–China Special Summit in November 2021, setting a precedent for the ASEAN–US Special Summit in May 2022 and the ASEAN–India Special Foreign Ministers' Meeting in June 2022. In each instance, the SAC refused to send a non-political representative, citing the aforementioned equality principle.

These instances indicate a gradual change in ASEAN's approach to recalcitrant members—though views may differ internally regarding the available options to overcome the current Myanmar impasse. Myanmar has been ASEAN's main recalcitrant member since it joined the association in 1979, with issues such as the generals' reluctance to cede power prior

---

8   In November 2021, a project-level activity coordinated by the ASEAN Foundation with international partners included the NUG minister for the environment in the advertised list of plenary speakers for an international conference on a climate and disaster resilient ASEAN, scheduled for 22–23 November 2021. However, the actual conference took place without any NUG participation at either plenary or technical level.

In November 2022, the Foreign Policy Community Initiative (FPCI), an Indonesian think tank, invited NUG foreign minister Zin Mar Aung to give opening remarks at the Global Town Hall 2022 virtual forum, which the FPCI organised in partnership with international education and advocacy organisation Global Citizen. Zin Mar Aung's deputy, Moe Zaw Oo, was invited to participate in a panel discussion at the same event. However, FPCI had to cancel both NUG representatives participation (and apologise to them separately) due to the UN's discomfort that featuring participants from the NUG might be interpreted as taking sides in the Myanmar crisis. Global Town Hall 2022 featured several high-level participants, including former UN secretary-general Ban Ki Moon, former Australian prime minister Kevin Rudd and US Assistant Secretary of State Daniel Kritenbrink.

9   Hun Sen, the incoming ASEAN chair, was especially vocal in stating that the SAC had brought about Myanmar's absence itself.

to 2010, the Thein Sein administration's refusal to consider the Rohingya issue, and the NLD administration's scoping of the ASEAN space and available institutional mechanisms to respond to the 2017 Rohingya crisis.

For the current political crisis in Myanmar, ASEAN still adheres to the broad rubric of the Five-Point Consensus despite the SAC's glaring lack of adherence to it. On the same day that ASEAN agreed on the Five-Point Consensus (24 April 2021), the military used lethal force against protesters. The military's violence resulted in increased levels of armed resistance against the SAC across the entire length and breadth of the country by several EAOs and localised militias known as People's Defence Forces (PDFs). Some of the PDFs and young people fleeing arrest sought EAO support for urban warfare training. The Myanmar public justifies and even applauds this armed resistance to the SAC as self-defence in the face of international inaction (or inability to take action) to intervene in Myanmar. Since 7 September 2021, this armed resistance has taken the form of a 'people's defensive war'. The SAC has labelled the EAOs and PDFs, and even the NUG, as terrorists in an attempt to justify its refusal to engage in any form of dialogue. In June 2022, however, the SAC seemed to backtrack on its rhetoric with an invitation—largely ignored—for PDFs to surrender and return to civilian life (*Irrawaddy* 2022c).

ASEAN's default position regarding the SAC's representation at key, high-level political meetings highlights its awareness of: 1) the SAC's attempts to influence ASEAN's processes towards its own interests, 2) the reputational damage caused by the SAC's disregard of ASEAN's processes and 3) the regional security implications arising from the continuing violence in Myanmar. ASEAN is clear about its ability to intervene in a situation that affects regional stability. In the past, such interventions have taken the form of statements of concern, at times accompanied by quiet diplomacy.

Before taking up her appointment as the UN secretary-general's special envoy on Myanmar, Dr Noeleen Heyzer observed in March 2021 (then in her capacity as a member of the UN Secretary-General's High-Level Advisory Board on Mediation) that 'we have to accept the fact that the age of quiet diplomacy is over in the age of social media', and that 'ASEAN's diplomacy needs to reflect this new reality' (Tan Hui Yee 2021). Heyzer was herself affected by this new reality in 2022 when a remark she made in an interview about 'power sharing' with the military drew a fierce reaction from Myanmar activists and civil society organisations supporting the anti-junta movement (Vaphual & Ratcliffe 2022). Her August 2022 visit to Naypyidaw as UN special envoy also provoked criticism for seeming to accord the SAC some legitimacy. Her statements to the media post-visit (UN 2022) did not endear her to the SAC, which asserted that she had not fully reflected the SAC's perspective. The SAC published a 'full description' of the meeting in the state-run newspaper *Global New Light of Myanmar* (2022).

ASEAN has also grappled with increasing criticism of its Myanmar response since the coup. ASEAN's earlier attempts, up to the point of the April 2021 ASEAN Leaders Meeting on Myanmar, were mainly efforts to keep up with the reality of what was happening on the ground in Myanmar, and the on-ground sentiments towards the SAC's promise of elections and restoration of stability. The intensity of these on-ground sentiments, reflected in the many protests across Myanmar—including burnings of the ASEAN flag in June 2021 signalling disagreement with the ASEAN chair's move to consult the SAC on the appointment of the special envoy on Myanmar—and the online activism on social media, constituted a wake-up call, jolting ASEAN to the new reality in Myanmar.

In this context, it is important to note the forces within ASEAN driving change in practice and policy towards Myanmar. Indonesia, Singapore, Malaysia, Brunei (which was the ASEAN chair in 2021) and (sporadically) the Philippines have treated the Myanmar crisis and ASEAN's response to it as a matter of principle. For these countries, adherence to the ASEAN Charter and upholding the centrality of regional decisions are paramount considerations. However, the SAC has challenged ASEAN with a narrow, one-dimensional interpretation of the charter's principles. These challenges have mainly taken the form of statements issued by the SAC's Ministry of Foreign Affairs in response to decisions made by ASEAN leaders and foreign ministers regarding Myanmar's representation at leaders' or foreign ministers' meetings. For its part, ASEAN's decisions have mainly been informed by the SAC's lack of commitment to address the Five-Point Consensus. In response, the SAC has resorted to making unilateral statements invoking ASEAN's noninterference principle and threatening 'negative impacts' on ASEAN's community-building efforts (MMoFA 2022a). It has also attempted to influence ASEAN's internal deliberations on Myanmar via its bilateral links with some countries in the region. This looks likely to continue unless either external or internal forces (or a combination of both) somehow compel the SAC to change its attitude towards mediation and reconciliation.

Myanmar and ASEAN in 2022

Focus on humanitarian assistance

Kicking off Cambodia's 2022 rotational chairmanship year, Prime Minister Hun Sen made much of his bilateral visit to Myanmar in January 2022—as did his military hosts in Naypyidaw (Tan Hui Yee 2022). The negative publicity from that visit gave Hun Sen pause to consider the import and broader implications of ASEAN's collective response to the Myanmar crisis, not least the credibility challenge that would redound to ASEAN if the situation continued to deteriorate (RFA 2022a).

Following Hun Sen's Myanmar visit, ASEAN expanded its October 2021 decision to the foreign ministers' level. The ASEAN Foreign Ministers' Annual Retreat, which usually kicks off ASEAN's key political discussions and agenda-setting for the year, followed the October 2021 precedent of inviting a non-political representative, drawing another retort from the SAC in a statement issued by Myanmar's foreign affairs ministry on 14 February 2022 (MMoFA 2022b).

After his Myanmar visit, Hun Sen's follow-up conversations with counterparts from other ASEAN member states, such as Indonesia and Singapore, revealed the seriousness with which these founding members viewed ASEAN's collective decision to send a clear message to the SAC about its adherence and commitment to the Five-Point Consensus priorities, not least those to cease violence and allow unfettered humanitarian assistance. In fact, in the first of his video calls with junta chief Min Aung Hlaing, Hun Sen made a four-point appeal, including to allow a visit by the ASEAN special envoy for 2022 and to provide 'full cooperation in support of ASEAN efforts' in order to provide humanitarian relief for people in Myanmar (CMoFAIC 2022a).

In 2022, ASEAN's focus on humanitarian assistance for Myanmar became more pronounced. ASEAN's secretary-general had led an appeal and a pledging conference in August 2021, but ASEAN was unable to coordinate aid delivery on the ground in Myanmar. The SAC instead designated the Myanmar Red Cross Society as the in-country coordinator for humanitarian assistance from ASEAN. In a statement issued at the one-year mark of the coup, the ASEAN chair voiced ASEAN member states' collective concern at the ongoing crisis in Myanmar, referring specifically to the 'continued violence and deteriorating humanitarian situation' (CMoFAIC 2022b). The statement, released by Cambodia's Ministry of Foreign Affairs and International Cooperation on 2 February 2022, also referred to the importance of the ASEAN special envoy's missions to Myanmar.

Hun Sen's January 2022 video call paved the way for ASEAN Special Envoy Prak Sokhonn's visit to Myanmar in March 2022. The Myanmar junta heavily circumscribed his visit, including determining who he could and could not meet. Unable to meet with senior NLD leaders, and finding no traction in his efforts to seek the cessation of violence and the 'engendering of an inclusive political dialogue that is Myanmar-owned and Myanmar-led', Prak Sokhonn prioritised facilitating ASEAN humanitarian assistance as his next deliverable (CMoFAIC 2022c). This has become his main deliverable to date.

The SAC agreed to Prak Sokhonn's proposal to convene a consultative meeting on humanitarian assistance, but then framed that proposal to its meet its own interests. The ASEAN consultative meeting was held on 6 May 2022, at the foreign minister level. It did not include UN Special Envoy to Myanmar Noeleen Heyzer, whose mandate included the facilitation of humanitarian assistance provision to Myanmar. Instead, Joyce Msuya, the assistant secretary-general for humanitarian affairs, and UN specialised agencies were present. The Special Advisory Council for Myanmar, which comprises former UN experts on Myanmar, shared that Heyzer was 'invited then disinvited' (*Irrawaddy* 2022a) to the meeting, which included representatives from all ASEAN member states, and some non-ASEAN countries such as the US, the UK and Japan. Heyzer's absence raised speculation that the junta may have blocked her participation in reaction to her earlier meetings with the NUG (*Irrawaddy* 2022a). Prior to the meeting, on 2 May, the junta had termed Saifuddin's proposal for 'informal engagement' with the NUG on humanitarian aid delivery as 'irresponsible and reckless' (*Irrawaddy* 2022b).

The ASEAN consultative meeting on 6 May identified certain states and regions in Myanmar, notably Kayah, Kayin, Magway, Sagaing and Bago, that were disproportionately in need of assistance due to fighting and civilian displacement. However, details on how those areas would receive priority assistance and how it would be delivered remained unclear. At a press conference following the meeting, Prak Sokhonn presented the meeting's outcomes as progress, though he noted that humanitarian assistance to Myanmar still faced numerous obstacles, including the junta's fear that aid would end up in the hands of resistance groups and the junta's desire to tax humanitarian assistance. While the latter issue was 'negotiated successfully', removing the requirement to tax humanitarian assistance, a lack of clarity on aid delivery remained (CMoFAIC 2022c). The outcome of the meeting also gave rise to the criticism that ASEAN seemed to be giving the junta control of aid delivery. At the meeting, the SAC's taskforce on humanitarian aid undertook to ensure that aid reached affected communities, especially those in areas under EAO control (*PPP* 2022). The NUG flagged its concern that the junta would 'continue to hamper urgent and effective delivery of humanitarian aid', and called for 'crucial stakeholders' such as 'Ethnic Resistance Groups' and local aid organisations to be involved in discussions on aid distribution (NUG 2022).

ASEAN–US Summit expectations

Prior to the ASEAN–US Special Summit in Washington on 12–13 May 2022, expectations ran high on how the Myanmar crisis would be approached. The Myanmar crisis was one of several pressing issues of geopolitical and regional importance competing for attention. The Joint Vision Statement of the ASEAN–US Special Summit (ASEAN 2022a) devoted an entire paragraph to Myanmar under the heading 'Preserving Peace, Building Trust'. Paragraph 26 covered all the broad priority points: 'timely and complete implementation' of the Five-Point Consensus; US support for ASEAN's response to the Myanmar crisis, including the work of the ASEAN special envoy in carrying out his mandate; and calls for humanitarian assistance to be 'without discrimination' and for the 'release of all political detainees including foreigners'. The call for close coordination between the ASEAN and UN special envoys suggested an awareness of the undercurrents of the 6 May ASEAN consultative meeting on humanitarian assistance for Myanmar. Meanwhile, increased publicity of the United States' informal engagement with the NUG[10] served as an indication of

---

10　Deputy Secretary of State Wendy Sherman met with NUG Foreign Minister Zin Mar Aung on 12 May 2022 for a second time (the first meeting was in August 2021). Zin Mar Aung also reportedly met with State Department Counsellor Derek Chollet (her third public meeting with Chollet, the first two being virtual sessions in September 2021 and January 2022) and the 'president's adviser for human rights', according to an interview with *RFA* (2022b). In that same *RFA* interview, Zin Mar Aung said that she had met 'a few ASEAN foreign ministers', but noted that the only publicised meeting was with the Malaysian foreign minister.

the Biden administration's attitude towards, and position on, the Myanmar crisis, despite its continued practice of not mentioning the NUG in official documents or statements.

Beyond these publicised instances of engaging with the NUG, the ASEAN–US Special Summit itself did not issue specific recommendations on the way forward for the Myanmar crisis. In June 2022, US State Department Counsellor Derek Chollet affirmed at the 19th Shangri-La Dialogue's special session on Myanmar that Myanmar remained a 'top priority' for the US but, echoing observations made at the same session by Heyzer and Saifuddin on the need to strengthen ASEAN's role and seek more inclusive dialogue, acknowledged that 'the road ahead is going to be very difficult' (Ng 2022).

All this seems to indicate that quiet diplomacy via a few key ASEAN members and informal consultations with experts and stakeholders on possible policy options may still be the United States' preferred approach. The Myanmar crisis may also rank lower in terms of priority and attendant policy attention in view of the United States' domestic policy concerns as well as the foreign policy and security implications of Russia's invasion of Ukraine.

In November 2022, at the 40th and 41st ASEAN Summits under Cambodia's chairmanship, the nine ASEAN heads of state/government issued a statement on their review of the Five-Point Consensus, reiterating that it remained a 'valid reference' to be 'implemented in its entirety' (ASEAN 2022b). At the time, four of the five points of the consensus agreement remained either unmet or only partially met. ASEAN leaders called for specific and time-bound indicators that measured the implementation, or lack thereof, of the consensus—an approach that failed to meet any of the expected ideals for stringent measures towards the SAC. The question of expanding non-political representation to other sectoral meetings was delegated to the foreign ministers to decide 'as the situation requires', leaving this open for interpretation (Moe Thuzar & Seah 2022).

What are the options?

Notwithstanding its own internal differences on how best to deal with the Myanmar crisis, ASEAN's default position at the summit and foreign minister levels looks likely to hold, with SAC leaders' attendance at key regional meetings being restricted to non-political representatives. The focus on humanitarian assistance seems to be ASEAN's other default priority, specifically, to identify and pursue a common objective in consultation with different stakeholder groups. If the October 2021 decision is ASEAN's 'stick' regarding the Myanmar crisis, then humanitarian assistance might be considered the 'carrot'. However, the 6 May 2022 consultative meeting outcome shows that ASEAN (and successive special envoys of the ASEAN chair) continue to face the dilemma of balancing diplomatic pragmatism with addressing the pressing needs of a populace whose resilience is crumbling daily. The emphasis on a 'Myanmar-led, Myanmar-owned' process (CMoFAIC 2022b) that external interlocutors, including ASEAN, could support is open to different interpretations by different stakeholder groups in Myanmar.[11] Determining who the key stakeholders are and how best to mediate between them presents ASEAN with another dilemma.

In theory, there are numerous options for ASEAN to promote peace and development in Myanmar. Few may be politically feasible. The option of expanding the decision to disinvite the SAC to other sectoral ASEAN meetings is not considered here due to its political infeasibility. A fundamental difference between pragmatic and principled approaches adds to, or underpins, the current complexities of ASEAN's Myanmar response. Nevertheless, three distinct options within the present reality can be readily described. These options are not mutually exclusive and may be considered in combination or parts thereof.

Humanitarian resistance?

As ineffective as it has been, most ASEAN member states would agree it would be worse to not have the Five-Point Consensus. As the points listed in the document are not in any order of priority, the current conflicts across Myanmar necessitate ASEAN's responsibility to coordinate and provide humanitarian assistance to communities in need. However, the main vehicle by which such assistance would be coordinated, the ASEAN Coordinating Centre for Humanitarian Assistance (AHA Centre), requires both a request by and the consent of the member state concerned, as well as access to all areas and communities. This means working within ASEAN's intergovernmental bounds and engaging with the SAC. Additionally, the AHA Centre does not have the technical expertise to deliver aid in a conflict situation. Even

---

11   This phrase was first mentioned in the ASEAN chair's statement on Myanmar issued on 2 February 2022, but the SAC foreign minister used it to impress upon the ASEAN special envoy that Myanmar (under the SAC) must lead the implementation of the Five-Point Consensus.

if ASEAN were able to boost, and contribute to, the AHA Centre's team on the ground in Myanmar, the Nargis experience indicates that the SAC would be the main interlocutor on aid delivery and coordination.

The immediate past executive director of the AHA Centre, Adelina Kamal, classified ASEAN's current response as a 'classic band-aid' approach, which, as it was taking place under the scrutiny of the SAC, could only provide limited results. By contrast, she described the 'pragmatic' approach by Myanmar's neighbour China as a proactive buffering of potential humanitarian spillovers that offered an alternative out-of-the-box 'humanitarian resistance' model that placed people at the centre of aid coordination and delivery (Kamal 2022). Malaysia's recent appeal to ASEAN to consider informally engaging with the NUG in relation to humanitarian assistance provision suggests that there is at least some consideration of alternative options (*Irrawaddy* 2022a).

The current high-level of cynicism in Myanmar towards ASEAN and the ASEAN-led response coupled with ASEAN's hesitancy thus far to engage with the NUG collectively may affect the ASEAN special envoy's mandated task to meet with, and consult, all stakeholders. Among those stakeholders, the EAOs have emerged as important in state- and peace-building in Myanmar, and are now asserting their voice more than in the past.

Engage with the NUG and EAOs?

The military's narrative of being the only organised institution in the country protecting national security is being challenged as never before. Anti-coup protests have continued despite brutal repression and violence, and the NUG has continued to engage in dialogue with various EAOs, political parties, civil society organisations and Civil Disobedience Movement representatives via the National Unity Consultative Council (NUCC) platform. The lack of headway in engaging with the SAC seems to have created more interest in engaging with the NUG, albeit informally. Even Thai Special Envoy Pornpimol Kanchalanak's caution in June 2022 on the 'diminishing returns' of isolating the SAC carried an underlying acknowledgement of the junta's recalcitrance (Ng 2022).

Foreign Minister of Malaysia Saifuddin's call for ASEAN to consider more engagement with the NUG and the NUCC may serve to awaken more interest in these bodies, which, in turn, will need to prepare for such engagement. Part of that preparedness requires a greater awareness and understanding of how an intergovernmental organisation such as ASEAN operates. The EAOs and other NUCC members may, thus, require more assistance in this journey of engagement with ASEAN than the NUG. Even the NUG still faces the challenge of asserting its status as an essential counterpart for dialogue, not least because of the SAC's domination of the foreign policy space in ASEAN and the grey areas governing the recognition of states over governments.

Further, many external interlocutors may be less aware of the NUCC's role in discussions on Myanmar's political future and of its intersection with the NUG. The NUG's challenge will be to show, and to prove, that its current set-up and dialogue with the NUCC is different from past parallels.[12] The NUG's Rohingya policy provides a good illustration of this difference, but the NUG also faces the challenge of capacity and necessary human resources to pursue its state-building and peace-building moves (Htet Myet Min Tun & Moe Thuzar 2022).

ASEAN member states should consider ways and means to engage with the NUG and the EAOs to identify where bilateral or third-party capacity support can assist efforts to address and undo decades of structural violence inflicted by the military. This is where ASEAN may consider opportunities and complementarities of working with the UN and other dialogue partners, including Myanmar's neighbours, in a broader 'ASEAN Plus' configuration.

Work with ASEAN's dialogue partners in a loose coalition?

Across ASEAN's various external partners—dialogue, sectoral and development—there is a broad spectrum of goodwill and expertise for ASEAN to leverage and coordinate in providing assistance and support to the Myanmar people. The UN and ASEAN are dialogue partners, and ASEAN has a separate seat at the UN. Annual ASEAN–UN ministerial meetings take place in October. However, current geopolitical tensions surrounding Russia's invasion of Ukraine, and the tendency to assign competency to

---

12   After the State Law and Order Restoration Council annulled the results of the 1990 elections, the elected NLD members formed a government in exile, the National Coalition Government of the Union of Burma. That exile government was also part of the National Council of the Union of Burma, which served as a platform for dialogue and discussion among armed groups and other pro-democracy forces.

ASEAN for dealing with the Myanmar crisis, seem to indicate that UN attention on Myanmar will largely fall on Special Envoy Heyzer and the UN agencies in Myanmar.

However, in light of the current sentiments towards ASEAN in Myanmar, it may be more beneficial if the grouping is part of a larger international effort. Given that both the SAC and the resistance movement are opposed to considering any form of pragmatic mediated dialogue, the challenge will be to come up with creative ways of assisting the Myanmar people. Still, such a coalition, with ASEAN as a convenor, could galvanise action and commitment from other countries, including ASEAN Dialogue Partners, with economic and strategic interests in Myanmar.

Concluding thoughts

Ultimately, ASEAN's responsibility to protect the Myanmar people from further distress and disaster must transcend the discomfort of taking up an issue that pushes ASEAN out of its self-imposed constraints and forces it to discuss and respond to the Myanmar crisis—beyond merely at leaders' or foreign ministers' meetings. The Myanmar question must become an agenda item for every sectoral ASEAN meeting or discussion; projects and programs must be formulated bearing in mind the need to assist Myanmar in overcoming its multifaceted challenges. Inputs from ASEAN's research community and from ASEAN parliamentarians and civil society for track two diplomacy must also be sought and considered in formulating policy responses bilaterally and regionally. In Myanmar, too, the role and capacity of civil society must be considered and boosted. Efforts by civil society to build bridges that ease the tensions have borne results in the past. But the antagonisms between communities that have existed for decades will require an equally long period of constructive engagement, nationally and regionally (Tin Maung Maung Than & Moe Thuzar 2012).

At present, ASEAN's ability to find solutions to the Myanmar dilemma is limited by what veteran ASEAN hands may deem as ASEAN's 'structural flaws' (Desker 2021) as well as its capacity (or not) to persuade the Myanmar military. The Myanmar crisis presents yet another reminder that ASEAN and its member states need to determine the value and import of ASEAN membership and the internal dimension (i.e. implementation) of ASEAN centrality. This is not the first time that Myanmar has created issues for ASEAN, and, sadly, it may not be the last, but ASEAN's response to the present crisis in Myanmar could still be the first time that clearer precedents and procedures are established for violations of membership obligations.

The Myanmar people, with their limited awareness of what ASEAN as an intergovernmental organisation can or cannot do, welcomed ASEAN's October 2021 decision. Yet, few are sanguine enough to believe that ASEAN, as a collective grouping, can effectively be relied upon to deal with the crisis in their country. To many protesters and participants in Myanmar's Spring Revolution, the international community's readiness to take the cue from ASEAN and its Five-Point Consensus came as a surprise. At the same time, the expectation that individual ASEAN members and international donors could do more to engage with the NUG seems to be quite common. This hope centres on supporting the NUG's humanitarian assistance effort via local community networks and channels, including in ethnic-controlled areas. The ASEAN leaders' decision in November 2022 to give more leeway to the AHA Centre and the ASEAN secretary-general may result in new and creative forms of humanitarian assistance.

Russia's invasion of Ukraine highlighted the question of appropriate responses by regional and international organisations and individual member states to acts of aggression or war. While the Myanmar and Ukraine crises are not directly comparable, from the perspective of the Myanmar people, the Myanmar military is behaving like a foreign occupier, robbing the country of its institutional development and its political future.

Even before the Ukraine crisis, Myanmar's prolonged troubles imparted some awareness of the limitations of international/regional diplomacy. In the 2022 State of Southeast Asia survey on ASEAN's response to the Myanmar crisis, the attitudes of the Myanmar people were markedly more negative than the regional average. Myanmar respondents (78.8 per cent) were largely dissatisfied with ASEAN's response, compared to a 33.1 per cent disapproval rating regionally. Compared to their ASEAN peers, more Myanmar respondents (39.9 per cent) wanted ASEAN to employ 'harder methods', such as targeted sanctions and suspension to 'curtail the SAC' (Moe Thuzar 2022). In 2023, Myanmar respondents to the survey question on ASEAN's response still mostly viewed the Five-Point Consensus as 'fundamentally flawed' (35.7 per cent compared to 19.6 per cent regionally). However, more Myanmar respondents (36.5 per cent) preferred the option of engaging in dialogue with all stakeholders, including the NUG, 'to build trust' rather than resort to harder measures (15.7 per cent) than in 2022 (Seah et al. 2023).

The people's defensive war since September 2021 is an illustration—albeit an extreme one—of supreme dissatisfaction and people taking matters into their own hands. However, it is possible to discern a change in the political sphere. Discussions about overcoming the trust deficit now extend to not only how different political actors and institutions interact with each other, but also to addressing the dynamics between individuals and groups of individuals. Fragile in its nascence, the capacity and desire to move beyond such discussion and take action perhaps adds to the dilemma of determining Myanmar's value to, and in, ASEAN.

References

AHA Centre (ASEAN Coordinating Centre for Humanitarian Assistance on Disaster Management). 2019. 'Preliminary Needs Assessment for Repatriation in Rakhine State, Myanmar'. May. Jakarta: AHA Centre.

ASEAN (Association of Southeast Asian Nations). 2021. 'Chairman's Statement on the ASEAN Leaders Meeting'. 24 April. asean.org/wp-content/uploads/Chairmans-Statement-on-ALM-Five-Point-Consensus-24-April-2021-FINAL-a-1.pdf

ASEAN (Association of Southeast Asian Nations). 2022a. 'Joint Vision Statement of the ASEAN–US Special Summit'. 14 May. asean.org/wp-content/uploads/2022/05/Final-ASEAN-US-Special-Summit-2022-Joint-Vision-Statement.pdf

ASEAN (Association of Southeast Asian Nations). 2022b. 'ASEAN Leaders Review and Decision on the Implementation of the Five-Point Consensus'. 11 November. asean.org/asean-leaders-review-and-decision-on-the-implementation-of-the-five-point-consensus/

ASEANSAI (ASEAN Supreme Audit Institutions). 2021. 'Handover ASEANSAI Chairmanship at the 6th ASEANSAI Summit'. 3 November. www.aseansai.org/2021/11/03/handover-aseansai-chairmanship-at-the-6th-aseansai-summit/

Asia Society. 2017. 'Indonesia's Foreign Minister Recounts Meeting with Aung San Suu Kyi'. 27 September. youtu.be/juakKVDl7Lw

BMoFA (Ministry of Foreign Affairs, Brunei Darussalam). 2021. 'Statement of the Chair of the ASEAN Foreign Ministers Meeting'. 16 October. mfa.gov.bn/Lists/Press%20Room/news.aspx?id=947&source=http://mfa.gov.bn/site/home.aspx?id=japan

CabSecRI (Cabinet Secretariat of Republic of Indonesia). 2017. 'Foreign Affairs Minister with Aung San Suu Kyi to Discuss Rakhine Humanitarian Crisis'. 4 September. setkab.go.id/en/foreign-affairs-minister-meets-with-aung-san-suu-kyi-to-discuss-rakhine-humanitarian-crisis/

Callahan, Mary. 2018. 'Myanmar in 2017: Crises of Ethnic Pluralism Set Transitions Back'. In *Southeast Asian Affairs 2018*, edited by Malcolm Cook and Daljit Singh, 201–20. Singapore: ISEAS-Yusof Ishak Institute. doi.org/10.1355/9789814786843-016

CMoFAIC (Cambodian Ministry of Foreign Affairs and International Cooperation). 2022a. 'Press Release on Outcomes of the Meeting between Samdech Akka, Moha Sena, Padei Techo, Hun Sen and Senior General Min Aung Hlaing, Chairman of the State Administration Council of the Republic of the Union of Myanmar'. 26 January. www.mfaic.gov.kh/Posts/2022-01-26-Press-Release-Outcomes-of-the-Virtual-Meeting-between-Samdech-Akka-Moha-Sena-Padei-Techo-HUN-SEN--Prime-Minister-o-19-13-17

CMoFAIC (Cambodian Ministry of Foreign Affairs and International Cooperation). 2022b. 'ASEAN Chairman's Statement on the Situation in Myanmar'. 2 February. www.mfaic.gov.kh/Posts/2022-02-02-Press-Release-ASEAN-Chairman-s-Statement-on-the-Situation-in-Myanmar--20-44-05

CMoFAIC (Cambodian Ministry of Foreign Affairs and International Cooperation). 2022c. 'Briefing Note by H.E. Deputy Prime Minister Prak Sokhonn, Minister of Foreign Affairs and International Cooperation, on the Outcomes of the First Visit of the Special Envoy of the ASEAN Chair 2022 to Myanmar'. 23 March. www.mfaic.gov.kh/Posts/2022-03-24-Speeches-Briefing-Note-by-H-E--Deputy-Prime-Minister-Prak-sokhonn--Minister-of-Foreign-Affairs-and-Internatio-10-38-13

CSIS-Indonesia (Centre for Strategic and International Studies-Indonesia). 2022. 'The Role of ASEAN in Dealing with the Myanmar Crisis: Are We Putting the Wrong Hope?' CSIS Myanmar Initiative Webinar, 24 January. www.linkedin.com/posts/csisindonesia_asean-initiatives-may-have-been-lauded-as-activity-6889854007091843072-Y3gA

Desker, Barry. 2021. 'ASEAN's Myanmar Dilemma'. *East Asia Forum*, 23 May. www.eastasiaforum.org/2021/05/23/aseans-myanmar-dilemma/

Global New Light of Myanmar. 2022. 'Full Description of Discussions between SAC Chairman Prime Minister Senior General Min Aung Hlaing and Special Envoy of United Nations Secretary General on Myanmar'. 20 August. www.gnlm.com.mm/full-description-of-discussions-between-sac-chairman-prime-minister-senior-general-min-aung-hlaing-and-special-envoy-of-united-nations-secretary-general-on-myanmar/

Irrawaddy. 2022a. 'Myanmar Junta Slams Malaysia's Call for ASEAN to Engage Shadow Govt'. 3 May. www.irrawaddy.com/news/burma/myanmar-junta-slams-malaysias-call-for-asean-to-engage-shadow-govt.html

Irrawaddy. 2022b. 'Junta Bars UN Special Envoy on Myanmar from ASEAN Meeting'. 9 May. www.irrawaddy.com/news/burma/junta-bars-un-special-envoy-on-myanmar-from-asean-meeting.html

Irrawaddy. 2022c. 'Myanmar Resistance Rejects Junta Calls to Surrender'. 13 June. www.irrawaddy.com/news/burma/myanmar-resistance-rejects-junta-calls-to-surrender.html

Kamal, Adelina. 2022. 'Myanmar Crisis: A Humanitarian Stalemate or Fresh Opportunities?' *Fulcrum*, 16 February. fulcrum.sg/myanmar-crisis-a-humanitarian-stalemate-or-fresh-opportunities/

Mahbubani, Kishore. 2017. 'ASEAN's Strategic Diplomacy Underpins Regional Stability'. *East Asia Forum*, 18 June. www.eastasiaforum.org/2017/06/18/aseans-strategic-diplomacy-underpins-regional-stability/

Marr, Selena. 2010. *Compassion in Action: The Story of the ASEAN-Led Coordination in Myanmar*. Jakarta: ASEAN Secretariat.

MMoFA (Myanmar Ministry of Foreign Affairs). 2022a. 'Press Release'. 14 February. www.mofa.gov.mm/press-release-14/

MMoFA (Myanmar Ministry of Foreign Affairs). 2022b. 'Press Release'. 11 November. www.mofa.gov.mm/press-release11-11-2022/

MMoI (Myanmar Ministry of Information). 2022. 'Myanmar Attends 40th ASEANAPOL Conference Held in Phnom Penh, Cambodia'. 8 March. myanmar. gov.mm/news-media/news/latest-news/-/asset_publisher/idasset354/content/myanmar-attends-40th-aseanapol-conference-held-in-phnom-penh-cambodia

Moe Thuzar. 2022. 'The State of Southeast Asia Survey: An Outlet for Myanmar Aspirations'. *Fulcrum*, 28 February. fulcrum.sg/the-state-of-southeast-asia-survey-an-outlet-for-myanmar-aspirations/

Moe Thuzar and Sharon Seah. 2022. 'Reviewing the Review: ASEAN's Five-Point Consensus Implementation'. *Fulcrum*, 17 November. fulcrum.sg/reviewing-the-review-aseans-five-point-consensus-implementation/

Moe Thuzar and Htet Myet Min Tun. 2022. 'Myanmar's National Unity Government: A Radical Arrangement to Counteract the Coup'. *ISEAS Perspective 2022/8*, 28 January. www.iseas.edu.sg/articles-commentaries/iseas-perspective/2022-8-myanmars-national-unity-government-a-radical-arrangement-to-counteract-the-coup-by-moe-thuzar-and-htet-myet-min-tun/

Ng, Eileen. 2022. 'Asean Needs More Detailed Plan for Myanmar Crisis: Malaysia'. *Straits Times,* 11 June. www.straitstimes.com/asia/se-asia/malaysia-suggests-asean-returns-to-drawing-board-to-tackle-myanmar-crisis

NUG (National Unity Government). 2022. 'Statement 9/2022, Response to the Consultative Meeting on ASEAN Humanitarian Assistance to Myanmar'. 7 May. twitter.com/NUGMyanmar/status/1523007617257287680

PPP (Phnom Penh Post). 2022. 'Prak Sokhonn Announces Progress on Myanmar Assistance Plans'. 16 May. www.phnompenhpost.com/national-politics/prak-sokhonn-announces-progress-myanmar-assistance-plans

Reuters. 2022a. 'Malaysia Foreign Minister Meets Counterpart from Myanmar Shadow Government in Washington'. 15 May. www.reuters.com/world/asia-pacific/malaysia-foreign-minister-meets-counterpart-myanmar-shadow-govt-washington-2022-05-15/

Reuters. 2022b. 'Myanmar Junta Leader Casts Doubt on Return of Rohingya'. 24 May. www.reuters.com/world/asia-pacific/myanmar-junta-leader-casts-doubt-return-rohingya-2021-05-24/

RFA (Radio Free Asia). 2022a. 'Cambodia's Hun Sen Gives up on Myanmar'. 16 February. www.rfa.org/english/news/myanmar/towel-02162022174658.html

RFA (Radio Free Asia). 2022b. 'Interview: "It's Time for ASEAN to Move Forward", Urges NUG Foreign Minister'. 12 May. www.rfa.org/english/news/myanmar/myanmar-nug-interview-05122022184741.html

Seah, Sharopn, Joanne Lin, Melinda Martinus, Sithanonxay Suvannaphakdy and Pham Thi Phuong Thao. 2023. *The State of Southeast Asia: 2023 Survey Report.* Singapore: ISEAS-Yusof Ishak Institute. www.iseas.edu.sg/wp-content/uploads/2025/07/The-State-of-SEA-2023-Final-Digital-V4-09-Feb-2023.pdf

Singapore Government. 2007. 'Statement by ASEAN Chair, Singapore's Minister for Foreign Affairs George Yeo'. 27 September. www.nas.gov.sg/archivesonline/data/pdfdoc/20070927974.htm

Tan Hui Yee. 2021. 'Diplomacy Will Be a High-Wire Act as Resistance to Military Regime Hardens in Myanmar'. *Straits Times,* 21 March. www.straitstimes.com/asia/se-asia/diplomacy-will-be-a-high-wire-act-as-resistance-to-military-regime-hardens-in-myanmar

Tan Hui Yee. 2022. 'Cambodian PM Hun Sen Meets Junta Chief on Two-Day Visit to Myanmar'. *Straits Times,* 8 January. www.straitstimes.com/asia/se-asia/cambodian-prime-minister-hun-sen-is-first-foreign-leader-to-visit-myanmar-after-coup

Tin Maung Maung Than and Moe Thuzar. 2012. 'Myanmar's Rohingya Dilemma'. *ISEAS Perspective* 1/2012. Singapore: ISEAS-Yusof Ishak Institute.

UN (United Nations). 2022. 'Note to Correspondents: Statement by the Secretary-General's Special Envoy on Myanmar, Noeleen Heyzer'. 17 August. www.un.org/sg/en/content/sg/note-correspondents/2022-08-17/note-correspondents-statement-the-secretary-general%E2%80%99s-special-envoy-myanmar-noeleen-heyzer

Vaphual and Rebecca Ratcliffe. 2022. 'Myanmar's UN Envoy under Fire for Proposing "Power Share" with Military'. *Guardian*, 3 February. www.theguardian.com/global-development/2022/feb/03/myanmars-un-envoy-under-fire-for-proposing-power-share-with-military

8

The Federal Democracy Charter: A Path to Inter-Ethnic Peace in Post-Coup Myanmar

Costas Laoutides

Associate Professor, School of Humanities and Social Sciences,
Deakin University, Australia

Abstract

This chapter analyses the Federal Democracy Charter in light of the question of ethnic minorities in Myanmar. Drawing on consociational and integrative patterns of power sharing, two issues are explored. First, I discuss the extent to which cultural differences can create problems for the federation, especially if the federal units aspire to cultivate further such differences. This is particularly important for the emerging minorities in a federal redrawing of the map. Crucial in this respect is how the charter creates mechanisms to counterbalance such developments. The second issue under examination is the way that federal units and ethnic minorities are treated in the charter. There is a tension between the right to self-determination granted to federal states and the collective rights granted to ethnic groups who may be more geographically dispersed. Accordingly, the ramifications towards the realisation of self-determination are discussed.

***

A few weeks after the February 2021 coup, the National Unity Consultative Council (NUCC), a decision-making body that brings together the pro-democracy forces and ethnic armed organisations (EAOs) shaping the parallel governance system of Myanmar spearheaded by the National Unity Government (NUG), was formed. Soon afterwards, the NUCC issued the Federal Democracy Charter (FDC), claiming it would pave the way for a peaceful federal Myanmar in their hoped-for, post-coup future (Su Mon Thazin Aung 2022).

Globally, power sharing arrangements are based on the understanding that the unequal distribution of resources between communities leads to internal conflict. The denial of equal access to power and resources leads to frustration and mobilisation by oppressed minorities. Thus, power sharing offers an alternative approach to the design of the state to mediate the potential harm of majoritarian democracy. The models of power sharing oscillate between integration and consociationalism—that is, the formation of proportional representation and grand coalitions that ascertain the equal participation of ethnic minorities into the political process. However, the underlying assumption of power sharing is that persons are primordially separated into identity groups that cannot find sufficient common ground and are, therefore, eternally bound to antagonistic relations.

Some of the clauses in the FDC have been seen as progressive, especially viz. offering ethnic minorities the right to self-determination—although, at the same time, criticism of the lack of equal recognition of certain other minorities, especially the Rohingya, has mounted. Taking stock of the international experience in power sharing agreements, this chapter assesses the FDC to determine whether it has the potential to end decades of ethnic conflict in Myanmar, and, if so, whether it could, perhaps, unify the ethnic minorities behind a campaign to oust the brutal military regime.

The chapter examines two issues. First, it analyses the extent to which cultural differences can create problems for the federation, especially if the federal units aspire to cultivate further such differences. This is particularly important for the emerging minorities in a federal redrawing of the map. Crucial in this respect is how the FDC creates mechanisms to counterbalance such developments. The second issue under examination is the way that federal units and ethnic minorities are treated in the charter. There is a tension between the right to self-determination granted to federal states and the collective rights granted to ethnic groups who may be more geographically dispersed. This friction raises two questions. First, to what extent does the right to self-determination include the right to secession, especially in light of Article 4 of the FDC which recognises that the federal units and their people are 'the original owners of sovereignty'? Second, how could the right to self-determination not be a collective right, given that it counts as the more fundamental right within the third generation of human rights in international practice (Laoutides 2019)? These issues and questions will be explored throughout the chapter.

Building consensus? The Federal Democracy Charter and the ethnic identity question

Broadly interpreted, power sharing political systems are those that foster governing coalitions inclusive of most, if not all, major mobilised ethnic groups in society. In most deeply divided societies, power sharing political systems are inclusive of generally legitimate representatives of all groups. Democratic rule has been seen as the solution to ethnic conflict if power sharing institutions are introduced to overcome politically motivated ethnic divisions and to ensure access to political power for all members of the society. In this context, decision-making is based on a consensus of coalitions that are widely inclusive, thus transcending strict ethnic boundaries. The central issue is the search for those institutions and practices that create an incentive structure for ethnic groups to negotiate their differences via the legitimate institutions of a common democratic state (Sisk 1996). Put differently, we might ask: what form should an inclusive and moderate democracy take in a deeply divided society like Myanmar?

The FDC constitutes the first step towards constitutional reform proposed by the NUG for a post-coup Myanmar. Similar to earlier historical phases, the international audience is more occupied with the struggle between the democratic forces led by the NUG and the dictatorship led by the military. Yet, the ethnic identity dimension has been a core element of the conflict and, therefore, a key constitutional debate since independence in 1948. The question of ethnic communities and their representation in the Union has been the cause of multiple prolonged civil wars, leading to the conclusion by some that Myanmar will have neither democracy nor peace unless the ethnic question is recognised in a power sharing constitutional agreement (Williams 2009).

Chapter I of the FDC frames the twofold root cause of conflict in the country as a lack of democracy and ethnic representation, and sets out the goal of the NUG to:

> ensure all ethnic nationalities–population can participate and collaborate and to build a prosperous Federal Democracy Union where all citizens can live peacefully, share the common destiny and live harmoniously together. (FDC 2021, Chapter I)

Accordingly, Chapter I outlines as key objectives: the eradication of dictatorship, the abolition of the 2008 Constitution, the building of a Federal Union and the emergence of Public Government. The FDC attempts to set the ethnic question on a new base that would be in tune with the wider vision of an open and democratic country through abolition of the 2008 Constitution (Raynaud 2021). The concurrent use of the term 'ethnic nationalities–population' can be seen as an attempt to bridge ethnic and civic notions of peoplehood towards a common political community, a common demos, of the post-coup, future democracy. This intention is also attested in Chapter II, in which members of the FDC (i.e. those responsible for implementing the charter) are the elected MPs; political parties; the Civil Disobedience Movement; forces of the General Strike Committee; members of civil society organisations, including women and youth organisations; and EAOs. However, as will become clear, this effort remains undeveloped without a clear terminological pathway that can break from past views entrenched in identity politics towards an inclusive, democratic and tolerant Myanmar. The Conclusion of Part I of the FDC sets the context within which the charter would operate, referring to the need for members of the FDC to implement 'the Panglong Agreement, Panglong Commitment and Panglong Principle … in order to build peaceful and prosperous Federal Union'.

In Chapter IV, Part I, the FDC outlines the core values of the NUG's union, which include self-determination, social harmony, diversity, protection of minorities and commitment to human rights. In the second part of Chapter IV, the FDC identifies the locus of sovereignty as belonging to the member states of the Union and their people. This is also repeated in Part III of the same chapter under the heading 'Power of the Union'. What is noteworthy is that the FDC does not mention which states constitute the Union. Despite the lack of clarity around territories and borders, the FDC ascribes to member states 'the right to develop and enact State Constitutions' (FDC 2021, Chapter IV, Art. 12). In addition, there is no provision for further devolution to self-administered zones and divisions as in the 2008 Constitution. The criterion for creating special administrative zones in the 2008 Constitution was based on an ethnic minority who did not have an ethnic state constituting the majority population in two or more adjacent townships. In the FDC, there is little reference to the people that inhabit those areas. The lack of reference to territories and peoples in the NUG's charter appears as an attempt to overcome the challenge of identity politics that is so deeply embedded in Myanmar politics. At the same time, however, there is no clear positive step to replace the language of ethnicity/nationality, and this reluctance indicates a deferral of the thorny issue to a future constitution drafting debate. This is also supported by a reference to the protection of minorities in state constitutions, again without a clear description of who those minorities are and how they may be recognised as minorities (FDC 2021, Chapter IV, Part. III, Art. 14).

The reluctance (or inability) of the NUG to transcend identity politics is also evidenced in relation to the protection of fundamental rights and the rights of ethnic minorities (FDC 2021, Chapter IV, Part. III, Art. 23, 24). The FDC insists on another division that generates potentially two types of members in the political community of the Union. Article 23 provides individual and collective rights to 'all ethnic nationalities … entitled as ethnic groups', but this progressive and inclusive, yet loosely defined, approach is cut short in Article 24, in which the FDC provides that:

> Every citizen who has adopted the citizenship of the Union *although they are not ethnic nationalities born in the Union*, shall have the full rights to fundamental rights of the citizens (citizen rights). (emphasis added)

This wording is particularly interesting as it indicates the future existence of two types of citizens in Myanmar: those with both individual and collective rights on the basis of ethnicity, and those who will bear only individual civil rights. Despite the willingness of the NUG to be inclusive, the insistence on ethnicity as a political marker that can generate two types of citizens is highly problematic, as it reproduces the precondition for ethnic discrimination.

Another interesting omission that has been a point of heated debate between EAOs and the central government for decades is the absence of a clause on the right to secession. If ultimate sovereignty lies with the states and their peoples, however ill-defined, and if 'ethnic leaders who built the Union have given up their right to build their own separate nationals and signed 1947 Panglong Agreement to build this Union as a federation' (FDC 2021,

Part I, Conclusion), it follows that the right to secession, as an expression of the right to self-determination, should be provided in the charter and any future constitution. The lack of such reference highlights the vulnerability of Myanmar as a divided society.

Myanmar as a divided society

Although there are a range of scholarly accounts seeking to describe the role of ethnicity in the political organisation of societies, it is possible to discern a set of common patterns that can assist with identifying how deeply divided societies are. In any particular case, three issues determine the presence and degree of division: the structure of social cleavages, the level of access to political power by different ethnic groups, and the phases of conflict escalation and de-escalation. The salience of ethnicity as a marker of political distinction and the intensity of ethnic ties are critical elements in the shaping of a divided society. Salience and intensity are closely interconnected to the perceived stakes of ethnic relations (Esman 1994). According to Esman, the stakes are higher when group identity is threatened, especially symbols of ethnic identity that are held as sacred and thus are seen as non-negotiable. Consequently, ethnic group claims on issues such as language or customary practices have been referred to as 'incommensurate goods' that are not amenable to change (Horowitz 2000, 219–24).

There is a broad consensus in the literature that when social cleavages are reinforced by vertical divisions based on religion, ethnicity or class, the possibility for violent conflict is higher. This is particularly so when one distinct group dominates others (Huntington 1981). Donald Horowitz offers a vantage point by depicting a very clear, ideal scenario that describes a divided society:

> Suppose a society contains two ascriptive (birth-derived) groups: the As with 60 percent of the population, and the Bs, with 40 percent. The groups have the same age structures and rates of natural increase; their proportions are not vulnerable to change through immigration; they vote at the same rates; and they vote for ascriptively defined political parties, the A party and the B party. Under virtually every form of fair majoritarian political arrangement and every electoral system, the As will dominate government and Bs will be in opposition for perpetuity. (Horowitz 2008, 1214)

Similarly, Arend Lijphart (2004) defines a divided society as one with strong ethnocultural divisions that have the potential to be politically salient and mobilising, threatening the stability of the state and the coexistence of the different groups that live within it. What needs to be underscored is that ethnocultural diversity is not itself problematic from a political point of view. What makes a divided society is when those differences become markers of political identity and mobilisation (Coakley 2009). In divided societies, core assumptions that underlie the competitive paradigm of democratic politics (the Westminster model) do not apply. The most important of these assumptions is the belief that cross-cutting cleavages of interests and outlooks among individuals prevent any permanent exclusion of segments of society from political power. It follows that there is always a possibility for opposition parties to win a share of power. However, the ethnic segmentation of divided societies based on politicised identity poses an impediment to the development of cross-cutting cleavages based on membership in multiple social groups, multiple outlooks and overlapping interests that can moderate the political process (Choudhry 2009).

Myanmar has been a deeply divided society since independence in 1948 in several key ways. First, the dominant cleavage between the state-controlling, ethnic Bamar majority and the ethnic minorities has been a permanent political marker, determining the level of access to political power based on ethnic identity. The takeover of the country by the military in 1962 created a second cleavage between the supporters of the military regime and those who envisioned a democratic polity for Myanmar. Being a friend or a foe of the regime would determine the interaction of individuals with the decision-making centre. A final line of division, which often but not always overlaps with ethnic divisions, runs along religious lines, with Buddhism as the predominant religion against a number of other religious groups in the country, including Muslims, Christians and Hindus (Walton 2016). These divisions have created multiple levels of segregation, raising challenging questions about the body politic in Myanmar and how the demos (i.e. the political community) should be defined to allow for a functional and inclusive democracy (Laoutides & Ware 2016).

Such conversations were underway after 2011, being fundamental to the peace process discussions attempted as the country entered into its democratic transition, but have now been interrupted by the military coup. The rise to power of the National League for Democracy (NLD) in the 2015 elections, and their Panglong II peace process created hope for a final peace agreement that would create a new Federal Union. The February 2021 coup brutally destroyed the (limited) progress made. The NUG's FDC, issued a few months after the coup, aims to revive the conversation about federal democracy and instil an even greater sense of hope and unity for the future. The FDC proposes creating a set of power sharing arrangements among the communities to bridge the dividing cleavages and create a coherent demos. In the following section, I outline the two basic models of power sharing in divided societies; in the subsequent section, I provide an assessment of the power sharing elements of the FDC that address the ethnic sociopolitical cleavages of Myanmar society and examine the chances of it ending decades of ethnic conflict in a post-coup Myanmar and, thus, unifying the ethnic minorities in a united campaign to oust the military.

Models of power sharing in ethnic conflicts

During the Cold War period, ethno-political conflict was the cause of many cases of intense armed violence resulting in minority oppression. Based on the principle of self-determination, many ethnic groups sought to address their grievance through the creation of ethnically homogenous nation-states. In that period there was a bias against political divorce that would lead to secession, evidenced by the fact that only Bangladesh was successful in obtaining international recognition as an independent state (Laoutides 2019). However, since the early 1990s the breakup of former Yugoslavia and the Soviet Union, the bifurcation of Czechoslovakia, the successful Eritrean struggle and the creation of South Sudan have given an impetus to secessionist movements. There is a growing perception, by aspiring ethnic groups, that the creation of new sovereign states as a means of fulfilling self-determination is an achievable goal. The almost absolute logic of denial to secession by the international community, however, has led to ongoing oppression, war, humanitarian crises and genocide. Thus, international decision-makers face a fundamental choice: allow partition and political divorce or create new and more viable structures for living together in a common polity. The latter option is informed by the promotion of democracy as the form of government that can accommodate ethnic tension and create a political environment of coexistence and harmony. Many policymakers and scholars believe that broadly inclusive government is essential to successful conflict management in deeply divided societies.

There are two classical models for building conflict-preventing democratic institutions in ethnically divided societies: the consociational and centripetal/integrative approaches. The former, mainly represented in the work of Arend Lijphart (1968, 1969, 1977, 1995, 2004), defends inclusion through representation and assurances for minority protection. It introduces a series of proportional representation mechanisms, a grand coalition of communal leaders, group autonomy and mutual vetoes to protect vital interests. The centripetal/integrative approach is mainly associated with Donald Horowitz (1990, 1991, 1993, 2008) and aims to alter the identity of the body politic, away from ethnic affiliations, towards an integrative common demos. To this end, it encourages moderation by advocating institutions that provide incentives for the electoral success of cross- and multi-ethnic parties and candidates. Both approaches share a belief in coalescent democracy as an alternative to the adverse effects of majoritarian politics. Crucially, both approaches transcend standard notions of procedural democracy, since an impeccable procedure does not prevent minorities from complete exclusion (Horowitz 1993).

Consociational democracy

Consociationalism relies on elite cooperation as the principal characteristic of successful conflict management in deeply divided societies. Even if there are deeply communal differences, overarching elite cooperation is a necessary and sufficient condition to resolve conflict (Nordlinger 1972). In this context, group leaders are seen to legitimately represent various ethnic segments and their actions aim at forging political ties at the centre. The central tenet of consociationalism is to share, divide, decentralise, limit and separate power; the nature of this model is that of a fragmented political representation that 'allows for legislative representation of territorially dispersed minorities who may be outvoted under First-Past-the-Post in single member districts' (Choudhry 2009, 19).

There are two key elements for establishing a successful consociational democracy. The first element is power sharing in the executive through a grand coalition that ensures the minority is not permanently excluded from the political power. In grand coalitions, political elites negotiate their differences in an effort to reach consensus, but public contestation among them is limited (Lijphart 2004). The most important feature is that decision-making takes place consensually at the top among elites representing underlying segments of the society (Lijphart 1977). The possibility of sharing power transforms all participant elites into stakeholders who will defend the viability of the constitutional system. Power sharing at the executive level is also supported by the minority veto through which each segment of the society is given a guarantee that it cannot be outvoted by the majority on crucial issues affecting vital interests of the minority. The minority veto is at the heart of the concrete assurances of consociationalism, but, most importantly, it offers each ethnic group the power to protect themselves. Similarly, the principle of proportionality facilitates consociational systems, as it is introduced at every level of decision-making to give minority groups access to power and influence that reflects their size within the society. Proportionality is manifested through the commensurate representation of the ethnic group in parliament, and through the allocation of material and human resources by the state to the ethnic communities.

The second element is autonomy of communal groups on the basis of territorial or non-territorial federalism that devolves decision-making authority to the segments and, thus, promotes the internal autonomy of all groups. There is a distinction between issues that concern the whole of the society and those that mainly concern the ethnic segments: for the former, decision-making occurs via consensus, whereas for the latter, decision-making is delegated to the autonomous ethnic groups. Group autonomy means that communal groups 'have authority to run their own internal affairs, especially in the areas of education and culture' (Lijphart 2004, 97). An important element of the call for entrenched minority group rights is the question of whether power sharing should be made on an ethnic basis or with ethnically neutral criteria. Accordingly, the different segments of society should have the option of voluntary affiliation, away from strict, predefined ethnic markers, through a proportional electoral system (Lijphart 1995).

There are three areas of criticism of the consociational model. The first is the inherent assertion that elites can regulate ethnic conflict in divided societies. This is part of a wider argument about ethnic conflict as an elite-driven process (Brass 1991; Gurr & Harff 1994). Although political elites may agree on a formula for accommodation, peace cannot endure without grassroots backing. In the context of Myanmar, this has been captured in the fallout of 'ceasefire capitalism'—when ethnic communities in the borderland areas became disillusioned with their elites, who were coopted by the Burmese regime, and resumed violence to defend their lands from exploitation (Woods 2011). This experience reinforces the argument that consociationalism overestimates the deference communal groups pay to their elites and downplays the power of popular dissatisfaction with intergroup compromise. Elites will not necessarily use their leadership to promote peace (Horowitz 1991, 141). The second drawback is the entrenching of ethnic identity in the political system by consociationalism, as it maintains and legitimises ethnic claims against the state. By hardening ethnic boundaries—for example, through the statutory reservation of offices for specific group representatives—consociationalism normalises ethnicity as a paramount part of the political process and the body politic (Andeweg 2000). This leads to a form of systemic sectarianism that denies citizens in divided societies peace and justice (Taylor 2009). A third point of criticism concerns the arguably anti-democratic character of consociational institutions. The model of grand ethnic elite coalitions minimises the possibility of vigorous opposition politics. In turn, the potential lack of a strong opposition party may detract from the accountability of the government (Borman 2017).

Consociational democracies are rare, with prime examples to be found mostly in Western Europe. Austria, Belgium, Switzerland and the Netherlands are all classic consociations that elect their parliaments with the help of list proportional representation (Lijphart 1991). Although there is no universal agreement, Bosnia and Herzegovina, Burundi, Lebanon and Northern Ireland are frequently mentioned as consociational democracies.

The centripetal/integrative approach

The integrative approach promotes a politics of moderation and compromise as a way for effective democratic governance in deeply divided societies. Democracy can be best managed by depoliticising ethnicity through institutional incentives for cross-ethnic voting that increase accommodation among competing ethnic segments (Reilly 2012). Whereas consociationalism seeks to guarantee that all groups are represented in the government and the state apparatus, the centripetal/integrative approach seeks to foster initiatives that capture the middle/moderate ground. To achieve the integrative spin, there is a need for electoral incentives for broad-based moderation by political leaders and disincentives for hardliners (Horowitz 2000, 597–600). The incentives will be provided to politicians who can appeal beyond their communal segment for support. The assumption behind this rationale is that politicians, as rational actors, will do whatever they need to do to get elected (Horowitz 1991, 291). If they are rewarded electorally for moderation, politicians will control their rhetoric and action. This line of argument opts for incentives, as these provide reasons for behaving moderately; by contract, consociational constraints provide obstacles to prevent politicians from becoming entrenched in their ethnic segments. In addition, rather than (over)relying on ethnic leaders, the integrative approach puts the constituency at the centre of the moderation process. The electoral system must be designed so that the leaders have to appeal to the moderate sentiments of the electorate, thereby cutting across ethnic rival groups. Moving the basis of moderation from the elites to the constituency allows politicians to make compromises at the centre to achieve democratic stability for the divided society. Constituency-based consent via moderation can function only if minority votes in the electoral system are designed to be influential, rather than merely representative, thereby safeguarding the interests of the minority. There are, arguably, three institutional practices that can have this effect: vote pooling, devolution of power and a presidential system of politics.

Vote pooling occurs when politicians are dependent on cross-communal support to get elected and voters exchange votes across group boundaries. Vote pooling is based on the assumption that divided societies need electoral systems that fragment support of one or more ethnic groups and induce inter-ethnic bargaining that encourage electoral candidates to adopt a moderate stance. To win, politicians must seek to obtain the second or third preference votes of those who, in all probability, would not vote for them because they do not represent the voter's community (Horowitz 1993). The key difference of the integrative approach is the formation of electoral conditions by constituents, as they specify their second and third preferences that will lie outside the boundaries of the ethnic brethren. However, it is easier for vote pooling to occur in heterogeneous electoral districts (Bogaards 2003).

Devolution of power can facilitate ethnic coexistence in deeply divided societies (Horowitz 2000, 601). It can combine with the electoral system to promote moderate political parties that pursue inter-ethnic coalitions. Regional and local levels of politics provide the ideal space for the fostering of intergroup ties at the centre that can be projected in higher-stakes issues at the level of central government. Similarly, a devolved structure can absorb and resolve conflict at lower levels of government while promoting cleavages within ethnically homogenous groups. In addition, federalism can block any party from attempting a hegemonic grip of the entire country.

The integrative approach has attracted considerable criticism. The scarcity of empirical examples of the system at work is an important point of critique. Elements of the integrative model have been identified and assessed in 11 cases (Reilly 2001; McCulloch 2013; Coakley & Fraenkel

2017).[1] In addition, there is an inherent assumption that politicians will respond to the incentive system for moderation and, in a similar vein, that voters be willing to vote for parties not based in their own ethnic group (Lijphart 2004). Most importantly, centripetalist electoral systems have been criticised as majoritarian, since the logic of the model advocates the benefits of aggregation in terms of votes, parties and issues. As such, the integrative model is underpinned by a 'majoritarian vision' of democracy in which aggregation matters at the expense of an equitable reflection of all points of view into the legislature (Powell 2000).

At the heart of the difference between consociational and integrative approaches to power sharing are the nature and formation of multi-ethnic coalitions. Consociationalism advocates the formation of coalitions by elites after an election, whereas centripetalism advocates the forming of coalitions before the election. To paraphrase Horowitz (2000, 365ff), it is a dilemma between coalitions of convenience versus coalitions of commitment.

Ethnic minorities and the Federal Democracy Charter

A deeply divided society, Myanmar has been marred by long periods of armed conflict between the military government and ethnic groups, resulting in rounds of displacement, persecution and ethnic cleansing. According to Horowitz (2004, 252), 'most divided societies have crafted no institutions at all to attend to their ethnic problems', and this certainly applies to Myanmar. Although the conflict in Myanmar has been depicted as a clash between militarism and democracy, it is foundationally a conflict about ethnic identity. Even if Myanmar returns to democracy after the 2021 coup, stability will not be secured unless the ethnic identity question is addressed. Although ethnicity is socially constructed, the ethnic minorities in Myanmar perceive their different identities as real in their consequence. Their experience since the country's independence in 1948 is one of oppression and war perpetrated by Bamar-dominated military governments. The response to the aggression from the centre has been the creation of strong ethnic communities and inter-ethnic cooperation, with solid structures that look after their own in a nexus of dynamically evolving forms of ethnic

---

1   Australia, Estonia, Fiji, Indonesia, Kenya, Nigeria, Northern Ireland, Papua New Guinea, Republika Srpska, Southern Rhodesia and Sri Lanka.

identity (Sadan 2013). The gradual increase in political importance placed on ethnicity by successive Myanmar governments since 1962 has influenced minorities' political perceptions and agendas. Thus, the expression of ethnic difference is something that needs to be clearly reflected in any future power sharing constitutional arrangement as an acknowledgement of the existence of different ethnic communities in the political space of the union.

There are three main issues behind the call for power sharing measures. The first is the cultural denialism of the Bamar majority and the cultural domination of the political system on the basis of majoritarian politics unsuited for culturally diverse societies. The ethnic minorities in Myanmar have a different sense of belonging—they speak different languages, they practise different religions and they have different political structures (Smith 1999; Sadan 2013). The military governments have systematically oppressed the ethnic communities through a series of measures—from the lack of equal opportunities to access high civil and military offices and ban on local languages, to the burning down of churches and mosques and the utter denial of existence of particular ethnic groups like the Rohingya in Rakhine State (South 2008; Ware & Laoutides 2018). Even during the democratic transition, which ended abruptly in 2021, the Bamar-dominated state and military apparatus continued many of these measures, leaving the ethnic minorities in a constant state of fear. It is noteworthy that ethnic violence escalated under the NLD's first term, with genocidal aggression against the Rohingya in 2017, the war in Rakhine between the Arakan Army and the military in 2018–20, and the intensification of violence in Chin, Kachin, Karen and Shan states (Mathieson 2021). Thus, the ethnic minorities look for constitutional guarantees to block similar future behaviour on the part of the Bamar majority.

The second issue builds on the deep distrust towards the Bamar by the ethnic minorities, especially after the shortcomings of the NLD government that, until then, had been seen as the force of political and social change in the country. The ethnic minorities feel that a narrative of superiority is still strong among the ethnic Bamar. Such a narrative assumes that the country should be run primarily by the Bamar majority, with insouciance towards the needs and suffering of the minority ethnic communities. This was evidenced by the way that the national reconciliation process under the NLD became a Bamar-dominated affair—an elite bargain between the Bamar civilian political party and the Bamar-dominated military: hence the need for power sharing constitutional boundaries to control what the ethnic majority can do to the ethnic minorities.

The third issue relates to the collective distinctiveness of the ethnic minorities in Myanmar. They feel different and they associate this difference with the lands in which they constitute a majority. Therefore, they put forward a claim for self-determination, both as a collective within the Union of Myanmar, and as separate ethnic groups. For the ethnic minorities, this is the unfinished business of decolonisation. Whereas in 1948 the Bamar majority saw themselves recognised and liberated from alien rule, this is still an unfulfilled promise for the ethnic minorities. This claim is not only in cultural/historical terms, but also is meaningful in current material terms, given the long-term exploitation of natural resources from these regions by the central state. The members of ethnic minorities have a very strong sense of common belonging and participating in a self-determined future gives them meaning and purpose as a community. To this end, power sharing constitutional arrangements are seen as a way of guaranteeing a path to self-determination within the boundaries of a federal polity.

Strong territorial manifestations of ethnicity render the configuration of territorial power division extremely important. The range of solutions varies from partition to a centralised unitary state with a number of options in between, such as confederal, federal and semi-confederal systems. The territorial division of power can be manifested in an array of policy issues, such as economic mechanisms for the distribution of resources and political tools to reduce the stakes of conflict at the centre. Among the several options, federalism has been extensively analysed for its conflict-management effects. Federalism can be structured to serve both consociational and integrative/centripetal purposes. It can potentially create incentives for inter-ethnic cooperation and encourage alignments along non-ethnic interests. Devolution of power can give minorities some degree of power when it is unlikely that they would achieve majority status at the centre.

Federalism denotes a division of power based on mutual consent. The central government is allocated a defined area of authority while the territorial units are provided degrees of autonomy; both levels of government enjoy some limited coordinated powers. The most distinctive characteristic of federalism is that neither the centre nor the regions can unilaterally amend the arrangement—consent is a sine qua non condition of federalism. The principle of unity through diversity, a core democratic principle for deeply divided societies, can be realised through federalism. This obtains stronger normative and political purchase when the protection of minorities is a priority through a number of federal tools, such as internal self-determination, semi-sovereign ancestral lands, autonomous rule and indigenous rights.

The FDC was published at an important juncture in terms of the history of constitutional battles between ethnic minorities and the central government in Myanmar (Williams 2009). The coup d'état in February 2021 followed a landslide victory of the NLD at the national elections, which resulted in a massive wave of resistance and led to the creation of the NUG, which, in turn, now leads the struggle for the restoration of democracy in the country. The FDC's aim is to create a federal democracy that will:

> bring an end to the conflicts and problematic root causes in the Union, to ensure all ethnic nationalities–population can participate and collaborate and to build a prosperous Federal Democracy Union where all citizens can live peacefully. (FDC 2021, Chapter 1)

The FDC is an attempt to both establish a roadmap for the restoration of democracy and recognise the participation of ethnic minorities in a new, post-coup democracy. In doing so, the charter addresses, at a preliminary level, civil–military relations as well as the deeper issue of the representation of ethnic minorities in the political realm.

However, a persistent problem with federal solutions like this is how to resolve questions of dual sovereignty. Which unit has sovereign power over the various functions of the states? The locus of sovereignty is of paramount importance because it determines the supreme authority and the ultimate holder of decision-making power. In its 'Guiding Principles', the FDC affirms that 'the member states of the Union and the people in these states are the original owners of sovereignty' (FDC 2021, Chapter 4, Part II, Art. 1), and that:

> the Federal Democracy Union is established with member states which have equal rights and right to self-determination in full. All the member states of the Union (all the federal units) are equal in terms of politics. (FDC 2021, Chapter 4, Part II, Art. 2)

Further, it asserts that 'member states of the Union have the right to enact their own respective State Constitution' (FDC 2021, Chapter 4, Part II, Art. 3). Neither the territories (states) nor the people are specified as the proteogenic source of sovereignty and power. Given the emphasis it places on ethnicity, the FDC veers towards an elite-driven, semi-consociational approach, in which power and authority are allocated to ethnic groups.

Yet, the ambiguity between states and ethnic groups is not resolved. In earlier efforts (e.g. the 2008 Constitution) there is reference to specific space, but in the FDC, the demographics—if ethnicity is to determine the boundaries of the units—are not clear in terms of majorities and minorities. Although there are certain perceptions of ownership, often based on narratives of ancestral land, the reality for a future territorial demarcation of federal units could be problematic. Many members of ethnic minorities want to live their culture and be responsible for the wealth of their land, but, at the same time, the high degree of ethnic mobility and intermarriage, and the presence of other minorities in ethnic states, means that an ethnic/territorial approach does not reflect the complexities on the ground. A case in point is Rakhine State; in a future scenario that involves a return to democracy along the NUG's framework, the United League of Arakan and the Arakan Army would want to see a sovereign Arakan State as member of the Union of Myanmar. The current FDC would ascribe the locus of sovereignty to ethnic Rakhine in the state, leaving in limbo both other ethno-religious groups of the region (predominantly the Rohingya) as well as ethnic Rakhine residing in other parts of the country. How would the Rohingya or the Bamar or the Daignet in Rakhine exercise their constitutional right of self-determination within such an Arakan State? And how would social harmony (FDC 2021, Chapter 4, Part I, Art. 4) be realised if ethnicity continues to separate communities? This same conundrum is replicated across the country.

Coupled with the lack of clarity on the definition of peoples and territories is the stipulation that the union exercises power sharing and revenue sharing based on the principle of subsidiarity (FDC 2021, Chapter 4, Part II, Art. 4):

> The original owner of all land and natural resources within a State is the people who live in the State. The State shall have the right to independently manage the exploration, extraction, selling, trading, preservation, and protection etc. of the natural resources within the State. (FDC 2022, Chapter 4, Part III, Art. 20)

The consociational underpinnings of this clause promote a new power equilibrium between the centre and the periphery that is further supported by the rights of ethnic minorities (FDC 2021, Chapter 4, Part III, Art. 23–4, 26–7). However, the overall scheme aims at the de-Burmanisation of politics—not through the downgrading of ethnicity as a critical factor for political discourse, but through an increased recognition of ethnic communities as such. The FDC moves towards a more consociational path as the basis for a post-coup democratic Myanmar. Yet, the labyrinth of ethnic definitions and territorial demarcations may lead more towards the Minotaur of conflict than Ariadne's thread of exodus to peace.

Since the publication of the FDC, the clash to oust the military junta continues. The NUG had originally hoped to complete a final draft of a new constitution by December 2021 (Saw Thonya 2021), but this did not eventuate. The lack of progress in finalising the union's constitution based on the FDC highlights the challenges that the NUG faces. It takes considerable effort to coordinate and hold together a unified campaign against the junta on the promise and vision of an ethnically based, semi-consociational polity. The NUG hopes the payoff will be an open, peaceful society for all, with an open democracy that resembles the established models of open liberal democracies around the world. However, the situation on the ground seems to be changing into a long-term, low-intensity civil war between the PDFs and the military. The issues outlined in this chapter highlight why the FDC has not offered a compelling vision for the EAOs to unite around. Without a clear victory, it remains for the NUG to convince the EAOs to unite with the progressive forces. Past experience through the ceasefire agreements in the 1990s indicate that ethnic elites may opt for a non-democratic regime as long as their interests are promoted. The recent decision by some less significant EAOs to start ceasefire talks with the military points in this direction (Moe Thuzar & Htet Myet Min Tun 2022). The semi-consociational approach adopted by the FDC moves towards a choice of convenience rather than a choice of commitment. Despite its progressive character, the charter seems to be locked in the past rather than paving the way forward for a future that unites the people.

References

Andeweg, Rudy B. 2000. 'Consociational Democracy'. *Annual Review of Political Science* 3: 509–36. doi.org/10.1146/annurev.polisci.3.1.509

Bogaards, M. 2003. 'Electoral Choices for Divided Societies: Multi-Ethnic Parties and Constituency Pooling in Africa'. *Commonwealth and Comparative Politics* 41 (3): 59–80. doi.org/10.1080/14662040412331310201

Borman, Nils-Christian. 2017. 'Ethnic Power-Sharing Coalitions and Democratization'. In *Power-Sharing: Empirical and Normative Challenges,* edited by Allison McCulloch and John McGarry, 124–47. Abingdon: Routledge. doi.org/10.4324/9781315636689-7

Brass, Paul. 1991. *Ethnicity and Nationalism: Theory and Comparison.* London: London.

Choudhry, Sujit. 2009. 'Bridging Comparative Politics and Comparative Constitutional Law: Constitutional Design in Divided Societies'. In *Constitutional Design for Divided Societies: Integration or Accommodation?*, edited by Sujit Choudhry, 3–40. Oxford: Oxford University Press.

Coakley, John. 2009. 'Ethnic Conflict Resolution: Routes towards Settlement'. *Nationalism and Ethnic Politics* 15 (3–4): 462–83. doi.org/10.1080/13537 110903392670

Coakley, J. and J. Fraenkel. 2017. 'The Ethnic Implications of Preferential Voting'. *Government and Opposition* 52 (4): 671–97. doi.org/10.1017/gov.2017.4

Esman, Milton J. 1994. *Ethnic Politics*. Ithaca: Cornell University Press.

FDC (Federal Democracy Charter). 2021. Part 1. Declaration of the Federal Democary Union. crphmyanmar.org/wp-content/uploads/2021/04/Federal-Democracy-Charter-English.pdf

Gurr, Ted Robert and Barbara Harff. 1994. *Ethnic Conflict in World Politics*. Boulder: Westview Press.

Horowitz, Donald L. 1990. 'Making Moderation Pay: The Comparative Politics of Ethnic Conflict Management'. In *Conflict and Peacemaking in Multiethnic Societies*, edited by Joseph V. Montville, 451–76. Lexington: Lexington Books.

Horowitz, Donald L. 1991. *A Democratic South Africa? Constitutional Engineering in a Divided Society*. Berkeley: University of California Press. doi.org/10.1525/ 9780520328884

Horowitz, Donald. 1993. 'The Challenge of Ethnic Conflict: Democracy in Divided Societies'. *Journal of Democracy* 4 (4): 20–38. doi.org/10.1353/jod.1993.0054

Horowitz, Donald. 2000. *Ethnic Groups in Conflict*. 2nd ed. Berkeley: University of California Press.

Horowitz, Donald. 2004. 'Some Realism about Constitutional Engineering'. In *Facing Ethnic Conflicts: Toward a New Realism*, edited by A. Wimmer, R. Goldstone, D. Horowitz, U. Joras and C. Schetter, 245–57. Lanham: Rowman & Littlefield.

Horowitz, Donald. 2008. 'Conciliatory Institutions and Constitutional Processes in Post-Conflict States'. *William and Mary Law Review* 49 (4): 1213–48.

Huntington, Samuel. 1981. 'Reform and Stability in a Modernizing, Multi-Ethnic Society'. *Politikon: South African Journal of Political Studies* 8 (2): 8–26. doi.org/ 10.1080/02589348108704792

Laoutides, Costas. 2019. 'Self-Determination and the Recognition of States'. In *Routledge Handbook of State Recognition*, edited by Gezim Visoka, John Doyle and Edward Newman, 59–70. London: Routledge. doi.org/10.4324/9781351131759-5

Laoutides, Costas and Anthony Ware. 2016. 'Re-Examining the Centrality of Ethnic Identity to the Kachin Conflict'. *Conflict in Myanmar: War, Politics, Religion*, edited by Nick Cheesman and Nicholas Farrelly, 47–65. Singapore: ISEAS–Yusof Ishak Institute.

Lijphart, A. 1968. 'Typologies of Democratic Systems'. *Comparative Political Studies* 1 (1): 3–44. doi.org/10.1177/001041406800100101

Lijphart, A. 1969. 'Consociational Democracy'. *World Politics* 21(2): 207–25. doi.org/10.2307/2009820

Lijphart, Arendt. 1977. *Democracy in Plural Societies*. New Haven: Yale University Press.

Lijphart, A. 1991. 'Constitutional Choices for New Democracies'. *Journal of Democracy*, 2 (1): 72–84. doi.org/10.1353/jod.1991.0011

Lijphart, Arendt. 1995. 'Self-Determination versus Pre-Determination of Ethnic Minorities in Power-Sharing Systems'. In *The Rights of Minority Cultures*, edited by Will Kymlicka, 275–87. Oxford: Oxford University Press.

Lijphart, Arendt. 2004. 'Constitutional Design for Divided Societies'. *Journal of Democracy* 15 (2): 96–107. doi.org/10.1353/jod.2004.0029

Mathieson, David S. 2021. 'Myanmar's Army of Darkness: The Military Was Never Interested in Peace or a Democratic Transition—and Neither Was Aung San Suu Kyi'. *Nation*, 12 February. www.thenation.com/article/world/myanmar-burma-coup-rohingya/

McCulloch, A. 2013. 'Does Moderation Pay? Centripetalism in Deeply Divided Societies'. *Ethnopolitics* 12 (2): 111–32. doi.org/10.1080/17449057.2012.658002

Moe Thuzar and Htet Myet Min Tun. 2022. 'Myanmar's National Unity Government: A Radical Arrangement to Counteract the Coup'. *Perspective*, no. 8. ISEAS – Yusof Ishak Institute.

Nordlinger, Eric A. 1972. *Conflict Regulation in Divided Societies*. Cambridge, MA: Harvard University Centre for International Affairs.

Powell, G. Bingham. 2000. *Elections as Instruments of Democracy: Majoritarian and Proportional Visions*. New Haven: Yale University Press.

Raynaud, Mael. 2021. 'Asymmetric Territorial Arrangements and Federalism in Myanmar'. *Perspective*, no. 160. ISEAS – Yusof Ishak Institute.

Reilly, B. 2001. *Democracy in Divided Societies: Electoral Engineering for Conflict Management.* Cambridge: Cambridge University Press. doi.org/10.1017/CBO 9780511491108

Reilly, Benjamin. 2012. 'Institutional Designs for Diverse Democracies: Consociationalism, Centripetalism and Communalism Compared'. *European Political Science* 11 (2): 259–70. doi.org/10.1057/eps.2011.36

Sadan, Mandy. 2013. *Being and Becoming Kachin: Histories beyond the State in the Borderworlds of Burma.* Oxford: Oxford University Press. doi.org/10.5871/bacad/9780197265550.001.0001

Saw Thonya. 2021. 'Draft Federal Union Constitution to be Finalized in December'. *Burma News International,* 24 May. www.bnionline.net/en/news/draft-federal-union-constitution-be-finalized-december

Sisk, Timothy D. 1996. *Power Sharing and International Mediation in Ethnic Conflicts.* Washington, DC: United States Institute for Peace.

Smith, Martin. 1999. *Burma: Insurgency and the Politics of Ethnicity.* 2nd ed. London: Zed Books.

South, A. 2008. *Ethnic Politics in Burma: States of Conflict.* London: Routledge. doi.org/10.4324/9780203895191

Su Mon Thazin Aung. 2022. 'Myanmar's Quest for a Federal and Democratic Future: Considerations, Constraints and Compromises'. *Perspective,* no.28. ISEAS –Yusof Ishak Institute.

Taylor, Rupert. 2009. 'The Injustice of Consociational Solution to the Northern Ireland Problem'. In *Consociational Theory: McGarry & O'Leary and the Northern Ireland Conflict,* edited by Rupert Taylor, 325–46. London: Routledge. doi.org/10.4324/9780203962565

Walton, Matthew. 2016. *Buddhism, Politics and Political Thought in Myanmar.* Cambridge: Cambridge University Press. doi.org/10.1017/9781316659144

Ware, Anthony and Costas Laoutides. 2018. *Myanmar's Rohingya Conflict.* London: Hurst and Oxford University Press.

Williams, David C. 2009. 'Constitutionalism before Constitutions: Burma's Struggle to Build a New Order'. *Texas Law Review* 87: 1657–93.

Woods, Kevin. 2011. 'Ceasefire Capitalism: Military–Private Partnerships, Resource Concessions and Military-State Building in the Burma–China Borderlands'. *Journal of Peasant Studies* 38 (4): 747–70. doi.org/10.1080/03066150.2011.607699

9

Rakhine State Post-Coup: Arakan Army State-Building and Its Implications for Rohingya and Aid

Anthony Ware

Associate Professor, School of Humanities and Social Sciences,
Deakin University, Australia

Costas Laoutides

Associate Professor, School of Humanities and Social Sciences,
Deakin University, Australia

Abstract

The conflicts in Rakhine State have taken a surprising backseat on the national and international stage since the 1 February 2021 coup in Myanmar. Obvious concerns about the wellbeing, citizenship and return of Rohingya aside, the most surprising events have been with regards to the Arakan Army's (AA) increasing moves to set up parallel state functions. There has been very little support for the National Unity Government in northern and central parts of Rakhine State, while the AA enjoys very strong popular support. Under the cover of COVID-19, and an ongoing ceasefire while the military are heavily stretched in other parts of the country, the AA has rapidly expanded its control through new de facto state institutional functionings. Since the coup, they have implemented new judicial, taxation, conflict resolution and security functions; taken a leading role in the COVID-19 response; and overturned major aspects of Rohingya policy at the local level. This signals a significant power shift in Rakhine State that is likely to reshape both state and (perhaps) national politics for decades to come. This chapter explores these changing dynamics, their likely trajectory and the implications for both domestic politics and international aid/peace-building. These developments will undoubtedly have significant implications for the Rohingya, but the nature of these implications is not yet clear or resolved, given that the underlying issues for the Rohingya remain unaltered.

***

Prior to the 1 February 2021 coup, international attention on Myanmar was squarely focused on the conflicts in Rakhine State—notably, the plight of the Rohingya and the culpability of the Myanmar military[1] in the Rohingya genocide. Since the coup, however, Rakhine State has taken an unexpected backseat on the national and international stage, and the region has surprisingly become one of the more stable parts of the country. Concerns about Rohingya wellbeing remain: there has been no progress on the fundamental issues of citizenship for, and repatriation of, the million-plus refugees sheltering in Bangladesh, and the military has not budged on issues of Rohingya identity, rights or access to services. Nonetheless, since the coup, Rakhine State has been on a significantly different trajectory to most of the rest of the country, and there have been some significant developments there that may well reshape both that part of the country and, possibly, Myanmar national politics for decades to come.

The most surprising and significant development since the coup has been the consolidation of power by the Arakan Army (AA) and its political arm, the United League of Arakan (ULA). This chapter explores that phenomenon and its implications. Under the cover of COVID-19, and capitalising on a de facto ceasefire while the Myanmar military was heavily stretched in other parts of the country, the AA/ULA rapidly consolidated control and expanded its influence across large parts of Rakhine State. Commencing in November 2020, barely two months before the coup, and while never formalised, the ceasefire ended a two-year period of intense

---

1   The Myanmar military calls itself the 'Tatmadaw', which literally translates as 'royal armed forces'. As Myanmar is no longer a kingdom, the contemporary use of the name implies 'glorious'. In solidarity with the resistance to the coup, this chapter simply uses the term 'Myanmar military'. See Desmond (2022).

fighting that only ever seemed to further the reach and capability of the AA/ULA and attract new recruits and support. The ceasefire broke down in late 2022; however, as a consequence of the ceasefire and the region's very limited participation in the Civil Disobedience Movement (CDM)—which explains the absence of military backlash against anti-coup activities—the situation in the state became relatively peaceful for almost two years. After the coup, the AA/ULA were apparently seen by the military as a less immediate threat—a group to be dealt with later or via a different approach—although that has clearly changed now. But, at least until late 2022, while state institutions have become increasingly fragile and unable to provide basic services, the AA/ULA rapidly expanded its institutional capacity, transiting itself from an armed liberation movement to an increasingly de facto state-like entity. While its control of territory remains contested, since the coup, the AA/ULA has implemented new judicial, taxation, conflict resolution and security functions, taken a leading role in the COVID-19 response and overturned major aspects of Rohingya policy at the local level. The AA/ULA have filled a vacuum created by a withdrawing state, consolidating their own position and legitimacy both domestically and internationally in the process. This is a significant power shift in Rakhine State. If accompanied by attitudinal shifts and a reduction in intercommunal tension, which appears to largely be the case, these shifts in policy have the potential to help reshape national political debates over identity and citizenship nationally. In so doing, Rakhine State may perhaps offer the tiniest glimmer of hope towards a possible eventual end to conflict and identity politics in Myanmar.

This chapter explores these changing dynamics in Rakhine State, their likely trajectory and the implications for both domestic politics and international aid/peace-building. These developments will undoubtedly have significant implications for the Rohingya, both the half a million plus still living in Rakhine State and the million plus sheltering across the border, although it is not yet clear what those implications will be beyond the short term. The AA/ULA have fastidiously avoided confrontation or harassment of Rohingya within Myanmar, seeking to portray themselves as representing a more inclusive politics, but how far they would go in reality if they gained full territorial control is far from clear. Nonetheless, with some 200,000 Rakhine having been displaced by fighting over the 12 months prior to the coup, narratives of greater solidarity through shared victimhood are emerging between Rakhine and Rohingya villages. The politics is further affected by the National Unity Government's (NUG) new-found support for the Rohingya. It is possible that this may be more a means to wedge the military and enhance support from the international community, while also leveraging international justice mechanisms to their side, than an example of real attitudinal change, but this is not yet clear. Certainly, the NUG's long silence on Rakhine/AA/ULA issues is noticeable. Nonetheless, this is all new in Rakhine State and potentially very positive. This chapter explores these changes with a focus on policy implications for international actors and aid agencies seeking to assist Rakhine State and resolve the Rohingya issue.

The findings presented in this chapter are based on a close following of local news media reports, regular monitoring of social media posts in both English and Burmese/Rakhine by prominent activists, and regular discussions with Burmese and Rakhine key informants via secure online communication (Signal). For the safety of those involved, only the news media reports are fully referenced. The remainder of this chapter is divided into six sections. The first two provide background context for the complex conflict in Rakhine State, and the rise of the AA/ULA pre-coup, their objectives and support. A third section then briefly looks at the literature about the path to recognition for autonomous regions—the path to de facto statehood. The fourth section then considers the amount of state-building and nation-building the AA/ULA have undertaken since the coup, in light of this theory. A fifth section then briefly explores the complex relationships the AA/ULA have with the (junta-led) State Administration Council (SAC), NUG and other armed minority groups, and what this means for the likelihood of achieving their objectives. The final section draws out the significant implications of the changed conflict and political dynamics for international actors, including bilateral donors and foreign states, as well as international agencies seeking to provide development, humanitarian and/ or peace-building support.

The Rakhine conflict: Complex and intractable

The conflict in Rakhine State is complex, an intractable conflict that dates back many decades, if not centuries. Significantly, it is a conflict between three parties, not two: the Bamar-dominated state, the Rakhine and the Rohingya. We have previously examined these intersecting conflicts in detail and here offer only the briefest summary by way of background (for further details and sources, see Ware & Laoutides 2018, 2019).

Driven by narratives about ethnicity that exacerbate social cleavages in an attempt to forge stronger group identities, these conflicts involve horizontal and vertical dimensions, and both armed and unarmed violence.

The first conflict dyad, and the most recognised by international audiences, is the campaign that has been waged by the state against the Rohingya, and counterattacks by some Rohingya on state security forces. This culminated in mass atrocities and ethnic cleansing in 2017, driving more than a million Rohingya refugees to Bangladesh. This conflict is not new; there are antecedents involving mass violence against Rohingya/Rakhine Muslims and mass exoduses in 1942, 1978 and 1991–92, each of which bear an eerie resemblance to recent events. This conflict is driven by narratives of the Rohingya being recent economic migrants, some versions suggesting that they arrived as labourers during British rule, others that most arrived illegally following independence. The reality is that large numbers of Muslims have lived in what is now Rakhine State for centuries; yet the narrative paints Rakhine State as a 'Western Gate' that needs to be firmly shut to prevent an even greater deluge of Muslims from the overpopulated subcontinent entering and overwhelming Buddhism and Burmese culture (Ware & Laoutides 2019). This is effectively Myanmar's version of the toxic great replacement theory.

The second dyad, widely propagated inside Myanmar, is an intercommunal conflict between Rakhine and Rohingya communities, into which the Myanmar government/military claim they must intervene to maintain order. The 2012 violence highlighted this long simmering dimension, and the narratives underlying it appeal to domestic, religious-oriented audiences and emphasise sectarian cleavages. Charney (1999) argues that this communal tension dates to the aftermath of the First Anglo-Burmese War (1824–26), and the return of large numbers of both Rakhine and Muslim refugees who had fled the harsh Burman occupation after their 1784 invasion. This intercommunal competition has a long history in Rakhine State, periodically boiling over into violence.

This chapter, however, is focused on the third dyad of this conflict, a dimension that has been largely overlooked by the international community until quite recently—namely, the struggle by Rakhine nationalists for autonomy or independence from the Bamar-led state. One of us (Ware 2015) flagged the significance of this dimension in a paper presented at a symposium in early 2013, just after the 2012 communal violence and well before the AA began moving troops to Rakhine State (see below). This conflict narrative harks back to the Bamar destruction of the Arakanese (Rakhine) kingdom at Mrauk-U in 1784, an event etched deeply into Rakhine collective memory. The principal grievance of the Rakhine ever since that time, popularised by late eighteenth and early nineteenth-century historical chronicles, has been Bamar domination. It is important to note that their principal grievance is not, and never has been, the presence nor actions of the Rohingya. Rakhine voters have demonstrated this deep distrust of Bamar authorities and desire for autonomy in every multi-party election in the country since independence, with support for Rakhine nationalist parties consistently as high or higher than any other minority in Myanmar in each of the 1951–52, 1956, 1960, 1990, 2010, 2015 and 2020 elections.

The growth of resentment against even the Bamar-led civilian National League for Democracy (NLD) government after a single term is attested in the 2020 election results. Even though elections were cancelled in many parts of Rakhine State due to armed clashes, preventing an estimated 73 per cent of Rakhine State's voters from casting a ballot (Kaung Hset Naing 2020), the NLD lost ground to Rakhine nationalist parties. Rakhine nationalist parties still won the fourth largest block of seats in the national Lower House, and third largest block in the Upper House. This included Rakhine nationalists winning in more southern areas of the state, where support for the nationalist parties has traditionally been weaker.

Adding to the conflict complexity, Rakhine State is the second poorest in the Union, and the northern townships where conflict has been focused constitute the poorest part of the country (World Bank 2015; also Ware & Laoutides 2018, 29). The region has suffered chronic underinvestment by the central government, and, despite Rakhine State being resource rich and strategically positioned between China and the Bay of Bengal, recent economic liberalisations have not translated into revenue and investment for the region. Further economic deterioration since the coup has hit key industries and increased the vulnerability of the population. In addition, around 148,000 Rohingya remain in internal displacement camps after the violence against them over the past decade, with a further 79,000 Rakhine also still displaced after the AA–Myanmar military conflict (UNHCR 2021). Most live in dilapidated or makeshift camps or are sheltering in monastery compounds.

Rise of the Arakan Army

From humble beginnings, and in the above context, the AA has become a leading actor in Rakhine State in under a decade, now controlling significant parts of the state and rapidly expanding its institutional capacity. The AA was formed as recently as April 2009. It drew its initial recruits from Rakhine working in the jade mines in upper Myanmar, and developed under the auspices of the Kachin Independence Army, a thousand kilometres from Rakhine State. The AA only existed in northern Myanmar until 2014. Indeed, the AA's first operations in Rakhine State were as recent as March 2015 (BNI 2017; *MPM* 2013), triggering a major operation by the Myanmar military.

Many observers believed the AA would be defeated or sink into obscurity at that time (Gaung 2022), but it prevailed in major battles and demonstrated its combat capability. Violence escalated in 2018, after the Rohingya clearance operations were concluded, until a de facto ceasefire was declared in November 2020 with Japanese mediation, less than two months before the February 2021 coup. Ko Oo (2022) speculates that this ceasefire was part of military preparations for the coup, and that if the coup had been quickly successful, they would have resumed the Rakhine war sooner. Either way, with the coup only partially successful at best, there was minimal armed confrontation with the AA for 18 months after the coup—until the AA's consolidation of power and growing alignment with resistance forces could no longer be ignored. What this has meant for the AA is discussed in detail later in this chapter. Where this heads next is uncertain. What is known is that, until recently, with the military preoccupied elsewhere in the country and seemingly relatively unconcerned about Rakhine State, the AA have consolidated their position and set up a range of activities that could best be described as institutional development, effectively state-building and nation-building, as they try to build the apparatus of a de facto state. We will discuss this more in subsequent sections.

The AA were excluded from the 2014–15 negotiations for a Nationwide Ceasefire Agreement (Aung Hla Tun 2015; Ye Mon & Lun Min Mang 2015). Both the military and the quasi-civilian NLD government branded the AA a terrorist organisation, easily dismissing them as new, small and opportunistic, and suggesting that they only formed in light of the peace process to try to gain a seat in negotiations and enhance the political voice of the Rakhine. Despite their growth and progress, they were excluded from the NLD government's 21st Century Panglong Peace Process and continued to be branded as terrorists until late 2020 (Htet Naing Zaw 2020; ICG 2020). Indeed, during its term in office, the NLD government called for the military to 'crush' the AA (Reuters 2019) and, with this in mind, imposed the world's longest internet shutdown in parts of Rakhine State (Kyaw Hsan Hlaing 2020).

The military and the NLD clearly misread the AA as a small and entirely new organisation, ignoring the long history of Rakhine nationalist armed struggle against Bamar domination, as we have documented elsewhere (Ware & Laoutides 2018). The AA is simply the most recent of many Rakhine nationalist armed groups (see also Smith 1994, 2007; Lintner 1999; South 2008), but this was not acknowledged by the Bamar-led state. Their analysis has also proven wrong in that the AA have grown rapidly in strength, organisation and popularity. Major General Twan Mrat Naing, leader of the AA, boasted in January 2022 that they had grown to over 100 battalions of 300 soldiers each, including 22,000 well-trained and battle-hardened soldiers now in effective control of 60 per cent of Rakhine State; 6,000 more soldiers deployed in allied territories; and an Auxiliary tasked with logistics and intelligence (Lintner 2022). More recent claims put the fighting force at over 30,000 troops (Gaung 2022; Ko Oo 2022). While those numbers may be inflated, and that level of control somewhat overstated, effective control of territory creates the conditions for the sort of transformation of an armed non-state actor into a state-like agent, as we are now seeing in Rakhine State, post-coup.

The political goal of the AA and its bureaucratic wing, the ULA, is summed up as the 'Arakan Dream', the long-held vision of the Rakhine people for collective self-determination. In promoting this goal, the AA/ULA appeal to a deep-seated sense of oppression, tapping into a vision of restored Rakhine sovereignty, lost when the Bamar conquered their Mrauk-U kingdom in 1784. While there has been some promotion of the idea of independent statehood, the official position is that Rakhine State could be a confederate member of a future post-coup Federal Union of Myanmar if the political arrangements are favourable, but this depends on being granted sufficient autonomy. This was recently restated by the leader of the AA, Major General Twan Mrat Naing, in January 2022:

> we are not requesting or asking for what we want from our enemy who has deprived us by force. We shall create our own destiny with our own hands, no matter what they think. We must build

on our own and earn what we deserve. My mission is to restore our sovereignty and reclaim a rightful political status for Arakan (Rakhine). (Lintner 2022)

It was restated by AA/ULA spokesperson Khaing Thu Kha during the first ever AA/ULA press conference in March 2022, highlighting it as policy not a single offhanded statement:

If there is no place for the political status we want in this union, we will have to create it ourselves and continue to build our government and our future nation-state together with the international community. (*Western News* 2022a)

The rise of the AA/ULA as a credible force has motivated a majority of people in Rakhine State to support the demand for self-determination and political autonomy. There have been several movements in the past that tried to promote political autonomy for Rakhine State, but none was able to generate mass support to the extent the AA/ULA have. After several years of intense fighting followed by a long de facto ceasefire, both political elites and the general population have become more confident in their support for the ULA/AA and the call for political autonomy.

State-building in emerging politico-territorial entities

Before providing an assessment of the extent and success of the AA/ULA in building new institutional structures, we need to review the role and basic components of state-building and nation-building in territories that seek international recognition. The first step of any national liberation movement towards having claims of autonomy recognised internationally is widely regarded as achieving a monopoly over the use violence in the territory they claim. Control of security is twofold: 1) keeping government forces out; 2) maintaining internal security among the population, thus preventing anarchy. Security allows the rebels to proceed with building institutions and infrastructure to deliver basic public services, then to create institutional structures and bodies that will exercise authority over the population. To this end, there is a gradual setting up of legislative, executive and judicial arms in tandem with the development of mechanisms for the collection and distribution of tax revenues. The next step in state formation is translating that authority over the population into a stable and systematic administration. Gradually, sections of a civil service apparatus develop and the administration seeks to reach all members of the community. The evolving bureaucracy provides a unified system of values, introduces the rule of law and gradually sets norms. In this bureaucratisation stage, the forming state becomes a centralised, impersonal systems of governance. A third potential step in the state-building process is the division of power between different institutions to facilitate a system of democratic governance, however, democratisation is not a necessary step in state formation. Several non-recognised entities have existed over a long period of time without a strong democratic footprint, while we increasingly witness an authoritarian turn in internationally recognised states (Ayoob 2001; Carbone 2013).

State-building is also coupled by a process of identity reconfiguration aiming at the creation of a coherent society in which the state will function—that is, nation-building. The emphasis is on the construction of a unified or inclusive identity as the core political identity of the people. National identity obtains a civic character that encompasses diverse ethno-linguistic and religious realities. This is an essential step for defining the political community. The challenge is how to achieve a successful coexistence of two different levels of identity: an overarching identity that brings the people together and diverse communal identities that reflect specific cultural and linguistic identities. Successful nation-building creates a sense of belonging to an all-embracing political dimension, while ethno-linguistic communities are seen as cultural (non-politicised) groups within this (Anderson 1991; Hobsbawm 1990; Smith 1998).

The AA/ULA since the coup: Consolidation, state-building and nation-building

Ko Oo (2022) recently suggested that the AA/ULA used the ceasefire and post-coup period to quickly develop four priority areas: 1) strengthen the army, 2) build a civil administration, 3) establish peaceful relations with the Rohingya, and 4) improve relations with Bangladesh and seek their help with the Rohingya living within Myanmar. In light of the above theoretical overview, these priorities make perfect sense. The following three subsections look at the first three of these in turn: the AA/ULA's consolidation, state-building and nation-building since the coup.

Consolidation: Strengthen the Arakan Army

The growth in size of the AA has already been noted, with AA leader Major General Twan Mrat Naing claiming over 30,000 troops (Lintner 2022; Gaung 2022; Ko Oo 2022). Recruitment has increased since the coup, with the AA being able to offer employment with hope and a purpose to young people who otherwise felt they lost their future in the coup. The growing legitimacy of the AA has also helped with recruitment, with experienced AA troops returning to their homeland from Kachin and Shan states providing training and support to the new recruits. Recent claims that over 100 junta soldiers have defected to the AA in Rakhine State has furthered such legitimacy (*Irrawaddy* 2022a). The bigger issue has been armaments, and, to that end, Twan Mrat Naing claims to have set up an arms and munitions factory in Rakhine (Ko Oo 2022). It is difficult to confirm if this is true, but Ko Oo believes it to be likely. Certainly, recent reports claim the NUG's People's Defence Forces have set up significant arms and munitions production within Myanmar since the coup, so it is quite plausible. Improved organisation and administration of the military has also allowed the AA/ULA to redirect staff to state-building functions (see next section).

The AA has simultaneously deepened its range of supports from the community. Rakhine entrepreneurs have become the main contributors of funding to the AA/ULA, while boatmen and truck drivers have helped transport weapons with their regular shipping. Weapons have been secretly stored in basements and other secret places, with local people, landowners, lawyers and local media outlets providing information and intelligence, all shaping and broadening the revolution.

The level of legitimacy of the AA is clearly increasing. Recently a number of rural schools raised the Arakan flag instead of the Union flag, a clear sign of where their loyalty and trust lies. On this note, the AA does not want to be hated by the people. When locals in Paletwa Township, Chin State, were reportedly beaten by AA troops in 2020, an official of the AA apologised to the public and punished the soldier who was responsible. The AA has also apologised for the killings of two Burmese traders accused of providing information to the Myanmar military during the armed conflicts in Rakhine State. Apology is a difficult choice, but optimal for developing its long-term credibility and status as accountable to its people. The same approach was followed towards soldiers when the AA captured prisoners of war, including the battalion commander from the Myanmar military; they were fed for several months and then elderly and sick soldiers were released. It can be said that these actions are building political prestige.

State-building: Build a civil administration

Some of Myanmar's other minority group armies, such as the Kachin Independence Army, United Wa State Army and Karen National Union, have provided many of the services of a government in the areas under their control for decades. However, this is a new development in Rakhine State. The AA/ULA has been working for some time to build processes of institutionalisation and bureaucratisation that would increase the legitimacy of their presence in the eyes of the local population.

In December 2019, the AA/ULA announced the formation of an Arakan People's Authority (APA) (Nan Lwin Hnin Pwint 2019), which would begin civil administration, policing and judicial functions in 2020, as well as collect taxes. More recently, the AA/ULA have begun referring to the APA as 'the Arakan People's Government' (e.g. spokesman Khaing Thu Kha during the first ever AA/ULA press conference, see Gaung 2022). Significantly, the APA is notionally centred in Mrauk-U (RFA 2020), the former capital of the Arakan Kingdom that prevailed in the region for centuries before the Burmese invasion in 1784. The symbolism in making Mrauk-U the administrative capital is important as a step along the road towards fulfilling the Arakan Dream. The commencement of tax revenue collection has allowed the AA/ULA to administer areas under its control, fund the AA/ULA's civil and political operations and increasingly rollout other services—although it has resulted in many residents currently being burdened by double taxation, to the AA as well as the SAC.

In May 2020, while still under NLD democratic rule, the AA/ULA demanded the immediate withdrawal of all government administrative offices and the military from northern Rakhine State. This was naturally ignored by the NLD government, but the APA has significantly expanded its administration since, setting up local structures that are different from Myanmar government divisions, and extending parts of its administration into southern Rakhine State, where its forces have less presence (Ko Oo 2022). The informal ceasefire implemented shortly before the coup was followed by the junta delisting the AA as a terrorist organisation in March 2021, that is, a few weeks after the coup (*GNLM* 2021). This, together with the military being preoccupied with conflicts in other parts of the country, allowed the AA/ULA to increase the role of the APA. After the coup, the civil administration in Rakhine State was faced with a wave of resignations and detentions of local administrators by Myanmar security. This situation created a gap in administration, as local communities rely on local administrators for leadership. In filling this void, the ULA/AA has increased its presence in policing, judicial services, public health and education.

The consolidation of the APA, and growth in policy and service capability, has been steady. In August 2021, the AA/ULA passed a law establishing a Justice Department and paid judiciary (DMG 2021a). Courts have been set up from the village-tract level up to district level, and wrongdoers are prosecuted in accordance with the new law. Although commencing online, some physical in-person courts are now appearing. The AA/ULA claim they received 3,838 cases in 2021, of which 50 per cent were resolved, and another 1,845 cases in the first quarter of 2022 (Gaung 2022; *Western News* 2022b). These include both civil and criminal cases, meaning it functions both in support of its own security function, and as a local conflict resolution mechanism.

At least some local lawyers suggest the ULA's judiciary are gaining trust by avoiding corruption (Gaung 2022). On the other hand, there have been complaints about abuse of power and unfair decisions. The AA/ULA response has been to suggest 'inexperience and public goodwill coexist. Mistakes are sure to be made along the way' (Gaung 2022). They have also sought to increase the quality and the quantity of the training required, to reprimand and penalise AA members who have abused their power and to encourage the public to continue reporting any wrongdoing by its members. The AA/ULA has sought to include people from all ethnicities in its justice system, and they claim these people are increasingly trusting them and seeking their intervention as required.

An interesting indirect measure of trust in AA/ULA administrative capability and legitimacy is the way people obeyed public health orders issued by the APA during the COVID-19 pandemic. Stay-at-home orders issued in June 2021 were widely followed and led to the control of the infection rate in Rakhine State. In the same area of policy, the AA/ULA has rolled out a COVID-19 vaccination program, and included both Rohingya and other remote minority communities, demonstrating commitment to its inclusive approach. Interestingly, at the time, they procured most of their vaccines from the military government!

Nation-building: Establish peace with the Rohingya

Concurrent with the AA/ULA's rapid progress in consolidating their position and state-building, they have also made significant progress in nation-building—and this development is most likely to have the greatest impact on national politics in the future, if consolidated. Nation-building in this context, as discussed above, is the process of reconfiguring the sense of identity in Rakhine State to create a more coherent society in which an alternate, potential state could actually function, a unified or inclusive identity that could gain national and international recognition and legitimacy. Again, this has been going on in other parts of the country for some time, but is a new and profound development in Rakhine State. The Kachin, for example, established a coherent sense of 'Kachin' identity out of the prior disparate tribal ethnicities over the past century or so, which particularly accelerated during the decades of conflict with the Burma/Myanmar state (Sadan 2013). In Rakhine State, the AA/ULA are now devoting considerable effort to redefining the competitive struggle between Rakhine and Rohingya into a more shared identity. They are hampered by the history of violent conflict, by the fact that the Rakhine and the Rohingya are not related in the manner of the Kachin tribes and by ongoing isolated incidents, but their attention to redefining identities appears considerable and deliberate.

Without wanting to overstate the situation, it is clear that the AA/ULA has adopted an approach to the Arakan polity that is distinctively more inclusive than the Burma/Myanmar state has previously done at any time since independence—including under the civilian-led NLD. Particularly significant in the AA/ULA's approach is their rhetoric of being inclusive of all ethnic and religious groups in Rakhine State. This is in stark contrast to the narrative of Rakhine–Rohingya hatred, and a significant distinction from other Rakhine nationalist parties, who have long pushed ethno-nationalism as a key to political autonomy. Notably, the AA has not attacked the Rohingya, either in rhetoric or physically, and has even issued calls for them to join the AA. The AA/ULA seems to have recognised since its beginning that anything other than transforming relations with the Rohingya would be counterproductive towards achieving the ultimate goal of the Arakan Dream. For example, in one of the first official statements by the AA, issued as early as 2014 in response to a *Foreign Policy Magazine* article that accused them of having an anti-Muslim agenda, they responded:

The author demonized and accused the Arakan Army as [an] armed gang against Muslims. [The] AA is not a safe haven for the extremists to do as they pleased [sic]. Nor do we intend to harm any innocent people or groups against humanity. We are highly disciplined with morals and strongly committed to freedom, justice, human rights and dignity. The Arakan Army was only established to strive for our right to self-determination and equality which no honest man shall lose in his/her life. More importantly, [the] AA is not a religion based armed group which is only formed with Buddhists but people with other religious faiths are also allowed to join [the] AA in order to share our cause. This alone proves our belief in religious diversity and our desire to create an open society where basic human rights are guaranteed. (AA 2014)

Although the term 'Rohingya' remains a point of friction, perhaps in part because the AA/ULA has to deal with the strong ethno-nationalism that has long been promoted by the Arakan National Party, the AA leader stated the following in an interview in January 2022 (answering a question about whether it is feasible for Muslims, Buddhists, Hindus and Christians to live together peacefully in Rakhine State):

It is achievable when we don't have outsiders manipulating us and using one group against another. Evidently, our Arakan (Rakhine) state never had the current level of social stability and racial harmony during 1941/2 to 2019. Now, we have more social stability, racial tension has started to decline and more positive social activities can be found. These are observable shifts and more changes should be started from within. (Twan Mrat Naing, cited in Lintner 2022)

During a recent interview in Rakhine, AA leader Twan Mrat Naing took this further, saying that everyone living in the state were citizens of Arakan, regardless of race or religion (*AK Media* 2021). Similarly, in a public statement of solidarity ahead of International Mother Language Day on 21 February 2022, the ULA, referring to the relationship between the people of Rakhine State and the people of Bangladesh, declared:

We deeply regard that both our societies are historically and culturally interlinked. The Arakanese community is part of the Bengali nation, and the same way the Bengali community is part of our Arakan nation. Since both territories are comprised of our brothers and sisters, we firmly believe that it is our responsibility to serve both our people for the best. (ULA 2022)

Certainly, shortly after the coup, reports began circulating of the Myanmar military threatening not only Rakhine, but also Rohingya villages, warning them not to support the AA (Kyaw Linn 2022), and rumours were spread by the military of Rohingya and Rakhine cooperating in armed resistance in Rakhine State. These rumours were intended to alarm Bamar audiences, tarnish the domestic reputation of the AA and reinforce the need for military intervention in the region. To us, however, they highlight the significant work done by the AA/ULA, and the profound change of polity it signals.

The AA/ULA's cause is thus not the removal of the Muslims from Rakhine but, it seems, the formation of a pan-Rakhine citizen identity out of the melting of ethnicities, cultures, languages and histories. In this nexus, the Rohingya Muslims have a role and place. The 'Arakan Dream', the vision of an autonomous Rakhine State, is undoubtedly primarily Rakhine-led, just as the Myanmar state they reject is primarily Bamar-led. There are no guarantees they will thoroughly address discrimination, equal rights and systemic injustices. Yet, their 'Arakan Dream' is very conciliary, now seeking to create space for Rohingya and Rakhine to live together, within a broader shared identify.

Significant work was done on this in the year or two prior to the coup, although not by the AA/ULA. A local process of dialogue and reconciliation occurred in Rakhine State through a series of meetings between Rakhine, Rohingya and other minority communities' representatives, running from October 2020 to January 2021. This resulted in a 'Declaration by the Diverse and United Communities of Arakan', sometimes translated as the 'Joint Declaration of Peaceful Coexistence in Rakhine State, Myanmar'. This declaration, completed and published on 18 January 2021, just two weeks prior to the coup (Nyi Nyi Lwin 2022a, 2022b), shows a social movement broader than simply the work of the AA/ULA.

Nonetheless, the AA/ULA have taken the lead in this space since the coup. Public communication by the AA/ULA has been consistent in their messaging about the inclusion of the Rohingya in their Arakan Dream. At a practical level, they have relaxed the central government's travel bans on Rohingya, effectively allowing almost free movement of Rohingya in the areas under their control, enhancing livelihood opportunities and furthering social cohesion. Supporters have repeatedly stressed the need to prevent the Rohingya issue causing problems for the AA/ULA, and the AA/ULA appear to be monitoring incidences of racial violence, concerned that military supporters will stir up intercommunal violence to undermine the AA/ULA (DMG 2021b). The AA is cautious to avoid any incidents being allowed to be framed as anti-Rohingya. For example, despite reports/complaints about a local Muslim outlaw (Abdul Hakim) whose gang committed kidnappings and drug trafficking, the AA have reportedly not taken action against him for fear of it being reported as abuse of a Rohingya. Instead, the AA/ULA made it known that they would only act if Rohingya elders and religious leaders made a formal complaint against the gang leader.

Marking a sharp break with a succession of central governments, the AA/ULA have included Rohingya representatives in local administration (Kyaw Hsan Hlaing 2021). Kyaw Hsan Hlaing notes that the Rohingya had never been allowed to participate in civil administration under the NLD administration, or any previous central government, but now the AA is giving priority to mobilising Muslims in order to gain the trust of the Muslim community and control Rohingya insurgent activity in the region. The AA/ULA have now recruited Rohingya policemen and administrators in some ULA positions, training them in administrative office work, management and law (AK Media 2021). Ko Oo (2022) points out that Rohingya have equal access to the AA/ULA legal system, and claims that the AA/ULA deserve credit for Muslim students being allowed to return to in-person studies at Sittwe University (although this was actually a SAC Ministry of Education decision and is subsequently being restricted again, it may have been influenced by the changing social context that the AA/ULA have helped foment).

Relations with the SAC and NUG

In a bid to placate the AA, the SAC military council removed the AA/ULA from its list of terrorist organisations on 11 March 2021, just weeks after the coup. Their motivation appears to have been to both stabilise the informal ceasefire and allow themselves space to direct military resources elsewhere in the country. It appears to have worked: the AA issued a statement condemning the coup and violence against civilians in March (AA 2021), but otherwise did little to oppose the coup itself or come out in support of the NUG or People's Defence Forces. This status quo, which allowed the AA/ULA to consolidate control and administration in Rakhine State as described above, continued until early 2022. In February 2022, AA/ULA officials attended Union Day celebrations in Naypyidaw, at the invitation of Min Aung Hlaing. For this, they were quite stridently criticised by some Rakhine, to the extent that the AA arrested one of the loudest critics, Arakan National Party central committee member U Khine Kyaw Moe (*Irrawaddy* 2022b). But then, on 24 March, the NUG extended an invitation to informal meetings (*Western News* 2022c), which the AA/ULA took up—and the military immediately responded by sending long convoys with 1,000 new troops and advanced weaponry into the AA stronghold of Paletwa, in southern Chin State (DVB 2022). The military chief, Min Aung Hlaing, countered by inviting the AA to peace talks on 22 April, which the AA declined, and things have spiralled since then. Unsurprisingly, AA/ULA officials proceeded with the meetings with the NUG on 16 May 2022; in its statement after the meetings, the NUG referred to the ULA/AA as the 'Arakan People's Government' (BNI 2022). The army responded with obstruction, arrests and roadblocks to intercept shipments and movement more than direct military confrontation (Ko Oo 2022). Regular armed clashes have escalated throughout 2022.

As early as May 2022, the AA accused the military of disrupting AA/ULA administrative, taxation and judicial activities, including by deploying additional troops near ULA courts and threatening and arresting members of the local ULA administration as well as persons involved in legal cases (RFA 2022). The military has also allegedly been attempting to destroy relations between the Rakhine and the Muslim communities through harassment and attacks. The Myanmar Army have reinforced their position, bringing in at least two brigades to support the three stationed in Rakhine State, and deployed air strike and navy capability on the Kaladan River. The number of armed engagements has continued to escalate during 2022, with the military blockading Sittwe and other major cities in the north, pushing civilian populations to the brink of starvation. This may have slowed further progress in state-building and nation-building, but has not, at this point, reversed the progress. Notably, while the Rohingya did not take sides during the 2019–20 fighting between the AA and military, as Ko Oo (2022) notes, both sides are now working hard to mobilise the Rohingya, a move that highlights the concerns the military have about the potential powershift if there is widespread reconciliation between the two communities.

Implications for international actors

So, what do these tectonic shifts in relations and power in Rakhine State mean for international actors? The first significant implication concerns access for humanitarian aid and other organisations. The rise of the AA/

ULA means access not only needs to be negotiated with the SAC, which is problematic enough, but also with the AA/ULA for most of the areas with the greatest need in Rakhine State. The junta will not want this to occur. There are several implications of this, including more complications for international agencies in negotiating memorandums of understanding (MoUs), visas, etc. And, of course, the junta is less likely to allow access to areas under AA control, citing security concerns. So, accessing displaced populations and those most affected by conflict is going to be increasingly difficult—especially the Rohingya populations in Rakhine State. A more flexible approach may be via increased cooperation with local non-government organisations (NGOs) and civil society organisations (CSOs) in design and delivery, as argued for by Décobert in this volume (see Chapter 12). However, for this to work, a good deal of thought and discussion needs to go into ways of minimising the additional security risk to staff in these organisations, and significantly relaxed accountability processes surrounding implementation need to be introduced. Any increase in use of local NGOs/CSOs in the provision of aid to the Rohingya is even more difficult and needs significant thought and planning.

A second major implication for international actors is around alignment and legitimisation. One of the key principles of international aid in normal situations is that it should align as closely as possible with national systems, rather than create duplicate, parallel systems. That, of course, strengthens the systems of the state, and helps build their legitimacy, something the international community is in virtual consensus about wanting to avoid. Negotiating MoUs and gaining access to run any programs in Myanmar is fraught enough in terms of legitimisation—there is no suggestion aid should align with, and in any way strengthen, the systems and bureaucracy behind the SAC. And while significant parts of the international community would like to strengthen the NUG and their processes, systems, departments and so on, they have little capacity in Rakhine State. Therefore, the question that needs significant debate is this: with the AA/ULA increasingly in effective control of significant territory and rapidly institutionalising, should or could international aid align with AA/ULA structures and processes and, if so, by how much? Either way, international actors will need to tread more carefully than usual in Rakhine State and take account of AA/ULA institutions and state-building.

Interrelated with this is the question of how much recognition, support or other means of boosting legitimacy the international community would like to give to the emerging AA/ULA. Indeed, it is not clear whether such recognition, support or boosts to legitimacy would help the people of Rakhine, including the Rohingya, or goad the military into more ferocious operations in the region. A further complication is the AA/ULA's reputation for engaging in illicit activities, notably, drug trafficking—although they are not alone in this, with most other armed militias and minority armies around the country similarly engaged.

A final implication for the international community was raised by Ko Oo (2022), and that is whether there is a tactical and practical advantage to improve relations between Bangladesh and the AA, to help with the Rohingya, both inside Myanmar and in laying a foundation for a long-term solution to the refugee problem in Bangladesh, through changed attitudes and communal dynamics in Rakhine State and along the border. This is an unresolved question, worthy of international consideration. The observations above highlight the strategic relevance of humanitarian engagement in Rakhine to all parties. Given the asymmetrical nature of the conflict, any engagement by international actors will convey strategic benefits for one of the sides to the conflict: therein lies the moral dilemma for international donors.

References

AA (Arakan Army). 2014. '"Condemnation Letter" by the Arakan Army Commander-in-Chief'. 5 August. www.thearakanarmy.com (page discontinued, but cited in Ware & Laoutides 2018).

AA (Arakan Army). 2021. 'Statement on the Ongoing Internal Conflicts in Myanmar after the Military Coup'. 31 March. at: www.arakanarmy.net/post/statement-on-the-ongoing-internal-conflicts-in-myanmar-after-the-military-coup

AK Media. 2021. 'ရက္ခိုင့်တပ်တော်တပ်မှူးချုပ် ဗိုလ်ချုပ်ထွန်းမြတ်နိုင်နှင့် အင်တာဗျူး အစီအစဉ်' ['Interview with General Tun Myat Naing Nant, Commander-in-Chief of Arakan Army'].

Anderson, Benedict. 1991. *Imagined Communities: Reflections on the Origin and Spread of Nationalism*. London: Verso Books.

Aung Hla Tun. 2015. 'Excluded Armed Groups Say They Want to Join Myanmar Peace Talks'. Reuters, 11 September. www.reuters.com/article/myanmar-rebels-idUKL4N11H22B20150911

Ayoob, Mohammed. 2001. 'State Making, State Breaking, and State Failure'. In *Turbulent Peace: The Challenges of Managing International Conflict*, edited by C. A. Crocker, F. O. Hampson and P. Hall, 127–42. Washington, DC: United States Institute of Peace Press.

BNI (Burma News International). 2017. *Deciphering Myanmar's Peace Process: A Reference Guide 2016*. Chiang Mai: BNI.

BNI (Burma News International). 2022. 'Will the AA be Involved in the Spring Revolution?' *Myanmar Peace Monitor*, 24 May. www.mmpeacemonitor.org/311030/will-the-aa-be-involved-in-the-spring-revolution-issue-54/

Carbone, Giovanni. 2013. 'Democratisation as a State-Building Mechanism: A Preliminary Discussion of an Understudied Relationship'. *Political Studies Review* 13 (1): 11–21. doi.org/10.1111/1478-9302.12020

Charney, Michael. 1999. 'Where Jambudipa and Islamdom Converged: Religious Change and the Emergence of Buddhist Communalism in Early Modern Arakan (Fifteenth to Nineteenth Centuries)'. PhD thesis, University of Michigan.

Desmond. 2022. 'Please Don't Call Myanmar Military Tatmadaw'. *Irrawaddy*, 25 May. www.irrawaddy.com/opinion/guest-column/please-dont-call-myanmar-military-tatmadaw.html

DMG (Development Media Group). 2021a. 'ULA Introduces Parallel Justice System for Arakan State'. 3 August. www.dmediag.com/news/3235-ula-introduces

DMG (Development Media Group). 2021b. 'လူမျိုးရေးပဋိပက္ခများကိုဦးတည်စေ နိုင်သော ထူးခြားဖြစ်စဉ်များကို ဆက်တိုက်တွေ့ရှိလာရ၍ ဆင်ခြင်သတိထားးကရန်ရှိန ULA ထုတ်ပန့်' ['ULA Statement Urging Caution as a Series of Significant Developments Have Led to Sectarian Violence']. Facebook, 17 December. www.facebook.com/dmgnewsagency/posts/2181966828622383

DVB (Democratic Voice of Burma). 2022. 'Huge Convoy Rolls into Southern Chin to Establish Bulwark against AA'. 30 March. english.dvb.no/aa-tensions-rise-southern-chin/

Gaung. 2022. 'Arakan Army Grows up Quickly'. Burma News International, 19 April. www.bnionline.net/en/news/arakan-army-grows-quickly

GNLM (*Global New Light of Myanmar*). 2021. 'Withdrawal from Declaration as Terrorist Group'. 11 March. www.gnlm.com.mm/withdrawal-from-declaration-as-terrorist-group/ (page discontinued).

Hobsbawm, Eric. 1990. *Nations and Nationalism since 1780: Programme, Myth, Reality*. Cambridge: Cambridge University Press.

Htet Naing Zaw. 2020. 'Myanmar Govt Says Arakan Army Not Invited to Union Peace Conference'. *Irrawaddy*, 6 August. www.irrawaddy.com/news/burma/myanmar-govt-says-arakan-army-not-invited-union-peace-conference.html

ICG (International Crisis Group). 2020. *From Elections to Ceasefire in Myanmar's Rakhine State*. Yangon/Brussels: ICG.

Irrawaddy. 2022a. 'Over 100 Junta Soldiers Defect to Arakan Army in Western Myanmar'. 14 June. www.irrawaddy.com/news/burma/over-100-junta-soldiers-defect-to-arakan-army-in-western-myanmar.html

Irrawaddy. 2022b. 'ANP ဗဟိုကော်မတီဝင်ကို AA ဖမ်းဆီး' ['AA Arrests ANP Central Committee Member']. 23 February. burma.irrawaddy.com/news/2022/02/23/250093.html

Kaung Hset Naing. 2020. '"The Referee Is Taking Bribes": Rakhine Candidates Fume over Vote Cancellations'. *Frontier Myanmar*, 28 October. www.frontiermyanmar.net/en/the-referee-is-taking-bribes-rakhine-candidates-fume-over-vote-cancellations/

Ko Oo (ကိုဦး). 2022. 'ရခိုင်စစ်ပွဲ ပြန်ဖြစ်တဲ့အခါ' ['When the Rakhine War Broke out Again']. *Irrawaddy*, 26 May. burma.irrawaddy.com/opinion/viewpoint/2022/05/26/252132.html

Kyaw Hsan Hlaing. 2020. 'People in Parts of Myanmar Are Living under the World's Longest Internet Shutdown. It's Putting Lives in Danger'. *Time*, 16 November. time.com/5910040/myanmar-internet-ban-rakhine/

Kyaw Hsan Hlaing. 2021. 'Arakan Army Seeks to Build "Inclusive" Administration in Rakhine State'. *Diplomat*, 31 August.

Kyaw Linn. 2022. 'Myanmar Army Fears the Arakan Army as It Strengthens Its Hold over Rakhine'. *Mizzima*, 24 February.

Lintner, Bertil. 1999. *Burma in Revolt: Opium and Insurgency since 1948*. Chiang Mai: Silkworm.

Lintner, Bertil. 2022. 'Rebel Yell: Arakan Army Leader Speaks to Asia Times'. *Asia Times*, 18 January. asiatimes.com/2022/01/rebel-yell-arakan-army-leader-speaks-to-asia-times/

MPM (*Myanmar Peace Monitor*). 2013. 'Rakhine State Crisis Efforts'. 6 February. www.mmpeacemonitor.org/1477/rakhine-state-crisis-efforts-2/

Nan Lwin Hnin Pwint (နန်းလွင်နှင်းပွင့်). 2019. 'စီးပွားရေးလုပ်ငန်းများကို ၂၀၂၀ မှစ၍ အခွန်ကောက်တော့မည်ဟု AA စစ်ဦးစီးချုပ် ပြော' ['AA Commander-in-Chief Announces Tax Collection on Businesses from 2020']. *Irrawaddy*, 9 December. burma.irrawaddy.com/news/2019/12/09/210296.html

Nyi Nyi Lwin. 2022a. 'Declaration by the Diverse and United Communities of Arakan', *Arakan Media*, 18 January. arakannewsnet.net/2021/01/18/declaration-by-the-diverse-and-united-communities-of-arakan/ (page discontinued).

Nyi Nyi Lwin. 2022b. 'Joint Declaration of Peaceful Coexistence in Rakhine State, Myanmar'. Canadian Rohingya Development Initiative. www.rohingya.ca/joint-declaration-of-peaceful-coexistence-in-rakhine-state-myanmar/ (page discontinued).

Reuters. 2019. 'Myanmar's Civilian, Military Leaders Meet, Vow to "Crush" Rakhine Rebels'. 8 January. www.reuters.com/article/us-myanmar-politics-idUSKCN1P118S

RFA (Radio Free Asia). 2020. 'Arakan Army Collects Taxes, Polices Streets in Parts of Myanmar's War-Torn Rakhine State'. 20 July. www.rfa.org/english/news/myanmar/arakan-army-07202020093940.html

RFA (Radio Free Asia). 2022. 'Myanmar's Shadow Government Holds Talks with Powerful Arakan Army'. 16 May. www.rfa.org/english/news/myanmar/talks-05162022175552.html

Sadan, Mandy. 2013. *Being and Becoming Kachin: Histories beyond the State in the Borderworlds of Burma*. Oxford: Oxford University Press. doi.org/10.5871/bacad/9780197265550.001.0001

Smith, Anthony. 1998. *Nationalism and Modernism*. London: Routledge.

Smith, Martin. 1994. *Ethnic Groups in Burma: Development, Democracy and Human Rights*. London: Anti-Slavery International.

Smith, Martin. 2007. 'Ethnic Conflicts in Burma: From Separatism to Federalism'. In *A Handbook of Terrorism and Insurgency in Southeast Asia*, edited by in A. T. H. Tan, 293–321. Cheltenham: Edward Elgar.

South, Ashley. 2008., *Ethnic Politics in Burma: States of Conflict*. Abingdon: Routledge. doi.org/10.4324/9780203895191

ULA (United League of Arakan). 2022. *Statement of Solidarity*. 20 February. www.arakanarmy.net/post/statement-of-solidarity

UNHCR (United Nations High Commission for Refugees). 2021. *UNHCR Operational Update: November-December 2021*. reporting.unhcr.org/document/1668

Ware, Anthony. 2015. 'Secessionist Aspects to the Buddhist-Muslim Sectarian Conflict in Rakhine State, Myanmar'. In *Territorial Separatism and Global Politics*, edited by D. Kingsbury and C. Laoutides, 153–68. London: Routledge.

Ware, Anthony and Costas Laoutides. 2018. *Myanmar's 'Rohingya' Conflict*. London: Hurst & Co. doi.org/10.1093/oso/9780190928865.001.0001

Ware, Anthony and Costas Laoutides. 2019. 'Myanmar's "Rohingya" Conflict: Misconceptions, Complexity, Intractability, Drivers'. *Asian Affairs* 50 (1): 60–79. doi.org/10.1080/03068374.2019.1567102

Western News. 2022a. 'ULA/AA ၏ပထမအကြိမ်မြိသတင်းစာရှင်းလင်းပွဲကို' ['ULA/AA First Press Conference']. Facebook, 5 March. www.facebook.com/westernnewsagency/posts/477361687403674

Western News. 2022b. 'ULA/AA မှ ၂ နှစ်တာ တရားစီရင်မှုကာလအတွင်း အမှုပဝါင်း ၃၈၀၀ ကျော်လက်ခံရရှိ' ['ULA/AA Receives More Than 3,800 Cases in First 2 Years']. Facebook, 5 March. www.facebook.com/westernnewsagency/posts/477286407411202

Western News. 2022c. 'NUG နှင့် တွေ့ဆုံရေး တပ်တော်နဒ္ဓပါ်မြ ဗဟိုကော်မတီတွင် ဆုံးဖြတ်မည်ဟု ULA/AA ဆို' ['ULA / AA Says Decision Will Be Made by the Central Committee after the Meeting with NUG']. Facebook, 5 April. www.facebook.com/westernnewsagency/posts/496828382123671

World Bank. 2015. *Data: Wealth Ranking World Bank*. Yangon: Myanmar Information Management Unit. www.themimu.info/search/node/World%20Bank%20Wealth%20Ranking

Ye Mon and Lun Min Mang. 2015. 'Ceasefire Pact Is "Historic Gift": President'. *Myanmar Times*, 16 October. www.mmtimes.com/national-news/17051-ceasefire-pact-is-historic-gift-president.html (page discontinued).

10

Evolution of Communal Tensions in Rakhine State after the Coup

Ye Min Zaw

Independent researcher

Tay Zar Myo Win

Lecturer, Faculty of Political Science,
Ubon Ratchathani University, Thailand

Abstract

The military coup in Myanmar has resulted in democratic backsliding, creating turmoil with nationwide uprisings and resistance, including armed conflict. The Arakan Army (AA), a prominent armed group based in Rakhine State, has not collaborated with the fight for restoring democracy led by the National Unity Government, which was founded by elected members of the 2020 general election. Instead, the AA has been implementing its vision of self-determination—the 'Way of Rakhita'—by expanding territorial control and installing its own administration system. Rakhine was already trapped in a protracted humanitarian situation with more than 800,000 people in need, mostly Rohingya, within the state alone, and almost 1 million Rohingya refugees in Bangladesh. The term 'Rohingya' is contested and highly sensitive in the intercommunal conflict between the Arakanese and Rohingya, who have lost citizenship and fundamental human rights. Employing the concepts of protracted social conflict and territorial autonomy, the findings of this chapter demonstrate that the underlying conditions of the conflict in Rakhine State are far from resolved and could even deteriorate further in spite of improved intercommunal relations.

***

Myanmar faced democratic backsliding after the military coup on 1 February 2021 due to unfounded accusations of electoral fraud (Goodman 2021). Pro-democratic forces and civilians opposed the military coup through nationwide protests and a Civil Disobedience Movement. This national movement against the coup turned to armed resistance following the military's lethal crackdown on unarmed and largely peaceful protesters. As a consequence of the military's coup and armed conflict across the country, a humanitarian crisis has occurred with almost 1.1 million people displaced by post-coup violence as of the end of October 2022 (UNHCR 2022). This has added to the difficulty of accessing public goods and services, including healthcare, as a result of the COVID-19 pandemic (ILO 2022). Before the coup, Rakhine State had already been trapped in a protracted humanitarian crisis with more than 800,000 people in need, mostly Rohingya, within the state and almost 1 million Rohingya refugees in Bangladesh (UNOCHA 2021).[1]

The international and domestic community have expressed serious concern over the political crisis in Rakhine State, making the unresolved issues of the communal conflict between the Arakanese (Rakhine) and Rohingya[2] a matter that requires particular and urgent attention. The National Unity Government (NUG), led by elected members of National League for Democracy (NLD), put the Rohingya issue on the agenda in national politics (NUG 2021), but key stakeholders in Rakhine have chosen not to align with the NUG and have ignored the NUG's efforts to open a dialogue (Kyaw Lynn 2021). The Arakan Army (AA) maintained a temporary ceasefire with the military, called the *sit-tat* (armed forces) by the Myanmar people, while a leader of the Arakan National Party, the largest party in Rakhine State, joined the State Administrative Council—a body formed by

---

1   The resumption of fighting between the Arakan Army and the military in late July 2022 has significantly worsened the situation, leading to severe casualties. This occurred after the fieldwork was completed for this chapter.

2   In this chapter, we use 'Rohingya' for non-Kaman Muslims, which is a self-identified name; 'Arakanese' for the Rakhine Buddhists, which is their historical name; and 'Rakhine State' to refer to present-day Rakhine State under the Union of Myanmar. Note that most non-Rohingya interviewees used the term 'Muslim' to refer to the Rohingya.

the coup makers (Nyein Nyein 2021). The Arakan National Party was one of the few political parties in Myanmar to recognise the coup d'état; later, following public pressure, the party said that it might end its association with the junta (*Myanmar Now* 2021b), but it has not done so. Now, a year and a half after the coup, the conflict in Rakhine State has deteriorated significantly with the resumption of fighting between armed forces.

Applying the concepts of protracted social conflict and territorial autonomy, this chapter investigates the post-coup intercommunal situation in Rakhine State, particularly the changes in social tension upon the expansion of territorial control by the AA and the resurgence of Rohingya identity. The larger questions of state persecution and military violence against the Rohingya, and armed conflict between the military and AA, are beyond the scope of this chapter. Instead, the focus is on how the political crisis has impacted intercommunal tensions between the Arakanese and Rohingya communities in Rakhine State. The chapter examines how these communities have responded to the crisis, and the expansion of territorial control by the AA, by looking at changes in the interaction between these two communities. In addition, we include the perspectives of the conflict-affected communities in Rakhine State—particularly the Rohingya and the Arakanese—on the elevation of the Rohingya issue to the national political agenda.

Protracted social conflict and territorial autonomy

The Rakhine conflict is a typical protracted social conflict that is intractable and multifaceted (Kocamis 2019; Ware & Laoutides 2019). A protracted social conflict has multiple causal factors and dynamics in which the goals, actors, targets and intensity are always changing. It is also characterised by a blurred demarcation between internal and external sources and actors (Azar 1985). According to Kriesberg and Dayton (2012), social conflicts are not only an inevitable and essential part of social life but also can be beneficial by challenging existing exploitative structures. At the same time, social conflicts tend to create, reinforce and deepen reciprocal images of deception, making it extremely difficult to resolve them (Azar, Jureidini & McLaurin 1978). Thus, protracted social conflicts always carry a risk of escalating and turning violent at any time. The major characteristic of protractedness (i.e. continuing over a long period) make perceptions harden, diverting them into different narratives and clashes at dangerous levels (Udayakumar 2004).

Protractedness and violence are the key features of intractable conflicts, which are perceived as mostly irresolvable and demanding extensive investment (Bar-Tal 2007). Settlements that are agreed upon and benefit both parties are difficult to achieve, especially when the conflicting parties have unequal power. Therefore, changes in the relationship between the parties are crucial to getting out of the conflict cycle. To have a way out of conflict, the weaker side, in this case the Rohingya, may apply a non-violent coercive approach by drawing outside allies to develop institutional arrangements. The stronger side (i.e. the Arakan community) will be required to acknowledge the grievances suffered by the minority community and set up a robust institution to handle conflict and injustice, as well as establishing control over hardliners from each side (Kriesberg 1993). Protracted conflicts are mostly based on resource sharing, self-determination and identity-related issues (Udayakumar 2004).

Self-determination has become a claim in many ethnically diverse countries in order to protect ethnic interests and identity (Benedikter 2009; Connor 1994; Choudhry 2011). The claim for self-determination may incorporate a wide range of elements, from autonomy to independent statehood, including secession (Choudhry 2011). It is also associated with conflict, the development of ethno-nationalism and the rights of national minorities (Connor 1994; Kymlicka 1995). Kymlicka (1995) defines national minorities as territorially concentrated cultures incorporated into a larger state who historically enjoyed self-government and who consider themselves distinct from the majority and wish to maintain some autonomy to preserve their identity. As Benedikter (2009) notes, ethnic minorities often attempt to enjoy self-determination through territorial autonomy; this can be seen in the actions of the AA.

Background on the conflict in Rakhine State

Many scholars have described the conflict in Rakhine State as multi-causation and multi-level (Burke 2016; Aye Chan 2005; Kipgen 2013; Smith 1995). The conflict is historical and contested and involves disputed claims of 'indigeneity', with one group claiming original ethnicity and the right to full and neutral citizenship (Thawnghmung 2016; Ware 2015). Certainly, intercommunal tension is one of the key facets. The colonial legacy, which allowed people to freely cross international borders, also plays a big role, as it provokes Arakanese concerns relating to demographic changes (Aye Chan 2005; Leider 2020). The Advisory Commission on Rakhine State described the situation as a 'clash of narratives' in which both Arakanese and Muslims[3] try to legitimise political claims by using the historical past, leading to exclusive and irreconcilable demands (ACRS 2017).

The Arakanese narrative focuses on the demographic threat caused by migration, sociocultural exclusion and grievances from the structural conflict under Myanmar's current political system. Like other ethnic groups in Myanmar, the Arakanese have been struggling in their relationship with the central state and the Bamar majority. At the same time, however, the Arakanese narrative is based on the fear (and pervasive belief) that migration and the higher birth rate of Muslims will result in them becoming a minority within Rakhine State (Burke 2016; ICG 2016; Leider 2020). Aron (2018) and Simbulan (2018) suggest that these grievances and the rise of ethno-nationalism—which mobilises the community as a whole—could be key factors in the conflict dynamic and should be carefully unpacked. The Arakanese assume that they must be protected from mass illegal migration to maintain their influential status. To this end, Rakhine political parties have deployed anti-Muslim chauvinism as part of a wider, but recent, semi-organised social movement, with clear political goals that partly overlap with the Myanmar military elite (van Klinken & Su Mon Thazin Aung 2017).

Since the emergence of the AA, the Arakanese's dream of reclaiming the sovereignty dismantled by the Bamar Konbuang Dynasty in 1784 has been revived through the 'Way of Rakhita' concept, which has self-determination at its core (Ye Min Zaw 2019). As a result, the more territory the AA controls, the louder the call for greater autonomy and self-determination among the Arakanese. The Arakanese community sees self-determination as a matter of earning both the respect they deserve and gaining equality with other groups. They look to attain self-determination via three different paths: armed struggle, electoral politics and the peace process (Clarke, Seng Aung Sein Myint & Zabra Yu Siwa 2019).

The term Rohingya is one of the central issues of the conflict, as it draws attention to the existence of different perspectives. Some of these perspectives hark back to the pre-colonial period, seeing the role of Muslims in the

---

3   The original report says 'Muslims from Rakhine State'.

Arakan Kingdom as justification for the presence of Muslims in Rakhine State. However, the Arakanese view the term as not specifically referring to Muslims, but to the people from Rakhine State for whom it was originally coined (Aye Chan 2005). This perspective is important when considering Myanmar's 1982 citizenship law, which defines citizens as nationals who settled in the territory of the country before 1823 and gives the power to the state to decide whether any ethnic group is national or not (SRUB 1982). The law largely falls short of international standards and customary practice. It was used to exclude the Rohingya from Myanmar citizenship due to their ethno-religious identity (Haque 2014). While Ware and Laoutides (2019) argue that citizenship is not a cause of conflict but a symptom, Nyi Nyi Kyaw (2017) insists that the lack of actual implementation of the laws by successive Myanmar governments deprived the Rohingya of their right to a nationality. Cheesman (2017) points out that the concept of national race, *taingyintha*, as defined by the state, excluded the Rohingya and that this influenced the majority population to deny the Rohingya identity as part of the society. With their citizenship status rejected legally and constitutionally, the Rohingya have faced statelessness and limited freedom of movement within Myanmar. In addition, being a Muslim minority, the Rohingya have suffered from a widespread anti-Muslim campaign (Thawnghmung 2016). The semi-organised movement targeting Muslims involved multiple actors, including political parties from Rakhine State (van Klinken & Su Mon Thazin Aung 2017), and was strong during Thein Sein's administration; both hardliners and reformists of the transitional regime were complicit with ongoing communal violence in the country to promote their own political interests (Min Zin 2015).

The Rohingya community was disproportionately affected by the intercommunal conflicts in 2012 in Rakhine State. Until then, apart from partial involvement in communal-level clashes, the Rohingya had remained non-violent. However, when the Arakan Rohingya Salvation Army (ARSA) staged two rounds of attacks against security force posts in Rakhine—against which the *sit-tat* fiercely retaliated—it dramatically changed the conflict landscape. During the so-called clearance operation by the Myanmar *sit-tat*, the Rohingya faced the destruction of lives and property and over 700,000 fled into Bangladesh. According to the UN Fact-Finding Mission, the *sit-tat*'s actions amounted to war crimes, crimes against humanity and genocidal intent (OHCHR 2018). Since 2012, there have been international criticisms of this genocide and calls for the international community to act (Maung Zarni & Cowley 2014; Southwick 2015; Lindblom et al. 2015).

To sum up, grievances from both sides have created a double minority complex in which both the Arakanese and Rohingya fear an existential threat and express their sense of exclusion from Myanmar's political process. The former fears assimilation from the Bamar and the massive Muslim population of Bangladesh, while the latter is a marginalised and disempowered group (Ware & Laoutides 2019; Burke 2016). Both groups have used armed struggle as part of their campaign, although the scale and scope varies. Competing narratives, which remain unreconciled, pose the risk of further widening the gap between the two communities, increasing the difficulty of finding common ground and making meaningful steps towards overcoming the underlying problems.

Conceptual framework

Based on the underlying definition of a protracted social conflict, we seek to understand the relationship between the two communities by examining the Rohingya's deprivation of basic needs—which Azar (1990) defines as acceptance, participation and security needs—as well as the claim of autonomy by the Arakanese. To analyse the AA's efforts to gain territorial control, we apply the four criteria developed by Benedikter (2009) to determine autonomy in the modern world—that is, 1) the rule of law in the state and autonomous entity, 2) the permanent devolution of a minimum of legislative and executive powers, 3) democracy and free elections, and 4) equality of civil rights and general citizenship rights. We also explore the conflict dynamics using Azar's analytical model of protracted social conflict, paying particular attention to the genesis component (which deals with the precondition of the conflict) and process dynamics (which deal with how each communal actor responds to the conflict) (Azar 1990).

The chapter draws on both documentary research and field research. The documentary research includes analysis of reports and statements by relevant organisations as well as media interviews with stakeholders. The field research includes 10 key informant interviews by purposive sampling with key civil society organisation leaders (n=7), activists (n=2) and a politician (n=1). For the sake of the interviewees' security, their names have been anonymised throughout. All data collection was undertaken before the resumption of armed conflict between the AA and *sit-tat*, but we contend that the intercommunal Rohingya–Arakanese dynamics discussed in the chapter remain unaltered.

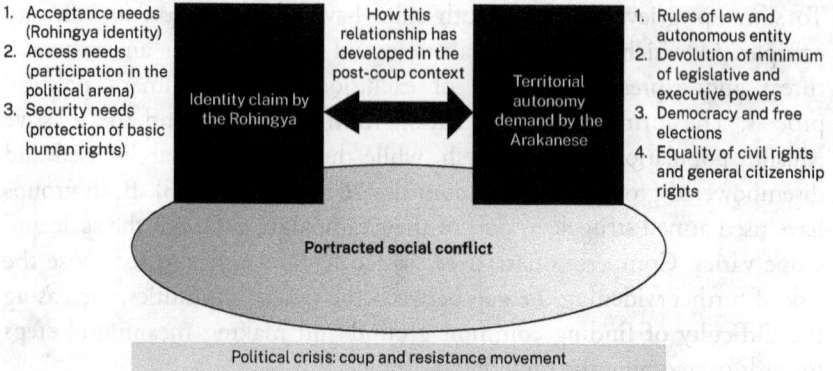

Figure 10.1: The effect of political destruction (military coup) on the protracted social conflict in Rakhine.
Source: Authors' summary.

Post-coup changes in Rakhine State

The situation in Rakhine State had started to calm down before the Myanmar *sit-tat*, led by Senior General Min Aung Hlaing, orchestrated the coup on 1 Feb 2021. The AA and the Myanmar *sit-tat* had agreed on a temporary ceasefire just after the nationwide election held on 8 November 2020 (*Myanmar Now* 2020). The armed conflict then de-escalated, with no major fighting for a year and a half, during which time the AA increased efforts to install a civil administration as part of the implementation of the Way of Rakhita (Kyaw Hsan Hlaing 2021a). While the rest of Myanmar responded to the coup with widespread protests and a Civil Disobedience Movement, Rakhine State did not see any major resistance, except in some southern townships where a swift anti-coup demonstration occurred (*Myanmar Now* 2021a). However, Arakanese from Yangon took part in the General Strike Committee of Nationalities—a loose coalition of ethnic groups formed to organise protests. A civil society organisation (CSO) leader in Rakhine State mentioned that the AA did not want those demonstrations to happen in Rakhine, because the people had already faced the hardships of long-term war and conflict (Interview, December 2021).

Several factors help to explain the limited participation of the Arakanese in the nationwide movement against the coup: the joining of the Arakan National Party to the putschists (the State Administration Council); the impact of war over two years; and the high level of trust in the AA leadership, who claim to be taking a unique path. Outstanding grievances over the

NLD government's handling of the conflict in Rakhine State also play a role. Many Arakanese see the Committee Representing the Pyidaungsu Hluttaw—a body formed by elected members of parliament—and the NUG as effectively being the NLD, and many Arakanese view the NLD and the military as being the same Bamar oppressors; consequently, they see the coup as a conflict among the Bamar. A director of a Rakhine-based peace organisation pointed out that the public in Rakhine showed sympathy when people from other parts of the country faced a brutal military crackdown, given their recent memories of the military's human rights violations in their own state. He also highlighted that since the majority of people were focused on survival issues they were not aware of political developments at a national level, particularly about the National Unity Consultative Council (NUCC)—a broad-based, inclusive platform with the specific aim of bringing together different forces around the federal democracy objective (Interview, December 2021).

Political parties from Rakhine State feel pressured to stand with the people from Rakhine State and face challenges in resisting the military's coercive measures as a result of its divide and rule approach (Interview, December 2021). According to one respondent, the Arakan League for Democracy openly opposed the military coup but most other parties showed oblique responses. A member of a non-profit organisation monitoring the conflict in Rakhine pointed out that, although the AA has not publicly joined the NUG and the NUCC, it is involved in fighting alongside other allies against the military in other parts of the country; allegedly, the AA is training local People's Defence Forces (PDF), which have been formed to fight against the military (Interview, December 2021). In addition, local youth in Rakhine State mobilised funds for the victims of Thantlang (BNI 2021), a town set on fire by the military, and there are cases of youths being arrested by the military for allegedly providing funding to the PDF (DMG 2021b, 2021c).

For the Rohingya community, the military coup has meant delaying the repatriation and settlement of refugees who fled to Bangladesh and internally displaced persons (IDPs) within Myanmar. The general Rohingya population from Rakhine State, like the Arakanese, was not fully aware of the political developments in the post-coup situation and, unsurprisingly, was unable to organise any resistance. They cautiously welcomed the NUG's statement announcing that 'the Rohingyas are entitled to citizenship by laws that will accord with fundamental human rights, norms and democratic federal principles' (NUG 2021). In contrast, the Arakanese were upset by the use of the term Rohingya; they accused the NUG of failing to engage in proper consultation (with them) and of political trickery (Interviews with CSO leaders, a youth activist and a political leader, December 2021 – January 2022). A Rohingya youth activist living in an IDP camp in Rakhine said that he fully supported the NUG's recognition of the Rohingya because of the military's action that provoked the atrocities they faced in the past, but he was not able to publicly state this (Interview, December 2021). Instead of looking to the NUG and other political developments, many Rohingya prioritise their relationship with the local Arakanese community and the AA.

Both the Arakanese and Rohingya have suffered severely during the violent conflict over the last decade. Armed conflict, access to basic needs, poverty and striving for identity are all associated with the conflict in Rakhine State. Although both communities have long contested their territorial autonomy, the Arakanese and Rohingya still need to interact to fulfil their physical and material needs. After the violent conflict of 2012, trust between the two communities was eroded, inevitably impacting interactions in social and economic activities. The conflict left 800,000 people in need of humanitarian assistance due to displacement and clashes within Rakhine State, while almost 1 million Rohingya fled to Bangladesh (UNOCHA 2021). According to some CSO leaders (Interviews, December 2021), in the post-coup environment, the Rohingya can now travel to cities, such as Sittwe and Mrauk-U, and between villages for basic needs, such as working and accessing medical treatment, but they cannot travel to Myaepone or Kyaukphyu. Proceeding with caution, the Rohingya travel only in the daytime, even though there are no restrictions on travel at night (Interviews, December 2021). Several respondents from CSOs expressed the view that communication and interaction between the two communities on the ground had improved and that the Arakanese welcomed Rohingya people who were travelling and fulfilling their basic needs (Interviews, December 2021). By contrast, the restrictions imposed by the military on the Rohingya limited travel both within Rakhine State as well as outside of it and required the Rohingya to fill out travel approval forms and obtain approval from the township administrative officer prior to any travel (CSO leader, interview, December 2021; DMG 2022; Myo Htun 2021).

Although freedom of movement has improved to a certain degree post-coup, no arrangements have been made for the repatriation of IDPs in the near future. People in IDP camps, both Rohingya and Arakanese, do not envisage returning to their villages. An Arakanese youth activist explained that the main concerns for Arakanese IDPs are the deployment of military troops and the existence of landmines, while Rohingya IDPs are concerned by the lack of durable solutions, such as guarantee of safety and livelihood and the right to return to their places of origin (Interview, December 2021). The resumption of armed conflict between the AA and the military since these interviews were conducted only accentuates the sense of instability of both sets of IDPs. There is no easy solution to the problem of IDPs in Rakhine State; meanwhile, the people in the camps face numerous challenges, including inadequate food.

If we look at intercommunal relations with this background of parallel priorities, we find improvements in relations between the two communities within Rakhine State. Certainly, it is clear that some progress has been made in terms of social relations and that initiatives for social harmony have had some good effects in both communities. Individuals and CSOs from both communities continue to attempt to build trust for peaceful coexistence. In a unique case, a Muslim teacher joined a monastery school in Mrauk-U Township to teach Arakanese students English (DMG 2021a). Similarly, a young Arakanese teacher now teaches Muslim students in primary schools at the Muslim villages in Maungdaw Township (*Western News* 2022b). In Pauktaw Township, Muslim villagers donated money for the construction and general expenses of a new pagoda (*Western News* 2022a). Many people have made positive and welcoming comments about these activities on social media. These examples demonstrate that both communities have endeavoured, and are endeavouring, to build mutual trust and peaceful coexistence after years of conflict.

A member of a youth organisation noted that, while some of the opposition to the Rohingya identity has decreased, the word 'Rohingya' continues to be problematic for some Rakhine community members who are not ready to accept it due to concerns about the presumed political motives behind it, such as demands for territorial rights and self-determination (Interview, December 2021). The Arakanese assume that most activists and advocates for the Rohingya identity are self-interested and unaware (or uninterested) in the views of community members on the ground (Interview, December 2021). While recognition and acceptance of the Rohingya identity is an important first step in granting the Rohingya meaningful participation in political and economic institutions, currently, the Rohingya prioritise basic material needs for their survival; therefore, they do not claim the identity strongly on the ground, instead accepting the term Muslim for the sake of better cooperation and interaction between the two communities (Interview, December 2021). This does not necessarily mean that they do not want acceptance of their identity. A Rohingya diaspora activist noted that Rohingya people from inside Rakhine State regularly contact activists from around the world to continue fighting for their identity (Interview, January 2022).

Restoration of autonomy in Rakhine State

The conflict in Rakhine cannot be analysed purely on the basis of the interaction between two communities, the Arakanese and the Rohingya, because it involves multi-causal factors and numerous other actors. The actions of the military and the armed conflict, for example, have also had a profound effect. The analysis should also consider the complexity of Myanmar's politics, and ethnic demands for territorial rights and self-determination. The country officially classified 135 ethnic groups, partitioned into eight major groups and subgroups, but Rohingya was not on the list (Kipgen 2018). The failure to adequately share power and accommodate diversity prompted several ethnic groups to take up arms to fight for territorial rights and self-determination against the Bamar-dominated central government (Kipgen 2018; Breen 2019).

The Arakanese are one such national minority in Myanmar who have demanded territorial rights and self-determination through armed struggle. Rakhine State enjoyed autonomy in the pre-colonial period until its kingdom fell under the Bamar Konbaung Dynasty, following the invasion of King Bodawphya in 1784 (Thawnghmung 2016). The claim of autonomy by the AA links back to the Arakan Kingdom with the strategy of the Way of Rakhita, the goal of which is to restore autonomy and self-determination (Ye Min Zaw 2019). In an interview with a media outlet, the AA chief admitted that the AA's ultimate goal was an independent Rakhine State (Parvez, Shafiqul Alam & Ashfaque Ronnie 2022).

After agreeing to an unofficial ceasefire with the military, the AA established its governing power through an administration, a judicial system and taxation (Parvez, Shafiqul Alam & Ashfaque Ronnie 2022). Rohingya people are invited to participate in the AA's administration system, but it is only at the village and ward level (Interviews, December 2021). While the Arakanese and Rohingya rely on the AA's administration more than the military regime's (even more so post-coup), there have been complaints and accusations of unfair treatment and power abuses by the authorities against

Rohingya people (Interviews, December 2021 – January 2022). Thus, the international community has concerns that the Rohingya will continue to be marginalised if the AA gains full control over the region (Fox 2021).

Fundamental civil and political rights for all group members are essential for establishing self-governance in a modern autonomous system (Benedikter 2009). If the Rohingya are prevented from meaningful and equal participation in the government of the Rakhine State, the challenge of fulfilling their developmental human needs will remain. Although the AA's plan to fully respond to the Rohingya people is not yet clear, some progress can be seen in the AA's emerging policy and actions. For example, General Twan Mrat Naing, leader of AA said:

> We recognize the human rights and citizen rights of the Rohingyas … It will take time to resolve this problem, especially with the arguments on both sides regarding the 'Rohingya' identity of the Rohingya people. (Parvez, Shafiqul Alam & Ashfaque Ronnie 2022)

According to Benedikter (2009), an autonomous territorial unit should be arranged by legal mechanism, domestic or international, in a modern autonomous system—not by territorial control by armed groups. The governance of Rakhine State is currently split between the Myanmar *sit-tat* and the AA, and is, therefore, highly contested. Nonetheless, since the military coup, both the Arakanese and the Rohingya choose to submit to the AA administration, rather than the military, wherever possible. Consequently, regulations imposed by the military have not been able to be enforced effectively in Rakhine State post-coup.

The NUG has attempted to coordinate with various ethnic armed organisations in the fight against the military, promising to build a genuine federal democracy (NUG n.d.). The AA refused the NUG's invitation to collaborate in this democratic revolution as they already have their own political agenda. Therefore, the direction of power sharing between the central government and the AA—even if the democratic forces win—cannot be anticipated yet, although the NUG has released a federal charter that would be its roadmap for state-building (NUCC 2021).

Meanwhile, the Arakanese fear that the Rohingya desire separation and territorial rights, and this fear informs the continued deprivation of the Rohingya identity. Though the Rohingya claim that they do not have any plans for separation, there is compelling evidence of a movement for territorial autonomy. For example, the Mujahid armed group, the Rohingya

Independence Force (now the Rohingya Patriotic Front), the Rohingya Solidarity Organization and the ARSA have all launched campaigns for self-determination and territorial autonomy over the last seven decades, including armed attacks. Some of these groups still remain active (Thawnghmung 2016; Ware 2015). The ARSA claimed that attacks against the military and police forces in Rakhine State in 2016 were aimed at defending the rights of the Rohingya people (Winchester 2017). These actions caused Rakhine nationalists to become fearful of recognising Rohingya identity. However, most Rohingya do not see the ARSA as representing their interests due its suspected affiliation with the *sit-tat* (Interview, January 2022).

Rohingya participation in the AA's administrative process is rare but not unheard of. The Arakanese claim that the AA gives everyone equal opportunity to become village administrators, regardless of ethnic background, and allows Rohingya people to be heads of their village (Interview, December 2021). This marks a sharp break with the central government (Kyaw Hsan Hlaing 2021b) and has helped to earn the trust of the Muslim community (Interview, December 2021). Lack of access to social superstructures, such as political participation and economic access, is one of the preconditions of protracted social conflict. The AA has claimed that it will treat everyone equally in terms of access to its administrative roles and police force, but it is too early to see whether this is the case. Moving forward, the strategies and actions the AA employs to influence the Rohingya community will become a key factor in determining the future dynamics of the protracted conflict.

The AA has been trying to enforce the rule of law, but issues on the ground, such as land disputes, tax collection and unequal treatment of Muslims, continue to make this difficult (Interview, December 2021). A Rohingya activist mentioned that some Rohingya within their community still feel unable to speak out due to fear of reprisal (Interview, December 2021). Such claims are criticised by Arakanese who believe that it is Rohingya from abroad who are making the problem worse by interfering while the two communities are trying to live together. Yet, many complaints about abuses of power and unfair decisions by the AA's administration for both Rohingya and Arakanese people are evident on social media emanating from within Rakhine State.

Conclusion

The underlying conditions of the protracted social conflict in Rakhine State remain unchallenged and unremediated. The multi-ethnic nature of Myanmar, the deprivation of basic needs—particularly for the Rohingya—and the role of the state, which is returning to a totalitarian regime after the coup in February 2021, combined with the mobilisation of an international diaspora, fulfils all the preconditions of a protracted social conflict. The return to armed conflict in Rakhine State poses further challenges for intercommunal relations. The claim of recognition and entitlements from within the political and social structure of Myanmar for the Rohingya identity was an outcome of collective action from a marginalised community. The clash of narratives on the Rohingya identity is still strong, particularly on the question of recognition as an indigenous people within Myanmar. Although the name is still used with caution, both the Arakanese and the NUG have agreed to the provision of fundamental human rights and citizenship for the Rohingya. It should be noted that, presently, and in accordance with the 1982 citizenship law, which the NUG has flagged it will amend, the most privileged citizenship status in Myanmar is still associated with indigenous ethnicity. Thus, currently, the Rohingya still have unequal status with other ethnic groups, although they can apply for other types of citizenship (e.g. associated or naturalised).

Meanwhile, the Arakanese community is steadily moving towards the claim of territorial autonomy by invoking historical narratives and using military power. The AA has become the leading force of the Arakanese political movement and claims to be building an inclusive Arakan in which the Rohingya will have a place and a role. But the Arakanese are still reluctant to officially recognise the Rohingya identity, citing concerns of separatist actions informed by historical evidence. The construction of identity by both the Rohingya and the Arakanese as a matter of 'communal actions and strategies' (which is a characteristic of protracted social conflicts) is an issue that remains unresolved. The former sees themselves as an indigenous ethnic group, while the latter promotes an 'Arakanese identity' based on historical grievances. Yet, there are indications that the current conflict may become latent, as both groups are motivated to avoid another round of violence, especially given the longstanding hardships both have suffered since the conflict of 2012.

Social relationships between the two communities have improved due to the conscious effort of both parties. The Rohingya have enjoyed a certain degree of freedom of movement with no antagonism from the Arakanese, although they are still unable to travel freely outside of Rakhine State owing to military-imposed restrictions. The Arakanese and the Rohingya have responded to Myanmar's political crises in different ways. The former distanced themselves from national politics and claimed they had their own way of working towards autonomy, while the latter covertly supported the NUG's recognition of the Rohingya identity, being unable to express their support explicitly, particularly within Rakhine State.

Recommendations for the international community

This analysis leads to several implications and recommendations for the international community. First, it highlights the need to engage directly with concerned stakeholders in Rakhine State, mainly the AA from the Arakanese side and representatives of Rohingya communities, both domestic leaders and exiled activists. The trust in the AA by the Arakanese is substantial, and the AA have huge leverage. For the Rohingya, local community leaders have extensive knowledge of on-the-ground situations but are limited in their capacity to speak freely due to safety concerns. Therefore, exiled Rohingya human rights activists should also be consulted. A second recommendation is to empower the civil society groups among the Rohingya communities. Students and youths in the IDP camps are initiating self-help groups and engaging informally with their Arakanese peers. These should be strengthened and supported, and, where possible, educational assistance and scholarships for youth from both communities should be provided.

Beyond this, the international community needs to support Myanmar's democratic transition. Myanmar is facing unprecedented challenges with democratic backsliding and is at risk of becoming a regional humanitarian catastrophe. The state and the majority group at the national level will continue to play a role and this will affect the situation in Rakhine State. Without addressing the structural issues and political impasse by which military and/or authoritarian regimes continue to control state power, both communities in Rakhine State are very likely to face another round of atrocities. Part of this requires closely monitoring the development of the ultra-nationalist movements that are backed by the military and opportunists. One of the root causes of discrimination against the Rohingya is nationalistic sentiments fuelled by fake news and hate speech. Such sentiments are seemingly still in the undercurrent but they could become overt at any time.

Finally, the international community needs to adhere to the 'do no harm' principle and try to reduce Myanmar's dependence on international aid. The international community is cognisant of the scale of support required for humanitarian reasons, but it must also explicitly understand the risk of creating a situation in which Myanmar becomes dependent on such aid, thereby undermining the capacity of the Myanmar people to build and rebuild their own relationships.

References

ACRS (Advisory Commission on Rakhine State). 2017. 'Towards a Peaceful, Fair and Prosperous Future for the People of Rakhine: Final Report of the Advisory Commission on Rakhine State'. 24 August. www.kofiannanfoundation.org/mediation-and-crisis-resolution/rakhine-final-report/

Aron, Gabrielle. 2018. 'Reframing the Crisis in Myanmar's Rakhine State'. *Peace Brief*, no. 242. www.jstor.org/stable/resrep20200

Aye Chan. 2005. 'The Development of a Muslim Enclave in Arakan (Rakhine) State of Burma (Myanmar)'. *SOAS Bulletin of Burma Research* 3 (2): 396–20.

Azar, Edward E. 1985. 'Protracted International Conflicts: Ten Propositions'. *International Interactions* 12 (1): 59–70. doi.org/10.1080/03050628508434647

Azar, Edward E. 1990. *The Management of Protracted Social Conflict: Theory and Cases*. London: Dartmouth Publishing Company.

Azar, Edward E., Paul Jureidini and Ronald McLaurin. 1978. 'Protracted Social Conflict: Theory and Practice in the Middle East'. *Journal of Palestine Studies* 8 (1): 41–60. doi.org/10.2307/2536101

Bar-Tal, Daniel. 2007. 'Sociopsychological Foundations of Intractable Conflicts'. *American Behavioral Scientist* 50 (11): 1430–53. doi.org/10.1177/00027642 07302462

Benedikter, Thomas. 2009. *The World's Modern Autonomy Systems: Concepts and Experiences of Regional Territorial Autonomy*. New Delhi: Anthem Press. webfolder. eurac.edu/EURAC/Publications/Institutes/autonomies/MinRig/Autonomies %20Benedikter%2009%20klein.pdf

BNI (Burma News International). 2021. 'Arakanese Youths Collect Donations for Fire Victims in Thantlang, Chin State'. 4 November. www.bnionline.net/en/news/arakanese-youths-collect-donations-fire-victims-thantlang-chin-state

Breen, Michael G. 2019. 'Asymmetry or Equality? Ethnic Nationalities in a Bamar-Dominated State. A Country Study of Constitutional Asymmetry in Myanmar'. In *Constitutional Asymmetry in Multinational Federalism*, edited by Patricia Popelier and Maja Sahadžić, 341–68. London: Palgrave Macmillan. doi.org/10.1007/978-3-030-11701-6_13

Burke, Adam. 2016. 'New Political Space, Old Tensions: History, Identity and Violence in Rakhine State, Myanmar'. *Contemporary Southeast Asia* 38 (2): 258–83. doi.org/10.1355/cs38-2d

Cheesman, Nick. 2017. 'How in Myanmar "National Races" Came to Surpass Citizenship and Exclude Rohingya'. *Journal of Contemporary Asia* 47 (3): 461–83. doi.org/10.1080/00472336.2017.1297476

Choudhry, Sujit. 2011. 'Federalism, Secession & Devolution: From Classical to Post-Conflict Federalism'. In *Research Handbook on Comparative Constitutional Law*, edited by Tom Ginsburg, 356–84. Cheltenham: Edward Elgar Publishing.

Clarke, Sarah L., Seng Aung Sein Myint and Zabra Yu Siwa. 2019. *Re-Examining Ethnic Identity in Myanmar*. Siem Reap: Centre for Peace and Conflict Studies. www.centrepeaceconflictstudies.org/wp-content/uploads/Re-Examining-Ethnic-Identity-in-Myanmar.pdf

Connor, Walker. 1994. *Ethnonationalism: The Quest for Understanding*. Princeton: Princeton University Press. doi.org/10.1515/9780691186962

DMG (Development Media Group). 2021a. '"Honesty and Love" Guide Interfaith English Lessons at Monastic School in Mrauk-U'. 23 November. www.dmediag.com/interview/3690-u-aung-khin

DMG (Development Media Group). 2021b. 'Eight People in Arakan State Arrested for Alleged Anti-Regime Links'. 6 December. www.dmediag.com/news/3749-eight-people-in-arakan-state-arrested

DMG (Development Media Group). 2021c. 'Students' Groups Condemn Recent "Acts of Sabotage" in Arakan State'. 24 December. www.dmediag.com/news/3838-%E2%80%98acts-of-sabotage%E2%80%99

DMG (Development Media Group). 2022. 'Military Tightens Security Checks on Travellers in Some Arakan Townships'. 4 January. www.dmediag.com/news/3873-mts?fbclid=IwAR3aTM7l9JX8OzoYsee3vJUOiGjB-JeijnMczYhrqkKlUhGhZZxykAiCd2s

Fox, Kyra. 2021. *Risk of Mass Atrocities against the Rohingya Post-Coup*. Washington: United States Holocaust Memorial Museum. earlywarningproject.ushmm.org/storage/resources/1454/The_Risk_of_Mass_Atrocities_against_the_Rohingya_Post-coup.pdf

Goodman, Jack. 2021. 'Myanmar Coup: Does the Army Have Evidence of Voter Fraud?' *BBC News*, 5 February. www.bbc.com/news/55918746

Haque, Md Mahbubul. 2014. '1982 Citizenship Law in Burma and the Arbitrary Deprivation of Rohingyas' Nationality'. *South Asian Journal of Policy and Governance* 25 (2): 23–40.

ICG (International Crisis Group). 2016. 'Myanmar: A New Muslim Insurgency in Rakhine State'. 15 December. www.crisisgroup.org/asia/south-east-asia/myanmar/283-myanmar-new-muslim-insurgency-rakhine-state

ILO (International Labour Organization). 2022. 'Employment in Myanmar in 2021: A Rapid Assessment'. www.ilo.org/yangon/publications/WCMS_835900/lang--en/index.htm

Kipgen, Nehginpao. 2013. 'Conflict in Rakhine State in Myanmar: Rohingya Muslims' Conundrum'. *Journal of Muslim Minority Affairs* 33 (2): 298–310. doi.org/10.1080/13602004.2013.810117

Kipgen, Nehginpao. 2018. 'The Quest for Federalism in Myanmar'. *Strategic Analysis* 42 (6): 612–26. doi.org/10.1080/09700161.2018.1557933

Kocamis, H. Methap. 2019. 'The Rohingya Minority in Burma/Myanmar: A Case of Protracted Social Conflict'. Master's thesis, Middle East Technical University.

Kriesberg, Louis. 1993. 'Intractable Conflicts'. *Peace Review* 5 (4): 417–21. doi.org/10.1080/10402659308425753

Kriesberg, Louis and Bruce W. Dayton. 2012. *Constructive Conflicts: From Escalation to Resolution*. 4th ed. Lanham: Rowman & Littlefield.

Kyaw Hsan Hlaing. 2021a. 'After Myanmar's Military Coup, Arakan Army Accelerates Implementation of the "Way of Rakhita"'. *Diplomat*, 20 April. thediplomat.com/2021/04/after-myanmars-military-coup-arakan-army-accelerates-implementation-of-the-way-of-rakhita/

Kyaw Hsan Hlaing. 2021b. 'Arakan Army Seeks to Build "Inclusive" Administration in Rakhine State'. *Diplomat*, 31 August. thediplomat.com/2021/08/arakan-army-rebels-seek-inclusive-administration-in-rakhine-state/

Kyaw Lynn. 2021. 'The Arakan Army, Myanmar Military Coup and Politics of Arakan'. Transnational Institute, 10 June. www.tni.org/en/article/the-arakan-army-myanmar-military-coup-and-politics-of-arakan

Kymlicka, W. 1995. *Multicultural Citizenship: A Liberal Theory of Minority Rights*. Oxford: Clarendon Press. doi.org/10.1093/0198290918.001.0001.002.004

Leider, Jacques P. 2020. 'Territorial Dispossession and Persecution in North Arakan (Rakhine)'. Torkel Opsahl Academic EPublisher, Policy Brief Series, no. 101: 1942–43.

Lindblom, Alina, Elizabeth Marsh, Tasnim Motala and Katherine Munyan. 2015. 'Persecution of Rohingya Muslims: Is Genocide Occurring in Myanmar's Rakhine State?' October. www.fortifyrights.org/downloads/Yale_Persecution_of_the_Rohingya_October_2015.pdf

Maung Zarni and Alice Cowley. 2014. 'The Slow-Burning Genocide of Myanmar's Rohingya'. *Pacific Rim Law & Policy Journal* 23 (3): 683–754. digitalcommons.law.uw.edu/wilj/vol23/iss3/8

Min Zin. 2015. 'Anti-Muslim Violence in Burma: Why Now?' *Social Research* 82 (2): 375–97. doi.org/10.1353/sor.2015.0024

Myanmar Now. 2020. 'Arakan Army Meets for Talks with Tatmadaw in Wa Capital'. 14 December. www.myanmar-now.org/en/news/arakan-army-meets-for-talks-with-tatmadaw-in-wa-capital (page discontinued).

Myanmar Now. 2021a. 'More Anti-Coup Protesters Arrested in Rakhine State'. 18 February. www.myanmar-now.org/en/news/more-anti-coup-protesters-arrested-in-rakhine-state?page=5&width=500&height=500&inline=true (page discontinued).

Myanmar Now. 2021b. 'ANP Chair Says Party May End Its Association with Junta'. 5 May. www.myanmar-now.org/en/news/anp-chair-says-party-may-end-its-association-with-junta (page discontinued).

Myo Htun. 2021. 'Rohingya in Buthidaung Hit with Even Tougher Travel Restrictions'. *Myanmar Now*, 29 November. www.myanmar-now.org/en/news/rohingya-in-buthidaung-hit-with-even-tougher-travel-restrictions (page discontinued).

NUCC (National Unity Consultative Committee). 2021. 'Federal Democracy Charter Part I, Declaration of Federal Democracy Union'. crphmyanmar.org/wp-content/uploads/2021/04/Federal-Democracy-Charter-English.pdf

NUG (National Unity Government). n.d. 'About NUG'. Accessed 23 February 2023. gov.nugmyanmar.org/about-nug/

NUG (National Unity Government). 2021. 'Statement of the National Unity Government of Myanmar on the 4th Anniversary of the Atrocity Crimes Against the Rohingya People in 2017'. 24 August. mofa.nugmyanmar.org/statement-of-the-national-unity-government-of-myanmar-on-the-4th-anniversary-of-the-atrocity-crimes-against-the-rohingya-people-in-2017/

Nyein Nyein. 2021. 'Anti-NLD Ethnic Politicians Picked by Military Regime for Governing Council'. *Irrawaddy*, 5 February. www.irrawaddy.com/news/burma/anti-nld-ethnic-politicians-picked-military-regime-governing-council.html

Nyi Nyi Kyaw. 2017. 'Unpacking the Presumed Statelessness of Rohingyas'. *Journal of Immigrant & Refugee Studies* 15 (3): 269–86. doi.org/10.1080/15562948.2017.1330981

OHCHR (Office of the High Commissioner for Human Rights). 2018. 'Myanmar: UN Fact-Finding Mission Releases Its Full Account of Massive Violations by Military in Rakhine, Kachin and Shan States'. Press release. www.ohchr.org/en/press-releases/2018/09/myanmar-un-fact-finding-mission-releases-its-full-account-massive-violations?LangID=E&NewsID=23575

Parvez, Altaf, Shafiqul Alam and Ashfaque Ronnie. 2022. 'We Recognise the Human Rights and Citizen Rights of the Rohingyas. Interview: Arakan Army Chief Twan Mrat Naing'. *Prothomalo*, English edition, 2 January. en.prothomalo.com/opinion/interview/we-recognise-the-human-rights-and-citizen-rights-of-the-rohingyas

Simbulan, Karen. 2018. *When Perceptions Define Reality: Implications and Challenges after the August 2017 Crisis in Rakhine State*. Yangon: RAFT Myanmar.

Smith, Martin. 1995. 'The Muslim "Rohingya" of Burma'. Conference paper, Burma Centrum Nederland, Amsterdam. www.burmalibrary.org/docs24/Martin_Smith-1995-12-11-The_Muslim_%27Rohingyas%27_of_Burma.pdf

Southwick, Katherine. 2015. 'Preventing Mass Atrocities against the Stateless Rohingya in Myanmar: A Call for Solutions'. *Journal of International Affairs* 68 (2).

SRUB (Socialist Republic of the Union of Burma). 1982. *Burma Citizenship Law*. 15 October. www.refworld.org/docid/3ae6b4f71b.html

Thawnghmung, Ardeth M. 2016. 'The Politics of Indigeneity in Myanmar: Competing Narratives in Rakhine State'. *Asian Ethnicity* 17 (4): 527–47. doi.org/10.1080/14631369.2016.1179096

Udayakumar, S. P. 2004. 'Reflections: Futures of Protracted Conflicts'. *Futures* 36: 379–84. doi.org/10.1016/S0016-3287(03)00161-7

UNHCR (United Nations High Commissioner for Refugees). 2022. 'Myanmar UNHCR Displacement Overview 31 Oct 2022'. data.unhcr.org/en/documents/details/96546

UNOCHA (United Nations Office for the Coordination of Humanitarian Affairs). 2021. 'Myanmar: 2021 Humanitarian Needs Overview'. January. reliefweb.int/report/myanmar/myanmar-2021-humanitarian-needs-overview-january-2021

van Klinken, Gerry and Su Mon Thazin Aung. 2017. 'The Contentious Politics of Anti-Muslim Scapegoating in Myanmar'. *Journal of Contemporary Asia* 47 (3): 353–75. doi.org/10.1080/00472336.2017.1293133

Ware, Anthony. 2015. 'Secessionist Aspects to the Buddhist-Muslim Conflict in Rakhine State, Myanmar'. In *Territorial Separatism in Global Politics: Causes, Outcomes and Resolution,* edited by Damien Kingsbury and Costas Laoutides, 165–80. London: Routledge.

Ware, Anthony and Costas Laoutides. 2019. 'Myanmar's "Rohingya" Conflict: Misconceptions and Complexity'. *Asian Affairs* 50 (1): 60–79. doi.org/10.1080/03068374.2019.1567102

Western News. 2022a. 'Pauktaw Tha Mie Win Zaydi Ah Thwet Muslim Layy Ywar Mha Ngwe Kyat 24 Thein Kyaw Hlu Dan' ['Four Muslim Villages Donate 24 lakh to Pautktaw Historical Pagoda']. Facebook, 8 January. www.facebook.com/westernnewsagency/posts/443088924164284

Western News. 2022b. 'Muslim Kyaung Tharr Twae Yae Mee Eain Shin Rakhine Kyaung Sayama Layy' ['"The Lady with the Lamp"—A Lady Teacher for the Muslim Student']. Video, Facebook. 9 January. www.facebook.com/watch/?v=330476328931276

Winchester, Mike. 2017. 'Birth of an Ethnic Insurgency in Myanmar'. *Asia Times*, 28 August. asiatimes.com/2017/08/birth-ethnic-insurgency-myanmar/

Ye Min Zaw. 2019. 'What Does the Arakan Army Bring to Rakhine State?' *Irrawaddy*, 11 January. www.irrawaddy.com/opinion/guest-column/arakan-army-bring-rakhine-state.html

11

Pandemic Weaponisation and Non-State Welfare in Pre- and Post-Coup Myanmar

Gerard McCarthy

Assistant Professor, International Institute of Social Studies
(The Hague) and Research Fellow, Asia Research Institute,
National University of Singapore

Saw Moo (pseudonym)
Independent scholar

Abstract

The Myanmar military's seizure of power in February 2021 led to a breakdown in the collaborative state–society relations that had characterised the COVID-19 response during the first year of the pandemic. This chapter examines the dynamics of cooperation and contention between successive administrations (civilian and military) and the enduring role of Myanmar's vibrant, non-state charitable sector in pandemic response prior to and following the coup. Assessing claims made prior to the coup that the intermediation of state pandemic social aid was weaponised by the National League for Democracy, the chapter focuses on how the junta's abandonment of the government's limited social stimulus initiatives, and their adoption of strategies to empower pro-military or neutral loyalists at a local level, has fractured the state–society collaboration that had helped contain and manage COVID-19 in 2020. The chapter identifies four key strategies through which the junta has sought to discipline Myanmar's vibrant, non-state social sector: suppressing perceived dissenters, empowering loyalists, disciplining charitable actors and partnering with neutral welfare groups. We conclude by reflecting on debates about the meaning of neutrality in the context of the new dictatorship, urging the need for greater international support to non-state welfare provision in the short term.

***

With the onset of the COVID-19 pandemic in early 2020, pre-existing dynamics of economic inequality, political polarisation and democratic decay were exacerbated globally and across Southeast Asia (Croissant 2020; Aspinall et al. 2021; Gadarian, Goodman & Pepinsky 2022). Myanmar is no exception in this regard, with the pandemic intensifying deeply ingrained political divides, especially over the distribution of government social aid to populations whose livelihoods were upheaved by the socioeconomic downturn and lockdowns. Throughout the pandemic, both the elected government of Aung San Suu Kyi and the military administration since February 2021 were accused of exploiting COVID-19 to benefit their political allies and entrench their social dominance. This chapter assesses these claims by examining the dynamics of what we term *pandemic weaponisation* before and after the military's return to power in February 2021. Initially enlisted by critics of the National League for Democracy (NLD) to describe pandemic response efforts in 2020, we use the concept of weaponisation to examine patterns of state–society relations before and after the military coup. We argue that, whereas the NLD government encouraged non-state social responses during 2020, after seizing power in February 2021, the State Administrative Council (SAC) brutally suppressed political opposition and disrupted non-state pandemic responses. The result has been the fracturing of state attempts to manage the pandemic via societal partners while paradoxically heightening reliance on neighbourhood and charitable response efforts to survive and resist the dictatorship.

This chapter draws on a national survey conducted in January 2021 by the co-authors and colleagues at The Australian National University, the University of Massachusetts and Innovations for Poverty Action, along with over 50 interviews with ordinary people, political candidates and welfare activists conducted prior to and after the 2021 military coup. Interviews with respondents in seven states and regions were conducted between

2020 and 2022 by a team of research assistants trained and coordinated by the co-authors. To manage COVID-19 and post-coup safety concerns, the bulk of discussions occurred virtually via encrypted communications. Transcripts were anonymised and translated into English and are available via a public archive.[1]

The sections of this chapter proceed by outlining the socioeconomic impacts of COVID-19 and governmental social responses, initially during the civilian government and then since the return to military dictatorship. The first section analyses the inadequacy and limitations of state social aid during 2020 and how these dynamics fed claims of politicisation and pandemic weaponisation by minority parties and interests against the NLD government in the months prior to the February 2021 coup. The second section highlights the junta's abandonment of the NLD government's limited social stimulus initiatives and examines how the collapse of state–society cooperation impacted pandemic health and social responses during 2021. Informed by interviews with grassroots welfare activists and businesspeople since the coup, the third section highlights how the junta's suppression of charitable COVID-19 response efforts and dismissal of striking government staff further entrenched the role of private, communal and ethnic social service providers both in providing aid and in sustaining resistance to the new dictatorship.

The chapter concludes that the nascent state–society cooperation of the NLD-era has come to a dramatic end since the coup, deepening the reliance of ordinary people on private and non-state providers. In this sense, the weaponisation of COVID-19 by the junta has compounded a process of state social outsourcing that has been ongoing for decades, entrenching societal reliance on non-state social actors both to survive and resist the dictatorship (McCarthy 2023).

---

1   English versions of transcripts from selected oral history interviews focusing on the pandemic and conducted with Myanmar respondents between 2020 and 2022, including several cited here, are accessible from the National University of Singapore Asia Research Institute archive for the 'Living with COVID-19 in Southeast Asia' project: ec2-54-169-180-248.ap-southeast-1.compute.amazonaws.com/omeka-s/s/living-with-covid-19-in-sea/page/welcome

Pandemic response under the NLD (January 2020 – January 2021)

Health and social impacts of COVID-19

The arrival of COVID-19 in Myanmar claimed fewer lives in the initial months of the pandemic than in global hotspots in Europe, the United Kingdom and the United States. A variety of factors helped reduce the transmission and severity of cases in the first few months of the pandemic. These included a rapid drop in incoming visitors from hotspot countries, along with community willingness to set up and run quarantine facilities and partner with local administrators to enforce health protocols.

Even though the initial wave of COVID-19 cases was relatively modest, by March 2020 Myanmar's historically under-resourced health system was strained. This was especially the case in Yangon where there were shortages of protective gear for medical personnel and overcrowding of hospital facilities. In response, the elected government, after initially downplaying the virus, began restricting non-essential entry to the country and expanded resourcing for the health response by redirecting domestic budgets to pandemic response and soliciting international aid.

In late March 2020, it became clear that Myanmar was experiencing a catastrophic economic downturn far worse than the direct and immediate health mortality of the virus. Disruptions to global supply chains, border closures and declining global demand in trade-exposed industries, such as garment manufacturing and tourism, prompted layoffs across major sectors of Myanmar's economy, precipitating rapid declines in Myanmar's agricultural exports (World Bank 2020). Meanwhile, the government's imposition of lockdowns and market closures in urban centres, along with the laying-off of Myanmar migrant workers abroad, hit the remittances on which many households had become reliant.

Just prior to the Burmese New Year (*Thingyan*) in April 2020, the NLD government announced its COVID-19 Economic Relief Plan. Informed by modelling that predicted significant shrinkage in Myanmar's economy and a spike in poverty rates in the absence of government action, the initial USD2 billion stimulus package, supported partly by international partners, comprised spending for emergency loans to businesses and trade financing (Bello et al. 2020). It also included around USD210 million in cash and food to support the most vulnerable (Kyaw San Wai 2020). The initial package accounted for 2.5–3 per cent of Myanmar's gross domestic product, below the average Association of Southeast Asian Nations (ASEAN) commitment of 3.7 per cent and significantly less than Thailand, which had committed close to 9 per cent by mid-2020 (Martinus & Seah 2020).

The design of the package was constrained by Myanmar's minimal tax revenue, skeletal social welfare state bequeathed by decades of autocratic austerity and the intimacy of business networks with the NLD who had advocated against tax reform. The vast majority of funds ultimately benefited large formal businesses, comprising less than half of Myanmar's economy. Meanwhile, assistance provided to the needy, initially ration packs during *Thingyan* in 2020 and later cash payments, were distributed on an explicitly one-off basis to deter expectations of ongoing entitlement to state support.

A severe wave of COVID-19 infections in July 2020 led to further degradation in the economic and health situation. Yet state aid remained insufficient, constrained by the reluctance of Myanmar's policymakers to accrue sovereign debt and the absence of a well-developed state social apparatus capable of distributing aid directly to needy households. As a result, few households and businesses received any state social aid during 2020. A January 2021 national survey of 700 respondents from across all states and regions conducted by the co-authors in partnership with The Australian National University and locals found that almost 80 per cent of households had reduced food intake in the seven days prior, while 30 per cent reported taking on new loans—often with interest—to pay for basic necessities (McCarthy, Ross & Myat The Thitsar 2021). Of the overall sample, fewer than 25 per cent of respondents reported having received government aid in January 2021, significantly less than in Thailand (68 per cent), Indonesia (46 per cent) and Malaysia (71 per cent) where the same questions were asked (McCarthy 2021). In Myanmar, those who received government support said it often lasted no more than a few days, with 60 per cent saying it lasted less than a week.

In addition to being insufficient to meet needs, government aid in 2020 was poorly targeted, leaving many confused as to why their equally poor neighbours received support while they did not. This pattern was borne out in the January 2021 survey, with households who were reducing meals in the seven days prior to the survey only slightly more likely (3 per cent) to have received government aid via rations or cash transfers than their less needy neighbours. For minority party supporters, the limitations of the state's social response fed a larger narrative about the NLD government's exploitation of the pandemic for political benefit and broader majoritarian approach to opposition. These perceptions were especially strong in Rakhine State, where, with the support of the civilian government, the intensification of conflict between the Myanmar armed forces (Tatmadaw or *sit-tat*)[2] and the Arakan Army throughout 2020 was seen as posing a far greater threat to the lives of ordinary people than COVID-19 (Khin Khin Mra 2020).

Political polarisation of government pandemic management

The inadequacy and poor targeting of government social aid became a partisan obsession for non-NLD party activists in the run-up to and following the November 2020 elections. Minority party supporters complained that the government was using the pandemic, especially the stimulus package, to reward supporters and punish critics. The polarisation of perspectives was borne out in more than 30 interviews and in the national survey conducted prior to the coup—both of which highlighted the mediating role of partisan identity in shaping perceptions of governmental social aid.

Respondents from NLD backgrounds recognised flaws in the government's management of COVID-19, with 40 per cent in the national survey saying that government aid was not being distributed fairly or to the neediest. However, in interviews, voters in NLD strongholds such as lowland Myanmar tended to attribute these flaws to local confusion and administrative inadequacy rather than systematic failure or corruption on the part of the NLD government. A 67-year-old ethnic Bamar (majority ethnic group) shopkeeper from central Myanmar, for instance, recounted how neighbours blamed their local administrators for their exclusion from state social aid:

> Some of my neighbours did not get the [government] assistance, which made some tensions in the neighbourhood. Some went to the ward office to complain regarding why some people got the assistance, and some were excluded. (Interview, October 2020)

---

2   Since the February 2021 military coup and subsequent atrocities against civilians, some Myanmar scholars have debated the linguistic politics of referring to Myanmar's state army with its chosen moniker of Tatmadaw given that the honorific '*daw*' implies royal or glorious status. Some have preferred to label it *sit-tat*, simply meaning 'military', though there are linguistic and analytical implications and limitations to using that term as well (see Aung Kaung Myat 2022). Consequently, we prefer to use the terms 'state army' or 'armed forces' to refer to the Tatmadaw.

Supporters of small political parties that won very few head-to-head races with the NLD at the 2015 and 2020 elections were more critical of government social aid. Some viewed it as an example of NLD malfeasance. For example, 69 per cent of Union Solidarity and Development Party (USDP) voters and 48 per cent of ethnic minority party supporters surveyed just prior to the 2021 coup said that government COVID-19 assistance was not reaching the households who needed it most. In interviews, several minority party supporters described the mediation of government aid via township COVID-19 response committees led by members of parliament, along with eligibility checks and distribution efforts led by ward and village-tract administrators, as a form of vote-buying. As many of the officials and informal community representatives involved were elected or appointed during the NLD term (and were often supporters of the party), those who missed out or received minimal state aid during 2020, especially ethnic minorities and supporters of the USDP, felt that NLD loyalists were exploiting their role to benefit supporters and exclude partisan opponents and non-Bamar voters. Social media posts claiming that NLD candidates were describing pandemic social aid as a gift from the party for which voters should be grateful reinforced these perceptions. A 31-year-old teacher and election booth staffer in Mon State described one such post she encountered online just prior to the November 2020 election:

> I heard people who received financial support are not all poor families and widows and that some middle-class people also received money. I also saw on social media a post from an ethnic Mon woman who said that the village administrator who is an NLD supporter used the COVID-19 support to buy votes from the villagers. The woman refused support and said, 'I cannot sell my vote to this peacock party [symbol of the NLD]'. She became famous and Mon people [on Facebook] praised her for being brave enough to speak out. (Interview, November 2020)

It is important to note that the mediation of state social aid by political officials prior to the November 2020 election—which some supporters of minority parties labelled as political corruption—is unlikely to have influenced the outcome of the election. After all, the majoritarian nature of Myanmar's first-past-the-post electoral system ensured that the NLD, which won a plurality of the vote in the vast majority of seats, secured more than 80 per cent of seats in parliament.

Despite this, stories about corrupt dispersal of state pandemic social aid are important as they circulated within USDP, military and some ethnic minority social media pages in the weeks and months prior to the November 2020 election and in the period immediately prior to the coup. These stories framed the NLD government as exploiting its response to the pandemic to weaken its rivals and further strengthen its political position, despite the spike in COVID-19 infections in the months prior to the election (Strangio 2020). Examples of alleged biases in state social aid along with restrictions on minority party campaigning, while NLD chief ministers and members of parliament travelled widely to coordinate the pandemic response, helped feed a narrative among non-NLD supporters that led to calls for military intervention into the electoral process. Social media posts detailing the movements of NLD politicians amid COVID-19 circulated widely among pro-military, USDP and some minority party Facebook pages in mid to late 2020 and early 2021 (Author, digital fieldnotes 2020). Indeed, the decision by the NLD-appointed Union Election Commission (UEC) to host the election in November 2020, despite complaints from USDP and military representatives about pandemic restrictions on campaigning and canvassing with voters, was cited repeatedly by non-NLD supporters in the oral history interviews. As a candidate for a pro-USDP party in Yangon stated prior to the coup:

> I believe that the government is biased toward the NLD party which is why we failed to implement effective campaigns … I have heard stories of vote-buying by candidates but there isn't any plan to investigate the allegations … the government together with the Union Election Commission did not listen to our voices [as minor parties] and conducted the election anyway. (Interview, December 2020)

For some non-NLD voters, the UEC's reluctance to investigate reports of vote-buying, along with irregularities during the election, were signs that the NLD was exploiting its incumbency to further strengthen its dominance while avoiding scrutiny. These concerns were echoed in complaints from ethnic Arakan political elites in October 2020 who viewed the UEC's decision not to run elections in the vast bulk of Rakhine State as the deliberate disenfranchisement of 1.5 million potential voters (Fishbein & Kyaw Hsan Hlaing 2020). These grievances, especially about the conduct of the election, were later cited by the military to justify its seizure of power in February 2021, and formed the basis for the junta's later charges of corruption and voter fraud against the NLD (Lee 2021). Though governance of the pandemic, and especially state aid, was highly politicised in 2020, alongside these controversies non-state social actors played a significant, albeit less high-profile, role in leading grassroots response efforts across the country.

Non-state pandemic response efforts

From the early days of the pandemic, the NLD government actively encouraged societal collaboration and partnerships in response efforts at both the national and local level. Political leaders encouraged diverse non-state actors to fill gaps in social welfare and public goods provision. In the weeks prior to the coup, the NLD government even established a fund for businesspeople and ordinary citizens to donate to Myanmar's efforts to procure vaccines (Zaw Zaw Htwe 2021).

Early in the pandemic, state officials encouraged township, neighbourhood and village welfare groups, charities, ethnic civil society groups, businesspeople and religious leaders to take on critical roles in the pandemic response at a sub-national level (Rhoads et al. 2020). These non-state networks assumed major roles in local response efforts, including quarantine, transport of patients, relief coordination, supplementation of service providers and enforcement of restrictions (Nay Yan Oo & Batcheler 2020). Armed groups and ethnic civil society groups coordinated with the Ministry of Health and Sport on public education and, later in 2020, vaccinations, building on ongoing collaboration over the five or so years prior (Si Thura & Schroeder 2018).

The leader of a social welfare group in a contested region of Karen State described being directly integrated into COVID-19 committee structures established by the government to coordinate response efforts across sectors:

> During the first and second wave [in 2020] we worked with the township committee to stretch resources given by government to meet local needs for oxygen, food, transportation … with support from General Administration Department [GAD] we also opened a health screening centre where general sickness were treated and those with more serious medical issues were referred to government public hospital … the GAD office provided allowances to volunteers during second wave, 4500 MMK were given to the volunteers for 60 days as a food allowance. (Interview, January 2022)

Similar dynamics of collaboration between societal actors and the state were described at a village level in a ceasefire area of Mon State. As the leader of a village welfare group recounted of response efforts in 2020:

> During the second wave [in mid-2020], the village COVID-19 committee included our *parahita* [social welfare] organisation and the local monk. Together we helped to raise funds and contribute oxygen canisters when the administrator's supply had run out. (Interview, February 2022)

These collaborative dynamics shifted markedly after February 2021 when the Myanmar military seized direct power once again. The coup, arrest of elected civilian leaders and subsequent brutal suppression of protests provoked an extraordinary civilian mobilisation against the dictatorship. It also ruptured the partnership between state and societal actors to manage the pandemic and extend state social aid through additional contributions and resource pooling at the community level. Since then, ordinary people have relied more than ever on non-state networks and practices of reciprocity, both to survive the economic collapse and the pandemic and to sustain resistance to the renewed dictatorship (Wittekind 2021). The following section examines these dynamics as they have developed in light of the February 2021 coup, identifying how the rupture of the pre-coup state–society pandemic response has been a crucial component of the junta's strategy to root out and discipline local administrative networks and social groups sympathetic to the NLD and democratic struggle more broadly.

Post-coup management of COVID-19

Since February 2021, the SAC, led by Senior General Min Aung Hlaing, has used COVID-19 to wrest control over local administration and weaken networks it views as affiliated with the previous NLD government. Four key strategies have been deployed to discipline Myanmar's vibrant, non-state social sector: suppression of perceived dissent, empowerment of loyalists, disciplining of charitable actors and partnerships with neutral welfare groups. These strategies have markedly altered pre-coup patterns of state–society cooperation around the pandemic, likely worsening the mortality and socioeconomic impacts of the Delta wave of COVID-19 and prompting intense debate within Myanmar's charitable sector over the meaning of neutrality in the context of the new dictatorship.

Suppression of dissent

Consistent with the junta's reliance on violence to maintain power and its refusal to tolerate dissent or negotiate with dissenters, since February 2021, military officials have engaged in the widespread suppression of non-state welfare groups perceived to be materially supporting the anti-junta resistance. This has fractured the national and sub-national health response that relied heavily on collaboration with societal actors and the public at large, particularly at a local level.

Immediately upon taking power, the junta arrested or suspended civil servants who had taken leading roles in the pandemic response, including coordinators of the national vaccination rollout that was just commencing in early 2021. In reaction to the coup, tens of thousands of medical staff at public facilities across the country walked off the job in an act of civil disobedience. Military personnel responded by harassing, coercing and, in some cases, directly attacking doctors and nurses, including some who had begun treating patients at charitable and private clinics or ambulance services that the junta viewed as aligned with the escalating protest movement (Dziedzic 2021). The Ministry of Health and Sport ultimately dismissed thousands of nurses, teachers and civil servants across ministries in response to their opposition to the coup, structurally undermining the already overstretched pandemic response.

Consistent with the broader boycott of government services and payment of taxes by the Civil Disobedience Movement, many patients also began to actively avoid government health facilities and resources following the coup (RFA 2021). This boycott became most obvious during the outbreak of the Delta wave of COVID-19 in mid-2021. Rather than seek care or supplies from state facilities, many patients and their family members instead sought treatment at charitable and private clinics, and attempted to procure oxygen canisters on the open market. In a context in which oxygen was already in short supply regionally due to the pandemic, junta officials attempted to counter the private procurement of breathing apparatuses and oxygen by centralising canister distribution through junta, USDP and military networks. Reports emerged of the forcible removal of oxygen canisters procured privately from critically ill COVID-19 patients, attracting domestic and international outrage (*Irrawaddy* 2021). These efforts were justifiably viewed by many in Myanmar as an attempt to weaponise the pandemic for political gain by forcing ordinary people opposed to the new dictatorship to engage with the junta's structures and networks if they wanted their family members to survive.

The spread of COVID-19 during the Delta wave was likely exacerbated by the junta's attempts to suppress dissent and coerce patients and their families into relying on state resources. Many patients who contracted COVID-19 were forced to stay in state-led quarantine or isolation centres or were hospitalised at public facilities where, due to the strikes caused by the coup and shortages of medical supplies, many subsequently died. The military also raided charity and underground clinics that provided healthcare to patients, including those with COVID-19 (Esther J 2021).

The junta's Ministry of Health recorded 14,401 deaths in public facilities across the country during the peak of the Delta wave between July and September 2021; however, this excluded those who died at home or in private and charitable facilities (*Frontier Myanmar* 2022). Regional government and welfare group data on burials and cremations at Yangon's four main cemeteries provide a snapshot of the massive, unacknowledged death toll of COVID-19 in Myanmar following the coup. Their data, cited by *Frontier Myanmar* (2022), suggest that more than 30,000 people died in Yangon alone during the peak of the Delta wave.

The dire human consequences of the coup further eroded faith in the remaining staff at government health facilities, deepening popular grievances against the junta and reinvigorating the Civil Disobedience Movement in the second half of 2021. As the leader of a *parahita* (social welfare) group, which coordinated treatment for COVID-19 patients in a contested region of Myanmar throughout the Delta outbreak, explained: 'People do not trust [the staff] at government facilities so they just simply avoid getting their help' (Interview, January 2022).

Empowerment of junta loyalists

Alongside junta attempts to coerce popular reliance on state networks has been the wholesale replacement of local governance and pandemic response teams with USDP and military loyalists. Across several contexts, including contested and ceasefire areas, welfare volunteers who had previously been members of village and township COVID-19 management committees in 2020 described being sidelined after the coup. Reflecting mutual distrust between regime loyalists and social actors previously involved in collaborative local pandemic response, junta administrators formed new committees at village and township levels and filled these positions with people affiliated with the USDP or who they viewed as apolitical or unlikely to align themselves with democratic resistance efforts. As one interviewee explained:

> We did some collaborative work with the [NLD] government previously, before the coup, and for that, they offered to donate some funds. However, for the work we have been doing after the coup, they [SAC administration] have never offered to work together or donate some money ... But a few other businesses in our group were contacted directly by the regime ... Maybe they [SAC officials] did not contact us because we currently chose to stay low profile and did not contact them. (Interview, January 2022)

The sidelining of local welfare groups involved in the COVID-19 response, and reliance instead on ostensibly neutral or loyalist businesspeople, broke the supplementary relationship between non-state charitable actors and government officials that had helped patch the significant gaps in resourcing throughout the first waves of COVID-19 in 2020.

The collapse of state–society trust as a result of the coup has been especially acute in contexts where junta administrators perceive monks to be supporting anti-coup resistance efforts; thus, local SAC COVID-19 committees have bypassed and sidelined local monastic networks. Fear of recrimination from the junta has also resulted in substantial declines in donations from wealthy businesspeople and private donors to local charitable efforts, as they are often unsure whether these groups are supporting the junta, opposing the coup or directly sustaining resistance efforts. As perceived support for resistance efforts can lead to the junta freezing bank accounts, boycotting businesses or arrest, some businesspeople have withdrawn from philanthropic efforts entirely in order to avoid such risks. Many *parahita* groups, meanwhile, have sought to prove that they are apolitical by regularly posting their charitable activities on Facebook as a means of appeasing their donors (Author notes, May 2022). Requiring local charitable actors to reframe their activities as 'apolitical' despite them directly supplementing for the social inaction of the state and responding to human insecurity created by its atrocities bears striking similarities to the depoliticisation of the *parahita* sector during the 1990s and 2000s (McCarthy 2016, 2023).

Dynamics of mutual distrust with local charitable and religious actors have also undermined the junta's attempted rollout of COVID-19 vaccinations. Several interviewees alleged that people loyal to the junta were the first to receive vaccinations in their communities. Others reportedly refused the vaccine, despite its availability, due to it being distributed by SAC representatives and because the Sinovax shot they were offered was viewed as inferior and riskier relative to other vaccines. Consequentially and worryingly, despite having regular and direct contact with COVID-19 patients, only a handful of the charity workers interviewed since the coup reported being fully vaccinated.

Disciplining charitable actors

At the same time as seeking to control and redirect the pandemic response and resources through loyalists, and suppressing networks it sees as supporting resistance, the junta has also sought to selectively partner with, and strategically regulate, non-state social actors to advance the regime's objectives. The most direct way that the military has surveilled the *parahita* sector is by requiring groups and volunteers to be endorsed by junta officials and tightening control over where they source their funds.

Since the coup, military checkpoints have been set up in many cities, towns and on significant inter-town arteries to monitor the movement of people and goods, ostensibly for both pandemic and security purposes. In some cases, local *parahita* groups have been enlisted to help run these checkpoints (Author notes, May 2022). The military and state personnel manning these checkpoints require letters of recommendation from local SAC-affiliated administrators to permit volunteers to pass through. Without such documentation, volunteers are harassed and, in some cases, accused of supporting the democratic resistance. Social workers seeking to engage in charitable action in the post-coup context are, thus, forced to cultivate workable relationships with village or township SAC officials to solicit endorsement letters they can then show at checkpoints. In addition to forcing charitable workers to accede to the regulatory power of SAC authorities, these requirements also place the onus on volunteers to avoid actions that may be viewed by local administrators as in any way supporting the democratic resistance.

As well as tightening financial flows into the country to starve funding for anti-coup activities, the SAC has become more stringent about requiring formal registration of any welfare group—large or small, local or national—

with the junta before they can receive international funds. The Central Bank also restricts the flow of funds from large humanitarian organisations to small community organisations by requiring extensive documentation justifying each transfer. These new constraints build on earlier moves by the USDP and NLD administrations to regulate local civil society and any international financial support they may receive. In the post-coup context, if the leaders of a group are found to be receiving funds from abroad without registration, they risk being accused of being financial supporters of the People's Defence Forces or other local resistance efforts. Despite the severe socioeconomic situation created by both the pandemic and the coup, many groups that had relied on funds wired from diaspora networks abroad or international donors to local Myanmar bank accounts to support pandemic response efforts in 2020 have scaled back their activities since the return to military rule. The pastor of a village church in a contested region of Myanmar that had received funds in 2020 from international Christian networks to support COVID-19 relief explained that they had had to cut back their aid considerably as they had not been able to receive or withdraw their funds easily since the coup. The tightening of financial regulation around foreign charitable donations has only been compounded by the catastrophic financial sector crisis brought about by the coup (see Chapter 3, this volume). Though it is understood that some welfare groups have turned to informal financial transfer networks (*hundi*) to funnel money from abroad to support their efforts, this channel was not mentioned by any respondents interviewed for this project. However, it is clear that the operational barriers to *parahita* and civil society work within Myanmar have sparked a new exodus of people and organisations to Thailand and India since the coup, as well as a growing reliance on informal networks to transfer funds to local partners and beneficiaries (Author notes, May 2022).

Strategic partnership

Within the larger context of the junta suppressing dissent and disciplining Myanmar's charitable sector, SAC officials have also sought to achieve their objectives by strategically partnering with, and resourcing, non-state social actors willing to accept a stringent notion of neutrality in the post-coup context. The clearest examples of such pragmatism are in contexts where local administrators and General Administration Department (GAD) staff have collaborated in the past with local social welfare groups or where the existence of ethnic armed organisations had led to a degree of flexibility about state engagement with diverse actors prior to the coup.

The closest relationship between SAC authorities and non-state social actors we encountered was in a contested area under mixed administration by an armed group and Myanmar government agencies. In this township, the *parahita* group reported receiving monthly stipends from the GAD township office during 2020 to support their role in COVID-19 treatment and transport. This cooperative relationship had continued beyond the coup. Volunteers shielded medical staff who did not join the Civil Disobedience Movement by guarding the local hospital from potential attacks by armed groups during the peak of the 2021 Delta wave. Members of the group also continued to be offered, and to accept, stipends from the GAD office for these efforts in mid-2021. Building on the role they played prior to the coup, these volunteers continued to act as mediators for patient transport between local armed groups, the People's Defence Forces and Myanmar's state army in 2021 and into 2022, much as non-state social actors such as churches have done in contested regions for decades.

The collaboration between charitable actors and local SAC officials appears to be highly contextual and seemingly dependent on pre-existing relationships developed between welfare volunteers and GAD officers stationed in the area prior to the coup. Numerous *parahita* groups that had played an active role in the pandemic response during 2020 reported being sidelined from local efforts in preference for loyalist local businesspeople. In a context of strict regulation of dissent and the tightening of state controls over non-state social actors, the willingness of some groups to engage with and directly endorse the junta has prompted intense debate within Myanmar civil society about the nature of humanitarian neutrality.

Neutrality tensions

Several local welfare activists interviewed for this project criticised groups for engaging with the SAC, as doing so had the appearance of taking sides in the larger political conflict. The leader of an ambulance and funeral group active in the COVID-19 response argued that the cooption of welfare groups by SAC officials ran the risk of undermining the popular respect and ethical consistency that Myanmar's charitable sector relied upon to function:

> I went to attend a government meeting in [the state capital] recently, and witnessed some of them had a very close relationship with the new [SAC] chief minister … Personally, just leaning toward one authority is something I would never do. Because of these *parahita*

groups that are partnering with the military, other non-partisan *parahita* groups are also negatively viewed and judged by people. (Interview, January 2022)

In addition to navigating the SAC's tightening surveillance, welfare groups are thus faced with difficult trade-offs between principles and pragmatism—both personally and organisationally—in order to operate in the post-coup context. As the leader of a township-focused group that directly engaged with GAD officials to transport patients explained, at stake is a question of humanitarian neutrality:

> For us it doesn't matter where the patients are coming from … whether NUG [National Unity Government], [armed group] or military areas, we will do our best to support those who need our help … we need to work with all authorities to get the work done. We take training from NUG online, review their COVID materials … Sometimes, if there is some support the military government can provide, we need to work with them too. We cannot just take sides as the organisation. (Interview, January 2022)

However, organisational neutrality did not constrain some volunteers who engaged pragmatically with SAC officials during the peak of the Delta wave from expressing personal grievances about the coup. Several welfare volunteers, who otherwise maintained pragmatic and open relationships with GAD township administrators after the coup, claimed to have publicly advocated a return to democracy on social media, with no obvious ramifications for them or the organisations with which they worked (Interview, January 2022).

The notion of separating personal ethics from organisational neutrality in the context of dictatorship is highly contentious within Myanmar's charitable sector. As Myanmar activist Khin Omar (2021) argued post-coup:

> Myanmar's humanitarian needs are overwhelming, but they cannot be met by engaging with the same perpetrators of the grave human rights abuses that relief aid intends to address … there is nothing neutral about engaging with the military junta.

Amid broader discussions about whether and how the international community can deliver urgently needed humanitarian aid across Myanmar without directing it through the SAC (see Décobert, Chapter 12, this volume), post-coup debates about the neutrality—both organisational and personal—of Myanmar's non-state welfare sector raise thorny questions about the ethical and practical risks of partnering with local charitable actors in townships where the SAC retains an administrative presence. Is it safe and feasible to partner with local non-state actors to disburse aid given the national context of rigid discipline within which such groups must operate? Or is the international community obliged to recognise and support the heroic work that many charitable groups are doing in the post-coup context rather than solely partnering with the junta?

The humanitarian agreement reached between the SAC and ASEAN in May 2022 suggests that regional neighbours are, for now, willing to partner with the SAC and the military in an attempt to distribute aid and relief as the post-coup humanitarian crisis intensifies (ASEAN 2022). The exclusion of the National Unity Government, ethnic armed organisations and local civil society in these dialogues and subsequent aid distribution risks compounding conflict in an already fractious political context. Given that the coercive developmental expansionism of Myanmar's state army into contested areas was stretching tenuous ceasefires to breaking point before the coup (McCarthy & Farrelly 2020), empowering the military to broker international aid will only enable the SAC to further discipline and neutralise its critics and depict itself domestically and internationally as a legitimate and compassionate authority. As Myanmar regional and international organisations argued in response to ASEAN's humanitarian partnership with the SAC in mid-2022, allowing the junta to 'weaponise humanitarian aid' is likely to result in the exclusion of many vulnerable people from urgently needed relief while implicating the regional bloc in the junta's ongoing atrocities (Progressive Voice 2022).

Conclusion

The pandemic and its management via collaborative state–society relations in 2020 exacerbated pre-existing fractures in Myanmar's society and political system. Comparing state–society cooperation in relation to the pandemic in 2020 with the junta's suppression of NLD-affiliated charity groups and empowerment of ostensibly neutral social partners, this chapter has argued that the perceived weaponisation of the pandemic by successive state authorities highlights the marked political and sociological impact of COVID-19, both prior to and after the February 2021 coup.

Non-state social actors affiliated with the NLD have been suppressed and disempowered, fracturing the pandemic response and likely worsening mortality during the peak of the Delta wave in the second half of 2021.

Meanwhile, the charitable sector as a whole has been simultaneously disciplined and strategically coopted by SAC officials to help manage both the pandemic and the humanitarian crisis created by the coup. In some respects, this technique echoes the approach taken in the 1990s and 2000s by the previous dictatorship that suppressed overly political civil society groups and outsourced social functions to non-state social actors and businesspeople. The most recent wave of post-coup outsourcing is likely to similarly shape and distort welfare politics in Myanmar for years and decades to comes (McCarthy 2023).

The urgent humanitarian crisis unfolding across Myanmar after the coup raises questions about the prospective role of Myanmar's vibrant non-state charitable sector in any substantive short-term response, especially in a context in which SAC administrators demand a degree of neutrality from *parahita* volunteers that many see as compromising both individual and organisational ethical integrity. ASEAN's initial agreement in May 2022 to partner with the junta on humanitarian aid comes with the risk that local welfare groups will be bypassed in flows of international support brokered and mediated by the Myanmar military despite their clear functional capacity to deliver urgent relief in the vexed political context.

In the medium term, the deepening of societal reliance on non-state social actors both to survive and resist dictatorship should compel strategic thinking about how a future civilian government can better address the precarity faced by ordinary people and put to rest the legacies of inequality bequeathed by past and current periods of dictatorship.

References

ASEAN. 2022. 'Press Release on the Outcomes of Consultative Meeting on ASEAN Humanitarian Assistance to Myanmar'. *ReliefWeb*, 6 May. reliefweb.int/report/myanmar/press-release-outcomes-consultative-meeting-asean-humanitarian-assistance-myanmar-6

Aspinall, Edward, Nicole Curato, Diego Fossanti, Eve Warburton and Meredith L. Weiss. 2021. *COVID-19 in Southeast Asia: Public Health, Social Impacts, and Political Attitudes*. Policy briefing, Southeast Asia Rule Based Order Project. Canberra: Australian National University. www.newmandala.org/wp-content/uploads/2021/08/SEARBO_COVID-19-in-Southeast-Asia_Public-health-social-impacts-and-political-attitudes_final.pdf

Aung Kaung Myat. 2022. 'Sit-Tat or Tatmadaw? Debates on What to Call the Most Powerful Institution in Burma'. *Tea Circle*, 3 October. teacircleoxford. com/politics/sit-tat-or-tatmadaw-debates-on-what-to-call-the-most-powerful-institution-in-burma/

Bello, Walden, Jennifer Franco, Pietje Vervest and Tom Kramer. 2020. 'How to Improve Myanmar's Covid-19 Emergency Relief Program'. *Transnational Institute*, 9 June. www.tni.org/en/article/how-to-improve-myanmars-covid-19-emergency-relief-program

Croissant, Aurel. 2020. 'Democracies with Preexisting Conditions and the Coronavirus in the IndoPacific'. *Asan Institute*, 6 June. theasanforum.org/democracies-with-preexisting-conditions-and-the-coronavirus-in-the-indo-pacific/

Dziedzic, Stephen. 2021. 'Doctors Accuse Myanmar's Military of Hoarding Oxygen as COVID-19 Crisis Deepens'. *ABC News*, 18 July. www.abc.net.au/news/2021-07-18/myanmar-doctors-military-junta-hoarding-oxygen-coronavirus/100297282

Esther J. 2021. 'Loikaw Church Closes Clinic after Military Arrests Medical Staff'. *Myanmar Now*, 24 November. myanmar-now.org/en/news/loikaw-church-closes-clinic-after-military-arrests-medical-staff/

Fishbein, Emily and Kyaw Hsan Hlaing. 2020. 'Vote Cancellations Trigger Outrage among Myanmar Minority Voters'. Al Jazeera, 28 October. www.aljazeera. com/news/2020/10/28/vote-cancellations-trigger-outrage-among-myanmar-minority-voters

Frontier Myanmar. 2022. 'COVID Cover up: Third Wave Death Toll May Be in Hundreds of Thousands'. 14 January. www.frontiermyanmar.net/en/covid-cover-up-third-wave-death-toll-may-be-in-hundreds-of-thousands/

Gadarian, Shana K., Sara W. Goodman and Thomas B. Pepinsky. 2022. *Pandemic Politics: The Deadly Toll of Partisanship in the Age Of COVID*. Princeton: Princeton University Press. doi.org/10.1515/9780691219004

Irrawaddy. 2021. 'Myanmar Military Seized Medical Oxygen Imported by Charities'. 27 July. www.irrawaddy.com/news/burma/myanmar-military-seizes-medical-oxygen-imported-by-charities.html

Khin Khin Mra. 2020. 'Fighting on Two Fronts: The Women Facing Conflict and COVID-19 in Rakhine State'. *Myanmar Now*, 20 May. www.myanmar-now.org/en/news/fighting-on-two-fronts-the-women-facing-conflict-and-covid-19-in-rakhine-state (page discontinued).

Khin Omar. 2021. 'There's Nothing Neutral about Engaging with Myanmar's Military'. *New Humanitarian*, 28 July. www.thenewhumanitarian.org/opinion/2021/7/28/theres-nothing-neutral-about-engaging-with-myanmars-military

Kyaw San Wai. 2020. 'Myanmar's COVID-19 Response Banks on Aung San Suu Kyi'. *East Asia Forum*, 31 July. www.eastasiaforum.org/2020/07/31/myanmars-covid-19-response-banks-on-aung-san-suu-kyi/

Lee, Ronan. 2021. 'COVID Coup: How Myanmar's Military Used the Pandemic to Justify and Enable Its Power Grab'. *Conversation*, 16 February. theconversation.com/covid-coup-how-myanmars-military-used-the-pandemic-to-justify-and-enable-its-power-grab-155350

Martinus, Melinda and Sharon Seah. 2020. 'Are ASEAN Stimulus Dollars Going towards Sustainability?' *ISEAS-Yusof Ishak Institute Perspective*, 19 August. www.iseas.edu.sg/wp-content/uploads/2020/08/ISEAS_Perspective_2020_87.pdf

McCarthy, Gerard. 2016. 'Buddhist Welfare and the Limits of Big "P" Politics in Provincial Myanmar'. In *Conflict in Myanmar: War, Politics, Religion*, edited by Nick Cheesman and Nicholas Farrelly, 313–32. Singapore: ISEAS-Yusof Ishak Institute. doi.org/10.1355/9789814695879-020

McCarthy, Gerard. 2021. 'Precarity, Debt and Taxes: Pandemic Politics and the Fiscal Social Contract in Southeast Asia'. Paper presented at Development Studies Conference, University of East Anglia, 30 June.

McCarthy, Gerard. 2023. *Outsourcing the Polity: Non-State Welfare, Inequality, and Resistance in Myanmar*. Ithaca: Cornell University Press. doi.org/10.1515/978150 1767999

McCarthy, Gerard and Nicholas Farrelly. 2020. 'Peri-Conflict Peace: Brokerage, Development and Illiberal Ceasefires in Myanmar's Borderlands'. *Conflict, Security & Development* 20 (1): 141–63. doi.org/10.1080/14678802.2019.1705072

McCarthy, Gerard, Nicholas Ross and Myat The Thitsar. 2021. *Myanmar COVID-19 Recovery Priorities Survey*. Southeast Asia Rule Based Order Project. Canberra: Australian National University.

Nay Yan Oo and R. Batcheler. 2020. *Government of Myanmar COVID-19 Response Committees*. Yangon: The Asia Foundation.

Progressive Voice. 2022. 'ASEAN: Decision on Humanitarian Assistance on Myanmar Must Include All Related Parties'. *Civicus*, 11 May. www.civicus.org/index.php/media-resources/news/5782-asean-decision-onhumanitarian-assistance-on-myanmar-must-include-all-related-parties-to-avoid-aid-weaponisation-by-the-junta

RFA (*Radio Free Asia*). 2021. 'Electricity Bill Boycott Denies Myanmar Military US $1 Billion in Power Revenues since Coup'. 15 September. www.rfa.org/english/news/myanmar/power-09152021192918.html

Rhoads, Elizabeth, Thang Sorn Poine, Cho Cho Win and Helen M. Kyed. 2020. *Myanmar Urban Housing Diagnostic & COVID-19 Rapid Assessment*. Yangon: Enlightened Myanmar Research Foundation.

Si Thura and Tim Schroeder. 2018. 'Health Service Delivery and Peacebuilding in Southeast Myanmar'. In *Myanmar Transformed? People, Places and Politics*, edited by Justine Chambers, Gerard McCarthy, Nicholas Farrelly and Chit Win, 85–108. Singapore: ISEAS-Yusof Ishak Institute. doi.org/10.1355/9789814818551-008

Strangio, Sebastian. 2020. 'COVID-19 Spirals Ahead of Myanmar Election'. *Diplomat*, 28 September. thediplomat.com/2020/09/covid-19-spirals-ahead-of-myanmar-election/

Wittekind, Courtney T. 2021. 'Crisis upon Crisis: Fighting COVID-19 Becomes a Political Struggle after Myanmar's Military Coup'. *ISEAS-Yusof Ishak Institute Perspective*, 11 May.

World Bank. 2020. *Myanmar Economic Monitor, December 2020: Coping with COVID-19*. Washington: World Bank. openknowledge.worldbank.org/handle/10986/34936

Zaw Zaw Htwe. 2021. 'Donations Pour in as People of Myanmar Dig Deep to Help Cover Cost of Vaccine'. *Irrawaddy*, 12 January. www.irrawaddy.com/specials/myanmar-covid-19/donations-pour-people-myanmar-dig-deep-help-cover-cost-vaccine.html

12

Localisation, Good Humanitarianism and Solidarity-Based Approaches to Aid in Myanmar

Anne Décobert

Lecturer in Development Studies, Faculty of Arts,
University of Melbourne

Abstract

Responses to the multifaceted humanitarian emergency precipitated by Myanmar's 2021 military coup demonstrate the effectiveness of localised aid. Yet localisation is not just about aid effectiveness, but about humanitarian autonomy, rights and justice. In Myanmar's Spring Revolution, we are seeing not just ongoing resistance against the military regime, but also growing resistance against unequal and unjust international aid systems. Recognising the political and moral imperative of localisation has implications for debates over the nature of, and principles that should shape, international humanitarian engagement in Myanmar. In Myanmar's political and humanitarian crises, community-based and civil society actors are striving not only to help their communities but also to shape their country's future—and they are calling for solidarity from international actors. In a context in which normative neutrality can do harm, defining 'good humanitarianism' as promoting local agency and autonomy provides a moral compass for international actors to navigate complex political and ethical dilemmas.

***

The 2021 military coup in Myanmar has triggered immense suffering across the country, with civilian populations impacted by escalating violence and displacement, an evolving civil war on multiple fronts, an economic and food security crisis, and a public health emergency within which the junta has weaponised COVID-19. The resulting multifaceted humanitarian emergency cannot be understood in isolation from Myanmar's protracted history of structural violence, injustice and conflict. Against the backdrop of a political crisis triggered by the coup but which has its roots in this long history, civil resistance movements across the country have continued to reject a violent and illegitimate regime. At the same time, in response to the current situation of volatile, concurrent and overlapping crises spanning the country, and within a context of shrinking humanitarian space, community-based and civil society actors have mobilised to provide critical assistance to their communities, demonstrating the strength and effectiveness of locally driven aid. National and local-level actors are now also calling for changes to international aid systems and practices, through their advocacy and everyday work demonstrating that localisation is not just about aid effectiveness but also—and more importantly—about humanitarian autonomy and justice.

In Myanmar's Spring Revolution,[1] we are seeing not just ongoing resistance against the overt violence of the military regime, but also growing resistance against what Bethia Burgess describes as the 'quiet violence' of unequal international aid and governance systems that perpetuate neo-colonial power relations (Burgess, forthcoming). In this context, debates about the localisation and decolonisation of aid are, at a deeper level, debates about rights, autonomy and justice. For members of Myanmar civil society, these are debates about who has the right and the authority to define the future of their country, and about their need to be recognised as equals by international counterparts. Localisation, as Hugo Slim demonstrates, is then 'about realising political rights and making humanitarian citizenship, and should be recognised as politically necessary' (Slim 2021).

In Myanmar today, debates about localisation are also often linked to deeply political questions over the nature of, and principles that should shape, international humanitarian engagement. Here again, issues of rights and

---

1   The popular protests and Civil Disobedience Movement, which began in early 2021 as a result of opposition to the military coup, are commonly referred to by local actors and analysts as Myanmar's Spring Revolution (see e.g. Ko Maung 2021).

justice are key, as community-based and civil society actors in Myanmar call for solidarity from international donors and aid agencies in a context in which, as one international aid worker acknowledged, 'there is a clear right and wrong here' (Interview, February 2022). While recognising that there are no simple answers to what remain difficult questions, I argue that, in a context in which normative neutrality can do harm, it is necessary to define 'good humanitarianism' as humanitarianism that promotes the autonomy and agency of local populations (Slim 2015).

This chapter is part of a broader, ongoing research project on opportunities and challenges for the localisation and decolonisation of aid in Myanmar's complex emergency. To explore debates on the localisation and decolonisation of aid, and their links to questions of international engagement and solidarity, I draw specifically here on 18 targeted semi-structured interviews with representatives of community-based organisations (CBOs), civil society organisations (CSOs), non-government organisations (NGOs), international NGOs (INGOs), donor agencies and the National Unity Government (NUG), as well as multiple, more informal discussions with community, national and international-level actors involved in humanitarian responses in Myanmar. I also draw on public documentation and discussions, as well as my work for over a decade as a consultant and researcher working on aid systems in Myanmar—work that has notably enabled me to take part in past and current debates about aid programs, localisation and the principles that should shape international humanitarian engagement in Myanmar. All individual sources and identifying details have been anonymised to protect the security and confidentiality of those involved. Organisations have been named only in cases where the activities described are already published or openly discussed in the public domain.

In the following sections, I discuss opportunities for the localisation and decolonisation of aid in Myanmar's complex emergency, highlighting the need to move beyond 'localisation by default' and towards long-term and sustained changes to the status quo of unequal and unjust international aid systems. I demonstrate that, for members of civil society and community-based organisations in Myanmar, localisation is not just a technical issue but a political and moral imperative: it is about the need to be recognised as agents of their own destiny. I then turn to ongoing debates about international humanitarian engagement in Myanmar, reassessing these debates through the lens of localisation as a political and moral imperative.

Ultimately, and while these debates have no simple answers, I argue that reframing 'good humanitarianism' can provide a moral compass to guide decision-making and much-needed reforms in aid systems and practices.

COVID-19 and the coup: From 'default localisation' to sustainable change

> We have very little [international] aid, but we are not going to plead and go down on our knees anymore … One of the slogans of this revolution is that we only have ourselves, to be much more self-reliant and less inclined to depend on outsiders. That means less inclined to be colonised. (CSO leader, Myanmar, interview, February 2022)

In Myanmar, aid practitioners and analysts had previously highlighted the strength of locally led emergency responses, which can be far more timely, effective, relevant and sustainable than those by international actors (e.g. L2GP n.d.; Walsh 2020). Yet, the COVID-19 pandemic and 2021 coup have together drawn increased attention to the importance of localised responses to humanitarian emergencies, and to the relationship between localisation and questions of humanitarian autonomy and emancipatory justice.

The COVID-19 pandemic meant that, to a large extent, as an international aid agency representative in Myanmar conceded in an interview in February 2022, 'the international community went into paralysis'. As a consequence of COVID-19, international agencies were forced to bring many expatriate workers back to their home countries, to make staff work more remotely and to suspend many operations on the ground. A civil society leader in Myanmar, frustrated with the reactions of international agencies, put it more bluntly when he said: 'The international aid community withdrew into their cocoons' (Interview, February 2022). Throughout 2020, as they grappled with COVID-19 restrictions, as well as their own occupational health and safety policies and other bureaucratic regulations, many international agencies that continued to support aid programs in Myanmar became increasingly dependent on working with and through local and national systems and organisations. Meanwhile, civil society actors as well as community-level and national-level organisations in Myanmar continued to work on the ground, serving their communities and providing essential services (for a detailed analysis of COVID-19 pandemic responses, see Chapter 11, this volume). Of course, similar trends have been noted throughout the world, the pandemic restricting international agencies' operations and providing a temporary window of opportunity for greater localisation (Barbelet, Bryant & Spencer 2021; Roche & Tarpey 2020; Ullah, Khan & Wijewickrama 2021).

In Myanmar, the impacts of the pandemic were then compounded by the military coup, impeding any return to business as usual by international aid agencies—for now at least. After the military seized power on 1 February 2021, and as Myanmar grappled with an escalating political and humanitarian crisis, community-level and civil society actors throughout the country mobilised their networks and devised creative solutions to channel vital assistance to affected communities. Responses to Myanmar's now multi-pronged complex emergency have, in turn, showcased the effectiveness of locally driven aid, as well as the bravery and resilience of local actors who have continued to assist their communities, despite huge risks to their own lives and security.

These locally led responses drew upon existing social networks and community-level systems—including self-help groups, CSOs, CBOs and religious groups. Some groups—particularly those in historically contested border areas or in areas of the Delta that were devastated by Cyclone Nargis in 2008—already had significant experience in emergency response. Others, such as those in Myanmar's historically more stable Dry Zone, were often previously involved in social and development work but had little emergency response experience; they learnt as they went, as a CSO member explained during a webinar by the Myanmar Local Humanitarian Network (MLHN) in January 2022 (MLHN 2022b). Others still were formed over the past year or two, comprising affected community members who exercised their own agency in mobilising resources and assisting their communities in highly localised, piecemeal and effective ways, without formal mechanisms or external support. At the same time, national-level NGOs in Myanmar ramped up their support for community-level and civil society networks in different parts of the country, and longstanding cross-border aid organisations worked to meet increasing humanitarian needs in border areas under mixed administration or ethnic armed organisation control.

Meanwhile, since the coup, escalating conflict and displacement, soaring humanitarian needs, ever more restricted humanitarian access and COVID-19 have continued to increase international agencies' reliance on national and local organisations and networks. Some international aid agencies that previously relied purely on models of direct implementation for their work in Myanmar were forced to shift towards indirect implementation, working with and through local and national partner agencies. As an INGO worker put it: 'It's been default localisation, because the international actors can't reach the populations that they want to' (Interview, December 2021). For actors on the ground in Myanmar, this is not just a time of crisis, but also one of opportunity. As one civil society leader explained:

> There is a high opportunity for us to show others the capacity of the local. And also, this is a very good time that international also recognises the power of the local—this is a kind of blessing in disguise. (Interview, February 2022)

The current 'default localisation' in Myanmar has showcased the feasibility, effectiveness and benefits of locally led aid approaches. As civil society and community-based actors across Myanmar have continued to lead humanitarian responses, they have also become increasingly connected and organised, sharing knowledge, experience and resources through networks that have developed within and across different states and regions, and calling for changes to international aid systems and practices. In early 2022, multiple regional networks, CSOs, CBOs and national NGOs came together to form the MLHN, which 'aims to render humanitarian assistance more strategic and coordinated in reaching the most vulnerable and far-fetched areas, while pushing the localisation agenda at the heart' (MLHN 2022a, 2). In a position paper on localisation published in January 2022, the MLHN, along with local intermediary actors, other humanitarian networks and 25 CSOs in Myanmar, called for institutional, systemic and behavioural changes by donors and international aid agencies. They asked for international actors to 'take into account the current power imbalance of existing internationalised humanitarian aid architecture and mov[e] towards a real equitable and equal partnership' (MLHN 2022a, 2).

At the same time, there has been increasing recognition within international donor and aid agency circles that the international aid architecture itself has inhibited a timely and effective response to the volatile, concurrent, overlapping and protracted humanitarian crises currently spanning the country. Meanwhile, frustration with the inadequacy of international responses and with ongoing challenges created by overly rigid, bureaucratic and top-down systems has led many to call out what one civil society leader in Myanmar called the 'chronic ailments' of international aid systems (Interview, February 2022).

As a result of these dynamics, actors on the ground in Myanmar are now increasingly calling on international donors and aid agencies to abide by commitments made in the 2016 Grand Bargain,[2] by putting more funding and decision-making power into the hands of local and national responders (IASC n.d.). They are also demanding reforms to overly rigid and top-down international funding mechanisms and compliance requirements—'those tools and systems that we have in place that create barriers, that create hierarchy', as one international aid worker described them (Interview, February 2022). Refusing to be treated as unequals in an international system of humanitarian governance[3] that has to date largely failed their people, civil society and community-based actors throughout Myanmar are, therefore, now uniting in a groundswell of support for the localisation and decolonisation of aid (MLHN 2022a).

In the current situation in Myanmar, this groundswell of increasingly loud and organised voices from community-based and civil society actors who are calling for change arguably presents a conjunctural moment for a more radical localisation and decolonisation of aid systems and practices. Indeed, in a situation where the shortcomings of international systems are only too apparent and where international donors and aid agencies have been forced into greater localisation by default, community-based and civil society actors themselves are now attempting to use the window of opportunity presented by the pandemic and complex emergency in Myanmar to define the terms and shape of localisation. This is in striking contrast to much of the international work on localisation to date, which, as Maha Shuayb (2022) laments, is all too often top-down, internationally driven and imposed on local actors and contexts, instead of being defined by those on the ground.

At the same time, and while the current situation in Myanmar has fostered some noteworthy evolutions through 'default localisation', there is a real need for international agencies and donors to commit to more radical,

---

2   The 2016 Grand Bargain is an 'agreement between some of the largest donors and humanitarian organisations who have committed to get more means into the hands of people in need and to improve the effectiveness and efficiency of the humanitarian action' (IASC n.d.). The Grand Bargain notably emphasises the need to give local and national humanitarian actors more direct funding, support and decision-making power.

3   In this chapter, I adopt Didier Fassin's definition of international humanitarian governance as 'a mode of governing that concerns the victims of poverty, homelessness, unemployment, and exile, as well as of disasters, famines, epidemics and wars—in short, every situation characterised by precariousness' (Fassin 2012, x). Its temporality is that of emergency, its object is to save lives, and 'the powerful legitimacy with which it is invested derives precisely from the fact that it can point to those rescued from death due to famine, epidemic or injury' (Fassin 2012, 189).

long-term and sustainable change. In a possible future scenario in which Myanmar's complex emergency is at least less acute (if not fully resolved), it would be hugely detrimental for international agencies to roll back to more internationally driven approaches. So while, in the current context in Myanmar, greater localisation is no longer really a choice for international actors, locally led aid programs must become a sustained reality. For this to happen, international actors cannot hide behind the idea of 'crisis' in Myanmar. This is not just because the label 'crisis' can deflect from the reality of long-term and deep-rooted political and systemic problems that need to be addressed in order to achieve lasting peace in Myanmar, but also because there is a tendency for international actors to maintain that times of crisis make it impossible to rethink existing systems and ways of functioning (Slim 2021; Interviews with international aid agency representatives, February 2022). Additionally, recognising the need for real and sustained change implies moving beyond seeing localisation as a technical advantage and towards recognising localisation as a political and moral imperative.

Localisation as a political and moral imperative

Within and beyond Myanmar, the need to localise aid systems and practices—to reorient the playing field by giving local and national actors more direct funding, support and decision-making power—is commonly justified in relation to operational effectiveness (Barbelet et al. 2021; IFRC 2018). With local actors and organisations being deeply embedded in crisis-affected contexts and communities, they can respond and address local needs more rapidly and effectively. But localisation is not just about aid effectiveness. As Hugo Slim (2021) argues, localisation is about realising political rights and defining humanitarian citizenship, with those affected by crises, their local organisations and their leaders driving decisions about humanitarian responses that will shape the long-term future of their communities.

Contemporary systems of humanitarian governance remain top-down and internationally biased. Despite commitments made in the Grand Bargain, most international humanitarian aid is still transferred to international organisations, with only small percentages of overall aid budgets going directly to national and local agencies (Slim 2021). This international trend is replicated in Myanmar, where members of civil society and community-based organisations are increasingly demanding that more funding be transferred directly to local and national responders (MLHN 2022a). At the same time, and as lamented by many aid workers in Myanmar, buzzwords like 'participation' and 'partnership' still too often obscure a reality where those affected by crises are reduced to objects of top-down and externally driven interventions, and where national, sub-national and community-level organisations become subcontractors implementing programs that they have not defined—programs that will, moreover, have profound and lasting effects on social and political dynamics in their societies.

This is not to say that there have not been notable attempts to implement Grand Bargain commitments in Myanmar. Even before the coup, some international agencies had initiated extensive programs aimed at promoting localisation. The Humanitarian Assistance and Resilience Programme Facility (HARP-F), for example, was established in 2016 to deliver the United Kingdom's commitments under the Grand Bargain and, specifically, to advance localisation. Through its work before and since the coup, HARP-F demonstrated how international agencies can (and indeed should) adopt a more peripheral and supportive role in humanitarian responses, absorbing much of the bureaucratic and financial management work associated with international donor funding, while giving local and national agencies the independence and flexibility to design, manage and deliver aid programs in their areas. HARP-F has also documented successes and challenges in its work with local and national partner agencies in Myanmar, as well as highlighting the types of institutional and systemic changes required to enable greater localisation (HARP-F n.d.-a).

Moreover, in Myanmar's conflict-affected border areas, systems of remote partnerships had for decades enabled international donors to support local aid agencies in ways that gave considerable decision-making power and operational independence to these local agencies. Remote partnerships entail a division of labour between the local organisation, which manages aid programs and their delivery, and the international partner organisation, which channels back-donor funding and deals with much of the more bureaucratic aspects of aid work. During a public webinar organised in August 2021 by HARP-F on localisation and remote partnerships in Myanmar, a representative of The Border Consortium—an INGO that has supported aid programs for decades in Myanmar's border areas by working with local agencies through remote partnerships systems—described this model as 'disruptive programming' (HARP-F n.d.-b). Remote partnerships can disrupt power imbalances since they allow for greater local leadership though decentralised and flexible approaches that are adapted to local needs. In this model, INGOs like The Border Consortium act as intermediaries, taking on much of the donor-facing aspects of aid work and managing upwards by attempting to push back against overly onerous donor compliance and other requirements that can cripple local agencies.

However, and despite all the efforts that have gone into localisation to date in Myanmar, the international aid architecture itself continues to impede changes to the status quo. For one, the rigid and bureaucratic systems of many international donors and aid agencies 'conceptually privilege and prioritise their own knowledge and expertise, often imposing Western-centric structures on contexts for which they are ill suited' (Walsh 2020). Moreover, as an INGO worker in Myanmar explained:

> It's not in the interest of the great proportion of the aid industry—localisation isn't in their own interests. Of course, there's going to be a lot of resistance to it! (Interview, December 2021)

Combined with institutional inertia and the disincentivising practices of many international agencies themselves, vested interests in the status quo produce a tendency towards minor tweaking of aid programs instead of real shifts in power relations—something documented well beyond the Myanmar context (e.g. Ayobi et al. 2017). Localisation is then all too often reduced to international agencies employing a few additional local staff, engaging in a few additional and often largely tokenistic consultations with local communities, or in other ways talking the talk without really walking the walk of change.

Overall, contemporary international aid systems and practices therefore still perpetuate systemic inequalities between international actors and their counterparts in Myanmar. These inequalities become visible notably in the differential pay structures, benefits and levels of protection accorded to international and local or national aid workers; or in the ongoing dominance of international actors in positions accorded greater decision-making power, mobility and agency. There remains, as one civil society leader in Myanmar noted, a 'core asymmetry' that 'includes incomes and perks and all the allowances that come with working with that [humanitarian system]' (Interview, February 2022). At a deeper level, these realities reveal systems of humanitarian governance to be fundamentally paradoxical, uniting a politics of solidarity with a politics of inequality, a relation of assistance with a relation of domination (Fassin 2012, 3). Humanitarian governance, then, not only accords value to bare life, in Giorgio Agamben's terms, but also accords different ontological values and unequal levels of agency to different human lives (Agamben 1998; Fassin 2012).

The unequal status quo in contemporary international aid systems and practices ultimately results, Hugo Slim (2021) maintains, in 'imposing a system of social welfare in [people's] societies which excludes them from its design, and prevents them from building their own social contracts and humanitarian institutions'—in turn breaching people's fundamental rights to what Slim describes as 'humanitarian self-determination' and to be treated as international equals. Genuine localisation, entailing changes to the status quo of unequal power relations, is then a political and moral imperative, not just a technical advantage. And this is precisely what members of Myanmar civil society and community-based organisations are demonstrating through their work and advocacy.

Today, much of the discussion about localisation among international agencies operating in Myanmar continues to be focused on more 'technical' issues—or at least technical-seeming issues, since many of these have significant political and ethical ramifications. There is, therefore, much focus on issues such as the 'absorption capacity' of local and national agencies, funding streams and modalities, and what are seen by international actors as potential financial risks and compliance issues posed by channelling increased international support to local and national responders. But for members of national, community-based and civil society organisations in Myanmar, the debate about localisation is inextricably linked with political questions about who has the right and authority to define the future of their country. As the leader of a national NGO in Myanmar stated:

> I think localisation, in a political sense, is another space where locals are able to voice against in this very, very unjust humanitarian architecture. When we look at the humanitarian architecture, it is very much an internationalised system … The thing about the self-determination means [the affected community] need to look at what they want to be in the future, about their country, about their community, about their society. Sometimes that might not be exactly the same as the international expectation, but we need to recognise the self-determination. (Interview, February 2022)

Recognising the reality of, and need to remedy, ongoing inequalities and injustices in international systems of humanitarian governance is the first step towards realising the type of genuine and sustained changes that actors on the ground in Myanmar are demanding. It also implies that, as the same national NGO leader in Myanmar explained of international actors: 'Maybe some of your privilege you may need to share—without sharing your privilege, as far as you talk, localisation is impossible' (Interview, February 2022).

Additionally, achieving genuine and lasting localisation means respecting and building systems, institutions and organisations that not only save lives and reduce human suffering, but also enhance the autonomy and agency of the very people impacted by crises. As Charlotte Dany highlights, localisation becomes a means by which 'humanitarian aid may help to achieve common goals among equals and thus to integrate a more solidarity-focused approach'—an approach historically at odds with the unequal nature of international systems of humanitarian governance (Dany 2021; Fassin 2012). Further:

> To make humanitarian aid a real tool for expressing global solidarity, one would have to regard the recipients of aid as equals and strengthen their agency, as well as that of local and grassroots organisations in the most affected areas. (Dany 2021)

Framing localisation in these ways, then, has important ramifications in relation to debates about how to deliver international aid within a complex emergency like Myanmar's, where international humanitarian engagement can have significant ethical and political consequences.

Localisation and debates about humanitarian engagement and solidarity in Myanmar

In Myanmar today, debates about localisation are often interlinked with questions over the nature of, and principles that should shape, international humanitarian engagement—with solidarity-based approaches challenging the type of normative neutrality long claimed to be the 'litmus test of humanitarianism' (Décobert 2016, 232). While acknowledging that there is no simple, one-size-fits-all solution to these debates, recognising the political and moral necessity of localisation and reframing 'good humanitarianism' provides a much-needed moral compass for navigating complex political and ethical dilemmas.

As mentioned above, it is essential to understand Myanmar's multi-pronged humanitarian emergency in relation to longstanding structural violence, injustices and conflict. Within the more acute emergency situation precipitated by the coup, a civil resistance movement is legitimately opposing an illegitimate and abusive military regime bent on terrorising local populations to retain power. As well as denying the democratic will of the people, the State Administrative Council (SAC) and Myanmar armed forces have continued to commit widespread and systematic abuses and attacks against civilian populations, which amount to crimes against humanity (OHCHR 2021). The junta has also restricted humanitarian operations, blocking the delivery of aid, deliberately destroying food and medical supplies, diverting aid away from its intended recipients, and attacking and even killing aid workers—acts that constitute violations of international humanitarian law.

Within this context, members of civil society and community-based organisations are calling for solidarity from international donors and aid agencies. Overwhelmingly, community-level and civil society actors continue to reject the SAC and denounce the suffering it is driving, and they are asking international actors to support them in their struggle for democracy and human rights. 'We cannot pretend we are neutral, we are not', one civil society leader stated (Interview, February 2022). Through their work, civil society and community-based actors are trying not just to assist civilians in need of aid, but also to define the future of their country. In so doing, they are asserting their agency as humanitarian citizens with the right and authority to shape their own humanitarian institutions and social contracts. And they perceive attempts at neutrality by international agencies as potentially doing real harm, particularly if—by not taking a stand or by having their aid politicised by the military regime—international actors end up legitimising, emboldening and enabling those behind the coup (Décobert 2021; Khin Ohmar 2021; Progressive Voice 2021). As one national NGO leader in Myanmar explained:

> Sometimes, you know, international humanitarian organisations, they are too narrow with the international so-called principles. If you are on that principle, you are with them. If you are not there, well … so, I think we need to go beyond that now … We need

solidarity. We are struggling, we are facing a lot of challenges, we need their understanding, empathy, and also the solidarity. (Interview, February 2022)

In the classic International Committee of the Red Cross definition, neutrality means 'not tak[ing] sides in hostilities or engag[ing] at any time in controversies of a political, racial, religious or ideological nature' (Haug 1996). It is worth noting that the *Code of Conduct for the International Red Cross and Red Crescent Movement and Non-Governmental Organisations in Disaster Relief* does not explicitly refer to neutrality, but instead focuses on the humanitarian imperative (reducing suffering) and impartiality (non-discrimination; see ICRC 1994). Nevertheless, and despite a long history of divisions over the viability of neutrality as a guiding principle for humanitarianism in complex emergencies, many international aid agencies still maintain that it is essential to humanitarian action (Décobert 2016; Fassin 2012; Redfield 2011). Moreover, international actors can be reluctant to support local and national agencies if they are not politically neutral, with the principle of neutrality then acting as a potential barrier to localisation. Yet, as Hugo Slim (2020) highlights, 'neutral humanitarian action is one version of humanitarianism—not the only version', and it is not absolutely necessary to be neutral to be a good humanitarian.

A commitment to localisation implies that international actors should engage with, listen to and respect civil society and governance systems that are deemed legitimate by the Myanmar people themselves. Moreover, in a context like Myanmar's complex emergency, where normative neutrality becomes morally questionable and can do very real harm, it logically implies adopting a solidarity-based approach. An international aid agency representative currently working in Myanmar mused:

> What civil society in Myanmar wants to do is overthrow the military. That's what they want to do and so if we really want to localise, if we really want to support these local organisations, we would take a line that says: we will support you in doing that because that is what you want ... I think, objectively, you could say the question of neutrality is irrelevant and if our role is really just to support people that are in need, these are mechanisms to be able to do that. That's the solidarity approach. (Interview, February 2022)

In their private capacities, many representatives of international donor and aid agencies support a solidarity-based approach—after all, to repeat the words of an international aid agency representative, there is 'a clear right and wrong here'. However, at the same time, international agencies that are still working officially inside Myanmar are having to balance calls for solidarity with the geopolitical agendas of their back-donors, and with concerns about protecting staff and programs on the ground. The same international aid agency representative who had voiced their personal support for a solidarity-based approach went on to explain that:

> The question is: given these restraints, what can we do to support in solidarity, without putting our people at risk or without putting the whole organisation at risk? I think it's a difficult line because, as long as we have an organisational presence in Myanmar, as long as we have staff in Myanmar, it's going to be really tough to take a really overt position on some of these issues … I think that's where we do need to differentiate, or we need to take a differentiated approach. (Interview, February 2022)

In contexts where normative neutrality may not be possible or may in fact do harm, it is important to rethink the principles shaping international humanitarian engagement and action. In *Humanitarian Ethics*, Hugo Slim (2015, 2) defines 'good humanitarian work' as work that:

> enables a person or a community to remain the subject of their lives, not objects in the lives and purposes of others. Good humanitarian action makes people its goal but does not objectify them as 'beneficiaries' or commodify them as 'recipients' of aid. On the contrary, good humanitarian aid and protection increase people's autonomy and agency as human beings. The best humanitarian action is that which respects people and works with them to prevent suffering, repair harm, and enable them to come through their suffering and flourish.

This reframing of principles to guide humanitarian action and engagement can then allow for differentiated but still 'good humanitarian' approaches in a context like Myanmar. Some of these approaches can—and indeed should—align explicitly with what Thomas Weiss calls a 'solidarist' approach, 'employing humanitarian action within a political strategy on behalf of victims' (Weiss 1999, 5). Others can be less *explicitly* political or aligned but should still respect the wishes of the Myanmar people and be founded on a definition of 'good humanitarianism' as increasing people's autonomy and agency as human beings.

Since the 2021 coup in Myanmar, international agencies have adopted different types of approaches to the provision of aid. Some international agencies have taken an explicitly solidarist stance, refusing to engage in any way with the SAC, and instead supporting humanitarian and human rights efforts from outside the country. To date, these types of explicitly solidarist approaches to international aid in Myanmar have generally entailed working with and through CBOs and CSOs operating inside Myanmar—including, but not limited, to longstanding cross-border aid organisations. Given escalating humanitarian needs in Myanmar, international donors and aid agencies must provide increased support to these local-level systems and organisations, which have 'the expertise, local legitimacy, and vision to offer an alternative to traditional aid distribution practices' (Khin Ohmar 2021). These types of approaches are necessary, not only to channel assistance to civilian populations in need of aid but also to help lay the foundations for longer-term democratisation, development and peace in Myanmar.

At the same time, a solidarist approach can extend to engaging with the NUG's Ministry of Humanitarian Affairs and Disaster Management. The NUG is currently channelling humanitarian aid to displaced populations, Civil Disobedience Movement participants and others in need by working with and through local networks and groups in different areas of the country. To date, however, very few international agencies have funded humanitarian aid through the NUG. International donor and aid agency representatives often cite concerns about the NUG's links with the People's Defence Forces and its support for armed resistance against the SAC—although of course, geopolitical concerns also play into the reluctance of some back-donor countries to be seen as supporting the NUG.

If recent responses by Western donor countries to the crisis in Ukraine show us anything, it is that international actors can and do at times support 'resistance humanitarianism' (Slim 2022). Such an approach is morally justified in contexts where the type of neutrality fostered by the Red Cross movement becomes unfeasible and where aid becomes a way to support legitimate local resistance and resilience against military violence and oppression. Of course, political interests and not just moral questions will inevitably continue to influence international actors' decisions about how to engage in Myanmar. But international humanitarian engagement with the NUG is justified from a solidarist perspective and any such engagement should be done in ways that support localised responses, that follow a definition of 'good humanitarianism' as increasing the Myanmar people's autonomy and agency, and that include systems to ensure that aid is used for humanitarian purposes and does no harm.

While some international agencies have rejected any kind of engagement with the SAC, others have maintained an official presence inside Myanmar, trying to access populations in need of aid by negotiating with the regime. Oftentimes, international agencies working in this manner have also been discretely ramping up support to civil society and community-based organisations that are, in various ways, opposing and are, therefore, targeted (or potentially targeted) by the military regime, with this very solidarist aspect of their work needing to remain below the radar. Of course, this approach is likely to become increasingly difficult as the junta further restricts humanitarian space and puts more pressure on international and local agencies to register and report on their activities—with the 2022 Registration of Associations Law creating a highly restrictive regulatory framework and anticipated to have wideranging negative impacts for NGO and CSO operations in Myanmar.

International donors and agencies maintaining communication channels with the military regime should use their position to push for increased humanitarian access and protection, as well as respect for international humanitarian law. Any kind of negotiation with the SAC, however limited, also requires honest, careful and ongoing assessment of the political risks and impacts of these activities. This means that international agencies operating officially inside Myanmar must not be blinded by what one long-time aid worker described as 'their self-preservation and their sense of their worth' (Interview, February 2022), which can lead to doing more harm than good—for example, if any good done in provided aid with restricted levels of access to populations in need is outweighed by the harm done through paying taxes to or in any way legitimising the SAC.

In short, given the nature of Myanmar's political and humanitarian crises, and the demands of the Myanmar people themselves, international humanitarian engagement should ultimately be guided by an overarching focus on solidarity. There can be a division of labour between international actors and agencies (or sometimes even between different branches of the same agency), with diverse but still 'good humanitarian' approaches taking place at the same time. Some of these approaches can be more *explicitly* aligned with, and supportive of, groups and organisations opposing the military junta. Other approaches may not be so explicitly opposed to the military regime and may instead maintain limited communication channels for the purposes of humanitarian diplomacy, while at the same time supporting civil society and community-based actors in less overt ways from inside the country. However, if they do adopt the latter approach, international donors and aid agencies must genuinely ensure that their aid programs do not end up legitimising, emboldening and enabling those behind the coup and ongoing systematic human rights abuses in Myanmar. And, whatever their approach, international donors and aid agencies must abide by a definition of 'good humanitarianism' as supporting the agency and autonomy of Myanmar's people.

Conclusion

Responses to the humanitarian emergency triggered by Myanmar's 2021 military coup demonstrate the strength and effectiveness of locally driven aid. Yet localisation is not just a technical advantage but a political and moral imperative. In Myanmar today, there remains a tendency for debates about localisation to depoliticise what is—for those on the ground—a deeply political issue, inextricably linked with systemic inequalities and injustices. So whereas, as one civil society leader put it, 'it is a power issue', many in international aid circles still emphasise effectiveness-related costs and benefits of localisation, focus on more technical advantages and barriers, and seem reluctant to acknowledge their own positions within unequal structures that they then often unintentionally perpetuate.

What is needed today in Myanmar is recognition of the inequalities and injustices that are reproduced by top-down international aid systems, and of the need for systemic changes through approaches that not only place local actors at the forefront of crisis response, but also realise a more emancipatory vision of localisation. Localisation is then not only about local actors helping their own communities. It is about these actors having the autonomy and agency to shape their own futures. Recognising the political and moral imperative of localisation is essential to start addressing one of the most problematic contradictions of contemporary systems of humanitarian governance—systems within which all human lives are supposed to be equally valuable, but that (re)produce inequalities between different human lives (Fassin 2012; Slim 2021).

In Myanmar today, there is a need to capitalise on and also move beyond the current 'default localisation', and for international donors and aid agencies to commit to long-term and sustainable changes to international aid systems and practices. Localisation in Myanmar 'should not be turning local actors into more cogs in the wheels of the international aid system', one aid worker emphasised. 'It's about respecting and understanding how local society responds to crisis, responds to issues' (Interview, February 2022). Approaches to localisation then need to go beyond simply recognising and working with national and local organisations that already have the types of systems in place that make it relatively easy for international agencies to engage with and support them. Genuine localisation in Myanmar also needs to recognise and enable the agency of the diverse local communities affected by crises, and their different leaders, systems and networks. The current political and humanitarian emergency in Myanmar is a time of opportunity in this respect—a time when international actors are being forced to recognise the strength of community-level responses, and to listen to civil society actors who are demanding changes to the status quo.

In practical terms, and given the escalating humanitarian needs in Myanmar, international donors and aid agencies must increase support to local-level systems and organisations that have the expertise, local legitimacy and systems to offer an alternative to top-down and internationally driven aid practices. These types of approaches are necessary, not only to channel assistance to civilian populations in need of aid, but also to help lay the foundations for longer-term democratisation, development and peace in Myanmar. At the same time, international donors and aid agencies must provide funding more directly to local and national responders—including multi-year core funding, which allows local and national actors to strengthen their systems and agencies in sustainable ways—and work to reduce overly rigid and burdensome reporting, financial and other bureaucratic and compliance requirements that continue to impede greater localisation.

In relation to ongoing debates over the nature of, and principles that should shape, international humanitarian engagement in Myanmar's complex emergency, international donors and aid agencies need to recognise that they have choices to make and that these choices will have important political and ethical ramifications. In a context in which normative neutrality can do very real harm, international humanitarian engagement should be guided by an overarching solidarity-focused approach. This is consistent with a commitment to genuine localisation and with the need for international actors to engage with, listen to and respect civil society and governance systems deemed legitimate by the Myanmar people themselves. While in practical terms, this may involve a range of different types of approaches— some more explicitly solidarist than others—ultimately international donors and aid agencies must ensure that their programs do not end up legitimising and enabling the military regime, but that they instead support the agency and autonomy of the Myanmar people.

Acknowledgements

The author would like to extend thanks to all the individuals who participated in interviews as part of this research, and to the three representatives of local and international aid agencies who provided feedback and comments on an earlier draft of this chapter. These individuals are not named for confidentiality reasons, but their input was invaluable in shaping the analysis and arguments presented in this chapter.

References

Agamben, Giorgio. 1998. *Homo Sacer: Sovereign Power and Bare Life*. Stanford: Stanford University Press.

Ayobi, Yaseen, Ayla Black, Linda Kenni, Railala Nakabea and Kate Sutton. 2017. *Going Local: Achieving a More Appropriate and Fit-For-Purpose Humanitarian Ecosystem in the Pacific*. Canberra: Australian Red Cross and Australian Government Department of Foreign Affairs and Trade. humanitarianadvisorygroup.org/wp-content/uploads/2020/12/ARC-Localisation-report-Electronic-301017.pdf

Barbelet, Veronique, John Bryant and Alexandra Spencer. 2021. *Local Humanitarian Action during Covid-19: Findings from a Diary Study*. London: Overseas Development Institute. cdn.odi.org/media/documents/C19__localisation_diary _methods_WEB.pdf

Barbelet, Veronique, Gemma Davies, Rosie Flint and Eleanor Davey. 2021. *Interrogating the Evidence Base on Humanitarian Localisation: A Literature Study*. London: Overseas Development Institute. odi.org/en/publications/interrogating-the-evidence-base-on-humanitarian-localisation-a-literature-study/

Burgess, Bethia. Forthcoming. 'Justice in Crisis: Pursuing Community-Based Liberation in Eastern Myanmar, Its Borderlands, and Beyond'. PhD thesis, University of Melbourne.

Dany, Charlotte. 2021. 'Solidarity through Localization? Humanitarian Responses to the COVID-19 Pandemic'. *Frontiers in Political Science* 3. doi.org/10.3389/fpos.2021.695654

Décobert, Anne. 2016. *The Politics of Aid to Burma: A Humanitarian Struggle on the Thai-Burmese Border.* Oxon; Routledge. doi.org/10.1355/cs38-3l

Décobert, Anne. 2021. 'Myanmar's Human Rights Crisis Justifies Foregoing Neutrality for a Solidarity-Based Approach to Humanitarianism'. *Melbourne Asia Review.* 7th ed. doi.org/10.37839/MAR2652-550X7.6

Fassin, Didier. 2012. *Humanitarian Reason: A Moral History of the Present Times.* Berkeley: University of California Press. doi.org/10.1525/9780520950481

HARP-F (Humanitarian Assistance and Resilience Programme Facility). n.d.-a. 'Knowledge Products'. www.harpfacility.com/our-work/share-knowledge/

HARP-F (Humanitarian Assistance and Resilience Programme Facility). n.d.-b. 'Webinar #3: "No Access, No Aid?" How Remote Partnerships Are Key to Delivering Humanitarian Aid in Protracted Crisis'. harpfacility.com/resources/webinar-no-access-no-aid-how-remote-partnerships-a/

Haug, Hans. 1996. 'Neutrality as a Fundamental Principle of the Red Cross'. *International Review of the Red Cross,* no. 315. www.icrc.org/en/doc/resources/documents/article/other/57jncv.htm

IASC (Inter-Agency Standing Committee). n.d. 'About the Grand Bargain'. interagencystandingcommittee.org/about-the-grand-bargain

ICRC (International Committee of the Red Cross). 1994. *Code of Conduct for the International Red Cross and Red Crescent Movement and Non-Governmental Organisations (NGOs) in Disaster Relief.* Geneva: IFRC. www.icrc.org/en/doc/resources/documents/publication/p1067.htm

IFRC (International Federation of the Red Cross and Red Crescent Societies). 2018. 'Localization—What It Means and How to Achieve It'. Policy brief. reliefweb.int/sites/reliefweb.int/files/resources/Localization-external-policy-brief-4-April.pdf

Khin Ohmar. 2021. 'There's Nothing Neutral about Engaging with Myanmar's Military'. *New Humanitarian,* 28 July. www.thenewhumanitarian.org/opinion/2021/7/28/theres-nothing-neutral-about-engaging-with-myanmars-military?fbclid=IwAR2eQzgC-QCd3RL5Z4IVVv7bPwtv31S-RkRbUJagydNCpwEOiN6huSCiz0M

Ko Maung. 2021. 'Myanmar's Spring Revolution: A History from Below'. *Open Democracy,* 15 December. www.opendemocracy.net/en/beyond-trafficking-and-slavery/myanmars-spring-revolution-a-history-from-below/

L2GP (Local to Global Protection). n.d. 'Myanmar'. www.local2global.info/research/countries/myanmar/

MLHN (Myanmar Local Humanitarian Network). 2022a. 'Positioning Paper on Localisation and Intermediary Role by Myanmar Civil Society'. static1.squarespace.com/static/5fc4fd249698b02c7f3acfe9/t/62344b7805620407528b354a/1647594360696/Myanmar+Positioning+Paper+on+Localization+and+Intermediary+role+by+CSO+31+January+2022+-+Eng.pdf

MLHN (Myanmar Local Humanitarian Network). 2022b. 'Launching of "Localisation and Intermediary Role by Myanmar CSOs Positioning Paper"'. Webinar.

OHCHR (Office of the High Commissioner for Human Rights). 2021. 'Special Rapporteur on the Situation of Human Rights in Myanmar Tells Human Rights Council that the International Community Is Failing the People of Myanmar'. www.ohchr.org/en/press-releases/2021/07/special-rapporteur-situation-human-rights-myanmar-tells-human-rights-council?LangID=E&NewsID=27284

Progressive Voice. 2021. 'Stop the Weaponization of Humanitarian Aid by the Myanmar Military Junta'. 20 June. progressivevoicemyanmar.org/2021/06/20/stop-the-weaponization-of-humanitarian-aid-by-the-myanmar-military-junta/

Redfield, Peter. 2011. 'The Impossible Problem of Neutrality'. In *Forces of Compassion: Humanitarianism between Ethics and Politics*, edited by Erica Bornstein and Peter Redfield, 53–70. Santa Fe: School for Advanced Research Press.

Roche, Chris and Fiona Tarpey. 2020. 'COVID-19, Localisation and Locally Led Development: A Critical Juncture'. *Dev Policy Blog*, 23 March. devpolicy.org/covid-19-localisation-and-locally-led-development-a-critical-juncture-20200323/

Shuayb, Maya. 2022. 'Localisation Only Pays Lip Service to Fixing Aid's Colonial Legacy'. *New Humanitarian*, 8 February. www.thenewhumanitarian.org/opinion/2022/2/8/Localisation-lip-service-fixing-aid-colonial-legacy?fbclid=IwAR0RubcamQWVfD9Vqt8Z9iSpnzsctK47htXWzmjkd68fZZWvqqz5_wT7F58

Slim, Hugo. 2015. *Humanitarian Ethics: A Guide to the Morality of Aid in War and Disaster*. Oxford: University of Oxford Press.

Slim, Hugo. 2020. 'You Don't Have to Be Neutral to Be a Good Humanitarian'. *New Humanitarian*, 27 August. www.thenewhumanitarian.org/opinion/2020/08/27/humanitarian-principles-neutrality

Slim, Hugo. 2021. 'Localization Is Self-Determination'. *Frontiers in Political Science* 3 (708584). doi.org/10.3389/fpos.2021.708584

Slim, Hugo. 2022. 'Solidarity, not Neutrality, Will Characterise Western Aid to Ukraine'. *Ethics and International Affairs*, 10 March. www.ethicsandinternational affairs.org/2022/solidarity-not-neutrality-will-characterize-western-aid-to-ukraine/

Ullah, Zaki, Saeed Ullah Khan and Eranda Wijewickrama. 2021. *Covid-19: Implications for Localisation. A Case Study of Afghanistan and Pakistan.* Humanitarian Policy Group Working Paper, Overseas Development Institute, London. humanitarianadvisorygroup.org/wp-content/uploads/2021/06/C19__localisation_Asia_case_study_WEB.pdf

Walsh, Matt. 2020. 'Time to Recentre Power to Northern Shan State's First Responders'. *Frontier Myanmar*, 27 January. www.frontiermyanmar.net/en/time-to-recentre-power-to-northern-shan-states-first-responders/

Weiss, Thomas. 1999. 'Principles, Politics, and Humanitarian Action'. *Ethics & International Affairs* 13 (1): 1–22. doi.org/10.1111/j.1747-7093.1999.tb00322.x

13

Relief as Resistance: (Re)Emergent Humanitarianism in Post-Coup Myanmar

Aung Naing

Independent researcher, Myanmar

Tamas Wells

Myanmar Research Network Coordinator, School of Social and Political Sciences, University of Melbourne

Abstract

This chapter presents the findings of a recent survey of civil society organisations (CSOs) in Myanmar that examines how new forms of accountability and cooperation can lead to highly efficient emergent relief. In the wake of the 2021 coup, Myanmar has become a failed state in which the current military authorities cannot fulfil the usual criteria of statehood. Besides a politicisation of humanitarianism, in effect sidelining all attempts to claim neutrality, the coup has also created a vacuum that multiple actors, including numerous local CSOs, have begun to fill, delivering a wide range of public services in ways that are rooted in popular claims to legitimacy. The results are expressions of resistance to military rule that are less about overt opposition and more about localised, alternative islands of state-building. This chapter urges a reorientation of humanitarian policy towards

Myanmar that embraces the complexity, ambiguity and latent potential of emergent, volunteer welfare groups as not only a means of delivering aid in ways that avoid entanglement and dependency on coup-controlled processes, but also enable and promote active citizenship in local communities, which is itself a critical step towards re-establishing community life and institutional integrity in Myanmar.

***

As discussed in Chapters 11 and 12, citizen organisations in Myanmar have a rich history of subversive humanitarianism. However, the impact of the recent COVID-19 pandemic and the 2021 military coup have reshaped the role of civil society organisations (CSOs)[1] in important ways. The response to COVID-19 enhanced the role of CSOs in providing services, yet public health restrictions limited their scope and voice. The frustration generated during the COVID-19 restrictions then served as emotional and organisational fuel for the widespread resistance to the 2021 military coup. In this context of state repression and vast humanitarian need, the work of local CSOs has become crucial. At the same time, the general collapse of state administrative and welfare mechanisms—due to both the Civil Disobedience Movement and the degradative effects of the military government's mismanagement—has resulted in a vacuum of statehood.

In this chapter we draw on a December 2021 survey of Myanmar CSOs and interviews with CSO leaders in January 2022. We argue that, through providing welfare, CSOs are demonstrating a particular form of resistance. They are embodying a viable, legitimate and internally sustainable alternative to the current military government's claims to statehood. CSOs are enacting their own form of statehood through providing consistent

---

1   The term CSO is used here to describe locally formed organisations, embracing a wide spectrum of organisational form. Some would be considered a local non-governmental organisation (NGO), with a more clearly defined structure and often (but not always) some form of registration. Others would fall into the *parahita* organisation category, which refers to a common form found in rural, but also some urban areas. These organisations are typically based loosely around Buddhist principles of welfare, rely on local donations, and engage in activities such as providing free funerals, healthcare, education, blood donation drives and emergency relief. Whilst some would have a more defined organisational structure, many would not. However, '*parahita* organisation' is an extremely well-recognised term when used to survey the presence of charity and welfare organisations, whereas the more imported terms like civil society organisation (CSO) or NGO are less well known. A third category would be even more loose associations of volunteers who have established themselves for a particular purpose, without any particular articles of association.

humanitarian assistance, using data and informal networks to ensure appropriate responses, and operating in ways that provide accountability to both international and local donors.

The first section of the chapter explores literature on failed states and humanitarianism and argues that post-coup Myanmar can be categorised as a failed state. The second section then explores the broader political dilemmas of humanitarian responses, including in Myanmar in the wake of the COVID-19 pandemic and the military coup. Drawing on our research with Myanmar CSOs, the third section explores three specific challenges for CSOs in Myanmar: safety and security, navigating operational space and finance. We conclude that, in the context of a failing Myanmar state in which civil society groups are taking on some of the functions of statehood, donor agencies need to take steps towards deeper engagement with CSOs.

Failed states and humanitarianism

One critical consideration of the embedded politics of humanitarianism relates to the appraisal of the state, for example, whether the state is viewed as weak and in need of assistance, support and legitimacy; whether the state is seen as malign and undeserving of assistance, thus justifying explicit solidarity with those considered its victims; or whether the state has essentially failed to the point of irrelevance. In the coming sections, we explore how different assumptions of the state—as failed or not, as malign or not—are crucial to the ways in which external agencies respond to humanitarian crises.

The definition and, indeed, the validity of the concept of failed states is both varied and contested (see Bøås & Jennings 2007). At what point is a fragile state considered to have failed or collapsed (Ware 2016)? Indices of fragile states express state capacity as a continuum (Fund for Peace 2021) measured in relation to the state's capacity and will to undertake key economic, social, political and security-related functions. Rotberg (2002) locates state failure beyond issues of territorial control, seeing it as the failure to deliver political goods. That failure in turn undermines legitimacy:

> Nation-states fail because they are convulsed by internal violence and can no longer deliver positive political goods to their inhabitants. Their governments lose legitimacy, and the very nature of the particular nation-state itself becomes illegitimate in the eyes and in the hearts of a growing plurality of its citizens. (Rotberg 2004, 1)

279

Frequently, illegitimacy fuels a cycle of oppressive policies, such that those in control of state apparatus abandon any attempt to implement policies to benefit citizens, and instead enact policies that exhibit:

> favour [towards] powerful elites, few budget controls and rampant corruption, cronyism and patronage arrangements that limit opportunity and siphon off public assets for private gain, and usually a combination of punitive use of existing regulations and exemptions to benefit the favoured few. (Brinkerhoff 2005, 6)

The exacerbation of inequalities coupled with a failure to deliver essential public goods and services contributes to perceptions of impotence and illegitimacy that, in turn, impact on wider security issues, for if citizens have little hope that 'their wellbeing will improve' they are more likely to 'engage in crime or be recruited into insurgency' (Brinkerhoff 2005, 6).

Reaching the conclusion that the state has failed, and enacting humanitarian aid based on that assumption, is itself inherently political. The residual state apparatus may contest the failed-state diagnosis, which serves to both codify the lack of legitimacy and further undermine it. If the state has essentially failed in terms of legitimacy, delivery of political goods and exercise of territorial control, the possibility emerges of humanitarian spaces that do not refer to state authority. The humanitarian mandate may be justified in several ways when working from the presumption of a failed state.[2]

First, if the state cannot provide for its citizens, then humanitarians must. Second, the failure of the state justifies the consequences of such an intervention, at least in the short term, while also serving to further undermine the legitimacy of the state. Third, the failure of the state—particularly where there is a collapse of legitimacy or, worse, evidence of abuse of citizens by the organs of the state—justifies a humanitarian approach that not only ignores any residual claims to authority by the state but also seeks to engage with other actors whose claims to legitimacy may be, albeit, perhaps, at a more local level, more robust, credible and constructive.

The relative absence of the state does not mean the absence of authority, merely that, in the fractured spaces of failed states, alternative power loci emerge, ranging from local armed militia, ethnic or religious affiliated

---

2   Dingli (2013, 91) questions the value of the failed state concept, pointing out its inherently Eurocentric perspective that leads to the employment of 'orientalist simplifications that mystify the complex, interrelated web of tribal governance and patronage', and allows regimes to manipulate the failed state label for their own interests.

organisations, localised welfare groups and the private sector (Coyne 2006), operating with various degrees of competition or cooperation. The acknowledgement of such alternative loci of statehood may, to some extent, circumvent the problematic aspects of the failed-state concept, and position humanitarian action in spaces where micro-level components of community, governance and legitimacy may be located—something that we explore later in this chapter in the context of Myanmar. This turns the attention of humanitarianism to the more 'nested games' (Coyne 2006, 341), where legitimacy, trust, authority, welfare, public services, political goods, territorial control and aspirations are located in a variety of actors, institutions and powerbrokers. It also signals an acceptance of the process of 'fundamental change and reordering', which, despite the significant degree of 'intrusion and social engineering' involved, is seen as 'both appropriate and reasonable, indeed, as reflecting the only realistic chance of a stable future' (Duffield 2005, 16).

Myanmar: A failed state?

To what extent does both external evidence and measure of public opinion support the categorisation of Myanmar as a failed state? Even prior to the COVID-19 pandemic and military coup of 2021, Myanmar was already ranked twenty-third in the list of fragile states (Fund for Peace 2021), and the only country in Southeast Asia listed in the top 40. Pandemic control measures for COVID-19 severely impacted an already fragile economy: research conducted towards the end of 2020 indicated that over 80 per cent of households had seen significant reductions in their household income since the start of that year (World Bank 2020), and economic forecasting projects that poverty rates are likely to double from 24 per cent (recorded in 2017) to 48 per cent. At the beginning of 2021, efforts were underway to commence a national vaccination program, as well as to slowly reopen business, education and travel sectors.

However, the coup d'état of 1 February 2021, and subsequent rapid spiral of violence, has instead wrought havoc on an already fragile society and economy, and, while the most recent data is yet to be published, is likely to have resulted in a negative trend in most, if not all, of the indicators of state fragility. Since the coup, leading personnel from the previously elected civilian government have either been incarcerated or are in hiding (or, in some cases, killed), removing their effective control over key levers of power. The subsequently formed Committee Representing the People's

Hluttaw and the broader-based National Unity Government (NUG) have attracted widespread popular support. However, despite the establishment of a government structure and the performance of certain key functions, including international relations, the NUG, at the time of writing, is not able to deliver necessary public goods and services to a significant extent across Myanmar.

The economic conditions have meanwhile deteriorated further. A survey conducted only two months after the coup found that the majority (79 per cent) of households reported a reduction of household income since the military coup; 25 per cent had not worked at all, while another 31 per cent had worked fewer hours since 1 February.[3] These trends continued to worsen in the year after the coup: monthly panel survey data conducted by local CSO organisations in mainly urban areas demonstrated increased rates of economic vulnerability, food insecurity and problem debt.[4]

In this context, the claims to legitimacy of the junta-led State Administrative Council (SAC) do not reach the standard of a functioning state.[5] In addition to the lack of public legitimacy, as evidenced by sustained, widespread protest and resistance, the Civil Disobedience Movement—whereby huge numbers of civil servants from key government departments such as health, education, transport and some administration departments effectively remain on strike—has severely constrained the SAC's ability to deliver public goods.[6] Moreover, the delivery of public goods, as described earlier, relates not only to services such as healthcare and education, but also to justice, security and the rule of law. The rapid and widespread militarisation of the administrative and justice systems[7] has enabled the process of detention, trial, sentencing and, in some cases, extrajudicial killing of political

---

3   Data taken from randomised sample of 500 households included in a phone survey undertaken in April 2021 by a Myanmar-based survey firm who requested anonymity.
4   Data taken from a sample of 800 households in five different locations between April 2021 and March 2022.
5   The criteria for statehood are varied, and not the same as that of effective government. However, while Article 1 of the Montevideo Convention refers to the 'capacity to enter into relations' as a significant criteria for independence and a prerequisite for statehood, additional criteria, particularly with respect to the human rights of the population within the territory, are also considered important (see Kreijen 2004).
6   This is not to ignore the ongoing delivery of some public goods by institutions under the SAC, such as electricity, some elements of public health (including COVID-19 vaccination), a limited reopening of schools and universities, some elements of administration, such as immigration and customs, and foreign relations and media.
7   Some would argue that, to some degree, these had never been demilitarised, with both the legal system and justice personnel reflecting conditions prior to the ascent of the civilian government, and, as such, that a reversion to those conditions was both swift and relatively straightforward.

opponents to take place relatively unchecked, which points not simply to a failure to provide such public goods, but a deliberate subversion of them. Beyond this, a mixture of strikes and mismanagement has resulted in a virtual collapse of the banking system and widespread economic inactivity in virtually every sector, effectively stalling any potential post-COVID-19 economic recovery. Armed militia groups, formed in response to attacks on protesters, and arbitrary detentions, have also significantly reduced the SAC's ability to provide security and order, even to senior officials. Added to this, various of the ethnic armed organisations (EAOs) in Myanmar have sought to use the political crisis to regain, consolidate or expand territorial control, sometimes in support of the aims of the NUG, but in many cases as a unilateral strategy.

Aside from more than 1 million internally displaced persons, mainly those fleeing military actions in central, eastern and western Myanmar, huge urban to rural remigration has placed increased burdens on already precarious rural livelihoods. The tentative steps that had been taken to establish social welfare systems, such as cash transfers to pregnant women, have now been destroyed, which, together with the collapse of the healthcare system, means that there are no wider safety nets for the poorest of the poor. Military actions to date have shown little concern for social welfare, with reports of elderly residents being left to burn alive in villages targeted by military reprisals.

In short: Myanmar is less of a failed state than an act of deliberate and wanton destruction—a torching of any residual state institutions that, in the past, had served the public. The consequences of this are beginning to be seen as an emerging catastrophe that could be described as humanitarian, except for its political origins. The targeting of charitable organisations, as well as restrictions on international humanitarian aid has, in conditions reminiscent of the early days of post-Nargis relief, left the majority of the burden of food and material assistance to informal networks, which have continued to flourish despite harassment by military and military-aligned forces.

The picture that emerges from the current crisis is one of multiple coping strategies formed either to resist, evade or undermine military control, or, in some cases, to survive within it. One consequence is the re-emergence, or, in some cases, the re-energising, of the numerous self-organisational capacities that were present for decades under previous military rule. Such capacities result in a prolific array of initiatives: for some EAOs, a consolidation of territorial control to include judiciary and administrative functions;[8] in areas not controlled by EAOs, the formation of local militia to provide protection against arrest and harassment by security forces under the SAC; volunteer groups providing healthcare; volunteer groups providing food aid and relief to local populations affected by the economic downturn; and numerous ingenious cooperative arrangements to maintain commerce in the absence of a functioning financial system and a cash crisis.[9] Even in some non-EAO areas, a coalescing of protection, provision of relief and enacting of basic administration provision by volunteer groups has resulted in what looks like micro-government. The argument here is that, if these three strands are taken together (consolidation of functions in EAO areas, the emergence of localised areas of micro-government and the multiple expressions of cooperation that enable the ongoing delivery of public goods outside of SAC control), then it follows that the state and state-building are located in multiple zones, representing an emergent, rather than centrally directed, phenomenon (South 2021).

The challenge to this approach is that, if legitimacy is established in multiple, diverse and often competing spheres, how can a single, legitimate state re-emerge? Brinkerhoff (2005, 5) rightly highlights the importance of re-establishing legitimacy. However, of critical importance are the foundations of that legitimacy:

> expanding participation and inclusiveness, reducing inequities, creating accountability, combating corruption and introducing contestability (elections) … re-establishment of the rule of law … institutional design … as well as civil society development. (Brinkerhoff 2005, 5)

At the heart of re-establishing legitimacy is trust. As Coyne (2006, 351) points out: 'Trust-enhancing institutions differ in complexity and magnitude. Some, such as reputation, may be effective in smaller groups while others … may be effective at facilitating interaction on a larger scale.' Our argument here is that, in the context of a failed state, particularly where the illegitimacy is rooted in oppression or abuse, re-establishing the legitimacy of the state requires more than a re-establishment of security and

---

8   The Arakan Army's consolidation of control over the judiciary and administrative bodies in Rakhine State being one of several examples. Other EAOs, such as the United Wa State Army have long exerted judicial, administrative and political control over their territories.

9   Such measures have taken on many forms, such as a revival of the *hundi* systems of money transfers, whereby money is transferred into an account held outside Myanmar, and the equivalent amount is released by a linked party in local currency within Myanmar. Such transactions enable rapid and safe transfer of funds, but are the stuff of nightmares for financial auditors.

adequate public service delivery. Core notions of citizenship, governance and accountability are required, and the rebuilding of these may need to take place in sites where alternative, constructive expressions of those are possible. This points to the increased importance of locally grounded forms of legitimacy, such as CSOs, which, in the absence of a legitimate state, represent a key modality for the distribution of political goods to the Myanmar population. In the next section, we describe the dilemmas faced by funding organisations in supporting humanitarian responses in a failed state such as Myanmar.

Humanitarian response in Myanmar

In responding to both the humanitarian and political crisis in Myanmar, various international actors, such as the Association of Southeast Asian Nations (ASEAN) (Chongkittavorn 2022) have proposed the establishment of 'humanitarian corridors' as a key element of assistance, although the nature of such a space has not been defined. Beyond this, the United Nations and international non-governmental organisations (NGOs) have sought to continue the provision of humanitarian assistance. However, given the already restricted nature of their activities, requiring substantial cooperation with government authorities, the continuance of such activities has, to a significant degree, been contingent on continued cooperation with government actors under the control of the military regime. This raises several issues and concerns. First, a coherent argument has been made by both activists and legal scholars that ongoing cooperation with state organs under the control of the military serves to enhance and entrench the legitimacy of what has been widely determined as an unlawful seizure of power (AMCDP 2021). Second, past experience of relief distribution in Myanmar where cooperation with military-controlled authorities was required featured a litany of obstacles, corruption and unnecessary restrictions that, in many cases, significantly hampered relief efforts (South et al. 2011). Third, the proposals by ASEAN and others argue that, for the people of Myanmar, the main priority is relief, and that the 'people' are by and large unconcerned with whether relief serves to legitimise a particular authority. This argument rests on an assumption that aid is viewed as neutral: an assumption that is, to a significant degree, unfounded. As Weiss (1999,12) succinctly puts it: 'The assumption that politics and humanitarianism can be entirely separated, as if they were parts of two different and self-contained worlds, is a fiction.'

Weiss (1999, 4) proposes a 'political spectrum' of humanitarians with regard to their operating principles, placing at one end the 'classicists' who seek to avoid 'taking sides' and approach consent as 'sine qua non' whereby the needs of the poor override any political concerns. At the other end of the spectrum, the 'solidarists' explicitly take the side of 'selected victims', eschew any attempts at impartiality and are prepared to override sovereignty 'as-necessary'. In between these extremes are 'minimalists' and 'maximalists' who tend either towards the classicist or solidarists position. While this is to some extent useful, the application of such a spectrum has a tendency towards labelling and blaming, rather than a constructive appraisal of how diverse aspects of humanitarian aid, even where politics are explicitly eschewed, nonetheless inevitably express and embody some form of politics.

The political nature of humanitarianism is determined from several angles: first, while the humanitarian agency may not possess an explicit political agenda, the practical delivery of aid is frequently enmeshed in complex processes of negotiations and permissions with either state or non-state actors. This means that decisions to deliver aid in ways that require cooperation and, to some degree, dependence on one or more group's authority are inherently political, as they legitimise the claims of that group.[10]

Second, while humanitarianism may purport to be non-political, this obscures the significance of the driving forces and motivations of humanitarianism, which may go beyond the desire to alleviate 'life-threatening suffering wherever it may be found' to more prosaic concerns regarding organisational priorities: 'the desire to continue operations and retain staff—or as a form of legitimization politics—showing the public that an agency is doing good work' (Hilhorst & Jansen 2010, 1121–2). Third, and critically for the claims and proposals of this chapter, humanitarian action does, by its modus operandi, serve to strengthen or erode capacities and systems, and, in doing so, effects changes on the wider political landscape.

The local partner conundrum

The standard narratives of development organisations emphasise the need to engage with local populations, institutions and partners, although the sincerity and efficacy of such engagement has been repeatedly challenged (see

---

10   Rich (1999) has explored this in the context of engaging 'warlords' in humanitarianism, which may be an appropriate framework for considerations of the political calculations of humanitarianism in Myanmar.

Smillie 2001; Gingerich & Cohen 2015). As Gizelis and Kosek (2005, 367) observes, 'pre-existing local institutions, structures and traditions are usually ignored in failing states, and NGOs fail to capitalize on opportunities to incorporate locals into relief work'. In considering humanitarian action in situations of conflict and failing states, the engagement of local populations and institutions is critical, not simply to enable more effective relief and development,[11] but also as part of the process of enabling the development and maintenance of governance functions.

However, engagement with local populations, actors and institutions in ways beyond simply using them as conduits for distribution will inevitably lead to the kind of political choices discussed earlier. In contexts in which the legitimacy of those claiming to be the state is contested or rejected, the maintenance of neutrality may be challenging and indeed unhelpful. In engaging with local organisations and populations, it is recognised that:

> local organizations are highly partisan, often for good reason. Justice may be as high on their agenda as relief … and [they] are therefore likely to have opinions that exist in tension with basic humanitarian principles. (Smillie 2001, 187–8).

Beyond that, where humanitarian needs are inseparable from basic protection against either a state or another non-state party, relief becomes intertwined with protection (South et al. 2011). Survival strategies enacted by local populations, and enabled by local organisations, thus encompass a range of activities, many of which represent a form of resistance enacted in self-preservation.

Aside from more formalised political or ethnic affiliation, which represents a more tangible source of partisanship, Tim Forsyth cautions against 'misplacing social or economic activities into pre-defined narratives of resistance' (Forsyth 2009, 274). Attempts at a neat framing of humanitarianism may unravel in contexts where survival strategies require protection as well as material support, and where humanitarian aid and human rights are inseparable.

---

11   Although this point should not be overlooked, as Gingerich and Cohen (2015, 38) point out:
Humanitarian response led by local and national actors (state and civil society) in affected countries is usually preferable to large international responses in a number of ways: it is likely to be faster and better grounded in local realities, and is frequently cheaper, thus will ultimately save more lives.

To summarise: the complexities of humanitarianism, particularly in contexts where the state is failing or collapsing—and particularly where the failing state is doing so due to malign intent and actions and not simply incompetence—call for a recognition that any related humanitarian space is inevitably and inherently political. In the advent of the collapse of the state, other actors and institutions become more prominent, and engagement with them is both necessary and advantageous, but also represents a choice in terms of political commitment (Décobert & Wells 2020). This presents agencies with a local partner conundrum. If such engagement is genuine, it will, of necessity, involve the humanitarian agency in the coping strategies of local populations and organisations, and, as such, offer little prospect of maintaining neutrality; further, it will require attention to justice, protection and the strengthening of systems that enable the circulation of material and political goods, even at a local level. The alternatives are either to focus on the strengthening of the displaced failed state, which can claim popular legitimacy but modest efficiency in terms of the delivery of public goods, or strengthening the in-situ failed state, which has little or no popular legitimacy and little or no efficiency in terms of delivery of public goods.

People have essentially chosen to express their citizenship, in relation to governance, in self-organised ways. Large and varied sections of Myanmar's population, having been denied the representative government based on their vote, have resorted to measures that would establish some form of self-organised system. In other words: 'If we can't get the government we want by voting, we'll just organise it ourselves.'[12] Aside from any value judgements on the competing claims to government, the reality is that this is what people are doing—a key part of everyday survival is self-organisation tactics that seek to evade central authority. The question for humanitarian assistance providers is: to what extent should humanitarian assistance work in tandem with those self-organised groups (and their strategies and tactics), given that they are posited, if not in direct opposition to the SAC, then at least in terms of evasion?

---

12   Three caveats need to be expressed here: first, that for a significant proportion of people, including many in areas controlled by EAOs, voting in recent elections was not possible or permitted and, for some, did not represent a genuine chance to secure adequate representation. Second, the statements here reflect what is commonly considered to be the majority public opinion. Third, the self-organising processes, as mentioned before, are not new, particularly in EAO controlled areas, but also, as Griffiths (2019) and others have highlighted, have long represented a significant element in the wider welfare system in Myanmar.

The view from below: Challenges for CSOs and the shrinking humanitarian space

This section presents findings from two sources: 1) a survey conducted in December 2021 of 40 CSOs on their operational status and challenges, and 2) in-depth follow-up interviews conducted with leaders and members of five of these organisations in January 2022. The interviews were conducted by locally recruited researchers in Burmese language.

The existence of self-organised welfare groups in Myanmar has been well documented (Griffiths 2019; McCarthy 2017). The recent decade of political reform saw a flourishing of such groups after decades of suppression by successive military regimes. However, the twin terrors of the COVID-19 pandemic and the 2021 coup have served to dramatically redefine and constrain the role and operating space of CSOs in Myanmar.

The COVID-19 pandemic was, in many senses, a double-edged sword. On the one hand, local *parahita* (social welfare) organisations were at the forefront of the COVID-19 response, mobilising and deploying considerable human and material resources to support ambulance services, quarantine centres, special COVID-19 field hospitals and innovative welfare distribution programs. During the initial period of the COVID-19 pandemic, local organisations in many cases expanded or changed their mandates to respond to COVID-19 restrictions and needs, and, in doing so, large numbers of young people were mobilised as volunteers and donor networks established and strengthened. A generation of CSO leaders developed through this period, with older, established leadership often providing a more hands-off, guiding role.

However, this also resulted in the shift of risk and burden to local organisations, who, in turn, were rarely 'counted' in the wider response strategy (Trócaire 2020). While providing the bulk of human and material resources in the COVID-19 pandemic response, local agencies were ignored or sidelined in strategic planning, despite having extensive local knowledge that could have enabled more tailored local responses. Thus, local organisations frequently found themselves with both an enhanced role and responsibility but a diminished voice.

The February 2021 coup further exacerbated this, as local organisations joined protests against the illegitimate seizure of power. All the organising capacity that served the COVID-19 response was now directed towards anti-coup resistance, fuelled by the pre-coup frustrations of being sidelined.

This, in turn, made local organisations visible targets for arrest by military authorities, which further diminished the humanitarian space (ICNL 2022). One CSO leader, whose organisation prior to COVID-19 focused more on civic education, described how 'because of COVID-19, we had to stop everything … we could only restart after the third wave. By then, because of the coup, we could not do as before' (Interview January 2022).

Despite some degree of expansion during the COVID-19 and post-coup period, many CSOs, particularly more established local NGOs, have faced considerable difficulties. Three major constraints were mentioned in both surveys and in-depth interviews: safety and security, navigating operational space and financial challenges. First, in situations in which, pre-coup, local CSOs were regarded as critical sources of human and material resources in the COVID-19 pandemic response, the vocal and vigorous response of the same CSOs and volunteers in protest against the coup resulted in harassment, arrest and seizure of property by military authorities. Humanitarian acts, including ambulance services and food distribution, were treated as hostile by the military. Previous collaborative networks became sources of vulnerability to infiltration and betrayal, resulting in a shrinking of horizons to ever more local spheres of operation: 'Our biggest issue now is safety. Now we have to be more careful with our networks. Every action now has to be carefully calculated, because of the risk' (Interview with staff of local CSO, February 2022).

A second challenge is one of navigating the narrow operational space with regard to dealings with the SAC. Operationally, many aspects of relief, healthcare and education, as well as finance and logistics, require some element of permission or facilitation by administrative bodies. Where these are under the control of the SAC, CSOs face a dilemma: cooperation with SAC-appointed bodies and personnel may enable more effective access to deliver aid but betrays the broader wishes of the very public to whom the aid is intended. Surveys of CSO volunteers and beneficiaries confirmed this: more than 90 per cent agreed strongly with the statement that: 'Relief organisations should avoid cooperation with SAC.' Again, 90 per cent of respondents strongly agreed that they would 'rather starve than accept help from [a] SAC-affiliated group'. Any sign of collaboration with the SAC at the local level risks, at best, undermining the legitimacy of the CSO, and, at worst, putting it in the crosshairs of local People's Defence Forces. Here, though, organisations use what Scott would call 'metis' (Scott 2020): that is, local knowledge and networks that enable them to undertake various civic functions without reference to state instruments and institutions:

> We avoid anything directly to do with SAC. With social, religious and other activities, we deal directly with the community, with people we know. In that way we can avoid dealing with SAC people. In these times, you do what you have to do, you avoid what you don't have to do. (Interview with CSO leader, January 2022)

New registration laws published by the SAC in 2022 required all local NGOs to register or re-register, or face penalties as unlawful associations. Beyond the wider principle of avoiding the SAC for ideological reasons, local CSOs recalled the experiences under the previous military regime in which official registration was further used as a tool of coercion.[13] Hence, all the organisations surveyed had opted for various forms of evasion, including reforming as underground associations, changing or removing names and office signboards, moving offices, switching to online/virtual operating modes, closing organisational bank accounts and switching to personal ones, or, in a few cases, suspending operations and supporting the activities of other groups. Such tactics come at a cost, particularly where donors prefer, or even require, registration, organisational bank accounts and a more visible, transparent operating presence.

Financial difficulties constitute a final challenge for CSOs. The survey of 40 organisations revealed that three-quarters had lower incomes in December 2021, compared with January 2020, and the median number of volunteers had decreased from 23 to 14. Some organisations had switched focus away from issue-specific advocacy to relief and humanitarian actions, but there was overall a 50 per cent reduction in the scale and scope of activities between January 2020 and December 2021. Along with loss of income and volunteers, the banking crisis (described earlier) also posed difficulties for CSOs, particularly those who operated with funds from institutional donors:

> Our biggest problem is banking. We can only withdraw our money from the banks with some brokerage fee, like five per cent or seven per cent. We have to negotiate with the donors for that. There needs to be more 'give and take' around the finance issue. (Interview with founder of local CSO, March 2022)

---

13   The odd paradox is that, by registration, an organisation becomes a legal entity, but is then subject to further restrictions in relation to what activities are permitted. This was in previous regimes enforced through a system of requiring regular activity and financial reports, with the threat of legal action if any activities were considered to be against the wishes of the authorities. Thus, many preferred simply to stay out of the legal framework altogether: as one leader of a local *parahita* organisation put it, 'If we register, then they can take action against us according to the law, as we are a legal entity. But if we don't register, we are neither legal nor illegal—we don't formally exist. It is better that way.'

The 2021 coup, combined with the broader impact of COVID-19 responses, has presented new challenges for CSOs. In particular, our field research revealed concerns about maintaining public legitimacy, safety and security, navigating operational space and financial challenges.

Conclusion: New spaces of statehood

We have argued in this chapter that there have been four turns for local CSOs—four transformative moments where responses have enabled a formative change. First, the constraints of COVID-19 enhanced their role while limiting their scope and voice. Second, the momentum and frustration generated during the COVID-19 period served as the emotional and organisational fuel for the massive outburst of resistance to the coup. Third, the subsequent repression of civic life and civil society by the military junta, including the targeting of charitable organisations and shooting and looting of ambulances and clinics, has once again defined the status of *parahita* welfare as political and therefore subject to arbitrary persecution from the perspective of the junta. Finally, the general collapse of state administrative and welfare mechanisms due to both the Civil Disobedience Movement and the degradative effects of SAC mismanagement has resulted in a vacuum of statehood into which CSOs have stepped.[14] There is ample evidence of not only continued but also expanded operations by myriad, loosely formed voluntary organisations, in which the operations of larger international NGOs and local NGOs have largely stalled. Voluntary associations provide food aid, medical care, education and refugee assistance to the hundreds of thousands displaced by conflict since the coup.

Following these turns, the space in which CSOs operate is not so much defined in terms of direct opposition to the state, but as a substitute for an absent or illegitimate state. This is nothing new. A key strand of the narrative of many of the *parahita* organisations that emerged under military and later quasi-military rule was self-organisation as legitimacy (Griffiths 2019).

In the post-coup environment, the absence of state provision is framed less in terms of benign neglect and incompetence, and more in terms of the wilful destruction of both the rudimentary welfare apparatus of the state and

---

14   We would pause here to acknowledge that this observation is somewhat centre-centric. In a number of the border areas under the control of EAOs, administrative and welfare systems are often administered by EAOs and their political wings (see e.g. well-documented examples of parallel judiciary and administrative systems in Rakhine State; Kyaw Linn 2022).

the emergent welfare organisations that were plugging the gaps. Our point here is that, in the process of providing welfare, CSOs are demonstrating a particular form of resistance: that of embodying a viable, legitimate and internally sustainable alternative to the state's claims to statehood.

However, statehood is contested by those who lay claim to the right of it by dint of force and by those whose claims are rooted in popular legitimacy and locality. These have different visions and means for development, and, as such, different trajectories and outcomes. Hence, what is important is not simply the role of local knowledge contra the state's organising power, but that the deployment of different organisational paradigms will result in different forms of development in the contested spaces of the 'local'. What this does is frame the welfare activities of CSOs, particularly under the current constraints, not simply as desperate attempts to ameliorate tragedy and suffering, or explicit/direct resistance to military rule, but as the implicit claiming of 'state space' and the embodiment of elements of statehood (especially the delivery of welfare and essential services). However, contesting such space involves many risks and challenges and requires extraordinary levels of adaptive capacity.

To that end, international cooperation needs to recognise three key principles as it seeks to engage with the process of ending violence and rebuilding society in Myanmar. First, humanitarian aid is not 'neutral' or 'apolitical'; to the contrary, it either explicitly or implicitly contributes to the enabling or constraining of alternative visions of society. Second, the ideal of a single, unitary and reproducible model of society implemented from above should be abandoned in favour of the kind of '"bottom-up federalism" that is emerging from the existing and actual local structures and practices of autonomy' (South 2021, 457). While South refers mainly to EAOs, we would argue here that the same principle applies to more central areas, where CSOs are also carving out small islands of statehood. The third principle is one of commensurate adaptation: if CSOs are adapting their modus operandi to continue to deliver humanitarian aid, then international donors should follow suit. In particular, issues around accountability frameworks being rigidly structured around financial audits rather than operational information should be addressed, and examples are emerging of how this could be implemented in practice, including through volunteers.[15]

---

15 We refer here to a program that has delivered monthly cash or in-kind support to a cohort of over 1,000 households since May 2021. International donations have been handled via complex payment networks, often involving third-party *hundi* (informal payment) trades.

In practice, this would require humanitarian donors to adopt more flexible approaches, including working with unregistered entities, allowing more creative means of transferring funds, such as the use of informal networks and *hundis*, and allowing leeway for local groups to address urgent, emergent needs without fear of incurring financial audit sanctions. Also, rather than predominately relying on international NGOs and the UN as financial intermediaries, bilateral donor agencies could enhance the role of large local NGOs as intermediaries who could channel funds to smaller local groups. Local intermediaries are, on the whole, far better placed to navigate the local politics of humanitarian aid in Myanmar than international agencies, as well as being more cost-effective. For this to occur, however, there will need to be significant growth in the operational flexibility and capability of bilateral donors.

In many cases, groups of volunteers are, in a small way, enacting a form of statehood: that is, providing humanitarian assistance in a consistent and transparent way, using data and informal networks to ensure appropriate responses and operating in ways that provide accountability to both international and local donors. In this way, recently displaced slum dwellers, people with disabilities, unemployed migrants and other vulnerable citizens are identified, a form of social contract is enacted and small steps are taken to maintain the essential conditions of life, for a few at least. It behoves the international donor community to consider its own capacity to adapt to the needs of local organisations and support the creation of multiple, alternative spaces of citizenry, from which a new state, or states, can emerge.

References

AMCDP (Australia-Myanmar Constitutional Democracy Project). 2021. 'AMCDP Statement in Support of Constitutional Democracy in Myanmar'. Media release, 10 February. www.medianet.com.au/news-hub-post?id=196753 (page discontinued).

Bøås, Morten and Kathleen M. Jennings. 2007. '"Failed States" and "State Failure": Threats or Opportunities?' *Globalizations* 4 (4): 475–85. doi.org/10.1080/14747730701695729

Brinkerhoff, Derick W. 2005. 'Rebuilding Governance in Failed States and Post-Conflict Societies: Core Concepts and Cross-Cutting Themes'. *Public Administration and Development: The International Journal of Management Research and Practice* 25 (1): 3–14. doi.org/10.1002/pad.352

Chongkittavorn, Kavi. 2022. 'Asean Tackling Aid for Myanmar People'. *Bangkok Post*, 3 May. www.bangkokpost.com/opinion/opinion/2303874/asean-tackling-aid-for-myanmar-people

Coyne, Christopher J. 2006. 'Reconstructing Weak and Failed States: Foreign Intervention and the Nirvana Fallacy'. *Foreign Policy Analysis* 2 (4): 343–60. doi.org/10.1111/j.1743-8594.2006.00035.x

Décobert, A. and T. Wells. 2020. 'Interpretive Complexity and Crisis: The History of International Aid to Myanmar'. *The European Journal of Development Research, 32* (2): 294–315. doi.org/10.1057/s41287-019-00238-y

Dingli, Sophia. 2013. 'Is the Failed State Thesis Analytically Useful? The Case of Yemen'. *Politics* 33 (2): 91–100. doi.org/10.1111/j.1467-9256.2012.01453.x

Duffield, Mark. 2005. 'Social Reconstruction: The Reuniting of Aid and Politics'. *Development* 48 (3): 16–24. doi.org/10.1057/palgrave.development.1100164

Forsyth, T. (2009). 'The Persistence of Resistance: Analysing Responses to Agrarian Change in Southeast Asia'. In *Agrarian Angst and Rural Resistance in Contemporary Southeast Asia*, edited by Dominique Caouette and Sarah Turner, 287–96. London: Routledge.

Fund for Peace. 2021. *Fragile States Index*. fragilestatesindex.org/country-data/

Gingerich, Tara R. and Marc J. Cohen. 2015. *Turning the Humanitarian System on Its Head: Saving Lives and Livelihoods by Strengthening Local Capacity and Shifting Leadership to Local Actors*. Oxford: Oxfam GB.

Gizelis, T.-I. and K. E. Kosek. 2005. 'Why Humanitarian Interventions Succeed or Fail: The Role of Local Participation'. *Cooperation and Conflict* 40 (4): 363–83. doi.org/10.1177/0010836705058224

Griffiths, Michael P. 2019. *Community Welfare Organisations in Rural Myanmar: Precarity and Parahita*. London: Routledge. doi.org/10.4324/9781003000464

Hilhorst, Dorothea and Bram J. Jansen. 2010. 'Humanitarian Space as Arena: A Perspective on the Everyday Politics of Aid'. *Development and Change* 41 (6): 1117–39. doi.org/10.1111/j.1467-7660.2010.01673.x

ICNL (International Centre for Not-For-Profit Law). 2022. 'Myanmar (Burma)'. Accessed 27 February 2023. www.icnl.org/resources/civic-freedom-monitor/myanmar

Kreijen, Gerard. 2004. *State Failure, Sovereignty and Effectiveness: Legal Lessons from the Decolonization of Sub-Saharan Africa*. Leiden: Brill. doi.org/10.1163/9789047405856

Kyaw Linn. 2022. *The Nature of Parallel Governance and Its Impact on Arakan Politics*. Amsterdam: Trans-National Institute. www.tni.org/en/article/the-nature-of-parallel-governance-and-its-impact-on-arakan-politics

McCarthy, Gerard. 2017. 'The Value of Life'. In *Citizenship in Myanmar: Ways of Being in and from Burma*, edited by Ashley South and Marie Lall, 167–87. Singapore: ISEAS.

Rich, Paul B. 1999. 'Warlords, State Fragmentation and the Dilemma of Humanitarian Intervention'. *Small Wars & Insurgencies* 10 (1): 78–96. doi.org/10.1080/09592319908423230

Rotberg, Robert I. 2002. 'Failed States in a World of Terror'. *Foreign Affairs*, July–August: 127–40. doi.org/10.2307/20033245

Rotberg, Robert I., ed. 2004. *State Failure and State Weakness in a Time of Terror*. Washington: Brookings Institution Press.

Scott, James C. 2020. *Seeing Like a State: How Certain Schemes to Improve the Human Condition Have Failed*. New Haven: Yale University Press, 2020, Chapter 9: 309–341. doi.org/10.12987/9780300252989-011

Smillie, I. 2001. *Patronage or Partnership: Local Capacity Building in Humanitarian Crises*. Bloomfield: Kumarian Press.

South, Ashley. 2021. 'Towards "Emergent Federalism" in Post-Coup Myanmar'. *Contemporary Southeast Asia: A Journal of International and Strategic Affairs* 43 (3): 439–60. doi.org/10.1355/cs43-3a

South, Ashley, Susanne Kempel, Malin Perhult and Nils Carstensen. 2011. *Myanmar—Surviving the Storm: Self-Protection and Survival in the Delta*. Local to Global Protection. www.local2global.info/wp-content/uploads/L2GP_Myanmar_Nargis_study.pdf

Trócaire. 2020. *Two Steps Forward, One Step Back: Assessing the Implications of COVID-19 on Locally-Led Humanitarian Response in Myanmar*. Maynooth: Trócaire.

Ware, Anthony, ed. 2016. *Development in Difficult Sociopolitical Contexts: Fragile, Failed, Pariah*. London: Palgrave Macmillan.

Weiss, Thomas G. 1999. 'Principles, Politics, and Humanitarian Action'. *Ethics & International Affairs* 13: 1–22. doi.org/10.1111/j.1747-7093.1999.tb00322.x

World Bank. 2020. *Myanmar Economic Monitor*. documents.worldbank.org/en/publication/documents-reports/documentdetail/9061716080866222905/myanmar-economic-monitor-coping-with-covid-19

14

Myanmar's Higher Education Sector Post-Coup: Fracturing a Fragile System

Charlotte Galloway

Honorary Associate Professor, College of Arts and Social Sciences,
The Australian National University

Abstract

The military coup has had a significant negative impact on human security in Myanmar. While the future remains uncertain, the effect of the coup on higher education (HE) and higher education institutions is more predictable, as history looks to repeat itself. Since February 2021, universities have been in stasis. Staff and student numbers have drastically declined and foreign engagement and capacity building has ceased. The consequences of another lost generation on Myanmar's future prosperity are dire. Without homegrown expertise there will, by necessity, be reliance on external actors to achieve any economic and social development. Global political responses to the coup suggest that, in the short to medium term, international linkages may favour nations friendly to Myanmar, which may further impact regional security. The consequences of the coup on international students from Myanmar is also unknown, as students either return to Myanmar or stay abroad, the latter path further eroding Myanmar's knowledge-based capacities. This chapter considers the impact of recent events on Myanmar's

HE system and likely future scenarios. The role of the international donor community is also discussed for if (or when) re-engagement with Myanmar starts to occur.

***

Myanmar's capability to achieve sustainable economic or social improvement requires a well-educated population. Recognising the need for capacity building in this field, prior to the military coup of 1 February 2021, Myanmar's education system was undergoing extensive reform and the outlook was positive. Yet, even in the pre-coup world, there was still a predicted lag of 20 years before Myanmar would see the full benefit of a generation of students who had experienced a modernised education system from primary through to tertiary level. It was anticipated that international donors would continue to support capacity building across the education sector, enabling Myanmar's ambition to have a population well equipped to engage with global workforce trends.

The coup has completely disrupted the progress made within the higher education (HE) sector over the last decade since Myanmar transitioned to quasi-democratic rule. However, even before the coup, human security and Myanmar's polarising political divides were an issue for HE reform. According to the United Nations' framework for human security, the HE sector should provide an environment whereby people—students and staff—can undertake their study and work free from fear and free from want (UNTFHS 2016). Myanmar has not shown any ability to deliver such an environment since the first military coup in 1962. With a keen connection between higher education institutions (HEIs), political activism and anti-government insurgency, the HE sector became politicised and has been closely controlled by the central administration for nearly 60 years. This has resulted in a brittle HE system that cannot be responsive to changing needs or innovation.

With the State Administration Council (SAC)—the military junta—in control of Myanmar's administration, the likely scenario for the post-coup HE environment is not positive (Galloway 2021). Superimposed on fundamental structural problems inhibiting sectoral reform is a central administration with dubious legitimacy to enact legislative change or implement new policies. In addition, there are the intractable issues of Myanmar's military leaders' lack of trust in institutional engagement with foreign democracies and their inability to accept even the mildest criticism of their own policy positions from their own people. With these issues in mind, this chapter considers the impact of the coup on the HE sector, Australian aid responses and the likely implications of future foreign engagement.

Background

Myanmar's HE sector has always held a fraught position within the country's social and political systems, as universities are viewed as sites for political activism by the central administration (Hellman-Rajanayagam 2020, 251–3). HEIs flourished briefly in the post-independence era (1948–62); however, the university sector was quickly targeted by the first military regime after the 1962 coup. HEIs were centralised, curricula nationalised, foreign academics expelled and autonomy removed. The decline in education standards in Myanmar was dramatic—from being regional leaders in literacy, Myanmar's education system became one of the weakest (Han Tin 2008; Lall 2008; Hayden & Martin 2013; Lee et al. 2020). Combined with multiple government-directed closures from 1988 to the early 2000s, several generations were lost to academic study, and continuity of education reform and capacity building was impossible.

In the 1990s, facing intense international pressure over the turmoil of the 1988 uprisings, the failure to accept the results of the 1990 election and the house arrest of Aung San Suu Kyi, the military junta opened engagement with the international community. In 2001, the junta enacted a 30-year education plan (2001–02 FY to 2030–31 FY) to raise standards across all levels of the education system. A decade later, evidence suggested that the plan's effectiveness was minimal. From 2000 to 2011, public expenditure on HE as a percentage of total education spending fell from roughly 28 per cent to 19 per cent, among the lowest in the world (UNESCO 2014). Myanmar was turning out the lowest numbers of masters and PhD students in Asia, apart from Timor-Leste (UNESCO 2014, 30). The number of masters and PhD graduates per 100,000 inhabitants in 2011 was also the lowest in the region.

Since 2011, international donor assistance has supported capacity building in Myanmar's education sector, seen as critical for Myanmar's future social development. Numerous independent sector reports were produced, including an Asian Development Bank study (ADB 2013) and a report by the Institute of International Education (IIE 2013). In 2012, the

Ministry of Education (MoE) commenced a comprehensive education sector review with support from international donor partners. This led to the endorsement of a National Education Strategic Plan 1—NESP1 (2016–21)—by the National League for Democracy (NLD) government in 2016. The overarching goal was: 'Improved teaching and learning, vocational education and training, research and innovation leading to measurable improvements in student achievement in all schools and educational institutions' (MoE 2016, 10).

Such ambitions attest to a commitment to bring Myanmar's education system into the modern era. However, key problem areas, including centralised administration, lack of autonomy, mandatory teacher transfers, dilapidated infrastructure and dated curricula, have been very slow to change. When COVID-19 became a global pandemic, the United Nations Educational, Scientific and Cultural Organization (UNESCO) assisted the MoE to develop an education recovery plan. The plan stated: 'If not properly addressed at the national level, the COVID-19 pandemic is expected to have a long-lasting negative impact on the education sector in Myanmar' (MoE 2020, 7). Identified risks highlighted the unpreparedness of the HE system to manage disruptions. Education quality was expected to decline and rates of inclusion to drop as access to online teaching was not available equally either geographically or financially. The document noted that COVID-19 response plans provided the MoE with the opportunity to fast-track some reforms, such as how examinations were held, revising the national curriculum and training staff in new pedagogical approaches (MoE 2020, 68).

Universities closed in March 2020 and, while there was a limited reopening later that year, many students had already returned to their hometowns ahead of nationwide lockdowns aimed at reducing the spread of COVID-19. Strategies for remote learning developed quite rapidly, particularly in urban centres. It was expected that the National Education Strategic Plan 2— NESP2 (2021–30)—would be ready for ministerial discussion in 2021 following the swearing-in of the new NLD government. The ambitions for HE in the NESP2 were high. The component pillars focused on developing curricula and competencies for the twenty-first century, pre-service teacher training, quality assurance and administrative reforms, and research capabilities. International collaborations would be enhanced through mutual recognition pathways for students, research scholar exchanges and industry partnerships. Then the military coup occurred.

The higher education system and the coup

The military coup provoked a rapid response from the HE sector. Student and staff protests against the junta's actions were followed by campus closures as the junta acted to quell public displays of discontent. Most international engagement had already transitioned to remote contact and the coup's timing meant that few foreigners were present to directly observe what was happening within the HE system. As the junta's position has stabilised, few firsthand accounts have been forthcoming. Internet restrictions and fear of reprisals for speaking out have inhibited our full understanding of the state of the sector. However, considering popular news reporting and the junta's past and present actions, some clear indicators have emerged.

Following their initial closure post-coup, universities were officially reopened to final-year students in May 2021, but attendance was very low. In January 2022, masters and third-year students were able to return, but news reports indicated that student turnout was still low. According to a Dagon University student union member: 'The Spring Revolution is almost two years and everything is getting harder and harder for some parents and students. However, the most students continue to boycott the military's slave education' (*Mizzima* 2022a). Myanmar's universities reopened to undergraduates on 12 May 2022, but there has been very little official reporting of student or staff numbers. At Hinthada Technological University, Civil Disobedience Movement (CDM) supporters reported that only 67 students enrolled compared to a pre-coup number of over 1,000. Staff numbers have almost halved (*Mizzima* 2022b). The absence of official comment suggests that this trend is repeated across the country. For returning students, the nature and quality of the education they receive will be questionable, as Myanmar's HE sector is in a weakened state post-coup due to internal factors and the withdrawal of international support. There is no indication that the SAC has any appetite for progressing HE reform. Indeed, early signals indicate that the former junta's education plan (2001–31) will be a model for Myanmar's future education policy.

Many of Myanmar's youth and academic staff participated in the CDM. Estimates suggest that 13,000–19,500 staff were suspended in May 2021, out of a total academic workforce of around 28,000 (Naw Say Phaw Waa 2021). Staff had until November 2021 to confirm their opposition to the CDM and return to work. It is unclear how many have since returned. Some retired or resigned, others died from COVID-19. Many applied for overseas scholarships. Returning staff face possible reprisals from CDM supporters who may view their decision to return as akin to support for the SAC; they may also face reprisals from the junta, with lecturers expressing fears of being closely watched when they resume teaching. For some, the decision will be financial—the decision to return to their university post may simply be one of providing for their family.

The junta has been quick to arrest anti-coup student and academic protesters and fast-track their trials. In December 2021, Yangon University Student Union committee member Aung Phone Maw was sentenced to three years hard labour, the maximum sentence for violating Section 505a of the Penal Code, despite what was reported as a lack of evidence (Esther J 2021). That week, another Yangon University student, Ko Aung Bone Kyaw, died in military custody (*Irrawaddy* 2021). With this sad pattern continuing, many students will stay away from university, preferring to forego their education rather than study under a SAC regime. The impact of their decision is obvious—personal loss and a loss of capacity to support Myanmar's future development needs.

Even with universities now open, not all are in a position to function. With civil unrest and armed conflict persisting, a percentage of staff and students will be isolated from HE education opportunities—firm statistics are not available. The future impact of this will further enhance social imbalances between ethnic groups and minorities. Without a full cohort of teaching staff, there will be an inevitable decrease in teaching quality. This was an issue prior to the coup with student numbers increasing but staff numbers remaining relatively stagnant. The withdrawal of international donors, the suspension of international partnerships and memorandums of understanding, and the absence of key senior academics who were actively engaged in the reform processes will see HE flounder and revert to pre-2011 teaching models.

The importance of education is not lost on the younger generations. In the wake of the coup, groups have established alternative HE options to enable learning outside of official systems. Support from international donors and educational institutions for these initiatives has been forthcoming and is gaining momentum. Enrolments have been encouraging. On the surface, these alternative education options may sustain engagement with HE and the international academic community. At the time of writing in mid-2022, there were four main HE entities aiming to provide education for students who did not wish to return to universities under junta control, or simply wanted to have an alternative way of continuing their studies.

The Virtual Federal University (VFU) owes its existence to student union members (Tharaphi Than 2021). It receives support from the International Institute for Asian Studies 'Humanities Across Borders' program, while linkages and support from other international organisations continue to evolve. Course materials are curated by international experts and online learning modules are available. Fees for courses can be waived according to need.

In June 2021, the NUG announced initiatives to support HE (NUG 2021; Nilar Aung Myint 2021) through a new body called Federal University (not connected to the VFU). Online lectures and seminars were posted on YouTube and Facebook; however, activity has slowed and there is no coordinated tertiary program running at present.

The initial enthusiasm for these alternative forms of education appears to have waned. The reality of developing and delivering online materials in Burmese is logistically challenging and resource intensive. While it is possible to replicate existing university curricula for many disciplines and deliver the material remotely, as many universities worldwide have done during the COVID-19 pandemic, there are real risks for those who associate directly with NUG activities, since the NUG is now considered a terrorist organisation by the SAC.

Spring University Myanmar (SUM) was established in May 2021 by local and foreign-educated Myanmar academics and offers a range of courses, with more being developed based on demand (SUM 2021). Students usually pay a fee for each course, which typically lasts for six weeks. SUM aims to pay its staff, many of whom are university academics who were sacked for participating in the CDM or resigned. Others are private sector experts. International donor funding has been received to develop models for the delivery of course materials when internet access is poor or restricted. SUM is expanding and enrolments are increasing.

The Yangon-based Parami Institute had a strong reputation for delivering continuing education courses prior to the coup. With close connections to Bard College, New York, the institute established Parami University in 2020. However, Parami University closed after the coup and its activities transferred back to Parami Institute. The institute is now working with the Open Society University Network to deliver courses to Myanmar students who have fled to Thailand, or who are in ethnic-controlled areas (Becker 2022).

These initiatives face numerous hurdles. First is the broad issue of accreditation. In the short term, it is expected there will be motivation for study. Certificates of completion are being issued by most of these entities, however, in the longer term there will be some expectation that the courses will be recognised as bona fide programs of study. This will be a challenge, but not an impossible one. Options include accreditation by a recognised international body that will take some responsibility for the oversight of quality control. Such accreditation will require evidence of appropriate teaching and learning outcomes and this will take time. Short-course and micro-credential certificates from reputable tertiary organisations are also viable possibilities. If optimism is given to a return to democratic rule in the medium term, the NUG may be able to accredit courses based on Myanmar's existing education accreditation standards. This may give some confidence to participants who would have expectations of their studies being recognised by a future democratically elected non-military government.

Another barrier to alternative education is reliable internet access for students and teachers. Each entity is set up to deliver programs remotely. Now, with the SAC shutting access to non-approved websites and increasing data costs, alternative course delivery methods must be devised. While possible, this requires intensive reworking of course materials and strategies to deliver materials in-country. A final issue is personal safety. There is no indication yet of the SAC targeting students who are studying with these organisations. However, it is possible that participants will be seen as CDM supporters by the junta and therefore risk arrest.

Another alternative to resuming state-run studies is enrolment in accredited and independent HEIs (Kyaw Moe Tun 2021). A number of private universities have gained accreditation in recent years and, currently, there is no barrier to their activities during junta rule—unless they are deregistered by the MoE. However, these are fee-paying organisations and relatively small in scale and number (the National Education Policy Commission registered 12 private HEIs in 2019) and it will take time to upscale course delivery and capacity. There are also many ways that private HE operations can be curtailed through bureaucratic edict, including the deregistration of teaching staff.

The junta and higher education

The SAC has recently turned its attention to the university sector and the rhetoric is not promising. Plans for NESP2 have been shelved. The absence of international partners and loss of skilled academic staff makes it impossible to sustain any of the gains of the past decade. However, it can be argued that deep change in the sector has continually been undermined by the central administration. The former junta's education plan has never been fully dismantled and is ready to be reactivated.

Both the Union Solidarity and Development Party (USDP), led by former general Thein Sein, and the NLD party, led by Aung San Suu Kyi, promoted education reform as a priority. However, even with international actors involved in evaluating and strategising capacity building pathways, the end goals were repeatedly inhibited by political issues. During the USDP's term from 2011 to 2015, education reform was complicated by a lack of cooperation with the major minority party, the NLD. A National Education Bill was submitted to parliament in July 2014, but President Thein Sein did not endorse it, instead favouring continuation of the 30-year military junta's plan (Wa Lone 2014). Twenty-five amendments were proposed and 19 were eventually accepted. According to dissenters, it was a divisive Bill that continued a path of centralised education control, no autonomy for universities, ongoing restrictions to student union activities and the continued exclusion of ethnic language instruction (Wa Lone 2014; Thu Zar 2014; Lall 2021, 58–85). In retrospect, this can be read as a signal that there was no widespread acceptance of the reform agenda, particularly among the military-backed USDP. Given the pervasive presence of military and former military personnel throughout the central administration, it must be considered that there were deliberate efforts to slow down change implementation.

The SAC has not released an education plan. However, the former junta's 2001–31 plan is likely to play a significant role in any new policy. Prior to the 2010 election, a 'Special Four-Year Education Development Plan' defined 21 programs to be implemented by HE sub-sectors, focusing on five core areas: promotion of quality education, introduction of information and communication technology in education, advancement of research, development of a lifelong learning society and enhancement of international collaborations (MoE 2012). By 2012, the plan had expanded to 36 programs, with a sixth core area added, namely 'preservation of national identity and national values' (MoE 2012).

After 15 years, the plan had resulted in no meaningful improvements in the education sector. Recent official communications herald a full return to the centralised control of education. On 15 January 2022, Min Aung Hlaing's speech at Dawei University was the lead article for the *Global New Light of Myanmar*, the official government English-language news publication. It asserted the need for every university to keep 'abreast of the international community', but no indication was given as to how this would occur, especially given the current state of sanctions (*GNLM* 2022a, 3). Min Aung Hlaing is quoted as saying that 'the government is fulfilling the needs of uplifting the education sector' (*GNLM* 2022a, 3). This is simply untrue, as there is no capacity in Myanmar to achieve such goals. It is also incompatible with recent junta-imposed draconian changes that restrict internet access, and a recent law making virtual private networks illegal (*Irrawaddy* 2022). Reports from people who have visited the University of Yangon indicate that it was like a return to the past. Only a handful of graduate students were present and, when seen taking photos, a guard appeared and told them it was prohibited to take photos in the compound. Such restrictions have fallen back into place easily, and apparently without protest (*Jurist* 2022).

In April 2022, the SAC minister for education, Dr Nyunt Pe, spoke with faculty at Myitkyina Education Degree College and:

> urged them not only to teach literacy to aspiring students, but also to educate them to be disciplined, patriotic and polite, only then can teachers trained by the degree colleges educate students to be disciplined, polite and patriotic. (*GNLM* 2022b, 3)

Such pronouncements indicate a return to the past, with a centralised nationalist approach to education that is in direct opposition to the recommendations of the previous decade's reports and education plans (Callahan 2022).

Other recent press releases forcefully discredit NLD members, CDM supporters and teachers who have refused to return to work under the SAC. Of concern is the language used that clearly threatens anyone who opposes the SAC:

> The security forces will take extraordinary measures to ensure the safety of teachers who are making efforts in the academic sector for the next generations in order to promote the education qualifications. The people should keep security awareness and cooperate with the security members in community peace and peaceful learning of children. (*GNLM* 2022c, 7)

Matriculation exams were held on 1 April 2022. The *GNLM* featured images of students attending examination centres and reported high numbers attending. This seems to have been an attempt to paint a picture of normality ahead of the reopening of universities on 12 May. Sadly for the education sector, the rhetoric only supports the continuation of systematic teaching methods. The junta's plans to increase the use of the internet and wi-fi further undermines the SAC's credibility as, at the time of writing, electricity supply was even more irregular, access to internet sites was becoming more restricted and inflation was soaring, putting the costs of laptops and tablets out of reach for most.

What does the future hold for Myanmar's higher education system?

As the coup continues, and with no resolution in sight, governments and international agencies are contemplating what re-engagement with Myanmar may mean. With many foreign governments boycotting direct funding to the junta, assistance for education will have to be directed through non-government organisations (NGOs). This is problematic, as the SAC is monitoring all NGO activity and has clamped down on many civil society organisations (Chapter 15, this volume; HRW 2021; Liu 2021). How effective NGOs can be in this environment is unclear. Prior to the coup, many governments were heavily invested in supporting Myanmar's education sector reform, including the United Kingdom, the European Union, Canada, Australia and the United States. As the Australian Government considers whether, how and when to engage with the SAC, the dilemmas it faces, as well as its responses, are typical. Australia's 'Aid Investment Plan 2015–2020' for Myanmar placed education as 'the flagship of Australia's aid program' (DFAT 2015). A team led by Australian experts, known as the Myanmar Quality Improvement Program or MyEqip, and local staff worked directly with the MoE to manage the implementation of Myanmar's NESP1 and to support the drafting of NESP2. However, MyEqip was suspended after the coup and closed in June 2021.

In 2020, Australia shifted its development assistance to respond to the needs presented by COVID-19 (Australian Government 2020). Since the coup, Australia's assistance to Myanmar has pivoted again:

> to meet the immediate needs of the country's most vulnerable people, including the poor and ethnic minorities. We have redirected development assistance away from regime entities and do not provide funding directly to the regime. To ensure our support benefits the people who need it most, we work through trusted non-government partners including multilateral and non-government organisations. Our program will remain under close review and be flexible to respond to the evolving situation to best meet the needs of affected populations. (DFAT n.d.)

Any country that has a policy of non-engagement with the junta, or will not provide direct funding to the SAC, will effectively end capacity building opportunities in the HE sector. Since the coup, Australian Government–endorsed statements have aligned with international partners in recognising the Association of Southeast Asian Nations' role in engaging with the junta. Australia has also endorsed the remarks of the United Nations General Assembly condemning human rights abuses in Myanmar, including the arbitrary detention of Myanmar nationals and foreigners.

Non-engagement policies have negatively affected Myanmar students studying internationally. Many are on foreign government scholarships and some are Myanmar government employees. Their position is difficult. Providing support for these students is challenging for foreign governments who may face internal criticism for supporting Myanmar public officials. So far, most students have shown solidarity and have taken the opportunity of being abroad to speak out against the military. But even this poses risks. In July 2021, it was reported that Myanmar students receiving Australian Government scholarships were given a letter from the Myanmar ambassador to Australia saying that they must declare their non-involvement with the CDM and state their support for the new government. Students were also warned of possible prosecution under Myanmar law if they were involved in any activities that were deemed anti-government or incited others (Dziedzic 2021). As reported in the press, students felt intimidated, with many concerned for the wellbeing of their families in Myanmar should they not comply. Individual universities have lobbied their own administrations for fee waivers and scholarship extensions with varying degrees of success. Meanwhile, the formal government response has been lacklustre. It was not until May 2021 that the Australian Government announced that visa extensions would be granted to existing students. However, recently graduated students could not automatically extend their visas. They were advised of their options and the official information encouraged the use of a migration agent to facilitate applications—at their own expense (Australian Government 2021; Gibbs 2021).

Since the coup, student groups have been quick to organise. The Myanmar Students' Association Australia became a registered charity in February 2021, an act that requires governmental approval (MSAA 2021). Registering organisations that are fundraising for humanitarian purposes is one way that governments can help international students support HE without direct involvement. Yet, without doubt, the activities of association members are being monitored and students are at risk (Wells, Breen & Décobert 2022). The SAC have tools to punish those who oppose them, even while abroad. This includes intimidation of family members in Myanmar and laying charges against Myanmar students and academics abroad and sentencing them in absentia. Some student activists have had their passports cancelled; others have had their passport renewals refused. Such tactics have also been used against members of the NUG (Handley 2022; Strangio 2022).

One avenue for continuing support for Myanmar's future HE system is through state party–funded scholarships. The Australia Awards, an Australian Government–funded university scholarship program, supports emerging leaders from developing countries primarily in the Indo-Pacific region and is continuing to accept applications from Myanmar citizens (Australia Awards n.d.). Myanmar applicants who are not serving military personnel can apply. However, also ineligible are those convicted of, or under investigation for, criminal activities—this may exclude many Myanmar citizens who have been convicted by the junta of supporting the CDM. Thus, the program has been criticised for educating applicants sponsored by the Myanmar government; however, this attitude ignores the principles of academic freedom and the benefits of international networks. A policy strategy could see governments direct scholarship funds to an independent organisation to administer. USAID's Lincoln Scholarship Program for Myanmar graduates focuses on further study in areas of need. Unfortunately, the 2022 guidelines stated that eligible applicants had to be residing in Myanmar, excluding those who have had to leave (USAID 2022a). How readily the SAC will approve student travel abroad is one of many unknowns.

Individual foreign academics may choose to re-engage with Myanmar on the basis of academic collaboration without borders. Barriers to this will include institutional and government restrictions. If the situation continues long term, the SAC may turn to 'friendly' nations for HE support and collaboration, most likely China and Russia. Should the models of these countries be adopted in Myanmar, HE will irrevocably shift away from its foundation of academic autonomy. Current geopolitics suggest that such a move would further isolate Myanmar from the rest of the world, resulting in significant regional and international effects. A destabilising factor in this scenario is the vast number of alumni from foreign institutions who have returned to Myanmar in recent years to participate in the country's development. Their motivation or ability to contribute to the collective disruption of the central administration, similar to the undermining tactics of the military during the previous government's rule, is unknown.

Should the situation with the junta ease, international aid could become conditional on continuing the implementation of the NESP1, which had been endorsed by the elected government. In this scenario, those who criticise any perceived support for the junta could be mollified. While Australia and other nations have maintained their distance and redirected funds without clear plans for future HE sector support, by mid-2022 some governments had taken targeted action. For example, the US government, through USAID, and the European Commission (EC) announced projects to support Myanmar's HE and technical and vocational education and training (TVET) sectors. These actions, which indicate an unwillingness to defer further engagement in the education sector, recognise the significance of maintaining access to education. In May 2022, USAID called for information to inform 'designing a new activity to increase access to inclusive higher education opportunities for youth in Myanmar' (USAID 2022b). The project will likely complement existing basic education support. The EC grant announced in June 2022 seeks 'to improve access to quality technical and vocational training, non-formal education and employment opportunities for youth in targeted communities in ethnic and crisis-affected border areas, including Rakhine' (EC 2022). It calls for in-country and external partners, though there will be difficulties in managing any projects. For example, local NGO partners must be registered. As noted, NGO activity is closely monitored and projects will be scrutinised by the SAC.

Alternatives to state-based universities would help fast-track reforms, allowing students to quickly engage with international educational models. This requires strong donor assistance to fill gaps in infrastructure, and to coordinate internationally recognised accreditation of study programs. International support for HE would be well directed towards preparing models for this option that could be implemented quickly. Funding international study for Myanmar students who have fled the country, and supporting employment opportunities in sectors relevant to Myanmar's development, would be an effective investment by donors. Should the situation change and the junta be ousted, a cohort of Myanmar graduates with international work experience could return to Myanmar and contribute to rebuilding the country. If there is no real change, the world will still benefit from having more young people educated.

Conclusion

With now over two years of interrupted education due to COVID-19 and the military coup, Myanmar's ability to be self-sustaining for their own HE research and development needs has been further hampered. It is difficult to see how the HE system can recover, then grow, in the medium term. Should some form of recognition be given to the junta after any future elections, tentative re-engagement by existing partners may be possible. However, there is no expectation that HE reform will be a government priority. With a decimated economy, much-needed infrastructure plans for the sector will be further delayed. There will be no curriculum reform and Myanmar's HE standards will fall further behind those of regional and global counterparts. Any aspirations for improved teaching will be quashed, as the environment to foster quality and creative teaching will be non-existent. There is no capacity within Myanmar to develop the HE system without international expertise. Yet, international sanctions may affect academics who wish to return to Myanmar and continue pre-coup teaching and research projects; they may find themselves prohibited from doing so by their own governments. For Australian academics, any re-engagement with Myanmar will require clearance under the *Foreign Relations Act 2020*. The absence of senior staff will also further exacerbate recovery in the HE sector. Many had benefited from foreign training, and their knowledge will be lost to the system.

Alternative education systems offer the potential to keep students engaged with learning. The international community can, and is, developing strategies to facilitate remote study. But in an environment of 'if you are not with us you are against us' there is the ever-present risk that participants will be deemed anti-state and suffer adverse consequences. This should not, however, deter such endeavours. There are still students and academics who are in areas outside of the junta's control, and some who are out of the country, who can benefit from these learning opportunities. Much more could be done by the international university community. Even if a fraction of the world's universities provided a fee waiver and living allowance for a single Myanmar student, significant demand would be met. From a strategic perspective, if foreign governments did the same, they would be shoring up Myanmar's future—surely a worthwhile investment.

While much attention has been given to students, there can be no future for HE if the academics who have left the system are not supported. For the younger generation of academics who had begun to experience foreign teaching methods, either through study overseas or directly from international visiting faculty to Myanmar, being part of a junta-controlled education system is not an option. Many have declared their support for the CDM and are blacklisted by the MoE. Their opportunity to return to academia is remote, especially given the most recent pronouncements in the *GNLM*. On 1 June 2022, the following appeared:

> Provisions of the national education law are being reviewed to amend something if necessary, not to mix education with politics. Students can learn political science at the university but they are not allowed to mix education with politics. If they wish to engage in politics, they need to join the political field. (*GNLM* 2022d)

There is no place for democratic debate under the current regime. This follows on from the recent dissolution of student unions, which have been replaced by student associations (*Frontier Myanmar* 2022b).

The ongoing education of university academics could be undertaken through international organisations such as Advance HE, formerly known as the Higher Education Academy. This would help academic staff keep abreast of contemporary teaching methods and approaches, and participate in international networks.

With the recent return to school and reopening of universities, Myanmar's youth are faced with a real conflict. On 24 January 2022, *Frontier Myanmar* published an article on the dilemmas faced by parents and students wishing to undertake their university entrance exams. Those who choose to do so fear a lifetime label of having taken exams under the junta (*Frontier Myanmar* 2022a). Yet how long do they put their studies on hold?

The outlook for HE in Myanmar is bleak. New relationships will need to be built between foreign agencies and donors, and the MoE. Given the events of the last decade, it will likely take at least three to five years for relationships to be re-established. However, donors will be cautious before committing resources at the levels seen in the 2016–20 period.

Should the junta remain in power, there is every indication that attempts at foreign engagement in the HE sector by governments critical of the regime will be viewed with suspicion, and potentially couched as foreign interference. Current global geopolitical shifts could work for or against the junta, depending on who aligns with whom. The role of third-party donor agencies will become more important as governments distance themselves from providing development aid to the SAC. Earlier plans for university autonomy and curriculum reform can only advance if HEIs are authorised to implement them—an unlikely prospect. The more likely outcome is the complete stasis of the HE system, causing Myanmar to fall even further behind in this development indicator. Yet, given the very real need to increase workforce skills, particularly in science and technology, one scenario could see the junta align itself with a foreign ally, in a way that may weaken Myanmar's independence and further erode human security. It is not yet known which foreign governments may decide to endorse the junta's administration. As this becomes clearer the threats to national and regional security will be more apparent. Regardless of the options that arise or the outcomes, the unpleasant certainty is that the aspirations of yet another generation of Myanmar students and academics will be thwarted by political upheaval.

References

ADB (Asian Development Bank). 2013. *Myanmar Comprehensive Education Sector Review Phase 1: Rapid Assessment: Technical Annex on the Higher Education Subsector.* Manila: ADB. www.adb.org/projects/documents/cesr-p1-rapid-assessment-annex-higher-education-subsector-tacr

Australia Awards. n.d. 'Myanmar'. Accessed 27 February 2023. www.australia awardsmyanmar.org/

Australian Government. 2021. 'Support for Myanmar Citizens'. Press release, 5 May, minister.homeaffairs.gov.au/AlexHawke/Pages/visa-arrangements-myanmar-nationals.aspx

Becker, Jonathan. 2022. 'It Takes a Higher Ed Network'. *American Association of Colleges and Universities*, 13 April. www.aacu.org/article/it-takes-a-higher-ed-network

Callahan, Mary. 2022. 'By the Book: Junta's Education Policy Follows 60 Years of Military Strategy'. *Frontier Myanmar*, 9 February. www.frontiermyanmar.net/en/by-the-book-juntas-education-policy-follows-60-years-of-military-strategy/

DFAT (Department of Foreign Affairs and Trade). 2015. 'Aid Investment Plan Myanmar 2015–2020'. www.dfat.gov.au/about-us/publications/Pages/aid-investment-plan-aip-myanmar-2015-20

DFAT (Department of Foreign Affairs and Trade). n.d. 'Australia's Development Assistance to Myanmar'. Accessed 27 February 2023. www.dfat.gov.au/geo/myanmar/development-assistance/development-assistance-in-myanmar

Dziedzic, Stephen. 2021. 'Myanmar Students in Australia Accuse Embassy of Intimidation'. *ABC News*, 28 June. www.abc.net.au/news/2021-06-28/myanmar-students-in-australia-accuse-embassy-of-intimidation/100249258

EC (European Commission). 2022. 'Strengthening Technical and Vocational Training and Non-formal Education in Ethnic and Conflict Affected Areas of Myanmar'. European Commission. ec.europa.eu/info/funding-tenders/opportunities/portal/screen/opportunities/topic-details/europeaid/174038/dd/act/mm (page discontinued).

Esther J. 2021. 'Junta Hands Yangon University Student Union Leader Three-Year Prison Sentence'. *Myanmar Now*, 24 December. myanmar-now.org/en/news/junta-hands-yangon-university-student-union-leader-three-year-prison-sentence

Frontier Myanmar. 2022a. 'Education vs. Revolution: School Reopenings Bring Hard Choices'. 17 January. www.frontiermyanmar.net/en/education-vs-revolution-school-reopenings-bring-hard-choices/

Frontier Myanmar. 2022b. 'Inside the Junta's War on Student Unions'. 18 May. www.frontiermyanmar.net/en/inside-the-juntas-war-on-student-unions/

Galloway, Charlotte. 2021. 'How Myanmar's Coup Will Affect Higher Education'. *Asia and the Pacific Policy Society Policy Forum*, 22 February. www.policyforum.net/how-myanmars-coup-will-impact-higher-education/

Gibbs, Nick. 2021. 'Myanmar Student Plea to Stay in Australia'. *Canberra Times*, 12 September. www.canberratimes.com.au/story/7426336/myanmar-student-plea-to-stay-in-australia/

GNLM (*Global New Light of Myanmar*). 2022a. 'Efforts Must Be Made for Establishment of Each University in Regions and States to Confer PhD on Students, Keeping Abreast of the International Community, Senior General Stresses'. 15 January, 1–3. www.mifer.gov.mm/storage/1642486720-newlight myanmar_15_01_2022.pdf

GNLM (*Global New Light of Myanmar*). 2022b. 'Only Then Can Teachers Trained by Degree Colleges Educate the Students to Be Disciplined, Polite and Patriotic'. 4 April. cdn.myanmarseo.com/file/client-cdn/2022/04/4_April_22_gnlm.pdf

GNLM (*Global New Light of Myanmar*). 2022c. 'Statement to Appreciate Teachers' Efforts'. 13 April, 7. cdn.myanmarseo.com/file/client-cdn/2022/04/13_April_22_gnlm.pdf

GNLM (*Global New Light of Myanmar*). 2022d. 'Efforts Were Made to Minimize the Casualties as Much as Possible in Performing the Counterattacks to Terror Acts: Senior General'. 1 June, 4–5. cdn.myanmarseo.com/file/client-cdn/2022/06/1_June_22_gnlm.pdf

Han Tin. 2008. 'Myanmar Education: Challenges, Prospects and Options'. In *Dictatorship, Disorder and Decline in Myanmar*, edited by Monique Skidmore and Trevor Wilson, 113–26. Canberra: ANU EPress. doi.org/10.22459/DDDM.12.2008.07

Handley, Erin. 2022. 'Myanmar Nationals in Australia Face Passport Limbo as Calls for Sanctions against the Military Junta Grow'. *ABC News*, 25 August. www.abc.net.au/news/2022-08-25/myanmar-passport-limbo-military-coup-junta-australia-sanctions/101339390

Hayden, Martin and Richard Martin. 2013. 'Recovery of the Education System in Myanmar'. *Journal of International and Comparative Education* 2 (2): 47–57. doi.org/10.14425/00.50.28

Hellman-Rajanayagam, Dagmar. 2020. 'From Rangoon College to University of Yangon – 1876 to 1920'. In *Southeast Asian Transformations*, edited by Sandra Kurfürst and Stefanie Wehner, 239–57. Bielefeld: Transcript Verlag.

HRW (Human Rights Watch). 2021. 'Myanmar: Junta Stops Lifesaving Aid. Donors Should Channel Assistance Via Local and Cross-Border Efforts'. 13 December. www.hrw.org/news/2021/12/13/myanmar-junta-blocks-lifesaving-aid

IIE (Institute of International Education). 2013. *Investing in the Future: Rebuilding Higher Education in Myanmar*. Report on the IIE Myanmar Initiative. New York: IIE. themimu.info/sites/themimu.info/files/documents/Report_RebuildingHigherEducationInMyanmar_IIE_Apr13.pdf

Irrawaddy. 2021. 'Student Activist Dies in Myanmar Junta Custody'. 29 December. www.irrawaddy.com/news/burma/student-activist-dies-in-myanmar-junta-custody.html

Irrawaddy. 2022. 'Myanmar Junta's New Cyber Law to Jail Anyone Using VPN'. 24 January. www.irrawaddy.com/news/burma/myanmar-juntas-new-cyber-law-to-jail-anyone-using-vpn.html

Jurist. 2022. 'Myanmar Dispatches: "It's Not the Same Anymore" – No Homecoming for Law Students at Yangon University'. 14 January. www.jurist.org/news/2022/01/myanmar-dispatch-its-not-the-same-anymore-no-homecoming-for-law-students-at-yangon-university/

Kyaw Moe Tun. 2021. 'We Need Authoritarian-Proof Higher Education Models'. *Times Higher Education Supplement,* 6 September. www.timeshighereducation.com/blog/we-need-authoritarian-proof-higher-education-models

Lall, Marie. 2008. 'Evolving Education in Myanmar: The Interplay of State, Business and the Community'. In *Dictatorship, Disorder and Decline in Myanmar,* edited by Monique Skidmore and Trevor Wilson, 128–49. Canberra: ANU EPress. doi.org/10.22459/DDDM.12.2008.08

Lall, Marie. 2021. *Myanmar's Education Reforms: A Pathway to Social Justice?* London: UCL Press. doi.org/10.14324/111.9781787353695

Lee, Zu Xian, Jana R. Glutting, Naing Lin Htet, Ngu Wah Win, Nyein Chan Aung, Thaint Zar Chi Oo and Zaw Oo. 2020. *Doing Research in Myanmar.* New Delhi: Global Development Network. www.gdn.int/sites/default/files/Myanmar%20Country%20Report.pdf

Liu, John. 2021. 'CSOs after the Coup: Operations Squeezed, Funding Crunched'. *Frontier Myanmar,* 28 September. www.frontiermyanmar.net/en/csos-after-the-coup-operations-squeezed-funding-crunched/

Mizzima. 2022a. 'Low College and University Enrollment under Myanmar Military Council'. 15 May. mizzima.com/article/low-college-and-university-enrollment-under-myanmar-military-council

Mizzima. 2022b. 'Only 67 Students Enrol at Hinthada Technical University for 2022–23 Academic Year'. 18 May mizzima.com/article/only-67-students-enrol-hinthada-technological-university-2022-23-academic-year

MoE (Ministry of Education). 2012. 'Education System in Myanmar: Self-Evaluation and Future Plans'. 203.81.81.180/dhel/education-system-in-myanmar/education-development-plans/ (page discontinued).

MoE (Ministry of Education). 2016. *National Education Strategic Plan 2016–21*. Naypyidaw: MoE. planipolis.iiep.unesco.org/sites/default/files/ressources/myanmar_nesp-english_summary.pdf

MoE (Ministry of Education). 2020. *Myanmar COVID-19 National Response and Recovery Plan for the Education Sector*. Naypyidaw: MoE. planipolis.iiep.unesco.org/en/2020/myanmar-covid-19-national-response-and-recovery-plan-education-sector-may-2020-%E2%80%93-october-2021.

MSAA (Myanmar Students' Association Australia). 2021. 'Myanmar Students' Association Australia'. Facebook. Accessed 27 February 2023. www.facebook.com/msaa.org

Naw Say Phaw Waa. 2021. 'Junta Suspends Thousands of Academics, University Staff'. University World News, 14 May. www.universityworldnews.com/post.php?story=20210514110259910

Nilar Aung Myint. 2021. 'Exiled Government Establishes Alternative HE Programs'. *University World News*, 24 July. www.universityworldnews.com/post.php?story=20210721150221771

NUG (National Unity Government). 2021. 'Ministry of Education'. Accessed 29 February 2023. moe.nugmyanmar.org

Strangio, Sebastian. 2022. 'Myanmar Junta Revokes Citizenship of Opposition Figures, NUG Ministers'. *Diplomat*, 7 March. thediplomat.com/2022/03/myanmar-junta-revokes-citizenship-of-opposition-figures-nug-ministers/

SUM (Spring University Myanmar). 2021. 'Spring University Myanmar'. Accessed 29 February 2023. springuniversitymm.com/

Tharaphi Than. 2021. 'Ruptured Space Allows Myanmar Youths Space to Reimagine a New Education System'. Humanities Across Borders, *Newsletter* 89, Summer. www.iias.asia/sites/default/files/nwl_article/2021-08/IIAS_NL89_5051.pdf

Thu Zar. 2014. 'I Consider Nothing to Have Changed'. *Irrawaddy*, 20 November. www.irrawaddy.com/in-person/interview/consider-nothing-changed.html

UNESCO (United Nations Educational, Scientific and Cultural Organization). 2014. *Higher Education in Asia: Expanding Out, Expanding up. The Rise of Graduate Education and University Research*. Quebec: UNESCO Institute for Statistics. uis.unesco.org/sites/default/files/documents/higher-education-in-asia-expanding-out-expanding-up-2014-en.pdf

UNTFHS (United Nations Trust Fund for Human Security). 2016. *Human Security Handbook. An Integrated Approach for the Realization of the Sustainable Development Goals and the Priority Areas of the International Community and the United Nations System.* New York: UNTFHS. www.un.org/humansecurity/wp-content/uploads/2017/10/h2.pdf

USAID (United States Aid). 2022a. 'USAID Lincoln Scholarship Program'. Accessed 28 February 2023. www.iie.org/Programs/USAID-Lincoln-Scholarship-Program/FAQs

USAID (United States Aid). 2022b. 'RFI-USAID/Burma HEA Request for Information on USAID/Burma's Higher Education Activity (HEA)'. 9 May. highergov.com/grantopportunity/request-for-information-on-usaid-burma-rsquo-s-higher-education-activity-hea-340185/

Wa Lone. 2014. 'President Seeks to Delay State Education Reforms for 8 Years'. *Myanmar Times*, 1 September.

Wells, Tamas, Michael G. Breen and Anne Décobert. 2022. 'Students Continue to Campaign for Change in Myanmar'. *Pursuit*, 31 January. pursuit.unimelb.edu.au/articles/students-continue-to-campaign-for-change-in-myanmar

15

The Aftermath: Policy Responses to Myanmar's Political and Humanitarian Crises

Monique Skidmore

Professor, Alfred Deakin Institute, Deakin University, Australia

Anthony Ware

Associate Professor, School of Humanities and Social Sciences, Deakin University, Australia

In the immediate wake of the 2021 coup, the world witnessed the depressingly familiar modus operandi of the Myanmar military. Promises made to restore a constitutional democracy through a 'reformed' Union Electoral Commission were made alongside those of a return to the status quo once corruption was rooted out by the saviour of the Union, the military. The shock was palpable to the generation of children and young adults who could only dimly remember a time of fear and repression before the 'transitional' period to democracy that began with national elections in 2011 and the release of Aung San Suu Kyi from house arrest. There was shock, too, among development organisations and governments that had believed that Myanmar was on an upward and linear trajectory to a democratic future, despite occasional setbacks and a gruellingly slow pace of reform. Many governments and organisations assumed that the Myanmar military, entrenched in the country as its dominant institution and intricately tied up in its economy, would somehow be won over by sheer passion and a sense of inevitability and agree to amend the constitution, removing its central role in the political and economic life of the country, as the military had done in Indonesia.

There was never any evidence for these assumptions. The last 60 years of Myanmar's history clearly show a trajectory of ongoing authoritarian rule in which the strategic use of political violence and widespread repression of basic rights have been regularly adopted by the generals, their cronies and families to allow them to limp along in power, even if they are despised.

Like in previous widespread pro-democracy protests (notably in 1988), a new generation of young people have been radicalised and taken up arms against the junta. Millions of civilians have been displaced, and hundreds of thousands have fled the country. And, as in previous purges, in 2022 the regime sought to rollout a military campaign to eliminate resistance to its rule and to break the nexus between the existing armed organisations and the newly formed People's Defence Forces (PDFs).

But this is not 1988 and much has changed in the world since the previous uprisings. Indeed, much has changed even since the attempted Saffron Revolution in 2008. As the contributors to this volume demonstrate, the roles of foreign companies, neighbouring countries, foreign governments, regional and political groups, aid organisations and disruptive technologies in the resistance to the reimposition of military rule, renewed civil war and ensuing emergency humanitarian crisis are different to any of the previous crises. The most important changes are local and regional, with the Association of Southeast Asian Nations (ASEAN) changing its narrative of noninterference in Myanmar and with the Myanmar people being more able to organise themselves to resist the imposition of military rule after having had a decade of relative freedom of association.

As the chapters of the volume illustrate, the political landscape has forever changed in Myanmar. The National Unity Government (NUG) is a significant evolution beyond the old National League for Democracy, with broader inclusivity, new policies and a new generation of leaders. Whatever happens now, significant change has been wrought. Likewise, formation of the Civil Disobedience Movement, then the PDFs, has added to the minority organisations and their armed wings, changing the status quo and power of the people to fight authoritarianism and oppression. Again, whatever happens next, these changes will impact the political landscape in Myanmar for generations.

Similarly, we see fundamental changes forced upon the delivery of development and humanitarian aid to Myanmar. For decades, aid donors and agencies have focused on development and tried to strengthen the capacity of state institutions; that is no longer desirable or possible. They have long preferred to fund multilateral organisations and international agencies, because of their capacity for large-scale projects and compliance with international accountability criterion, usually only bringing in local organisations as implementing partners or as part of consortia; most of those large programs have now been curtailed, and local groups are doing the most effective work. Aid donors and agencies have long considered development and humanitarian aid separately, formulating different policies and insisting on the neutrality of humanitarian aid. But now, local non-government organisations are delivering humanitarian aid and all local civil society activity is inherently political—even while meeting humanitarian need.

The opening up of Myanmar's communications sector over the past decade, in particular the widespread adoption of mobile phones and rapid internet uptake, has made it much easier to communicate, plan and mobilise civil society. This facilitated not only the Civil Disobedience Movement and PDFs, but also the mobilisation of humanitarian aid to the most vulnerable, such as internally displaced persons, in an agile response by dispersed local civil society groups. Myanmar civil society has changed. International principles no longer seem to apply. Instead, the changes demand that the global aid architecture significantly revamp its policy and practice.

Insights about the likely direction of the conflict and its key actors

Farrelly (Chapter 2) notes that, in Naypyidaw, the expectation remains that the international community will become increasingly exhausted with Myanmar's tragic situation and, together with the related inability of ASEAN to build a more proactive policy position, the post-coup government will have sufficient time to consolidate its rule. Kironska and Jiang (Chapter 6) add that China is already moving from a position of ambiguous neutrality to support for, and engagement with, the military—a move the generals are no doubt banking on.

If, as it is looking likely, the coup is further consolidated, the country's democratic activists are likely to face years, even decades, of dismay and punishment. Atrocities will continue and the space for resistance will become tighter and tighter. Simpson and McIntyre (Chapter 5) argue that the situation in Myanmar will get worse before it gets better, and that international justice mechanisms will have little if any ability to hold the generals to account. There are no quick fixes, no international processes or mechanisms to force change. The heavy burdens of forced displacement, poverty, food shortages and unemployment, along with the collapse of the healthcare and education systems, as well as the pressure of COVID-19, will continue unabated for the foreseeable future; not to mention climate change, which is already disrupting the monsoon, causing droughts, reducing agricultural returns, and threatening severe catastrophe at any moment.

Echoing Simpson and McIntyre's concerns, McCarthy and Saw Moo (Chapter 11) conclude that, in the medium term, the deepening of societal reliance on non-state social actors both to survive and resist dictatorship should compel strategic thinking about how a future civilian government can better address the precarity faced by ordinary people, and put to rest the legacies of inequality bequeathed by past and current periods of dictatorship. Farrelly proposes a frightening possible scenario in which centrifugal forces ultimately unravel claims to a single union in Myanmar. Some areas and leaders would be better placed to take advantage of the comprehensive failure of the central authorities to maintain the current order; this vision of state collapse and fragmentation paints a dire warning of one possible outcome of the current chaos.

Ware and Laoutides (Chapter 9) as well as Ye Min Zaw and Tay Zar Myo Win (Chapter 10) argue that we can already see this occurring in Arakan State. They conclude that the Arakanese community is steadily moving towards the claim of territorial autonomy by invoking historical narratives and the use of armed force. The state- and nation-building work of the Arakan Army since the coup has certainly consolidated their power and strengthened their claim of autonomy, and they have declared that they will take their claim of sovereignty outside the Union if there is no room for them within the Union. Similar centrifugal forces will surely pull on other ethnic minority organisations unless the NUG are seen to succeed in the near to medium term. In Bamar-majority areas of central Myanmar, the possibility of ongoing discontent and conflict is very real, especially given the mixed population patterns across most areas of Myanmar. Any process of partition on the basis of ethnicity would create messy and probably violent upheavals.

Amid the scramble for control, communications have become critical, with new possibilities for informing communities of impending military actions opening up with the uptake of mobile phones, VPNs and encrypted social media channels. Ye Min Zaw and Tay Zar Myo Win (Chapter 10) remind readers of the violence that has also been fuelled through the social media propaganda promulgated by the Myanmar military and ultra-nationalist groups against the Rohingya. They warn the international community of the need for ongoing vigilance against technology companies enabling violent hate speech and fabricated stories circulating in Myanmar. But, as Jadyn, Skidmore and Medail (Chapter 3) note, at the same time, new communication technology has enabled new ways of mobilising and supporting the resistance, including crowdfunding and digital financing. This inflow of money and arms is having results on the ground, and the PDFs are far better equipped in 2022 than they were in 2021. Nonetheless, Jadyn, Skidmore and Medail caution against drawing overly optimistic conclusions from the internet-savvy youth regarding Myanmar's resistance to the junta. They suggest that, although cyberspace currently offers a way to even the stakes on the ground, techno-totalitarianism in Myanmar may eventually look like it does in China. New cyber-surveillance technologies purchased by the junta will result in more measures designed to deny Burmese citizens access to the cyber-world as the junta learns to navigate and create their own cyber-sphere.

The contributors to this volume have provided insights that have policy implications for foreign governments, both neighbours and those further afield. Detailed analysis, drawing out implications and recommendations, are provided in each chapter. The following section summarises just a few of the key implications and policy recommendations from the analysis.

Implications for governments

Farrelly (Chapter 2) reminds governments of the importance of ASEAN, once again, as a primary international link between Myanmar and its regional neighbours. Moe Thuzar (Chapter 7) believes ASEAN's ability to find solutions to the current dilemma in Myanmar is limited by its own structural flaws and diminished capacity to persuade the Myanmar military; however, ASEAN is changing its narrative of noninterference. The Myanmar crisis presents yet another reminder that ASEAN and its member states need to determine the value and import of ASEAN membership, as well as the importance of implementing the mentality of ASEAN centrality. Arguing that ASEAN should lead a coalition of UN and other dialogue parties, Moe Thuzar points to the consultative meeting held on 6 May 2022 as a first step. She notes that hopes for individual ASEAN members' engagement with the NUG currently centre on supporting the NUG's humanitarian assistance efforts via local community networks and channels, including in ethnic-controlled areas.

The role and ability of China to protect the Myanmar regime from the effects of international pressure, sanctions and embargoes is not straightforward, as considerable anti-China sentiment has been evident in the response to the coup by the Myanmar population. The potential of Myanmar to become a collapsed state, the potential involvement of China, Russia and North Korea in Myanmar's development, and the enormous resources required to rebuild Myanmar as a nascent democratic state if the junta steps back, are all scenarios that will require Myanmar to be a higher political and aid priority than it has been since the coup.

Coppel (Chapter 4) reminds Western nations of the limited effectiveness of sanctions during previous eras of military dictatorship in Myanmar, and points to their inability to distinguish between hurting the regime's upper echelons and the most vulnerable of the population. He argues that foreign activist organisations need to think beyond the standard action playbook focused on large Western corporations and devise Myanmar-focused strategies—that is, strategies that directly assist agents and conditions for change in Myanmar. It is the businesses, organisations and people who remain, not those that have left, that will ultimately influence change in Myanmar.

Galloway (Chapter 14) focuses on the education system as one sector among many that has been upended by the coup, and one that will require not just significant rebuilding but also fundamental reform. International sanctions may have adverse impacts here; for example, they might prevent academics from returning to Myanmar to continue pre-coup teaching or from resuming research projects that could potentially be viewed by the regime as foreign interference. She also notes the new security environment in Australia, pointing to complications for educational institutions and researchers re-engaging with Myanmar who require clearance under the *Foreign Relations Act 2020*.

Simpson and McIntyre (Chapter 5) argue that the 'Responsibility to Protect' policy offers the best guide to the levers available for the international community to influence and pressure the military regime. They also argue that Australia should join other nations as in intervenor in the International Court of Justice genocide case, even though the jurisdiction of international courts remains limited. However, they conclude that foreign governments recognising the NUG may, in the long term, be the most effective option for holding the generals to account, because the NUG has committed to joining the Rome Statute, which would give the International Criminal Court jurisdiction in Myanmar.

Kironska and Jiang (Chapter 6) argue that China's new assertiveness in its foreign policy, as well as its geostrategic two-ocean objectives, comprise new areas of analysis that complicate the traditional view of China's peaceful rise to power. They conclude that, when dealing with China, Western countries need to understand that there has been a change in behaviour and that China is likely to be more assertive and, possibly, more extreme. Further, when dealing with Myanmar, they argue that countries such as Australia need to be aware that China is likely to become a stronger ally to the Tatmadaw as time goes by. China is unlikely to contribute to, and will possibly oppose, any moves by international actors to engage with the Myanmar shadow government.

Insights for donors

The companies, institutions and foreign investors that committed resources during Myanmar's brief liberalisation period are unlikely to return with substantial investments in the short or medium term, according to Farrelly (Chapter 2). However, material support can be given to the NUG. Simpson and McIntyre (Chapter 5) argue that the US could release the USD1 billion of assets frozen by the Federal Reserve to the NUG as a major show of concrete support for the country and its elected representatives.

More contentiously, Simpson and McIntyre argue that, if the international community and donors want to do things differently to try to end the cycle of violence and repression, it would be justifiable to support the anti-junta PDFs that have emerged, often in conjunction with existing ethnic minority militias, to militarily challenge the Tatmadaw. While many governments are hesitant to arm or support non-state militias, arguing that non-violent methods should be employed, Myanmar's military has shown throughout history that it has no qualms about ruthlessly and brutally crushing non-violent opposition movements. The alignment of the PDFs with a multi-party, unified shadow government, recently elected in a landslide, and the international war crimes cases being pursued against the junta's military leaders, perhaps makes this case very different to other cases. While the conflicts and crises in Myanmar are only likely to be resolved by groups within the country, Simpson and McIntyre conclude that international aid and diplomatic support may well provide the opposition movement with the resources, resolve and recognition it needs to force a negotiated settlement.

To this end, and almost as contentiously, Décobert (Chapter 12) calls for the funding and provision of emergency aid to be directed primarily to local-level systems and organisations, and for any preconditions of 'normative neutrality' to cease. This would be a major change to the 'business as usual' approach to aid to Myanmar—and one that many would argue is long overdue. It is simply not possible in the current environment for international agencies to work in-country. Décobert argues that, in practical terms, and given the escalating humanitarian needs in Myanmar, international donors and aid agencies must increase their support to civil society organisations and local non-government organisations, which have the expertise, local legitimacy and systems to offer alternatives to top-down aid and internationally driven aid practices. She concludes that these types of approaches are necessary, not only to channel assistance to civilian populations in need of aid but also to help lay the foundations for longer-term democratisation, development and peace in Myanmar. Décobert is clear that, in a context in which normative neutrality can do very real harm, international humanitarian engagement should be guided by an overarching solidarity-focused approach, and international donors and aid agencies must ensure that their programs do not end up legitimising, emboldening or enabling the military regime, but, rather, support the agency and autonomy of the Myanmar people.

Aung Naing and Wells (Chapter 13) draw the same broad conclusions and policy directions as Décobert, urging donors to end any allegiance to the concept that providing humanitarian aid can be a neutral or apolitical act, and that a single unitary and reproducible model of society can be implemented from above. They argue strongly that if civil society organisations and local non-government organisations are adapting their modus operandi to deliver humanitarian aid that embeds political resistance, then international donors should follow suit. Issues such as accountability frameworks being rigidly structured around financial audits rather than operational information should also be addressed. Aung Naing and Wells believe that it behoves the international donor community to consider its own capacity to adapt to the needs of local organisations, and to support the creation of multiple, alternative spaces of citizenry from which a new state, or states, can emerge.

The education sector provides a good illustration of the needs and opportunities for donors, many equally applicable to other sectors. Galloway (Chapter 14) notes that new relationships will need to be built between foreign agencies and donors, and that the relationship with the Myanmar Ministry of Education will need to be redefined. Given the events of the last decade, it will likely take three to five years for these relationships to be re-established. However, donors will be cautious before committing resources at the levels seen in the 2016–20 period. On a more positive note, Galloway argues that much more could be done by the global university community for international students from Myanmar. Even if a fraction of the world's universities provided fee waivers and living allowances for some Myanmar students, significant demands would be met. From a strategic perspective, if foreign governments did the same, they would be shoring up Myanmar's future.

Insights for the aid sector

Similar to the insights discussed above for donors, the most effective way for multilateral and international non-government organisations to provide aid is via closer partnerships with local organisations. Such aid should be provided in innovative ways that enhance the autonomy and decision-making agency of local organisations. As Décobert (Chapter 12) and Aung Naing and Wells (Chapter 13) point out, local responses to the humanitarian crisis demonstrate both the strength and effectiveness of locally driven aid in Myanmar and the capacity of the sector to deliver. Décobert argues for a version of localisation that is not only about local actors working in their own communities but also about those actors having the genuine autonomy and agency to shape their own programs. Aung Naing and Wells highlight the strength of responses by traditional *parahita* welfare groups as well as civil society organisations and local non-government organisations. There is substantial evidence of not only continued but also expanded operations by a myriad of loosely formed voluntary organisations, whereas the operations of larger, international NGOs and local NGOs have largely stalled. Voluntary associations of all descriptions are providing food aid, medical care, education and refugee assistance to the hundreds of thousands of people displaced and harmed since the coup. Both Décobert and Aung Naing and Wells argue for more empowering partnerships with these organisations (i.e. partnerships that hand over greater decision-making power and operational control) as well as recognising and explicitly supporting them in their rejection of expectations that aid should be apolitical. For those on the ground, aid is a deeply political issue; their support for others is an act of resistance (not just compassion), not so much in direct opposition to the state but as a substitute for, and rebuke of, an absent or illegitimate state. To deliver that aid with passion and motivation, they demand that the inequalities and injustices perpetrated by top-down international aid systems and partnerships be overturned. Further, they demand the autonomy and agency to shape their own programs, responses and futures. For that, multilateral and international non-government organisations must reverse the current power inequalities in aid partnerships.

There is an opportunity here to significantly strengthen the role and capacity of civil society and its international linkages and partnerships. But there is also a danger. McCarthy and Saw Moo (Chapter 11) demonstrate how the local, charitable, civil society sector has been simultaneously disciplined and strategically coopted by State Administration Council officials to help manage both the pandemic and the humanitarian crisis created by the coup. McCarthy and Saw Moo see the non-state, charitable sector as being in a difficult position with regard to state demands for their neutrality. Most continue in defiance of such demands, using aid as an act of resistance, but international bodies need to be aware of these pressures on local organisations and the significant risks they face in their work. Contesting such space requires extraordinary levels of adaptive capacity.

Ye Min Zaw and Tay Zar Myo Win (Chapter 10) likewise call for more aid to be channelled directly to civil society groups in Rakhine State for work among both the Rakhine and Rohingya communities. Further, they highlight the need to empower those groups. This is not just a new way of providing aid locally, but is a means of keeping both communities connected to the ongoing situation throughout the country. Like others in this volume, Ye Min Zaw and Tay Zar Myo Win argue for the ability of aid provision to empower civil society groups. Like Galloway (Chapter 14), they make a case for scholarships for youth from Arakanese and Rakhine communities. And, like Moe Thuzar (Chapter 7), they urge ongoing community support for integrated social cohesion and community-level, livelihood-based economic activities and peace-building programs across Rakhine State.

The future

As Farrelly (Chapter 2) notes in this volume, no matter which potential scenario eventuates, Myanmar will spend many years lagging behind its neighbours. It is clear now that the military is settling in and will not contemplate any gestures towards 'dialogue' or replacing the constitution until it is satisfied that its political control is unassailable. These new threats come from the battlefield, where, once again, the military junta is fighting itself into a standstill; other threats are economic, with the military needing to ensure it has enough money through the sale of oil and gas to fund its rule. Unless the NUG and PDFs can pull off an unlikely and overwhelming victory over the military forces, or other leadership dramatically emerges and leads the Myanmar military in a new direction, or some other unforeseen event occurs, the military are likely to remain intransient and bloody-minded.

Politically, the military are determined to neutralise the threat of Aung San Suu Kyi and the National League for Democracy by ensuring the organisation no longer exists and its leader languishes in prison. It is likewise trying to limit the power of the NUG and undoubtedly has the NUG high on its list. On the international stage, the military must fend off ASEAN's occasional demands for dialogue, and, in this respect, must neutralise the NUG's political lobbying to be recognised as the legitimate government of Myanmar. And it must increase its control of cyberspace to limit both the funding of opposition through digital financing and the coordination of resistance.

The diehard pragmatists will, of course, argue that the Myanmar people should resign themselves to ongoing servitude to their brutal military in order to decrease the number of deaths due to conflict. Conversely, at the other end of the political spectrum, some will as passionately argue for the arming of the PDFs by the international community. Both ends of the spectrum see peace as an end that justifies the means.

We believe that the reimposition of military rule through the brutal coup of February 2021 will only come to an end when enough of the population rises up against their rulers. Most likely, this will require the provocation of internal changes within the military itself. Aung San Suu Kyi once paraphrased Joseph de Maistre by saying that the people get the government they deserve, but no-one deserves this longstanding and brutish regime. In the years that come, the international community must not forget the brave people of Myanmar. Coppel (Chapter 4) argues that regime collapse is not a strategic goal if it results in, once again, the immiseration of the population. It is clear, however, that governments, multilateral agencies, development and humanitarian organisations, and democracy and human rights activists must join with the resistance movement in new ways to ensure that this period of military rule is shorter than all those that have preceded it. As Décobert (Chapter 12) notes, this is a time of opportunity: the contributors to this volume have shown many potential pathways by which purposeful and principled policy and collaboration can occur.